Web Services Security and E-Business

G. Radhamani
Multimedia University, Malaysia

G. S. V. Radha Krishna Rao
Multimedia University, Malaysia

IDEA GROUP PUBLISHING

Hershey • London • Melbourne • Singapore

Acquisitions Editor:	Kristin Klinger
Development Editor:	Kristin Roth
Senior Managing Editor:	Jennifer Neidig
Managing Editor:	Sara Reed
Assistant Managing Editor:	Sharon Berger
Copy Editor:	Angela Thor
Typesetter:	Cindy Consonery
Cover Design:	Lisa Tosheff
Printed at:	Integrated Book Technology

Published in the United States of America by
    Idea Group Publishing (an imprint of Idea Group Inc.)
    701 E. Chocolate Avenue
    Hershey PA 17033
    Tel: 717-533-8845
    Fax: 717-533-8661
    E-mail: cust@idea-group.com
    Web site: http://www.idea-group.com

and in the United Kingdom by
    Idea Group Publishing (an imprint of Idea Group Inc.)
    3 Henrietta Street
    Covent Garden
    London WC2E 8LU
    Tel: 44 20 7240 0856
    Fax: 44 20 7379 0609
    Web site: http://www.eurospanonline.com

Library of Congress Cataloging-in-Publication Data

Web services security and e-business / G. Radhamani and G.S.V.
  Radha Krishna Rao, editors.
    p. cm.
  Summary: "This book provides an insight into uncovering the security risks of dynamically created content and looks at how proper content management can greatly improve the overall security. It also looks at the security lifecycle and how to respond to an attack, as well as the problems of site hijacking and phishing"--Provided by publisher.
  Includes bibliographical references and index.
  ISBN 1-59904-168-5 -- ISBN 1-59904-169-3 (softcover) -- ISBN 1-59904-170-7 (ebook)
    1. Computer networks--Security measures. 2. Web services. 3. Electronic commerce--Security measures. 4. Computer security.
  I. Radhamani, G., 1968- . II. Radha Krishna Rao, G.S.V., 1973- .
  TK5105.59.W434 2007
  005.8--dc22
                        2006027712

British Cataloguing in Publication Data
A Cataloguing in Publication record for this book is available from the British Library.

Dedication

to Venkatesa

Web Services Security and E-Business

Table of Contents

Foreword viii
    S. S. Jamuar, Universiti Putra Malaysia, Malaysia

Preface x

Chapter I
Wireless LAN Setup and Security Loopholes 1
    Biju Issac, Swinburne University of Technology, Malaysia
    Lawan A. Mohammed, Swinburne University of Technology, Malaysia

Chapter II
Wireless Web Security Using a Neural Network-Based Cipher 32
    Isaac Woungang, Ryerson University, Canada
    Alireza Sadeghian, Ryerson University, Canada
    Shuwei Wu, Ryerson University, Canada
    Sudip Misra, Cornell University, USA
    Maryam Arvandi, Ryerson University, Canada

Chapter III
RFID Systems: Applications vs. Security and Privacy Implications 57
    Dennis M. L. Wong, Swinburne University of Technology, Malaysia
    Raphael C.-W. Phan, Swinburne University of Technology, Malaysia

Chapter IV

Mobile Code and Security Issues **75**

    E. S. Samundeeswari, Vellalar College for Women, India

    F. Mary Magdalene Jane, P. S. G. R. Krishnammal, India

Chapter V

A Survey of Key Generation for Secure Multicast Communication Protocols **93**

    Win Aye, Multimedia University, Malaysia

    Mohammad Umar Siddiqi, International Islamic University Malaysia, Malaysia

Chapter VI

Security in Mobile Agent Systems **112**

    Chua Fang Fang, Multimedia University, Malaysia

    G. Radhamani, Multimedia University, Malaysia

Chapter VII

Intrusion Detection System: A Brief Study **129**

    Robin Salim, Multimedia University, Malaysia

    G. S. V. Radha Krishna Rao, Multimedia University, Malaysia

Chapter VIII

Node Authentication in Networks Using Zero-Knowledge Proofs **142**

    Richard S. Norville, Wichita University, USA

    Kamesh Namuduri, Wichita University, USA

    Ravi Pendse, Wichita University, USA

Chapter IX

Web Services Security in E-Business: Attacks and Countermeasures **165**

    Wei-Chuen Yau, Multimedia University, Malaysia

    G. S. V. Radha Krishna Rao, Multimedia University, Malaysia

Chapter X

Verifiable Encryption of Digital Signatures Using Elliptic Curve Digital

Signature Algorithm and its Implementation Issues **184**

    R. Anitha, PSG College of Technology, India

    R. S. Sankarasubramanian, PSG College of Technology, India

Chapter XI

An Introductory Study on Business Intelligence Security **204**

    Chan Gaik Yee, Multimedia University, Malaysia

    G. S. V. Radha Krishna Rao, Multimedia University, Malaysia

Chapter XII

Secure Trust Transfer Using Chain Signatures 218

    Amitabh Saxena, La Trobe University, Australia

    Ben Soh, La Trobe University, Australia

Chapter XIII

Distributed Intrusion Detection Systems: An Overview 231

    Rosalind Deena Kumari, Multimedia University, Malaysia

    G. Radhamani, Multimedia University, Malaysia

Chapter XIV

Subtle Interactions: Security Protocols and Cipher Modes of Operation 239

    Raphael C.-W. Phan, Swinburne University of Technology, Malaysia

    Bok-Min Goi, Multimedia University, Malaysia

Chapter XV

Generic Algorithm for Preparing Unbreakable Cipher: A Short Study 262

    R. A. Balachandar, Anna University, India

    M. Balakumar, Anna University, India

    S. Anil Kumar, Anna University, India

Chapter XVI

A Robust Watermarking Scheme Using Codes Based on the Redundant Residue Number System 271

    Vik Tor Goh, Multimedia University, Malaysia

    Mohammad Umar Siddiqi, International Islamic University Malaysia, Malaysia

Chapter XVII

A Framework for Electronic Bill Presentment and Off-Line Message Viewing 306

    Ezmir Mohd Razali, Multimedia Univerisity, Malaysia

    Ismail Ahmad, Multimedia Univerisity, Malaysia

    G. S. V. Radha Krishna Rao, Multimedia Univerisity, Malaysia

    Kenneth Foo Chuan Khit, NetInfinium Sdn. Bhd., Malaysia

Chapter XVIII

Propagation and Delegation of Rights in Access Controls and Risk Assessment Techniques 328

    Saravanan Muthaiyah, George Mason University, USA and

    Multimedia University, Malayasia

Chapter XIX
IPSec Overhead in Dual Stack IPv4/IPv6 Transition Mechanisms:
An Analytical Study 338
  M. Mujinga, University of Fort Hare, South Africa
  Hippolyte Muyingi, University of Fort Hare, South Africa
  Alfredo Terzoli, Rhodes University, South Africa
  G. S. V. Radha Krishna Rao, University of Fort Hare, South Africa

Chapter XX
An Approach for Intentional Modeling of Web Services Security Risk
Assessment 363
  Subhas C. Misra, Carleton University, Canada
  Vinod Kumar, Carleton University, Canada
  Uma Kumar, Carleton University, Canada

About the Authors 380

Index 390

Foreword

There has been a dramatic impact on our society due to multifold increases in the use of personal computers. Computer networking plays a crucial role in building a wireless information society. Internet services and their applications have provided us with tools to obtain any kind of information in a flash of time, and the real world has been converted into a virtual world due to the proliferation of computers. Web sites are now a key asset to organizations of all sizes, providing information and services to clients, suppliers, and employees. Unfortunately, these developments have also opened new security threats to the enterprise networks, and opened the door to an increasing number of threats to individual and business computers. There is a growing trend of hackers attacking networks via home and remote users. These attacks can be range from partial loss of data to making the system nonusable, and privacy can be completely violated. Unauthorized users can use their computer to attack other computers by gaining access through the Internet. In the year 2005, new threats increased by almost 50%, as cybercriminals joined forces to create targeted malware attacks for financial gain.

Being *security aware* means that computer system users understand the potential threats: that it is possible for some people to deliberately or accidentally steal, damage, or misuse the data that is stored within their computer systems and throughout their organization. Therefore, it would be prudent to support the assets of their institution (information, physical, and personal) by trying to stop that from happening. By following the recommended security practices, the user has knowledge of the potential hole in the system, and the capabilities to block the hole in their defenses. There has never been a greater need for early, integrated, threat-management solutions because organized criminals are now working more closely together than ever before to infect computers.

Bringing together the understanding of security problems related to the protocols and applications of the Internet, and their contemporary solutions to these problems in this book, *Web Services Security and E-Business,* is both timely and purposeful. Cryptography has been introduced to understand the security protocols. The focus of the book is on architectures and protocols. Authors have provided an insight into uncovering the security risks of dynamically created content, and looks at how proper content management can greatly improve the overall security. They have also looked at the security life cycle and how to respond to an attack, as well as the problems of site hijacking and phishing.

Professor S. S. Jamuar

Preface

The proliferation of Internet services and applications is bringing systems and Web services security issues to the fore. There is a consensus that a key, contributing factor leading to cyberthreats is the lack of integrated and cohesive strategies that extend beyond the network level, to protect the applications and devices at system level as well. Many techniques, algorithms, protocols, and tools have been developed in the different aspects of cybersecurity, namely, authentication, access control, availability, integrity, privacy, confidentiality, and nonrepudiation as they apply to both networks and systems.

The IT industry has been talking about Web services for many years. The benefits of having a loosely coupled, language-neutral, platform-independent way of linking applications within organizations, across enterprises, and across the Internet, are becoming more evident as Web services are used in pilot programs and in wide-scale production. Moving forward, customers, industry analysts, and the press identify a key area that needs to be addressed as Web services become more mainstream: *security*.

The purpose of this book is to bring together the technologies and researchers who share interest in the area of e-business and Web services security. The main aim is to promote research and relevant activities in security-related subjects. It also aims at increasing the synergy between academic and industry professionals working in this area. This book can also be used as the textbook for graduate courses in the area of Web services security. This book is comprised of 20 chapters that cover various aspects of Web services security and e-business. The scope of the chapters is summarized hereunder.

The first chapter gives a practical overview of the brief implementation details of the IEEE802.11 wireless LAN and the security vulnerabilities involved in such networks. Specifically, it discusses the implementation of EAP authentication using RADIUS server with WEP encryption options. The chapter also touches on the ageing WEP and the cracking process, along with the current TKIP and CCMP mechanisms. War driving and other security attacks on wireless networks are also briefly covered. The chapter concludes with practical security recommendations that can keep intruders at bay. The authors hope that any reader would thus be well informed on the security vulnerabilities and the precautions that are associated with 802.11 wireless networks.

The increasingly important role of security for wireless Web services environments has opened an array of challenging problems centered on new methods and tools to improve existing data encryption and authentication techniques. Real-time recurrent neural networks offer an attractive approach to tackling such problems because of the high encryption capability provided by the structural hidden layers of such networks. In the second chapter, a novel neural network-based symmetric cipher is proposed. This cipher releases the constraint on the length of the secret key to provide the data integrity and authentication services that can be used for securing wireless Web services communication. The proposed symmetric cipher design is robust in resisting different cryptanalysis attacks. Simulation results are presented to validate its effectiveness.

In the third chapter, the business implications, as well as security and privacy issues of the widespread deployment of radio frequency identification (RFID) systems, were discussed. At first, the components that make up an RFID system to facilitate better understanding of the implications of each were discussed, and then the commercial applications of the RFID were reviewed. Further, the security and privacy issues for RFID systems, and what mechanisms have been proposed to safeguard these, were discussed. The topics discussed in this chapter highlight the benefits of using RFIDs for user convenience in ubiquitous and pervasive commercial services and e-businesses, while maintaining the integrity of such systems against malicious attacks on the users' security and privacy. This is vital for a business establishment to coexist with peers, and remain competitively attractive to customers.

Over the years, computer systems have evolved from centralized monolithic computing devices supporting static applications, into client-server environments that allow complex forms of distributed computing. Throughout this evolution, limited forms of code mobility have existed. The explosion in the use of the World Wide Web, coupled with the rapid evolution of the platform-independent programming languages, has promoted the use of mobile code and, at the same time, raised some important security issues. The fourth chapter introduces mobile code technology, and discusses the related security issues.

Multicast communication demands scalable security solutions for group communication infrastructure. Secure multicast is one such solution that achieves the efficiency of multicast data delivery. Key generation plays an important role in enforcing secure and efficient key distribution. The fifth chapter addresses the issues focused on the area of key generation on key management cryptographic algorithms that support security requirements in multicast group communications. These issues are of importance to application developers wishing to implement security services for their multicast applications. The three main classes: centralized, decentralized, and distributed architectures, are investigated and analyzed here, and insight is given to their features and goals. The area of group key generation is then surveyed, and proposed solutions are classified according to the efficiency of the cryptographic algorithms and multicast security requirements. The open problems in this area are also outlined.

Agent technologies have grown rapidly in recent years as Internet usage has increased tremendously. Despite its numerous practical benefits and promises to provide an efficient way of mitigating complex distributed problems, mobile agent technology is still lacking effective security measures, which severely restricts their scope of applicability. The sixth chapter analyzes and synthesizes the different security threats and attacks that can possibly be imposed to the mobile agent systems. The security solutions to resolve the problems and the research challenges in this field are presented.

The seventh chapter introduces the intrusion detection system (IDS). It started with a brief explanation of history of IDS, proceeded with generic components of IDS. Besides highlighting current advances in IDS, the chapter describes recent challenges to the system. The authors hope that this chapter will shed a light for readers who are unfamiliar with this domain.

ZKP-based authentication protocols provide a smart way to prove an identity of a node without giving away any information about the secret of that identity. There are many advantages, as well as disadvantages, to using this protocol over other authentication schemes, as well as challenges to overcome in order to make it practical for general use. The eighth chapter examines the viability of ZKPs for use in authentication protocols in networks. It is concluded that nodes in a network can achieve a desired level of security by trading off key size, interactivity, and other parameters of the authentication protocol. This chapter also provides data analysis, which can be useful in determining expected authentication times based on device capabilities. Pseudocode is provided for implementing a graph-based ZKP on small or limited processing devices.

Web services enable the communication of application to application in a heterogeneous network and computing environment. The powerful functionality of Web services has given benefits to enterprise companies, such as rapid integrating between heterogeneous e-business systems, easy implementation of e-business systems, and reusability of e-business services. While providing the flexibility for e-business, Web services tend to be vulnerable to a number of attacks. Core components of Web services such as simple object access protocol (SOAP), Web services description language (WSDL), and universal description, discovery, and integration (UDDI) can be exploited by malicious attacks due to lack of proper security protections. These attacks will increase the risk of an e-business that employs Web services. The ninth chapter aims to provide a state-of-the-art view of Web services attacks and countermeasures. This chapter also examines various vulnerabilities in Web services, followed by the analysis of respective attacking methods. Further, this chapter also discusses preventive countermeasures against such attacks to protect Web services deployments in e-business, and finally address future trends in this research area.

The 10th chapter presents a new simple scheme for verifiable encryption of elliptic curve digital signature algorithm (ECDSA). The protocol presented is an adjudicated protocol, that is, the trusted third party (TTP) takes part in the protocol only when there is a dispute. This scheme can be used to build efficient fair exchanges and certified e-mail protocols. In this chapter, the authors also present the implementation issues. The chapter presents a new algorithm for multiplying two $2n$ bits palindromic polynomials modulo $x^p - 1$ for prime $p = 2n + 1$ for the concept defined in Blake and Roth (1998) and it is compared with the Sunar-Koc parallel multiplier given in Sunar and Koc (2001). Finally, the chapter concludes that the proposed multiplication algorithm requires $(2n^2 - n+1)$ XOR gates, which is approximately 34% extra, as compared to $1.5(n^2-n)$ XOR gates required by the Sunar-Koc parallel multiplier, and 50% less than the speculated result $4n^2$ XOR gates given by Sunar and Koc (2001). Moreover, the proposed multiplication algorithm requires $(2n^2 - n)$ AND gates, as compared to n^2 AND gates which is doubled that of the Sunar-Koc method

Firstly, the fact that business intelligence (BI) applications are growing in importance, and secondly, the growing and more-sophisticated attacks launched by hackers, the concern of how to protect the knowledge capital or databases that come along with BI or, in another words, BI security, has thus arisen. In the eleventh chapter, the BI environment, with its security features, is explored, followed by a discussion on intrusion detection (ID) and intrusion prevention (IP) techniques. It is understood, through a Web-service case study, that it is feasible to have ID and IP as counter measures to the security threats; thus, further enhancing the security of the BI environment or architecture.

In the 12th chapter, the concept of "trust transfer" using chain signatures will be presented. Informally, transferring trust involves creating a trust (or liability) relationship between two entities, such that both parties are liable in the event of a dispute. If such a relationship involves more than two users, we say they are connected in a chained trust relationship. The members of a chained trust relationship are simultaneously bound to an agreement with the property that additional members can be added to the chain, but once added, members cannot be removed thereafter. This allows members to be incrementally and noninteractively added to the chain. We coin the term "chained signatures" to denote signatures created in this incremental way. An important application of chained signatures is in e-commerce transactions involving many users. We present a practical construction of such a scheme that is secure under the Diffie-Hellman assumption in bilinear groups.

The recent increase in the malicious usage of the network has made it necessary that an IDS should encapsulate the entire network rather than at a system. This was the inspiration for the birth of a distributed intrusion detection system (DIDS). Different configurations of DIDSs have been actively used, and are also rapidly evolving due to the changes in the types of threats. The thirteenth chapter gives an overview and the structure of DIDS. The various agents that are involved in DIDS, and the benefits are given in brief. In the end, directions for future research work are discussed.

In the 14th chapter, we discuss how security protocols can be attacked by exploiting the underlying block cipher modes of operation. This chapter presents a comprehensive treatment of the properties and weaknesses of standard modes of operation. Further, this chapter shows why all modes of operation should not be used with public-key ciphers in public-key security protocols. This includes the cipher block chaining (CBC) mode, when there is no integrity protection of the initialisation vector (IV). In particular, it was shown that it is possible in such instances to replace a block at the beginning, middle, or end of a CBC-encrypted message. This chapter demonstrates that the security of single-block encryptions can be reduced to the security of the electronic codebook

(ECB) mode, and show that in the absence of integrity, one could exploit this to aid in known- and chosen-*IV* attacks. Finally, this chapter also presents chosen-*IV* slide attacks on counter (CTR) and output feedback (OFB) modes of operation. Results show that protocol implementers should carefully select modes of operation, be aware of the pitfalls in each of these modes, and incorporate countermeasures in their protocols to overcome them. It is also important to realize that modes of operation only provide confidentiality, and that when used in the context of security protocols, these modes should be combined with authentication and integrity protection techniques.

The 15th chapter addresses the need of cryptographic algorithm to prepare unbreakable cipher. Though the performance of symmetric key algorithms is far better than asymmetric key algorithms, it still suffers with key distribution problem. It is highly evident that there is always a demand for an algorithm to transfer the secret key in a secure manner between the participants. This chapter argues that by providing the randomness to the secret key, it would be increasingly difficult to hack the secret key. This chapter proposes an algorithm effectively utilizes the random nature of stock prices, in conjunction with plain text, to generate random cipher. This algorithm can be used to exchange the secret key in a secure manner between the participants.

In the 16th chapter, a watermarking scheme that utilizes error correction codes for added robustness is proposed. A literature survey covering various aspects of the watermarking scheme, such as the arithmetic redundant residue number system and concepts related to digital watermarking, is given. The requirements of a robust watermarking scheme are also described. In addition, descriptions and experimental results of the proposed watermarking scheme are provided to demonstrate the functionality of the scheme. The authors hope that with the completion of this chapter, the reader will have a better understanding of ideas related to digital watermarking, as well as the arithmetic redundant number system.

A security framework for secure message delivery and off-line message viewing of the electronic bills is presented in the seventeenth chapter. This framework is implementable towards smart applications such as electronic bill presentment and payment systems.

Chapter XVIII, introduces the concept of access control and its objectives in fulfilling security requirements for the computing world. The main arrears in access control, namely DAC, MAC, and RBAC, will be covered; thus, giving enough background knowledge to the reader on existing policies and framework. Hence, the reader will be able to comprehend the concept of task delegation with regard to access control policies, and how delegated tasks or roles can affect existing risk levels in an organization. Measuring risk has a two-fold benefit: one is that it enables security officials to be prepared with more accurate security measures with higher granularity and secondly, this will certainly be useful for security plans for mitigating potential risks.

Internet protocol version 6 (IPv6) is the next generation Internet protocol proposed by the Internet Engineering Task Force (IETF) to supplant the current Internet protocol version 4 (IPv4). Lack of security below the application layer in IPv4 is one of the reasons why there is a need for a new IP. IPv6 has built-in support for the Internet protocol security protocol (IPSec). The nineteenth chapter reports work done to evaluate implications of compulsory use of IPSec on dual stack IPv4/IPv6 environment.

Finally, in the last chapter provides a conceptual modeling approach for Web services (WS) security risk assessment, which is based on the identification and analysis of stakeholder intentions. There are no similar approaches for modeling Web services security risk assessment in the existing pieces of literature. The approach is, thus, novel in this domain. The approach is helpful for performing means-end analysis; thereby, uncovering the structural origin of security risks in Web services, and how the root causes of such risks can be controlled from the early stages of the projects. The approach addresses "why" the process is the way it is, by exploring the strategic dependencies between the actors of a security system, and analyzing the motivations, intents, and rationales behind the different entities and activities in constituting the system.

This book aims to help toward technical strategy and a roadmap whereby the industry/academia can produce and implement a standards-based architecture that is comprehensive, yet flexible enough to meet the Web services security needs of real businesses.

References

Blake & Roth. (1998)

Sunar & Koc. (2001)

Acknowledgments

We would like to thank all contributors/authors who worked very hard to complete their chapters in time. Without each of their contributions, this book would have never been accomplished.

Our grateful thanks to the external reviewers for their valuable comments and constructive criticism, which developed and improved the overall content of this book.

We would like to thank Professor Datuk, Dr. Ghauth Jasmon, president of Multimedia University, and Dr. Ewe Hong Tat, dean of Faculty of Information Technology for kind assistance and support.

Special thanks to Dr. Mehdi Khosrow-Pour, senior academic editor, and Kristin Roth, development editor, of Idea Group Inc., for production of this book. Their efficiency and amiable manner made working together a pleasure.

We are grateful to all others who have indirectly helped us in bringing out this book to be successful.

Dr. G. Radhamani
Dr. G. S. V. Radha Krishna Rao

Chapter I

Wireless LAN Setup and Security Loopholes

Biju Issac, Swinburne University of Technology, Malaysia

Lawan A. Mohammed, Swinburne University of Technology, Malaysia

Abstract

This chapter gives a practical overview of the brief implementation details of the IEEE802.11 wireless LAN and the security vulnerabilities involved in such networks. Specifically, it discusses about the implementation of EAP authentication using RADIUS server with WEP encryption options. The chapter also touches on the ageing WEP and the cracking process, along with the current TKIP and CCMP mechanisms. War driving and other security attacks on wireless networks are also briefly covered. The chapter concludes with practical security recommendations that can keep intruders at bay. The authors hope that any reader would thus be well informed on the security vulnerabilities and the precautions that are associated with 802.11 wireless networks.

Introduction

Over the recent past, the world has increasingly becoming mobile. As mobile computing is getting more popular each day, the use of wireless local area network (WLAN) is becoming ever more relevant. If we are connected to a wired network, our mobility is undoubtedly affected. From public hotspots in coffee shops to secure WLAN in organizations, the world is moving to ubiquitous and seamless computing environments. IEEE 802.11 has been one of the most successful wireless technologies, and this chapter would be focusing more on this technology.

Mobility and flexibility has been the keynote advantages of wireless networks in general. Users can roam around freely without any interruption to their connection. Flexibility comes in as users can get connected through simple steps of authentication without the hassle of running cables. Also, compared to the wired network, wireless network installation costs are minimal as the number of interface hardware is minimal. Radio spectrum is the key resource, and the wireless devices are set to operate in a certain frequency band. 802.11 networks operate in the 2.4 GHz ISM band, which are generally license free bands. The more common 802.11b devices operate in the S-band ISM.

In the next sections, we will be explaining the wireless LAN basic setup and implementation, WEP encryption schemes and others, EAP authentication through RADIUS server and its brief implementation, WEP cracking procedure, war driving, 802.11b vulnerabilities with security attacks, and finally concluding with WLAN security safeguards.

Wireless LAN Network and Technologies Involved

Network Infrastructure

To form the wireless network, four generic types of WLAN devices are used. These are wireless station, access point (AP), wireless router, and wireless bridge. A wireless station can be a notebook or desktop computer with a wireless network card in it. Access points act like a 2-port bridge linking the wired infrastructure to the wireless infrastructure. It constructs a port-address table and operates by following the 3F rule: flooding, forwarding, and filtering. Flooding is the process of transmitting frames on all ports other than the port in which the frames were received. Forwarding and filtering involve the process of transmitting a frame based on the port-address mapping table in AP, so that only the needed port is used for transmission. Wireless routers are access points with routing capability that typically includes support for dynamic host control protocol (DHCP) and network address translation (NAT). To move the frames from one station to the other, the 802.11 standard defines a wireless medium that supports two radio frequency (RF) physical layers and one infrared physical layer. RF layers are more popular now (Held, 2003, pp. 7-14).

Modes of Operation

IEEE802.11 WLAN can operate in two modes, namely ad hoc (or peer-to-peer) and infrastructure mode. These modes come under the basic service set (BSS), which is a coverage area of communication that allows one station to communicate to the other. *Ad hoc* mode has WLAN stations or nodes communicating with one another without an access point to form an independent basic service set (IBSS). In contrast, *infrastructure* mode has WLAN nodes communicating with a central AP that is, in turn, linked to a wired LAN to form a basic service set. Here, the AP acts as a relay between wireless stations or between wired and wireless stations. A combination of many BSS with a backbone distribution system (normally ethernet) forms an extended service set (ESS).

IEEE 802.11 Architecture and Standards

802.11 is a member of IEEE 802 family, which defines the specifications for local area network technologies. IEEE 802 specifications are centered on the two lowest layers of OSI model, namely the physical layer and the data link layer. The base 802.11 specification includes the 802.11 MAC layer and two physical layers namely, the frequency hopping spread spectrum (FHSS) layer in the 2.4 GHz band, and the direct sequence spread spectrum (DSSS) layer. Later revisions to 802.11 added additional physical layers like high-rate direct-sequence layer (HR/DSSS) for 802.11b and orthogonal frequency division multiplexing (OFDM) layer for 802.11a.

The different extensions to the 802.11 standard use the radio frequency band differently. Some of the popular 802.11 extensions are as follows: 802.11b— specifies the use of DSSS at 1, 2, 5.5 and 11 Mbps. The 802.11 products are quite popular with its voluminous production. 802.11a specifies the use of a frequency multiplexing scheme called orthogonal frequency division multiplexing (OFDM), and it uses a physical layer standard that operates at data rates up to 54 Mbps. As high frequencies attenuate more, one needs more 802.11a access points compared to using 802.11b access points. 802.11g specifies a high-speed extension to 802.11b that operates in 2.4 GHz frequency band using OFDM to obtain data rates up to 54 Mbps as well as backward compatibility with 802.11b devices. 802.11i recognizes the limitations of WEP and enhances wireless security. It defines two new encryption methods as well as an authentication method. The two encryption methods designed to replace WEP include temporal key integrity protocol (TKIP) and advanced encryption standard (AES). The authentication is based on the port-based 802.1x approach defined by a prior IEEE standard. Other 802.11 extensions include 802.11c (focuses on MAC bridges), 802.11d (focuses on worldwide use of WLAN with operation at different power levels), 802.11e (focuses on quality of service), 802.11f (focuses on access point interoperability) and 802.11h (focuses on addressing interference problems when used with other communication equipments) (Held, 2003, pp. 27-32).

Joining an Existing Cell

There are three stages that a station has to go through to get connected to an existing cell, namely scanning, authentication, and association. When a station wants to access an existing BSS (either after power up, sleep mode, or just entering the BSS area), the station needs to get synchronization information from the access point (or from the other stations when in ad-hoc mode). The station can get this information by one of two modes: passive scanning and active scanning. In *passive scanning mode*, the station just waits to receive a beacon frame from the AP and records information from it. The beacon frame is a periodic frame sent by the AP with synchronization information. This mode can save battery power, as it does not require transmitting. In *active scanning mode*, the station tries to find an access point by transmitting probe request frames, and waiting for probe response frames from the AP. This is more assertive in nature. It follows the simple process as follows. Firstly, it moves to a channel to look for an incoming frame. If incoming frame is detected, the channel can be probed. Secondly, it tries to gain access to the medium by sending a probe request frame. Thirdly, it waits for a predefined time to look for any probe response frame and if unsuccessful, to move to the next channel.

The second stage is authentication. It is necessary, when the stations try to communicate to one another, to prove their identity. Two major approaches that are specified in 802.11 are open system authentication and shared-key authentication. In *open system authentication*, the access point accepts the mobile station implicitly without verification and it is essentially a two-frame exchange communication. In *shared key authentication*, WEP (wired equivalent privacy) encryption has to be enabled. It requires that a shared key be distributed to stations before attempting to do authentication. The shared-key authentication exchange consists of four management frame exchanges that include a challenge-response approach.

The third stage is association, and this is restricted to infrastructure networks only. Once the authentication is completed, stations can associate with an access point so that it can gain full access to the network. Exchange of data can only be performed after an association is established. The association process is a two-step process further involving three stages: unauthenticated-unassociated stage, authenticated-unassociated stage, and authenticated-associated stage.

All access points (AP) transmit a beacon management frame at fixed intervals. A wireless client that wants to associate with an access point and join a BSS listens for beacon messages that contain information regarding service set identifier (SSID) or network names to determine the access points within range. After identifying which AP to associate with, the client and AP will perform mutual authentication by exchanging several management frames as part of the process. After getting authenticated, the client moves to second stage and then to third stage. To get associated, the client needs to send an association request frame, and the AP needs to respond with an association response frame (Arbaugh, Shankar, & Wan, 2001).

Association helps to locate the position of the mobile station, so that frames destined for that station can be forwarded to the right access point. Once the association is complete, the access point would register the mobile station on the network. This is done

Figure 1. CISCO access point association table screen

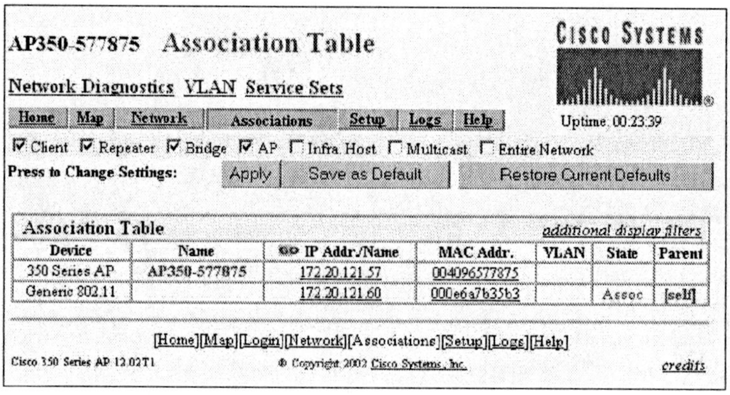

by sending gratuitous ARP (address resolution protocol) packets, so that the mobile station's MAC address is mapped with the switch port connected to the access point. Reassociation is a procedure of moving the association from an old access point to a new one. It is also used to rejoin a network if the station leaves the cell and returns later to the same access point.

WLAN Association Table on CISCO Access Point

Figure 1 shows the details of a wireless node that is connected in a wireless LAN cell. The figure shows the details of CISCO Aironet 320 series AP and another client connected within the cell. This is a very simple wireless connection between a station and AP, with no encryption enabled and no authentication enabled. The forthcoming section shows how to make the setup more secure.

Encryption Mechanisms in IEEE 802.11b and 802.11i

As WLAN data signals are transmitted over the air, it makes them vulnerable to eavesdropping. Thus, confidentiality of transmitted data must be protected, at any cost, by means of encryption. The IEEE 802.11b standard defines such a mechanism, known as wired equivalent privacy, which uses the RC4 encryption method. However, various security researchers have found numerous flaws in WEP design. The most devastating news broke out in 2001, which explained that the WEP encryption key can be recovered when enough packets are captured. Since then, this attack has been verified by several others and, in fact, free software is available for download that allows for capturing WEP packets and using those to crack the key.

Wired Equivalent Privacy

Wired equivalent privacy is a standard encryption for wireless networking. It is a user authentication and data encryption system from IEEE 802.11 that is used to overcome security threats. Basically, WEP provides security to WLAN by encrypting the information transmitted over the air, so that only the receivers who have the correct encryption key can decrypt the information. If a user activates WEP, the network interface card encrypts the payload (frame body and CRC) of each 802.11 frame, before transmission, using an RC4 stream cipher provided by RSA security. The receiving station, such as an access point, performs decryption upon arrival of the frame. As a result, 802.11 WEP only encrypts data between 802.11 stations. Once the frame enters the wired side of the network, such as between access points, WEP no longer applies. As part of the encryption process, WEP prepares a key schedule ("seed") by concatenating the shared secret key supplied by the user of the sending station with a randomly generated 24-bit initialization vector (IV). The IV lengthens the life of the secret key because the station can change the IV for each frame transmission. WEP inputs the resulting "seed" into a pseudorandom number generator that produces a key stream equal to the length of the frame's payload plus a 32-bit integrity check sum value (ICV). The ICV is a check sum that the receiving station eventually recalculates and compares with the one sent by the sending station to determine whether the transmitted data underwent any form of tampering while in transient. If the receiving station calculates an ICV that does not match the one found in the frame, then the receiving station can reject the frame or flag the user (Borisov, Goldberg, & Wagner, 2001). The WEP encryption process is shown as follows:

1.   Plaintext (P) = Message (M) + Integrity Check Sum of Message (C(M))

2.   Keystream = RC4(v, k), where v is the IV and k is the shared key

3.   Ciphertext (C) = Plaintext (P) $\oplus$ Keystream

4.   Transmitted Data = v + Ciphertext

The decryption is done by using the reverse process as follows:

1.   Ciphertext (C) $\oplus$ Keystream $\Box$ Plaintext (P)

What is Wrong with WEP?

WEP has been part of the 802.11 standard since initial ratification in September 1999. At that time, the 802.11 committee was aware of some WEP limitations; however, WEP was the best choice to ensure efficient implementations worldwide. Nevertheless, WEP has undergone much scrutiny and criticism over the past couple of years. WEP is vulnerable because of relatively short IVs and keys that remain static. The issues with WEP do not really have much to do with the RC4 encryption algorithm. With only 24 bits, WEP eventually uses the same IV for different data packets. For a large busy network, this reoccurrence of IVs can happen within an hour or so. This results in the transmission of frames having key streams that are too similar. If a hacker collects enough frames based on the same IV, the individual can determine the shared values among them; for instance, the key stream or the shared secret key. This leads to the hacker decrypting any of the 802.11 frames. The static nature of the shared secret keys emphasizes this problem. 802.11 does not provide any functions that support the exchange of keys among stations. As a result, system administrators and users generally use the same keys for weeks, months, and even years. This gives mischievous culprits plenty of time to monitor and hack into WEP-enabled networks. Some vendors deploy dynamic key distribution solutions based on 802.1x, which definitely improves the security of wireless LANs (Giller & Bulliard, 2004).

The major WEP design flaws may be summarized as follows (Gast, 2002, pp. 93-96):

- Manual key management is a big problem with WEP. The secret key has to be manually distributed to the user community, and widely distributed secrets tend to leak out as time goes by.

- When key streams are reused, stream ciphers are vulnerable to analysis. Two frames that use the same IV are almost certain to use the same secret key and key stream, and this problem is aggravated by the fact that some implementations do not even choose random IVs. There are cases where, when the card was inserted, the IV started off as zero, and incremented by one for each frame. By reusing initialization vectors, WEP enables an attacker to decrypt the encrypted data without ever learning the encryption key or even resorting to high-tech techniques. While often dismissed as too slow, a patient attacker can compromise the encryption of an entire network after only a few hours of data collection.

- WEP provides no forgery protection. Even without knowing the encryption key, an adversary can change 802.11 packets in arbitrary, undetectable ways, deliver data to unauthorized parties, and masquerade as an authorized user. Even worse, an adversary can also learn more about an encryption key with forgery attacks than with strictly passive attacks.

- WEP offers no protection against replays. An adversary can create forgeries, without changing any data in an existing packet, simply by recording WEP packets and then retransmitting later. Replay, a special type of forgery attack, can be used to derive information about the encryption key and the data it protects.

- WEP misuses the RC4 encryption algorithm in a way that exposes the protocol to weak key attacks and public domain hacker tools like Aircrack, and many others exploit this weakness. An attacker can utilize the WEP IV to identify RC4 weak keys, and then use known plaintext from each packet to recover the encryption key.

- Decryption dictionaries, which consist of a large collection of frames encrypted with the same key streams, can be built because of infrequent rekeying. Since more frames with the same IV come in, chances of decrypting them are more, even if the key is not known or recovered.

- WEP uses CRC for integrity check, encrypted using RC4 key stream. From a cryptography viewpoint, CRC is not secure from an attack of frame modification, where the attacker modifies the frame data contents as well as the CRC value.

In view of these WEP shortcomings, the IEEE 802.11 Task Group i (TGi) is developing a new set of WLAN security protocols to form the future IEEE 802.11i standard. These include the temporal key integrity protocol (TKIP) and the counter mode with CBC-MAC protocol (CCMP). The TKIP is a short-term solution that will adapt existing WEP implementations to address the WEP flaws while waiting for CCMP to be fully deployed. CCMP is a long-term solution that will not only address current WEP flaws, but will include a new design incorporating the new advanced encryption standard (AES).

The New 802.11i Standard

The new security standard, 802.11i, which was confirmed and ratified in June 2004, eliminates all the weaknesses of WEP. It is divided into three main categories (Strand, 2004):

1. *Temporary key integrity protocol (TKIP):* This is, essentially, a short-term solution that fixes all WEP weaknesses. It would be compatible with old 802.11 devices, and it provides integrity and confidentiality.

2. *Counter mode with CBC-MAC protocol (CCMP):* This is a new protocol designed with planning based on RFC 2610, which uses AES as cryptographic algorithm. Since this is more CPU intensive than RC4 (used in WEP and TKIP), new and improved 802.11 hardware may be required. Some drivers can implement CCMP in software. It provides integrity and confidentiality.

3. *802.1x port-based network access control:* Either when using TKIP or CCMP, 802.1x is used as authentication.

TKIP and CCMP will be explained in the following sections. 802.1x is explained in detail in the section titled Radius Server and Authentication Mechanisms.

Temporary Key Integrity Protocol (TKIP)

TKIP is part of a draft standard from the IEEE 802.11i working group. TKIP is an enhancement to WEP security. The TKIP algorithms are designed explicitly for implementation on legacy hardware, hopefully without unduly disrupting performance. TKIP adds four new algorithms to WEP (Cam-Winget, Housley, Wagner, & Walker, 2003):

- A cryptographic message integrity code, called Michael, to defeat forgeries has been added. Michael is an MIC algorithm that calculates a keyed function of data at the transmitter; sends the resulting value as a CRC check or tag with the data to the receiver, where it recalculates the tag value; and compares the computed result with the tag accompanying the data. If the two values match, the receiver accepts the data as authentic. Otherwise, the receiver rejects the data as a forgery.

- A new IV sequencing discipline to remove replay attacks has been added. TKIP extends the current WEP format to use a 48-bit sequence number, and associates the sequence number with the encryption key. TKIP mixes the sequence number into the encryption key and encrypts the MIC and the WEP ICV. This design translates replay attacks into ICV or MIC failures.

- A per-packet key mixing function, to decorrelate the public IVs from weak keys is added. TKIP introduces a new per-packet encryption key construction, based on a mixing function. The mixing function takes the base key, transmitter MAC address, and packet sequence number as inputs, and outputs a new per-packet WEP key. To minimize computational requirements, the mixing function is split into two phases. The first phase uses a nonlinear substitution table, or S-box, to combine the base key, the transmitter MAC address, and the four most significant octets of the packet sequence number to produce an intermediate value. The second phase mixes the intermediate value with the two least-significant octets of the packet sequence number, and produces a per-packet key.

- A rekeying mechanism is added to provide fresh encryption and integrity keys, undoing the threat of attacks stemming from key reuse. The IEEE 802.1x key management scheme provides fresh keys (Cam-Winget et al., 2003).

Counter Mode with CBC-MAC Protocol (CCMP)

CCMP (counter mode with cipher block chaining message authentication code protocol) is the preferred encryption protocol in the 802.11i standard. CCMP is based upon the CCM mode of the AES encryption algorithm. CCMP utilizes 128-bit keys, with a 48-bit initialization vector (IV) for replay detection. The counter mode (CM) component of CCMP is the algorithm providing data privacy. The cipher block chaining message authentication code (CBC-MAC) component of CCMP provides data integrity and authentication. CCMP is designed for IEEE 802.11i by D. Whiting, N. Ferguson, and R. Housley.

CCMP addresses all known WEP deficiencies, but without the restrictions of the already-deployed hardware. The protocol using CCM has many properties in common with TKIP. Freedom from constraints associated with current hardware leads to a more elegant solution. As with TKIP, CCMP employs a 48-bit IV, ensuring the lifetime of the AES key is longer than any possible association. In this way, key management can be confined to the beginning of an association and ignored for its lifetime. CCMP uses a 48-bit IV as a sequence number to provide replay detection, just like TKIP. AES eliminates any need for per-packet keys, so CCMP has no per-packet key derivation function (Cam-Winget et al., 2003).

Table 1. Summary of WEP, TKIP, and CCMP comparison (Cam-Winget et al., 2003)

	WEP	TKIP	CCMP
Cipher	RC4	RC4	AES
Key Size	40 or 104 bits	128 bits encryption, 64 bits	128 bits
Key Lifetime	24-bit IV, wrap	48-bit IV	48-bit IV
Packet Key Integrity	Concatenating IV to base key	Mixing Function	Not needed
Packet Data	CRC-32	Michael	CCM
Packet Header	None	Michael	CCM
Replay Detection	None	Use IV sequencing	Use IV sequencing
Key Management	None	EAP-based (802.1x)	EAP-based (802.1x)

Comparing WEP, TKIP, and CCMP

WEP, TKIP, and CCMP can be compared as in the following table. As it is quite obvious from the previous discussion, CCMP is the future choice, and TKIP is only an interim solution.

Radius Server and Authentication Mechanisms

To address the shortcomings of WEP with respect to authentication, a solution based on 802.1x specification is developed that, in turn, is based on IETF's extensible authentication protocol (EAP) as in RFC 2284. Its goal is to provide a foundation of architecture for access control, authentication, and key management for wireless LANs.

Figure 2. Authenticated wireless node can only gain access to other LAN resources (Strand, 2004) (See steps 1, 2, and 3 in the diagram)

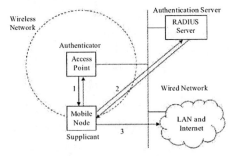

EAP was designed with flexibility in mind, and it is being used as a basis for various network authentication protocols. WPA (wi-fi protected access) is proposed to enhance the security of wireless networks through specifications of security enhancements that increase the level of authentication, access control, replay prevention, message integrity, message privacy, and key distribution to existing WiFi systems. RFC 2284 states that, in general during EAP authentication, after the link establishment phase is complete (i.e., after establishing connection), the authenticator sends one or more requests to authenticate the peer (client). Typically, the authenticator will send an initial identity request, and that could be followed by one or more requests for authentication information. The client sends a response packet in reply to each request made by authenticator. The authentication phase is ended by the authenticator with a success or failure packet. Figure 2 shows a general EAP diagram.

RADIUS Overview

Remote authentication dial-in user service (RADIUS) is a widely deployed protocol enabling centralized authentication, authorization, and accounting for network access. RADIUS is originally developed for dial-up remote access, but now it is supported by virtual private network (VPN) servers, wireless access points, authenticating ethernet switches, digital subscriber line (DSL) access, and other network access types. A RADIUS client (here is referred to access point) sends the details of user credentials and connection parameter in the form of a UDP (user datagram protocol) message to the RADIUS server. The RADIUS server authenticates and authorizes the RADIUS client request, and sends back a RADIUS message response. To provide security for RADIUS messages, the RADIUS client and the RADIUS server are configured with a common shared secret. The shared secret is used to secure the traffic back and forth from RADIUS server, and is commonly entered as a text string on both the RADIUS client and server (Microsoft, 2000).

Simple 802.1x Authentication with RADIUS Server

The following steps show the necessary interactions that happen during authentication (Gast, 2002).

1. The Authenticator (Access Point) sends an EAP-Request/Identity packet to the Supplicant (Client) as soon as it detects that the link is active.
2. The Supplicant (Client) sends an EAP-Response/Identity packet, with its identity in it, to the Authenticator (Access Point). The Authenticator then repackages this packet in the RADIUS protocol and passes it to the Authentication (RADIUS) Server.
3. The Authentication (RADIUS) Server sends back a challenge to the Authenticator (Access Point), such as with a token password system. The Authenticator unpacks

Figure 3. Step-by-step extensible authentication protocol (EAP) sequences that include the client or user computer, the Access Point, as well as the RADIUS server

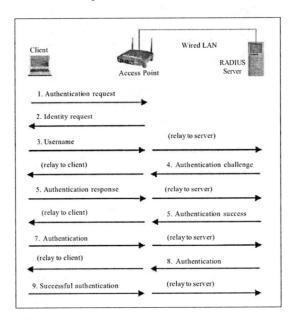

this from RADIUS, repacks it into EAPOL (EAP over LAN), and sends it to the Supplicant (Client).

4.   The Supplicant (Client) responds to the challenge via the Authenticator (Access Point), which passes the response onto the Authentication (RADIUS) Server.

5.   If the Supplicant (Client) provides proper credentials, the Authentication (RADIUS) Server responds with a success message that is then passed on to the Supplicant. The Authenticator (Access Point) now allows access to the LAN, restricted based on attributes that came back from the Authentication Server.

Figure 3 shows the details in a pictorial way, where client, AP, and RADIUS server interact. There are a few EAP types of authentication that include EAP-MD5, EAP-TLS, EAP-TTLS, LEAP, and PEAP with MS-CHAPv2. The PEAP authentication process consists of two main phases. Step 1: Server authentication and the creation of a TLS (transport layer security) encryption channel happens in this step. The server identifies itself to a client by providing certificate information to the client. After the client verifies the identity of the server, a master secret is generated. The session keys that are derived from the master secret are then used to create a TLS encryption channel that encrypts all subsequent communication between the server and the wireless client. Step 2: EAP conversation and user and client computer authentication happens in this step. A complete EAP conversation between the client and the server is encapsulated within the TLS encryption channel. With PEAP, you can use any one of several EAP authentication methods, such as passwords, smart cards, and certificates, to authenticate the user and client computer.

PEAP-Microsoft challenge handshake authentication protocol version 2 (MS-CHAP v2) is a mutual authentication method that supports password-based user or computer authentication. During the PEAP with MS-CHAPv2 authentication process, both the server and client must prove that they have knowledge of the user's password in order for authentication to succeed. With PEAP-MS-CHAPv2, after successful authentication, users can change their passwords, and they are notified when their passwords expire.

Implementing EAP Authentication with RADIUS Server

This section shows the implementation of 802.1x port-based authentication of PEAP (protected extensible authentication protocol) with MS-CHAPv2 (Microsoft challenge handshake authentication protocol version 2) by setting up RADIUS servers on Win-

Figure 4. Wireless network implementation. The WLAN is connected to the LAN where RADIUS server is used for authentication purpose

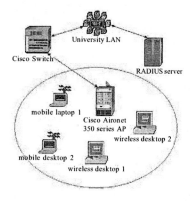

Figure 5. AP association table shows that the clients are EAP authenticated

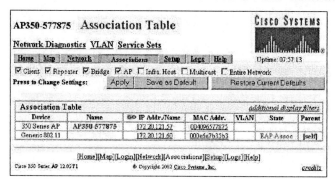

dows 2000 server and Linux Red Hat 9 as shown in Figure 4. Like what has been discussed in the authentication part, the purpose of this implementation is to allow authorized users to login to the WLAN. Authorized users are those users who are to register their usernames and their passwords with RADIUS server before they are allowed to access the WLAN.

The RADIUS server can be configured, as briefly explained next, on Windows 2000 server (with service pack 4) by configuring the IAS (Internet authentication server). In the IAS authentication service, there is a need to register the RADIUS client. Typically, that would be an access point, and its name and IP address with the shared secret are entered into IAS. Remote access policy needs to be configured to give proper access rights. EAP authentication needs to be selected as PEAP (protected EAP). Certificate services need to be configured, and certification authority details need to be entered to create the certificate that has to be used with IAS. The user account that uses wireless network needs to be given remote access rights in the active directory user management.

On the access point, there is a need to do the authenticator configuration by adding the IP address of the RADIUS server and the shared secret details. On the client's side, windows XP workstation has to be configured with a wireless card to negotiate with the AP that is doing RADIUS authentication through IAS server. The association table on CISCO AP in Figure 5 shows the details after the client's EAP authentication with RADIUS server. Note the words *'EAP Assoc'* under the State column.

An example setup used by the authors can be explained as follows. The user guest who had an account in the RADIUS/Windows 2000 server, risecure.isecures.com (with IP address 172.20.121.15), had connected from a client, PC.isecures.com (with IP address 172.20.121.60), through a CISCO Aironet 350 access point (with IP address 172.20.121.57). The event viewer output (only selected lines are shown) after successful EAP authentication was as follows:

IAS event viewer output on Windows 2000 Server:

```
Event Type: Information
Event Source: IAS
Computer:   RISECURES
Description:
User ISECURES\guest was granted access.
Fully-Qualified-User-Name = isecures.com/Users/Guest
NAS-IP-Address = 172.20.121.57
NAS-Identifier = AP350-577875
Client-Friendly-Name = isecureslab
Client-IP-Address = 172.20.121.57
Policy-Name = Allow access if dial-in entry enabled
Authentication-Type = EAP
EAP-Type = Protected EAP (PEAP)
```

To implement the RADIUS configuration in Linux platform, a GNU RADIUS software, known as *FreeRADIUS,* can be downloaded and be configured as the RADIUS server. The details of that can be found at the Web site http://www.freeradius.org. The details of the authentication messages (only selected lines are shown) when FreeRADIUS is run in a debug mode (i.e., radiusd - X) in Linux after successful EAP authentication can be as shown.

FreeRADIUS authentication output on red hat Linux:

```
rad_recv: Access-Request packet from host
172.20.121.57:1151, id=119, length=195
    User-Name = "guest"
    Cisco-AVPair = "ssid=isecureslab"
    NAS-IP-Address = 172.20.121.57
    Called-Station-Id = "0040965778XX"
    Calling-Station-Id = "00097c6f1dXX"
    NAS-Identifier = "AP350-577XX" ...
rlm_eap: EAP/peap
rlm_eap: processing type peap
rlm_eap_peap: Authenticate
rlm_eap_tls: processing TLS
rlm_eap_peap: EAPTLS_OK
rlm_eap_peap: Session established.
rlm_eap_peap: Received EAP-TLV response.
rlm_eap_peap: Tunneled data is valid.
rlm_eap_peap: Success
Login OK: [guest] (from client isecureslab port 37 cli 00097c6f1dbc) ...
```

The authors had used FreeRADIUS 1.0.0 to setup the RADIUS server. The source was compiled and executable was created. Some configuration files were edited, like radiusd.conf, eap.conf and clients.conf, to allow user permission with password to configure PEAP-MS-CHAPv2 functions.

The WEP Cracking Procedure

Problems with WEP

Generally, attacks on WEP were based on the design of the system, which many people thought was sound. However, a paper written by Fluhrer, Mantin, and Shamir (2001) dispelled that notion. The authors found a flaw in the "key scheduling algorithm" of RC4 that made certain RC4 keys fundamentally weak, and they designed an attack that would allow a passive listener to recover the secret WEP key simply by collecting a sufficient number of frames encrypted with weak keys. Though they did not implement the attack, others did. The first public description was in 2001 from an AT&T Labs technical report (Stubblefield, Ioannidis, & Rubin, 2001).

Aircrack is a WEP key cracker that the authors used. It implements the so-called Fluhrer-Mantin-Shamir (FMS) attack, along with some new attacks by KoreK. When enough encrypted packets have been gathered, Aircrack can almost instantly recover the WEP key. Every WEP encrypted packet has an associated 3-byte (24 bits) initialization vector. Some IVs leak information about a certain byte of key and, thus statistically, the correct key emerges when a sufficient number of IVs have been collected. To recover a WEP key, it really depends on the way the IVs are distributed. Most of the time, one million unique IVs (thus about 2 million packets) are enough.

Practical Cracking

Both the 64-bit and 128-bit WEP key cracking were tested and analyzed by the authors. The cracking was done using an ACER laptop client station with appropriate software. Huge files from the Internet (around 650 MB) were downloaded by the wireless laptop to create sufficient packets for capturing. The laptop had a built in wi-fi network adapter used for connection to the Internet through access point network. An additional CISCO Aironet 350 series PCMCIA card was used on the same laptop for packet capturing on channel 6. The packet capturing was done using Link Ferret software (version 3.10). Once the PCMCIA card is configured for promiscuous capturing, it cannot be used for connecting to a wireless network. The list of equipment (hardware or software) used is shown in Table 2.

The 128-bit WEP key (alphanumeric) was cracked by capturing around 3- to 4-million packets with 264674 unique IVs. The cracking took only 2 seconds and is shown in Figure 6. Other random 128-bit alphanumeric keys were also cracked easily.

Thus, WEP does not use RC4 encryption algorithm in a proper way, in that it exposes the protocol to weak key attacks, and free software hacker tools like Aircrack or Airsnort or others exploit this weakness.

Table 2. Hardware and software used for WEP cracking

Equipment/Item	Specification
Laptop	Acer Laptop with Mobile Centrino Intel processor, 256 MB RAM and 20 GB HDD with Windows XP.
Network Detection Software	NetStumbler 0.4.0
Packets Capturing Software	Link Ferret 3.10 (also used as analyzer)
Wireless Network Adapters	Onboard wireless network adapter and CISCO Aironet 350 series PCMCIA
WEP Cracking Software	Aircrack 2.1

Figure 6. WEP key (128 bits or rather 104 bits) cracked using Aircrack software

```
                          aircrack 2.1
  * Got   264674! unique IVs ! fudge factor = 2
  * Elapsed time [00:00:02] ! tried 1 keys at 30 k/m

  KB     depth    votes
   0     0/  2    01(  38) 7E(  24) 8C(  15) 63(  12) E6(   8) E4(   6)
   1     0/  1    23( 125) 64(  12) AE(   8) EC(   5) EF(   5) 84(   4)
   2     0/  3    45(  22) 74(  12) 32(  12) 3C(  10) 96(   5) D1(   5)
   3     0/  1    67(  59) 50(  15) 00(  12) 7B(   7) 7F(   6) F6(   6)
   4     0/  1    89(  77) A5(  24) C6(  23) 04(  12) F1(  12) 9D(  12)
   5     0/  4    AB(  19) BF(  10) 51(  10) 2F(   9) DF(   8) 60(   6)
   6     0/  1    CD(  74) B9(  15) 3E(  14) BA(  13) 01(  10) 40(   9)
   7     0/  2    EF(  57) E3(  45) 54(  20) 8A(  20) 34(  12) 76(  12)
   8     0/  1    01(  47) DA(  15) EC(  15) EA(  13) 42(  11) FF(   8)
   9     0/  3    23(  40) E9(  28) F2(  20) 62(  18) 55(  18) E1(  14)
  10     0/  1    45(  83) EB(  21) 9B(  18) 53(  12) BE(  11) 34(  10)
  11     0/  1    67( 126) 4B(  24) FF(  13) 5B(  12) 4A(  12) FD(  11)
  12     0/  1    89(  60) E9(  26) ED(  23) C1(  20) 3C(  15) FA(  13)

               KEY FOUND! [ 0123456789ABCDEF0123456789 ]

  Press Ctrl-C to exit.
```

War Driving and Packet Analysis

War driving is the process of driving around a place or city with a PC or laptop with a wireless card, running some wireless detection software and, preferably, connected to a global positioning system (GPS). The software detects the presence of wireless networks, and the war driver associates his device to the wireless network. This is due to the nature of all wireless networks, as they need to announce their existence so that potential clients can link up and use the services provided by the network. However, the information needed to join a network is also the information needed to launch an attack on a network. Beacon frames are not processed by any privacy functions, and that means that the 802.11 network and its parameters are available for anybody with a 802.11 card. War drivers have used high-gain antennas and software to log the appearance of Beacon frames and associate them with a geographic location using GPS.

Packet capturing can be done in various spots where wireless networks are detected through NetStumbler software alerts. Anyone would be quite surprised to see that quite a number of wireless networks were working without encryption. They simply had not enabled the WEP option. The authors had done war driving and packet capturing in eight different sessions for an average duration of around 30 minutes from different locations. The captured packet files are mainly from different locations that include petrol stations, banks, financial institutions, shopping complexes, and government organizations. It is unfortunate that the header of the wireless packets can reveal some interesting information, as it is transmitted in the clear. Sniffing and getting such details on a wired network is not that easy. Wireless frames/packets captured were a combination of control frames, management frames, and data frames. Control and management frames were much more in comparison to data frames. Some critical information captured were source, destination, and BSSID (or AP) MAC addresses; source and destination node IP addresses; source and destination node open port numbers; checksum details; initialization vector (IV) value; and so forth. This information in itself is not very sensitive, but some of it can be used to launch attacks against a wireless LAN, especially the DoS attacks.

Encrypted packets showed signs of using a set of WEP keys (against using one static key), and in some packets, TKIP protocol was used.

Some data packets were captured that were not even encrypted. Even though some APs were using WEP encrypted transmission with TKIP enabled, quite a number of unencrypted fragmented IEEE 802.11 data frames (with frame control type=2, i.e., type=data frame) could still be collected. These can be used to get meaningful or sensitive information that can interest an intruder, if one uses appropriate tools and shows some patient effort. For example, EtherPEG and DriftNet are free programs (EtherPEG, 2005 and DriftNet, 2005) that show you all the image files, like JPEGs and GIFs, traversing through our network. It works by capturing unencrypted TCP packets, and then grouping packets based on the TCP connection (i.e. from details determined from source IP address, destination IP address, source TCP port, and destination TCP port). It then joins or reassembles these packets in the right order based on the TCP sequence number, and then looks at the resulting data for byte patterns that show the existence of JPEG or GIF data. This is useful when one gets connected "illegally" to a wireless LAN.

Overall, 50 access points or peers in wireless networks without WEP encryption, and 21 access points or peers with WEP encryption using NetStumbler were located. It is similarly easy to even connect to an encrypted peer wireless network by typing in a random password. The PC or laptop thus connected can be assigned an IP address. Packet Analyzers like Ethereal (2005), Packetyzer (2005) and Link Ferret monitor software (Link Ferret, 2005) can be used for the detailed analysis of packets. Using filters, one could simply list out the interested packets. Each of those packets could then be analyzed with its detailed contents.

Table 3 gives some statistical information on data frames/packets that are unencrypted, and Figure 7 shows the related graph. The captured packet files (pkt1 to pkt8) are from seven different locations during different times (Issac, Jacob, & Mohammed, 2005).

Table 3. Details of captured packet files

Packet file name	No. of total packets	No. of unencrypted data packets (UDP)	Average unencrypted data packet size (in bytes)	No. of unencrypted data packets/sec
pkt1.cap	32767	2532	1081.86	3.31
pkt2.cap	32767	7482	108.17	2.42
pkt3.cap	19321	1397	428.34	1.05
pkt4.cap	32767	1465	228.15	0.45
pkt5.cap	6073	2385	173.85	1.30
pkt6.cap	32767	3527	83.57	4.71
pkt7.cap	32768	1558	84.79	1.13
pkt8.cap	39607	2550	77.25	1.81
Merged file	228837	22896	241.08	2.02

Figure 7. The graph showing the percentage of unencrypted data packets (UDP) captured from eight different sessions, based on Table 3.

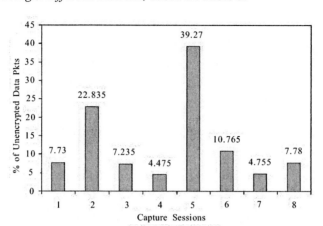

The data frames considered for tabular analysis fall into the following categories or groups — Data (frame type 32), Data + CF-Acknowledgement (frame type 33), Data + CF-Poll (frame type 34) and Data + CF-Acknowledgement/Poll (frame type 35). These data packets will be referred to as unencrypted data packets (UDP) from henceforth. Data frame type 32 dominates the population. The sample considered for analysis consists of unencrypted data frames and unencrypted fragmented data frames, both containing visible data sections in HEX format as viewed through Ethereal. The packet samples are *only indicative*, and they are not very exhaustive.

Frames of type Data + Acknowledgement (No data, frame type 37), Data + CF-Poll (No data, frame type 38), Data + CF-Acknowledgement (No data, frame type 39), QoS Data (frame type 40) and QoS Null (No data, frame type 44) are not considered for tabular analysis, since they contain no data payload or irrelevant data. From Table 3, one can see that the average number of unencrypted data packets per second is 2, and the average unencrypted data packet size is around 241.

Using *conditional probability* on the eight samples collected, the following is observed. Given an unencrypted packet, there exists a 15% average chance that it is a data packet.

Thus mathematically, $P_{avg}(DP \mid UP) = \dfrac{P(DP \cap UP)}{P(UP)} = 0.15$, where DP is data packet and

UP is unencrypted packet. Grouping the captured packets based on the source company/organization yielded Table 4. The 95% confidence interval was also calculated, assuming 5% error in captured packets. The results are quite revealing (Issac et al., 2005).

Table 4. Source of captured packets with 95% confidence interval calculation

Packet File name	Type of Company/ Organization	95% Confidence Interval for the proportion of unencrypted data packets
pkt1.cap	Petrol Station & Private Installations	(7.44%, 8.02%)
pkt2.cap	Bank/ Financial Institution	(22.38%, 23.29%)
pkt3.cap	Petrol Station	(6.87%, 7.60%)
pkt4.cap	Multistoried Shopping Complex	(4.25%, 4.70%)
pkt5.cap	Bank/ Financial Institution	(38.04%, 40.50%)
pkt6.cap	Bank/ Financial Institution	(10.43%, 11.10%)
pkt7.cap	Government Organization/ Office	(4.52%, 4.99%)
pkt8.cap	Government Organization/ Office	(7.49%, 8.07%)

IEEE802.11b Vulnerabilities and Other Attacks

This section presents some vulnerabilities that are present in the wireless networks. While most of these also apply to wired-networks as well, they are particularly important in wireless networks. This is not because the same risks are present, but also because of the nature of wireless networks that has made it more vulnerable than wired networks. The main focus will be in the areas such as interception, impersonation, denial-of-service, theft-of-service, and the like.

Issues with Default Access Point Setup

Access points (AP) are like base stations; they are the nonmobile unit that connects the wireless network into a wired network. They behave like a bridge or router. Usually, APs from manufacturers come with a set of default configuration parameters. These default parameters need to be changed in line with the corporate security policies, or else the default setup may leave some loopholes for attacks. For instance (depending on the manufacturer), most APs have a default administrator password, SSID, channels, authentication/encryption settings, SNMP read/write community strings, and so forth. Since these default values are available in user manuals, vendor's websites, and installation guides, they are well known to the general public, and may be used by wireless hackers to compromise WLAN security. Some default SSID based on different vendor products are shown in Table 5.

Table 5. Types of default SSID and their vendors

Vendor	Default SSID
Cisco Aironet	tsunami
3Com AirConnect	comcomcom
Symbol Technologies	101
Compaq WL -100/200/300/400	Compaq
D-Link DL -713	WLAN
SMC SMC2652W/SMC2526W	WLAN
SMC SMC2682	BRIDGE
Intel Pro/Wireless 2011	intel

A *service set identifier* (SSID) is a 32-byte case-sensitive text string that identifies the name of a wireless local area network (WLAN). All wireless devices on a WLAN must employ the same SSID in order to communicate with each other. SSID can be set either manually, by entering the SSID into the client network settings, or automatically by leaving the SSID unspecified or blank. A network administrator often uses a public SSID that is set on the access point and broadcast to all wireless devices in range. War drivers can scan for the SSIDs being broadcast by wireless LANs using software tools such as Netstumbler, Wellenreiter, and the like. Once they gain knowledge on the SSID, then they set that SSID on their client to attempt to join that WLAN. However, knowing the SSID name does not necessarily mean that rogue clients will be able to join the network, but it is part of the primary information required to carry on different forms of attacks.

The use of a Web browser or Telnet program to access the setup console of an access point can be a possibility from default values used in an AP setup. This allows the attacker to modify the configuration of the access point. Unless the administrator creates user-ID and password for authentication for AP's management console access, the network is in deep trouble with open access to the AP setup facility.

Rogue Access Point Installation

Easy access to wireless LANs is coupled with easy deployment. Any user can purchase an access point and connect it to the corporate network without authorization. Rogue access points deployed by end users pose great security risks. Many end users are not security experts and may not be aware of the risks posed by wireless LANs. Most existing small deployments mapped by war drivers do not enable the security features on products, and many access points have had only minimal changes made to the default settings. Unfortunately, no good solution exists to this concern. Software tools like NetStumbler allow network administrators to wander their building looking for unauthorized access points, though it is quite an effort to wander in the building looking for new access points. Moreover, monitoring tools will also pick up other access points in the area, which may be a concern if two or more organizations are sharing the same building or a floor. Access points from one organization may cover part of another organization's floor space.

DoS (Denial of Service) Attacks

Wireless networks based on 802.11b have a bit rate of 11 Mbps, and networks based on the newer 802.11a/g technology have bit rates of up to 54 Mbps. This capacity is shared between all the users associated with an access point. Due to MAC layer overhead, the actual effective throughput tops at roughly half of the nominal bit rate. It is not hard to imagine how local area applications might overwhelm such limited capacity, or how an attacker might launch a denial of service attack on the limited resources. Radio capacity can be overwhelmed in several ways. It can be swamped by traffic coming in from the wired network at a rate greater than the radio channel can handle. If an attacker were to launch a ping flood attack, it could easily overwhelm the capacity of an access point. Depending on the deployment scenario, it might even be possible to overwhelm several access points by using a broadcast address as the destination of the ping flood. Figure 8 shows a ping flood attack and the network utilization graph for a victim wireless node.

Attackers could also inject traffic into the radio network without being attached to a wireless access point. The 802.11 MAC is designed to allow multiple networks to share the same space and radio channel. Attackers wishing to take out the wireless network could send their own traffic on the same radio channel, and the target network would accommodate the new traffic as best as it could. DoS attacks could, thus, be easily applied to wireless networks, where legitimate traffic cannot reach clients or the access point because illegitimate traffic overwhelms the frequencies. Some other DoS attacks are TCP SYN flooding, Smurf attack, and fraggle attack. Distributed DoS attacks can do greater damage to network resources. Some performance complaints could be addressed by

Figure 8. Network utilization (y-axis) vs. time (x-axis) graph that shows the target equipment status during and after the ping flood attack (note that the graph drops after attack)

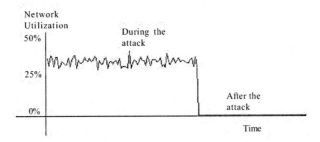

deploying a traffic shaper at the point at which a wireless LAN connects to the network backbone. While this will not defend against denial of service attacks, it may help prevent heavy users from monopolizing the radio resources in an area.

MAC Spoofing

In MAC spoofing, the attacker changes the manufacturer-assigned MAC address of a wireless adapter to the MAC address he wants to spoof, say by using tools like Mac Makeup software (Mac Makeup, 2005). Attackers can use spoofed frames to redirect traffic and corrupt ARP tables. At a much simpler level, attackers can observe the MAC addresses of stations in use on the network, and adopt those addresses for malicious transmissions. To prevent this class of attacks, user authentication mechanisms are being developed for 802.11 networks. By requiring mutual authentication by potential users, unauthorized users can be kept from accessing the network. Mac Makeup software can be used to do the MAC spoofing.

The MAC spoofing attack can be shown as in the outlined three steps in Figure 10.

Attackers can use spoofed frames in active attacks as well. In addition to hijacking sessions, attackers can exploit the lack of authentication of access points. Access points

Figure 9. Mac Makeup software. One can enter the MAC address to spoof and press Change button to change the original MAC address. Later, by pressing the Remove button, the original MAC address can be restored.

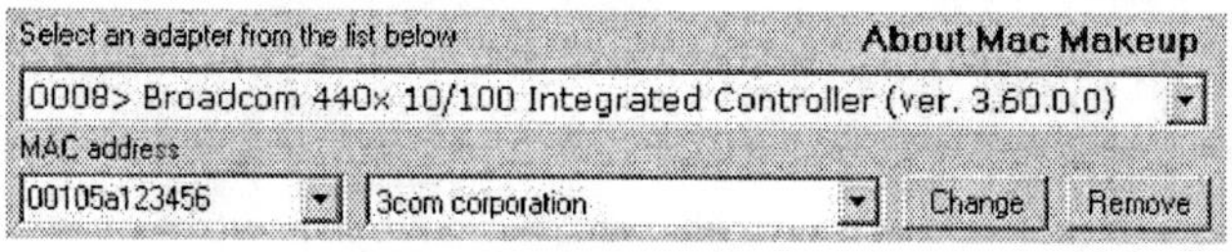

Select an adapter from the list below	About Mac Makeup
0008> Broadcom 440x 10/100 Integrated Controller (ver. 3.60.0.0)	
MAC address	
00105a123456	3com corporation	Change	Remove

Figure 10. MAC spoofing attack. Steps 1 to 3 are followed by the attacker.

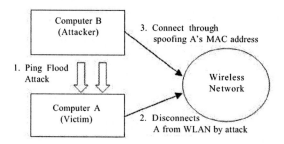

are identified by their broadcasts of Beacon frames. Any station that claims to be an access point and broadcasts the right service set identifier will appear to be part of an authorized network. Attackers can, however, easily pretend to be an access point because nothing in 802.11 requires an access point to prove it really is an access point. At that point, the attacker could potentially steal credentials and use them to gain access to the network through a man-in-the-middle (MITM) attack. Fortunately, protocols that support mutual authentication are possible with 802.1x. Using methods based on transport layer security (TLS), access points will need to prove their identity before clients provide authentication credentials, and credentials are protected by strong cryptography for transmission over the air.

Disassociation and Session Hijacking Attack

By configuring a wireless station to work as an access point, attackers can launch more effective DoS attacks. They can the flood the airwaves with continuous disassociate commands that compel all stations within range to disconnect from the wireless LAN. In another variation, the attacker's malicious access point broadcasts periodic disassociate commands that cause a situation where stations are continually disassociated from the network, reconnected, and disassociated again. Session hijacking is said to occur when an attacker causes the user to lose his connection, and the attacker assumes his identity and privileges for a period. An attacker temporarily disables the user's system, say by DoS attack or a buffer overflow exploit. The attacker then takes the identity of the user. The attacker now has all the access that the user has. When he is done, he stops the DoS attacks and lets the legitimate user resume. The user may not detect the interruption if the disruption lasts no more than a couple of seconds or few minutes. Such hijacking can be achieved by using a forged disassociation DoS attack, as explained previously.

Figure 11. ARP poisoning. The attacker C monitors the communication between Computer A and B by getting in between them.

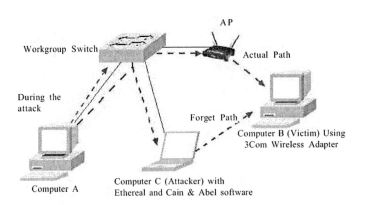

Traffic Analysis and Eavesdropping

Unlike in wired networks, a major problem with wireless networks is the ease of signal interception. Signals are broadcast through the air, where any receiver can intercept. Traffic can be passively observed without any protection. The main risk is that 802.11 does not provide a way to secure data in transit against eavesdropping. Frame headers are always unencrypted and are visible to anyone with a wireless network analyzer. Security against eavesdropping was supposed to be provided by WEP (as discussed earlier). WEP protects only the initial association with the network and user data frames. Management and control frames are not encrypted or authenticated by WEP, leaving an attacker wide latitude to disrupt transmissions with spoofed frames. If the wireless LAN is being used for sensitive data, WEP may very well be insufficient. It is therefore recommended to employ strong cryptographic solutions like SSH, SSL and IPSec. These were designed to transmit data securely over public channels, and have proven resistant to attack over many years, and will almost certainly provide a higher level of security. However, even when data is encrypted, attacker can gain insight about the meaning of the data by observing some properties such as message sizes, communication parties, and sequence of encrypted back-and-forth conversation. This technique is called traffic analysis, and can be effective (Frank, Sandeep, Golden, & Loren, 2005).

ARP Poisoning

In order to perform ARP poisoning, two desktop computers and one laptop can be used as shown in Figure 8. The two desktop computers (Computer A and Computer B) acted as the victims while the laptop (Computer C) acted as the attacker. A can be the source while B can be the destination. C can be equipped with the Ethereal (2005) packet capturing software and the ARP poisoning software known as Cain and Abel (2005).

In ARP poisoning, an attacker can exploit ARP cache poisoning to intercept network traffic between two devices in the WLAN. For instance, let us say the attacker wants to see all the traffic between computer A and B. The attacker begins by sending a malicious ARP "reply" (for which there was no previous request) to B, associating his computer's MAC address with A's IP address. Now B thinks that the attacker's computer is A. Next, the attacker sends a malicious ARP reply to A, associating his MAC address with B's IP address. Now A thinks that the hacker's computer is B.

Finally, the hacker turns on an operating system feature called IP forwarding. This feature enables the hacker's machine to forward any network traffic it receives from Computer A to B. Instead of enabling IP forwarding, the attacker has the choice of drowning Computer B with any DoS attack, so that the communication actually happens between A and the attacker, whom A thinks to be Computer B (Mohammed & Issac, 2005).

Operating System Weakness

Another security problem lies in the operating system. For instance, NetBIOS and SMB services allow unauthenticated users to create NULL sessions, thus permitting attackers to gain access to information about the machines they exploit. These services are enabled by default on Windows systems. Windows 2000 and Windows XP use ports 135 through 139, and port 445. When improperly configured, NetBIOS service can expose critical system files or give full file system access to any hostile party connected to the network. Many computer owners and administrators use these services to make their file systems readable and writable, in an effort to improve the convenience of data access. When file sharing is enabled on Windows machines, they become vulnerable to both information theft and certain types of quick-moving viruses. The same NetBIOS mechanisms that permit Windows file sharing may also be used to enumerate sensitive system information from Windows NT systems. User and group information (usernames, last logon dates, password policy, etc.), system information, and certain registry keys may be accessed via a NULL session connection to the NetBIOS session service. This information is typically used to mount a password guessing or brute force password attack against a Windows NT target.

Flipping Bits

Research has proved that an attacker could flip certain bits (bit flipping) in the frame and change the integrity check value without the knowledge of the user. At the receiving end, no error on tampering would then be reported. Though difficult to carry out this attack, it is possible to do it and has been proved. Encrypt the 802.11 frames within layer 3 (network layer) wrappers, so that any tampering cannot go undetected. IPSec tunnel or TKIP (temporal key integrity protocol) can be used to thus strengthen the security.

WLAN Security Safeguards

Wireless networks can never be security-risk free. Being risk free is an ideal concept that just does not exist. But we can try our best to minimize the possible attacks. Some security steps are listed here (Held, 2003; Hurton & Mugge, 2003; Issac et al., 2005).

1.   To start with, WEP 104-bit encryption should be enabled, with possible rotation of keys. WPA, with TKIP/AES options, can be enabled. Upgrade the firmware on AP to prevent the use of weak IV WEP keys. This is the first line of defense. The WEP key shall be a very random alphanumeric combination. In order to overcome the weakness in the current 802.11b WLAN standard, IEEE Task Group i has come out with draft version of 802.11i standard. The 802.11i standard explains the usage of 48-bit IV in temporal key integrity protocol (TKIP) that helps to minimize

cryptographic attacks against WEP key, brute force attack, and the weakness of static key. TKIP is a short-term solution to the WEP key (Walker, 2002). TKIP also helps to prevent undetected modification to the WEP key by providing an 8-byte message integrity code (MIC). Furthermore, counter mode cipher block chaining with message authentication codes (counter mode CBC-MAC or CCMP), which will be the long term security solution introduced by 802.11i standard, uses advanced encryption standard (AES), which encrypts data in 128-bit chunks using cipher block chaining (CBC) mode, and provides data integrity checks via medium access control (MAC) (Vocal Tech. Ltd., 2003). However, the emergence of equipments bundled with the 802.11i standard has yet to step into the market.

2. Ensure that mutual authentication is done through IEEE802.1x protocol. Client and AP should both authenticate to each other. Implementing IEEE802.1x port based authentication with RADIUS server (with PEAP/MS-CHAPv2) can be a second level of defense. There is now a regular rotation of key and per client WEP key.

3. Turn off the SSID broadcast by AP and configure the AP not to respond to probe requests with SSID "any" by setting your own SSID. Knowledge of SSID can be a stepping-stone to other attacks.

4. Change default WEP settings, if any. For example, Linksys AP WAP-11 comes with default WEP key one: 10 11 12 13 14 15, default WEP key two: 20 21 22 23 24 25, default WEP key three: 30 31 32 33 34 35 and default WEP key four: 40 41 42 43 44 45.

5. It is always better to change the default SSID (service set identifier, like the network name for WLAN) to a difficult one, and to disable any SSID broadcast in control frames. Knowledge of SSID itself may not cause direct harm, but it can be the first step for an attacker to proceed further.

6. Change the default IP address in the access point to a different one. For example, CISCO WAP54G AP comes with a built-in IP address 192.168.1.245 and DLink AP DWL-G730AP comes with a default IP address of 192.168.0.30. Enable dynamic IP addressing through DHCP.

7. Also, change the default login/password details for console access that comes along with an access point. For example, CISCO WAP54G AP uses a blank username and the word "admin" as password, CISCO Aironet 350 AP (802.11b) does not use any login/password by default, and DLink AP DWL-G730AP comes with a default user name, "admin," and no password.

8. Enabling the MAC filtering in AP level or in RADIUS server, or in both, can tighten the security more, as there is a restriction in the use of MAC addresses. Though MAC spoofing can be a possible attack, MAC filtering definitely tightens the security.

9. Positioning and shielding of antenna can help to direct the radio waves to a limited space. Antenna positioning can help the radio waves to be more directed and antenna shielding, with radio transmission power adjustment (5mW to 100mW), can confine it to a restricted environment. In order to limit the transmission range of the AP, shielding the AP with aluminum foil can be carried out.

10. Limiting DHCP clients can restrict the number of clients that can get hooked to the WLAN. The DHCP server can be configured to limit the number of clients

connecting concurrently. This can prevent an intruder getting connected when the total number is used up.

11. Data transmitted over a local wireless link should be secured. To secure only the data transmitted over the wireless link, the dedicated security server(s) can be placed anywhere within the enterprise network. Authentication is used to restrict which users are allowed to establish encrypted links with the security server. Similarly, data transmitted over local and public wireless links should be secured. Most enterprises are concerned about preventing unauthorized users from gaining access to their corporate network through wireless access points. We recommend putting a firewall between the wireless access points and the rest of the enterprise's wire line network. Using firewall between AP and the wired LAN can secure the wired LAN from further intrusion. Firewall can be configured to filter based on IP address, port numbers, MAC address, and so forth.

12. Enabling of accounting and logging can help to locate and trace back some mischief that could be going on in the network. Preventive measures can then be taken after the preliminary analysis of the log file. Allow regular analysis of log files captured to trace any illegal access or network activity.

13. Using an intrusion detection software can help to monitor the network activity in real time. Using an intrusion-prevention software can, to some extent, prevent access to intruders. It would thus be suggestive to use monitoring tools to police the activities on WLAN like intrusion and rogue access points. One such example would be IBM's Distributed Wireless Security Auditor, which can be accessed at http://www.research.ibm.com/gsal/dwsa/. Even big enterprises can be breached if employees within the office set up rogue APs themselves, or if they turn their wireless laptops into what is known as soft APs. Using commonly available freeware tools such as Host AP, which can be accessed at http://hostap.epitest.fi/, a laptop with a wireless card can be transformed into an access point, allowing anyone within range to connect through the laptop's wired ethernet connection. In any case, an intelligent WLAN monitoring tool can help to locate suspicious activities.

14. Implement VPN on WLAN. VPN technology has been used successfully in wired networks, especially when using Internet as a physical medium. This success of VPN in wired networks and the inherent security limitations of wireless networks have prompted developers and administrators to deploy VPN to secure wireless LANs. IPSec tunnel can thus be implemented for communication between nodes.

15. Use honey pots or fake APs in the regular network to confuse the intruder so that he/she gets hooked to that fake AP without achieving anything. Thus, the NetStumbler WLAN detection software, if used by the hacker, would then list the fake AP, and could get him/her into wasting his/her time.

16. The security management of the access points can be made better, especially when the WLAN deployment is large, with many AP installations across a campus. In such a situation, security configuration and other policies need to be done on individual APs, and that can be a hassle when the number of APs increase. We propose to make the APs less intelligent from what it is now, and to have an intelligent central switch to control a limited set of APs configuration, policy, and

security settings, like in any client-server environment. For example, let us say the ratio be one intelligent switch for n less-intelligent access points. Hence, the management of security settings can be done centrally.

17. Access points need to be secured from unauthorized access. In this case, the access point network, and in particular the wireless devices on it, may still be accessible by any device within range. To prevent unauthorized devices from communicating with other devices and resources, we recommend using access points with built-in protocol filtering (such as the Cisco Aironet Series).

18. Physical security is also important, and steps can be taken to limit the physical access to any networking resources (say by locking it within a box or within a room), thereby preventing other forms of attacks.

19. Enabling biometric finger print authentication on the top of existing schemes can really tighten the security, especially for accessing super-sensitive data.

Conclusion

Although we cannot make any network fully secure, we can try our best to minimize the anticipated attacks. A wireless LAN security checklist would include checking on features like access control, access point, antenna operation, authentication, encryption, firewall, network scan, physical security, SNMP, and VPN. The challenge ahead is to make the network and system administrators security conscious; thereby, allowing them to use the highest level of security in an implemented wireless LAN. Many a time, ignorance holds the key to various information thefts and other attacks, and eventual loss to businesses in hefty sums. The authors feel, as a general precaution, that an intelligent intrusion, detection, or prevention software can help locate many mischiefs in a wireless network.

References

Arbaugh, W. A. (2001). An inductive chosen plaintext attack against WEP/WEP2. *IEEE Document 802.11-01/230*. Retrieved July 20, 2005, from http://grouper.ieee.org/groups/802/11/Documents/index.html

Arbaugh, W. A., Shankar, N., & Wan, Y. C. J. (2001). Your 802.11 wireless network has no clothes. Retrieved July 20, 2005, from http://www.cs.umd.edu/~waa/wireless.pdf

Badrinath, B. R., Bakre, A., Imielinski, T., & Marantz, R. (1993). Handling mobile clients: A case for indirect interaction. In *Proceedings of the 4th Workstation Operating Systems*, CA, USA.

Borisov, N., Goldberg, I., & Wagner, D. (2001). Intercepting mobile communications: The insecurity of 802.11. Published in *Proceedings of the Seventh Annual Interna-*

tional Conference on Mobile Computing and Networking. Retrieved July 20, 2005, from http://www.isaac.cs.berkeley.edu/isaac/mobicom.pdf

Cain & Abel software. Retrieved August 15, 2005, from http://www.oxidt.it

Cam-Winget, N., Housley, R., Wagner, D., & Walker, J. (2003) Security flaws in 802.11 data link protocols. *Communications of the ACM*, 35-39.

Campbell, P., Calvert, B., & Boswell, S. (2003). *Security+ guide to network security fundamentals.* CA: Thomson Course Technology.

Chan, F., Ang, H. H., & Issac, B. (2005). Analysis of IEEE 802.11b wireless security for university wireless LAN design. *Proceedings of IEEE International Conference on Networks (ICON 2005)*, Malaysia (pp. 1137-1142).

Chen. T. (2005). Signaling for secure and efficient QoS-aware mobility support in IP-based cellular networks., MSc Thesis. Retrieved August 7, 2005, from http://edocs.tu-berlin.de/diss/2004/chen_tianwei.pdf

DriftNet software. Retrieved August 10, 2005, from http://www.ex-parrot.com/~chris/driftnet/

Ethereal software. Retrieved August 10, 2005, from http://www.ethereal.com/

EtherPEG software. Retrieved August 5, 2005, from http://www.etherpeg.org/

Fluhrer, S., Mantin, I., & Shamir, A. (2001). *Weaknesses in the key scheduling algorithm of RC4.* Paper presented at the Eighth Annual Workshop on Selected Areas in Cryptography. Retrieved July 25, 2005, from http://downloads.securityfocus.com/library/rc4_ksaproc.pdf

Frank, A, Sandeep, K. S. G., Golden, G. R., & Loren, S. (2005), *Fundamentals of mobile and pervasive computing.* McGraw-Hill.

freeRADIUS software. Retrieved August15, 2005, from http://www.freeRADIUS.org

Gast, M. (2002) *Wireless LAN security: A short history.* Retrieved July 25, 2005, from http://www.oreillynet.com/pub/a/wireless/2002/04/19/security.html

Gast, M. S. (2002). *802.11 wireless networks: The definitive guide.* CA: O'Reilly Media.

Giller, R., & Bulliard, A. (2004). *Security Protocols and Applications 2004: Wired Equivalent Privacy.* Lausanne, Switzerland: Swiss Institute of Technology.

Held, G. (2003). *Securing wireless LANs.* Sussex: John Wiley & Sons.

Hurton, M., & Mugge, C. (2003). *Hack notes: Network security portable reference.* CA: McGraw-Hill/Osborne.

IEEE Recommendation. (2003). *Recommended practice for multi-vendor of access point interoperability via an inter-access point protocol across distribution systems supporting IEEE 802.11 operation, IEEE 802.11F- 2003.*

Issac, B., Jacob, S. M., & Mohammed, L. A. (2005). The art of war driving: A Malaysian case study. In *Proceedings of IEEE International Conference on Networks (ICON 2005)*, Malaysia (pp. 124-129).

LinkFerret Software. Retrieved August 5, 2005, from http://www.linkferret.ws/

Mac Makeup software. Retrieved August 15, 2005, from http://www.gorlani.com/publicprj/macmakeup/macmakeup.asp

Microsoft Corporation. (2000). *Microsoft help in Windows 2000 server*. Retrieved July 20, 2005, from http://www.microsoft.com

Mohammed, L. A., & Issac, B. (2005). DoS attacks and defense mechanisms in wireless networks. In *Proceedings of the IEE Mobility Conference 2005* (Mobility 2005), Guangzhou, China (pp. P2-1A-4).

NetStumbler software. Retrieved August 5, 2005, from http://www.netstumbler.org

Packetyzer software. Retrieved July 25, 2005, from http://www.networkchemistry.com/products/packetyzer/

Strand, L. (2004). *802.1X Port-Based Authentication HOWTO*. Retrieved July 15, 2005, from http://www.tldp.org/HOWTO/8021X-HOWTO

Stubblefield, A., Ioannidis, J., & Rubin, A. D. (2001). Using the Fluhrer, Mantin, and Shamir attack to break WEP. *AT&T Labs Technical Report TD-4ZCPZZ*. Retrieved July 25, 2005, from http://www.cs.rice.edu/~astubble/wep

Vocal Tech. Ltd. (2003). *Counter CBC-MAC protocol (CCMP) encryption algorithm*. Retrieved July 28, 2005, from http://www.vocal.com/CCMP.pdf

Walker, J. R. (2000) Unsafe at any key size: An analysis of the WEP encapsulation. *IEEE Document 802.11-00/362*. Retrieved July 20, 2005, from http://grouper.ieee.org/groups/802/11/Documents/index.html

Walker, J. (2002). *802.11 security series Part II: TKIP*. Retrieved July 25, 2005 from http://cache-www.intel.com/cd/00/00/01/77/17769_80211_part2.pdf

Chapter II

Wireless Web Security Using a Neural Network-Based Cipher

Isaac Woungang, Ryerson University, Canada

Alireza Sadeghian, Ryerson University, Canada

Shuwei Wu, Ryerson University, Canada

Sudip Misra, Cornell University, USA

Maryam Arvandi, Ryerson University, Canada

Abstract

The increasingly important role of security for wireless Web services environments has opened an array of challenging problems centered on new methods and tools to improve existing data encryption and authentication techniques. Real-time recurrent neural networks offer an attractive approach to tackling such problems because of the high encryption capability provided by the structural hidden layers of such networks. In this chapter, a novel neural network-based symmetric cipher is proposed. This cipher releases the constraint on the length of the secret key to provide the data integrity and authentication services that can be used for securing wireless Web services communication. The proposed symmetric cipher design is robust in resisting different cryptanalysis attacks. Simulation results are presented to validate its effectiveness.

Introduction

With the widespread availability of the 802.11b standard and products, and their deployment in wireless networks supporting a host of telecommunication services, including multimedia services, there is a clear demand for network layer security, in recent years. In a wireless setting, any host within physical communications range can intercept and spoof network packets; therefore, corporate as well as wireless residential users face a substantial security threat. Resolving these problems at the application layer alone is not a desirable solution (Stubblefield et. al., 2002). For example, all applications would have to be upgraded on both the client and server sides to use authenticated protocols, which would take a considerable amount of time. However, network layer security protocols, such as the Internet protocol security (IPSec, 2004), provide the capability to solve these problems, since it secures end-to-end communications between hosts (Kent & Atkinson, 1998). As encryption is at the core of this framework, as well as many other security and authentication protocols, this chapter proposes a novel neural network-based symmetric cipher for message encryption. This novel cipher block chaining mode (CBC)-based encryption scheme is robust in resisting different cryptanalysis attacks, and provides efficient data integrity and authentication services that can be beneficial to wireless Web services. The design of the proposed symmetric cipher is presented, and its security is analyzed by examining two types of attacks: one against the message authentication code (MAC), and the other against the data encryption scheme itself. Simulation results are also presented to validate the effectiveness of the proposed symmetric cipher design.

The rest of the chapter is organized as follows. First, a background work sustaining the topic discussed in this chapter is presented as follows: (1) Cryptographic as a motivation for this study; (2) Review of previous research pertinent to applying neural network in cryptography. Second, the main thrusts of this chapter are discussed, which include (1) The proposed novel symmetric cipher design; (2) A security analysis of the proposed cipher design; and (3) Simulation results validating the proposed cipher design. Third, the future and emerging trends of the studied topic are discussed, which include a viability study, and foreseen research issues related to the aforementioned symmetric cipher design. Finally, the conclusion is presented.

Cryptography as a Motivation
for this Study

The boundary of interaction between communicating systems has significantly increased from intranets to the Internet with the adoption of Web services. In this context, information security (understood here as authentication, access control, confidentiality, integrity, and nonrepudiation) has become a top priority due to the existence of threats such as viruses, hackers, electronic eavesdropping, frauds, and so forth. One way to protect the secrecy of the information is by using *cryptography*, known as the science and study of secret writing (Deming, 1982). The basic objective of cryptography is to enable two peers (persons or computers) to communicate over an insecure channel while preserving the secrecy of the information. In this correspondence, the originated message is known as *plaintext*, while the coded message is referred to as the *ciphertext*. *Confusion* and *diffusion* (Schneier, 1996) are basic techniques used for obscuring the redundancies in a plaintext (diffusion disperses parts of the letters throughout the ciphertext, while confusion prevents the cryptanalyst from using ciphertext to figure out the secret encryption key). The process of transforming a plaintext into ciphertext is called *encryption*, and the process of turning ciphertext back to plaintext is called *decryption*. In general, a cryptosystem comprises five components: a plaintext message, a ciphertext message, a key, an encryption scheme, and a decryption scheme; and is characterized by (1) the type of operations used for transforming plaintext to ciphertext (these operations are bit-stream based or block-stream based); (2) the number and type of keys used (symmetric or secret key encryption, and asymmetric or public key encryption); and finally (3) the manner in which the plaintext is processed (block cipher scheme, in which an n-bit plaintext block is mapped onto an n-bit ciphertext, or stream cipher scheme, in which a plaintext stream is mapped onto a ciphertext stream). Cryptography methodologies are of two groups: (1) conventional cryptography [known as private key cryptosystems and public key cryptosystems; examples are Data Encryption Standard, Advanced Encryption Standard, Rivest-Shamir-Adleman algorithms (Stallings, 2003)]; and (2) *nonconventional* cryptography. The latter involves complex algebraic and theoretical problems that often require the use of a broad range of mathematical and computational intelligent techniques to be resolved (Meletiou, Tasoulis, & Vrahatis, 2003). One of these methods is the application of *artificial neural networks in cryptography*, which has just been explored in recent years (Meletiou, Tasoulis, & Vrahatis, 2002 and the references therein). This idea constitutes the foundation of the novel symmetric cipher design that is proposed in this chapter.

What is an Artificial Neural Network?

In contrast to the conventional concept of programmed computing, an artificial neural network (ANN) can be defined as a type of *information processing paradigm* inspired by the way biological nervous systems, such as the brain, operate. The key element of this paradigm is a novel structure of the information processing system, composed of a large number of highly interconnected units called *artificial neurons* (an example of neuron model is shown in Figure 1).

In an ANN architecture, each unit has an input/output characteristic, and implements its own local computation while keeping track of its interconnection to other units. The unit's architecture is mainly composed of (1) a set of weighted *synapses* (i.e., connecting links); (2) an *adder* for summing the input signals; and (3) an *activation function;* here, thresholds are often defined to lower the activation function's input. In other words, a neuron k (as shown in Figure 1) can be described by writing the following pair of equations:

Figure 1. Nonlinear model of a neuron

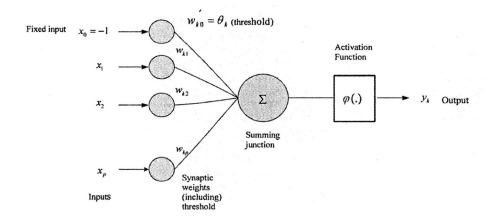

$$v_k = \sum_{j=0}^{p} w_{kj} x_j$$

$$y_k = \varphi(v_k),$$

where x_1, x_2, x_p are the input signals; w_{k1}, w_{k2}, ..., w_{kp} are the synaptic weights of neuron k; v_k is the linear combiner output; θ_k is the threshold; $\varphi(.)$ is the activation function; and y_k is the output signal of the neuron. A rigorous mathematical definition of these concepts can be found in Haykin (1998).

Real-Time Recurrent Neural Networks

In this chapter, a particular type of ANNs, known as *real-time recurrent neural networks (RRNNs)*, is used. RRNNs are ANNs with at least one *feedback loop*. For example, an RRNN may consist of a single layer of neurons, with each neuron feeding its output signal back to the inputs of all the other neurons (it should be noticed that the proposed RRNN architecture, as shown later in Figure 2, satisfies the aforementioned requirement). An ANN is usually configured for a specific application through a learning process. In this case, the proposed RRNN is designed for data encryption and decryption purposes, and the corresponding learning process involves adjustments to the synaptic connections that exist between the neurons. The operation of the network consists of iterative steps.

At the beginning, the states of the input layer neurons are assigned to generally real inputs, and the remaining hidden and output layers are passive. In the next step, the neurons from the first hidden layer collect and sum their inputs, then compute their output. This procedure is then propagated to the subsequent layers until the final outputs of the network are computed. Here, the training process is based on patterns for which the desired output is known a-priori. More often, an *adaptation procedure* is needed to adjust the patterns in order to obtain the required network outputs. The adaptation process starts by presenting all the patterns to the network, then computing and minimizing a total error function, E, defined as the sum of squared discrepancies between the actual network outputs and the desired values. One popular way of achieving this is by using the back propagation methods (Haykin, 1998). Each full pass of all the network patterns is referred to as a *training epoch*.

Since the application of ANNs as a tool for cryptography is at the core of the proposed design methodology, it is necessary to discuss the existing neural network approaches for cryptography, while highlighting some of their limitations or usability scope.

Previous Research Pertinent to Applying Neural Network in Cryptography

In the course of the last decade, a number of researchers have attempted the application of neural network-based techniques for cryptography purposes. More recently, Scott et al. (2000) and Su, Lin, and Yen (2000) proposed to use unpredictable outputs of a neural network, together with a dedicated hardware to encrypt digital signals. The randomness of the output of the system, built using a specific VLSI architecture, determines whether the encrypted data is predictable or not. These cipher designs involve complex bit operations, as pointed out by the authors themselves. Yee and De Silva (2000) suggested the use of multilayer perceptron (MLP) for key scheduling that employs a mutating algorithm comprising a modular arithmetic and a Feistel cipher. This method has a fixed key length. They also proposed the use of MLP networks in public key cryptography and as a one-way hash function. The feasibility of employing their MLP-based ciphers as both software and hardware solutions to some cryptanalysis attacks, such as differential/linear attacks, are not studied. Meletiou et al. (2002) proposed the use of feed-forward neural networks (in multilayer feed-forward networks, the inputs form an input layer, while the output neurons form the output layer. All other neurons are assigned to a number of hidden layers. Finally, in a given layer, each neuron is fully connected to all other neurons in the next layer) for computing the Euler function in RSA cryptosystems. As pointed out by the authors themselves, their ANN construction may be suitable for use in RSA cryptosystems, but more work is needed with regard to the normalization portion of their training algorithms. Kinzel and Kanter (2002) and Rosen et al. (Rosen, Kanter, & Kinzel, 2002) have proposed an analytical study of a neural cryptography scheme based on a mutual learning process between two parity feed-forward neural networks with discrete and continuous weights. The synchronization process is claimed to be non-self-averaging, and the analytical solution is based on random auxiliary variables. The learning time of an attacker that is trying to imitate one of the networks has been examined analytically, and is reported to be much longer than the synchronization time. Klimov et al. (Klimov, Mityaguine, & Shamir, 2002) have shown that Kinzel's protocol can be broken by geometric, probabilistic, and genetic attacks; thus, it is not entirely secure. Karras and Zorkadis (2003) have proposed the construction of robust random number generators based on MLP networks to be used in security mechanisms. Their MLP networks construction is useful in public key cryptography, but more research is needed to use their MLP networks as an authentication tool. Contrasted to all of the ANNs design approaches, the proposed ANNs-based cipher has at least three advantages: (1) its architecture is *relatively simple* (a detailed description follows in subsequent sections), (2) it satisfies both the diffusion and confusion properties; and (3) there are no constraints on the secret key length.

Moreover, in cipher design-related literature, a considerable amount of effort has been focused towards finding a means for knowledge representation using neural networks. Towards this end, popular algorithms were developed based on the pruning methods (Cant'u-Paz, 2003; Reed, 1993, and the references therein). The objective of a pruning method is to optimize the ANN architecture that, in turn, is determined by a trial-and-error process. Pruning methods can be classified either as sensitivity-based or penalty-term methods. In sensitivity methods, the error sensitivity to the removal of an element is estimated, and according to this, the elements to be removed are selected. In penalty-term methods, a cost function is used to drive unnecessary weights nearly to zero. In this study, this latter type of pruning method is used, and it is explained in the following subsection.

Neural Network "Black Box" as a Tool for Security

While selecting the structure of a network to be trained in an application environment, determining the *size* (i.e., the number of hidden layers, and the number of neurons per hidden layer) is a challenging problem. If the neural network size is less than what the application requires, that is, fewer hidden layers for instance, then the learning data with higher-order dynamics and nonlinearities might not be achievable. On the other hand, if the neural network size is more than what the application requires, it may result in *overfitting*, meaning that the learning error for the training data is minimized, but the error for the sets of testing data may be significantly increased.

One approach to avoid over-fitting is to use a neural network of *robust size* for a specific application, which has the capability to learn the training data fairly well while maintaining an acceptable generalization capability for the testing data. One method to identify that *robust size* of the neural network is by *pruning the weights* of the neural network. In reality, many pruning algorithms exist (Almeida, 1987; Cant'u-Paz, 2003; Reed, 1993; Williams & Zipser, 1989). Most of these algorithms are usually brute force and arbitrary. They treat the network as *a black box* solution (Benitez, Castro, & Requena, 1997), and tend to find its optimum size and structure based on the observation of the network input-output behaviors. The core problem is still not touched, since the *knowledge representation* of neural networks is unknown in such a case. In other words, neural networks have been applied successfully for training and learning purposes in a variety of applications; yet, they are considered a *black box* solution. A *black box* can be considered as having the potential capability of providing secure wireless Web services, and in general any network security, due to its lack of transparency.

In the case of wireless security, the advantage of a wireless network is that it uses airways instead of wires to communicate, but the price of this flexibility is that the network traffic can be intercepted by anyone with a scanning device (Coyle, 2001). To secure wireless transactions, wireless applications protocols use the wireless transport layer security (WLTS) protocol, and a wireless version of the public key infrastructure (PKI). Secure communication from a cell phone to a wireless access point (WAP) travels with WTLS until it reaches a gateway, where it is converted to secure sockets layer (SSL) as it continues its path to a Web server. Before a WAP gateway can convert a WTLS to an encrypted SSL, it must first decrypt the WTLS packets. As well, secure data transmission across Bluetooth networks depends on the link and application layers that are part of the protocol stack. At the link layer, the Bluetooth radio system provides authentication, encryption, and key management of users' public and private keys. Once other Bluetooth devices are assured about the identity of whom they are communicating with, the data can be encrypted at various key lengths, depending on requirements. This discussion reveals that encryption is at the core of many approaches to securing access to wireless voice and data. This leads to the fact that new data encryption technologies are always desirable. In the next section, a novel symmetric cipher based on RRNNs is proposed, which provides data integrity and authentication services that can be used for securing wireless Web services communication.

The Proposed Novel Symmetric Cipher Design

This section describes an innovative attempt to apply neural network learning techniques for cryptography purpose by means of such capability. The proposed symmetric cipher design is based on real-time recurrent neural networks (RRNN), as shown in Figure 2.

This real-time recurrent neural network has a multilayer structure with two constraints: (1) the dimension of the input vector X is twice that of the output vector Y; (2) one of the hidden layers has only one neuron with an output denoted by ξ. The symmetric cipher operates in two stages: key extension and data encryption/decryption. A popular pruning method (Haykin, 1998) is used to determine a neural network of *robust size* that has the capability to learn the training data fairly well, and still maintain an acceptable generalization capability for the tested data. A robust size is identified by pruning the weights of the neural network. In specific terms, at the beginning of the learning process, a large-size neural network is used; then, the irrelevant weights and nodes of the network are removed in an iterative process until a smaller-size network is derived.

This simple architecture satisfies the confusion and diffusion properties of the cipher. These are two basic techniques for obscuring the redundancies in a plaintext message.

Figure 2. Proposed recurrent neural network for cipher design

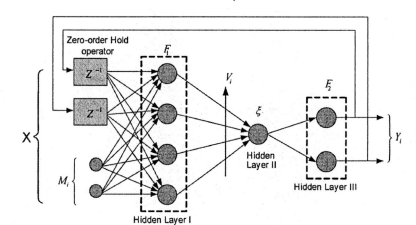

From the input layer up to the hidden layer II-the layer with only one neuron ξ-confusion is achieved, which is similar to the effect of substitution. Then, by applying the simple nonlinear function (sigmoid function in this case) to the inputs, diffusion is gained, which is similar to transposition. In addition, keeping the structure of the network *simple* can help with its analysis.

Key Extension

Suppose there are two users at the different ends of a communication line with an identical symmetric cipher based on a neural network similar to that in Figure 2. They will exchange a secret key S that contains the following three parts of information: (1) the input vector X; (2) the training target Y; and (3) the critical value of the self-adaptive procedure α. Vectors X and Y will then be presented to the neural network for training. The purpose of the training process is to make the neural network detect, store, or even "remember" the secret key information. The trained neural network parameters will be kept unrevealed and become the extended secret key for the subsequent encryption and decryption procedures. The last actual output of the network during the key extension will be the initial vector, M_0, for the encryption. It is commonly assumed that the weight distribution of the hidden layers is chaotic and unpredictable without the knowledge of the training data (i.e., the original secret key). Therefore, it is not feasible for a cryptanalyst to analyze the extended key. By changing the length of the secret key and the dimension or the hierarchy of the hidden layers, the user can adjust the security level accordingly. A major advantage of the proposed cipher design is its capability to release the constraints imposed on the length of the secret key.

Encryption

The structure of the symmetric cipher design (shown in Figure 2) ensures that among the hidden layers of the neural network, there exists at least one that has only one neuron (denoted as neuron ξ). This feature is used to decompose the feed-forward operation of the neural network into two functions, F_1 and F_2. In this decomposition, F_1 is the feedforward operation over the weight and bias matrices performed from the input layer to neuron ξ, and F_2 is the similar type of operation performed from neuron ξ to the output layer. These functions are then used in the encryption process that consists of two steps: (1) ciphertext generation; and (2) one-epoch training.

Ciphertext Generation

The plaintext should first be mapped to vectors $M_{i(i=1,...,n)} = \{M_1, M_2, M_3, ... M_n\}$ according to the dimension of input vectors. The first vector of the message M_1 is combined with the initial vector M_0 from the key extension procedure to build the following initial input vector:

$$X_1 = \left(M_0 \| M_1\right) \tag{1}$$

where $\|$ denotes a vector concatenation operator, that is, two $(n \times 1)$ vectors M_0 and M_1 are concatenated to form a $(2n \times 1)$ vector. Next, X_1 is presented to the neural network to produce both the intermediary neuron output V_1 in the hidden layer and the output Y_1. The error signal is calculated as $E_1 = M_1 - Y_1$, where M_1 is the target of the identity mapping. Finally, E_1 and V_1 are considered as the first block of the ciphertext referred to as $C_1\{V_1, E_1\}$.

One-Epoch Training

After the first ciphertext block C_1 is constructed, the neural network can be trained for one-epoch using X_1 as the input vector and M_1 as the training target. From the second and all following plaintext blocks, the preceding time instant output $Y_{i-1}(i=2,...,n)$ of the neural network is combined with the current plaintext block M_i to yield the current input vector. In order words, the input vectors can then be built according to:

$$X_i = \left(Y_{i-1} \| M_i\right), \quad i = 2, 3,...,\text{n} \tag{2}$$

Figure 3. Symmetric cipher in CBC mode (MLP: multilayer perceptron)

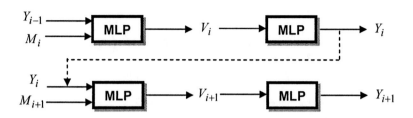

These two steps of encryption are repeated to generate values for V_i and Y_i and hence, train the neural network for one-epoch at a time. In fact, this encryption procedure will result in a symmetric cipher working in the cipher block-chaining (CBC) mode, as implicitly shown in Figure 3.

To summarize this procedure, the ciphertext blocks C_i are constructed as follows:

$$V_i = F_1(X_i) \tag{3}$$

$$Y_i = F_2(V_i) \tag{4}$$

$$E_i = M_i - Y_i \tag{5}$$

$$ST = C\{V_i, E_i\} \tag{6}$$

where ST refers to the ciphertext at the instant i. The recurrent neural network structure in Figure 3 is a schematic representation of equations (3) to (6). The first hidden layer defines F_1 in equation (3). The second hidden layer has one neuron ξ. The third hidden layer implements the function F_2 that computes the output Y_i as shown in equation (4). Finally, the output at time instant i is fed back through a zero order hold to construct the input to the network at the following time instant.

Decryption

The decryption procedure (Figure 4) works in a similar fashion as that of the encryption. When the symmetric cipher receives the ciphertext $C_i\{V_i, E_i\}$, the output Y_i is computed as:

$$Y_i = F_2(V_i) \tag{7}$$

Figure 4. Decryption process

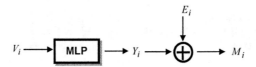

Next, the original plaintext block can be restored using:

$$M_i = Y_i + E_i \tag{8}$$

After the message block M_i is restored, the one-epoch training step is performed using $X_i = (Y_{i-1} \| M_i)$ as the input vector and M_i as the training target.

The output V_i of the final block can be used as the Message Authentication Code (MAC) for the whole ciphertext. After calculating Y_i from V_i during decryption, M_i can be produced, and hence $X_i = (M_i \| Y_i)$ is once again reconstructed. Then, V'_i is computed:

$$V'_i = F_1(X_i) \tag{9}$$

Next, V'_i is compared with V_i to verify data integrity and authentication. In general, at the end of the data encryption/decryption stages, the cipher block chaining-message authentication code (CBC-MAC) (Schneier, 1996) is prepared (or examined if already exists) to ensure data integrity. The CBC mode encryption and decryption is illustrated

Figure 5. CBC mode encryption (left) and decryption (right)

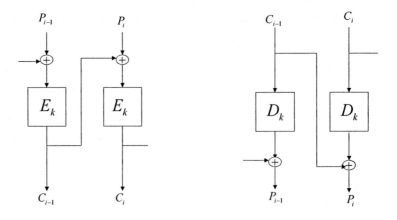

in Figure 5, where the P_is are plaintext blocks, and the C_is are ciphertext blocks. CBC-MAC is a simple method that uses the last encrypted block as the MAC for the ciphertext chain.

RRNN and Symmetric Cipher Design

By means of the RRNN (shown in Figure 2), the symmetric cipher uses the forward dynamics equations (3) to (6) to generate the ciphertext and the message authentication code. In specific terms, the output of the network forward dynamics is computed as:

$$Y_j(n+1) = \varphi\left(\sum_{i=A\cup B} w_{ji}(n)U_i(n)\right), \quad j \in B \tag{10}$$

where φ is a nonlinear activation function, and the variable w_{ji} represents the synaptic weight of the neuron j. In (10), $U_i(n)$ is the input vector to the RRNN, defined as in Haykin (1998):

$$U_i(n)\begin{cases} X_i(n) & if \ i \in A \\ Y_i(n) & if \ i \in B \end{cases} \tag{11}$$

where A denotes the set of indices i for which $X_i(n)$ is an external input, and B denotes the set of indices i for which $U_i(n)$ is the output of the neuron. Furthermore, the term representing the argument of the linear activation function in equation (10) is the neuron internal activity function V_i defined in equation (3). To define the initial values for the weight $w_{ji}(0)$, a set of uniformly distributed random numbers is chosen. Next, the dynamic process for updating the network weights in real time is defined by means of the following triple index:

$$\vartheta_{kl}^j(n+1) = \varphi'\left(V_j(n)\right)\left[\sum_{i\in B} w_{ji}(n)\vartheta_{kl}^j(n) + \delta_{kl}U_l(n)\right] \tag{12}$$

where $j\in B$, $k\in B$, $l\in A\cup B$, and $\varphi'(.)$ is the derivative of the nonlinear activation function. In (12), δ_{kl} is the Krönecker delta equals to one when $k = l$ and 0 otherwise. The triply index is initialized such that $\vartheta_{kl}^j(0) = 0$. The index in (12) is used to update the RRNN weights as follows:

$$\Delta w_{ki}(n) = \eta \sum_{j} E_j(n) \vartheta_{kl}^{j}(n) \tag{13}$$

where Δw_{kl} denotes the update to the weight w_{kl}, and the parameter η refers to the learning rate of the network. In equation (13), the error function E_j at time instant n is computed as:

$$E_j(n) = M_j(n) - Y_j(n) \tag{14}$$

Finally, the weight w_{kl} is updated according to the following equation:

$$w_{kl}(n+1) = w_{kl}(n) + \Delta w_{kl}(n) \tag{15}$$

Both forward and backward dynamics vary in time to ensure that the learning procedure of the RRNN has the capability to detect temporal patterns of the training data. Consequently, the symmetric cipher can prepare the message authentication code to maintain both the data integrity and the data authentication.

Security Guarantee of the Proposed Symmetric Cipher Design

This section examines two possible types of attacks against the proposed symmetric cipher: (1) attacks against the MAC; (2) attacks against the data encryption scheme itself. A self-adaptive learning procedure for the symmetric cipher is also introduced.

Attacks against the MAC

Several features of the message authentication code can be viewed as potential targets for the cryptanalysis attacks. Among those features are (1) message authentication code needs to be a one-way function — For any given input x, it is easy to compute the authentication code by the secure hash function H, but it is computationally not feasible to arbitrarily guess x from the message authentication code, even if H is known; (2) message authentication code needs to be collision-resistant — It is not computationally feasible to find a pair (x, y) such that $H(x) = H(y)$; and (3) message authentication code needs to be capable of data authentication — Only the secret key owner can prepare or verify the code because the hash value is encrypted by the secret key.

Most of the cryptanalysis attacks against MAC focus on the collision resistance feature. The attacker tries to substitute the text x with the alternate text x' such that $H(x) = H(x')$. In doing so, the attacker can target either the key space of the MAC or its actual value. Also, without attempting to recover the secret key, the attacker may try to find a message that matches a given MAC value, and then use that message to replace the original one. When a ciphertext message $C_i\{V_i, E_i\}$ in equation (6) is changed, one of the following two scenarios arises: (1) either E_i or V_i is changed; or (2) both E_i and V_i are changed.

Now suppose that either E_i or V_i are changed during a cryptanalysis attack. The decryption process will produce $^*M_i$ from $^*C_i$ according to equations (7) and (8). Then the attacker will calculate $^*V_i$ according to equation (9). Furthermore, due to the fact that the value of $^*V_i$ and V_i will not match, data corruption may be detected. However, it is possible for the attacker to choose a ciphertext $^*C_i\{^*V_i, ^*E_i\}$ so as to pass the message authentication code (MAC) check. Yet, this attack will be detected when the next MAC is checked because of the CBC mode. This is due to the fact that $^*Y_i$ is not only used for the MAC check of the current block, but also for one step ahead check. In other words, the input vector will be changed from $X_{i+1} = Y_i \| M_{i+1}$ to $^*X_{i+1} = ^*Y_i \| M_{i+1}$ and the data integrity corruption of ciphertext C_i will be detected by the MAC check of the next ciphertext C_{i+1}. Hence, the attacker will be forced to identify a chain of messages to replace the whole document of plaintext for the attack against the CBC-MAC to be successful. Also, if the length of the plaintext is n bits, the effort will require approximately 2^n operations.

Now, let us consider the case of an attack against the key space of the MAC. If the attacker successfully determines the secret key, she/he can generate a valid MAC value for any given message. If the attacker has the knowledge of some sets of both the plaintext and ciphertext, she/he can try every possible secret key to generate the MAC. By comparing the results, she/he may then try to break both the MAC and the cipher. Suppose the total key size of the extended key is k bits and the length of the plaintext is n. Since the MAC is usually a many-to-one mapping, for the first-round attack, it is expected that the attacker will find about $2^{(k-n)}$ matching keys. It is necessary for the attacker to perform multiple rounds of attacks. For the second round, the attacker will search within the remaining $2^{(k-n)}$ keys and will probably find $2^{(k-2n)}$ keys, and so on. Such an effort will be reduced quickly for the consecutive rounds. The overall effort of this type of attack will consist in searching 2^k keys roughly. In summary, the effort of the attacks against the message authentication code will be in finding $\beta = min(2^k, 2^n)$ keys. According to modern cryptanalysis, the strength of the key is required to be at least 128 bits.

Attacks against the Data Encryption Scheme

The encryption procedure of the proposed symmetric cipher can be viewed as a nonlinear mapping in which the ciphertext is the nonlinear transformation of the plaintext. If this function is static, the nonlinear equations can possibly be solved when the cryptanalyst has large volumes of plaintext with the corresponding ciphertext available. In comparison to other existing algorithms such as the data encryption standard (Schneier, 1996), the extended key length k of the proposed symmetric cipher is much longer. Because the symmetric cipher makes use of the learning procedure of neural network to encrypt data, it is assumed that a key stream encrypts the plaintext blocks. As a result, the extended key length *k* should be the total sum of all these keys within the same key stream period. The longer the key stream period is, the longer the extended key length *k* will be. This will result in a stronger symmetric cipher. If it can be guaranteed that the learning procedure will not converge quickly, the symmetric cipher can then generate long period key stream. Consequently, the nonlinear transform function should be dynamic when it is applied for data encryption. The feedforward dynamics of the RRNN must keep varying in time to provide security protection of the plaintext. Furthermore, since the learning procedure usually tends to be convergent, a cryptanalysis attack based on the stability of the neural networks during learning may be an issue of importance. This is studied in the next section.

Attack against Data Confidentiality

Let *G* denote the set of plaintexts, *Z* the set of local and global minima, and *L* the largest invariant set in *Z*. *L* will contain all of the possible points at which the solution might converge and the trajectory can be trapped. Assume *L* contains only one fixed-point *y*. A cryptanalyst will repeatedly train the symmetric cipher with the known plaintext until the symmetric cipher converges to *L*. After the symmetric cipher is stabilized, all the secret plaintexts input that belongs to *G* will converge to this fixed point. Although the cryptanalyst has no knowledge of the weight matrix and the initial state of the symmetric cipher, she/he can obtain the convergent point *y* in *L* by means of the known plaintext. Then the cryptanalyst can restore the following secret plaintext *M* via the error signal *E* using $M = Y + E$. It shows that the stability of the neural networks will eventually help the cryptanalyst to break the symmetric cipher without the knowledge of the weight matrix. To resist such an attack, the learning procedure needs to guarantee that convergence will not drift towards an invariant set *L* after the training of large volume of plaintexts. This consideration is directly related to the stability problem of neural networks discussed as follows.

An RRNN can be modeled as nonlinear dynamic system, and the direct Lyapunov function (Pointcheval, 1994) can be used to analyze the stability of neural networks, providing such a function be found and used for the back-propagation algorithm processing (Haykin, 1998). This problem is difficult. Alternatively, through a *local* analysis of the learning procedure of neural networks, it can be assumed that the local stability of the forward propagation is a sufficient condition for the local stability of the backward propagation, and vice versa (Townley, Iichmann, Weib, Mcclements, Ruiz, Owens, & Pratzel-Wolters, 2000). Consequently, there is only need to guarantee the instability of the backward propagation (equation 11), so that the forward propagation (used to generate the ciphertext) is ensured to be chaotic and unpredictable. According to equation (11), the instability of the backward propagation depends on both the error signal and the weight matrix. An estimate of the gradient has been used to approximate the *true* gradient curve of the cost function in order to perform real-time learning. If the learning rate η is set to a large value, a small mismatch between the output and the learning target will have a dramatic effect on the weight update process; hence, will cause the forward propagation to be unstable, that is, chaotic. This chaotic oscillation of the learning behavior can then be generated in order to provide the desired data security.

A Self-Adaptive Learning Procedure

The self-adaptive function of the symmetric cipher is a necessary component to resist possible cryptanalysis attacks. This algorithm implements such a function, and it detects the trend of the learning procedure via monitoring the mean squared error performance function (*MSE*), and then adjusts the learning rate by a multiplicative-increase gradual-decrease (MIGD) method, that is, the TCP Vegas congestion control protocol (Hengartner, Bolliger, & Gross, 2000). At first, a low-pass filter for the *MSE* learns the trend detection as follows:

$$T(k) = \delta T(k-1) + (1-\delta) * MSE(k) \tag{16}$$

where δ is often selected between 0 and 1, $T(k)$ is the output of the low-pass filter of *MSE* at time k and the initial state $T(0)$ is set to be zero. The learning stop condition MSE^{stop} (also referred to as the learning goal) is defined as:

$$MSE^{stop} \leq \alpha \tag{17}$$

where α is the critical value of $T(k)$. The learning rate will adapt itself according to the MIGD method based on one of the following three cases:

1. Case 1: $T(k) \leq \alpha$

   The condition shows that the learning procedure tends to be convergent to the learning goal. To avoid the stability of the learning and restore the chaotic behavior, the learning rate is increased aggressively by a factor λ, that is $\lambda = 2$. In this case: $\eta = \lambda \cdot \eta$

2. Case 2: $T(k) > \alpha$ and $T(k) > T(k-1)$

   The condition shows that the learning procedure tends to be oscillating. Hence, to maintain the learning rate close to the maximum allowable value, it should be gradually decreased by a factor θ, for example $\theta = 0.9$. In this case: $\eta = \theta \cdot \eta$

3. Case 3: $T(k) > \alpha$ and $T(k) \leq T(k-1)$. In this case, the learning rate keeps the same value.

The above self-adaptive procedure can be performed at the conclusion of each epoch of training in both the encryption and decryption procedures. The critical value α can guarantee that the learning procedure will not settle at a stable point. At the same time, it helps maintain the learning rate close to the maximum allowable value so that the learning trajectory is closely related to the training data. More precisely, it will make the learning trajectory behave more randomly, which in turns makes the analysis of the learning procedure more difficult without the knowledge of the initial state of the network.

Simulation Results Validating the Proposed Symmetric Cipher Design

To validate the symmetric cipher design, a simulation software program in MATLAB environment is developed. The simulation contains an encoder to encrypt the plaintext and a decoder to restore the plaintext from ciphertext. The encoder model and encryption flowchart are shown in Figures 6 and 7. The decoder model and decryption flowchart are given in Figures 8 and 9.

A script file is used to control the configuration of the cipher. This file defines some crucial parameters such as the dimension of the input/output vectors, the dimension of the hidden layer, the learning stop condition, the initial values for the weights and bias, and so forth. The symmetric cipher is constructed using a multilayer perceptron network (Yee and De Silva, 2000). In order to perform the recurrent real-time learning, the output

Figure 6. Encoder model

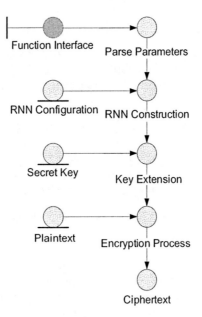

of the symmetric cipher is fed back as part of the input vector. The dimensions of the input and output vectors are, respectively, four and two. The hidden layer has only one neuron, and its output represents the first part of the ciphertext. A sample plaintext is used as the external input signal for the symmetric cipher. The plaintext contains a long string of character "a," followed by a short string of character "z," then followed again by a long string of character "a." The plaintext is first translated to the corresponding ASCII code, and then scaled between 0 and 1. These values are permuted and padded by 0 (if necessary) to form several ($4x1$) vectors as input data for the symmetric cipher. The first two simulation experiments are carried out to analyze the effect of the learning rate on the network learning performance, while in the third experiment, the effect of the self-adaptive algorithm for updating the network's learning rate is investigated. The configuration parameters for all the experiments are given in Table 1.

For the first two experiments, the ciphertext output is illustrated in Figure 10 in terms of V_i and E_i. Figure 10(a) is the first part of the ciphertext V_i as described in equation (6). Since V_i is actually the output of the neural network, it is a value in the interval (0, 1). In Figure 10(b), the second part of the ciphertext in E_i (as described in equation (6)) is presented. Since E_i is the two-dimensional error signal between the input and the output, it may assume negative values. The only difference between the 1st and 2nd experiments is in the

Figure 7. Encryption flowchart

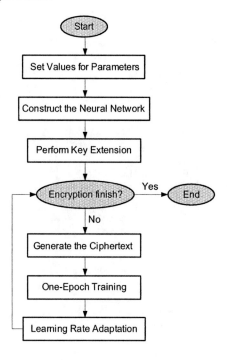

Figure 8. Decoder model

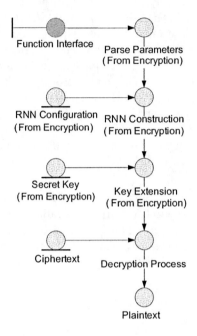

Figure 9. Decryption flowchart

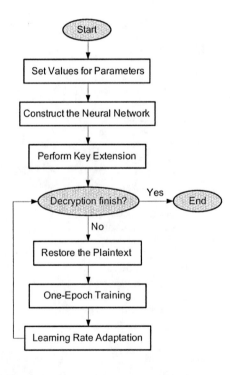

learning rate (set to a large value in the 2nd experiment). The ciphertext output for the 2nd experiment is illustrated in Figure 11.

Comparing the results of these two experiments, it is observed that the second part of the ciphertext, E_i, has weaker protection than the first part when the learning rate is small. Hence, the first part of the ciphertext output can be the MAC for the corresponding plaintext blocks. Therefore, it will be much more difficult for a cryptanalyst to perform an attack based on the first part of the ciphertext. Since the weakest point on the text can be used to examine the security of the symmetric cipher, the focus should be on the analysis of the second part of the ciphertext.

Based on experiments, when the learning rate is small, the second part of the ciphertext, E_i, will expose the temporal pattern of the plaintext. The cryptanalyst can then perform the attacks discussed earlier to guess the new character "z". But when the learning rate is set to a large value, the learning procedure can be prevented from convergence, and the temporal structure of the plaintext input can be protected because the ciphertext is chaotic. Even though the ciphertext looks chaotic, it is difficult to determine whether it has a limited number of states. It is often desirable for the error signal to have an unpredictable number of states so that further cryptanalysis is impossible. This can be achieved by introducing more random factors into the ciphertext generation process (i.e., the learning process of the neural network). A suitable source for random factors would be the plaintext itself. This is illustrated in the third experiment. The two parts of the ciphertext output for this experiment are shown in Figure 12.

When the learning error reaches the critical value α, the self-adaptive procedure will be triggered. In that case, the learning rate value is multiplied by an increase factor λ. Afterwards, if the learning procedure oscillates according to the case 2 of the MIGD method previously studied, the learning rate value is multiplied by the decrease factor θ. On the other hand, the learning rate value is sustained if the learning procedure is in accordance with case 3 of the MIGD method. In the third experiment, when the learning rate is set to a large value, the error signal will diverge away from the critical value and learning goal. Consequently, the parameter α can be used as a knob to control the learning and make it unpredictable; thus, guaranteeing a desirable instability. Large learning rate can help to hide the temporal structure of the plaintext input data, and force the symmetric cipher to generate chaotic ciphertext.

Table 1. Configuration parameters for the first, second, and third experiments

Experiment	Weight initial value	Epochs for key extension	Dimension of input vector	Learning rate for encryption	Learning stop condition	Learning rate adaptation
1	0.5	4	2	0.05	1e-50	Disabled
2	0.5	4	2	35	1e-50	Disabled
3	0.5	4	2	1	1e-50	Critical value α: 0.04 Increase factor λ: 2 Decrease factor θ: 0.9

Viability of the Proposed Models and Future Work

In this chapter, the study of an artificial neural networks approach to design a novel cryptographic cipher has shown that it is possible to train the networks to perform encryption/decryption while achieving a satisfactory level of data security and integrity (as shown by simulation results in Figures 10, 11, 12). This work is among the first few attempts towards this direction, and several issues remain unsolved that deserve more investigations in order to obtain a comprehensive view of the tremendous potentials of using artificial neural networks for security purposes:

1.   The proposed symmetric cipher is based on an error-correcting learning algorithm (i.e., the self-adaptive procedure). Because of the nature of this algorithm, the reliability of the symmetric cipher is not as strong as it should be. This might be due to the authors' observation that the speed of the change of the gradient of the learning trajectory is sometimes much faster than the change of the error. Therefore, when the precision limit is met before the threshold, the learning procedure is broken, and thus stops suddenly. In general, it is not possible for the algorithm to

Figure 10. Small fixed learning rate effect (Learning rate = 0.05, learning rate adaptation disabled)

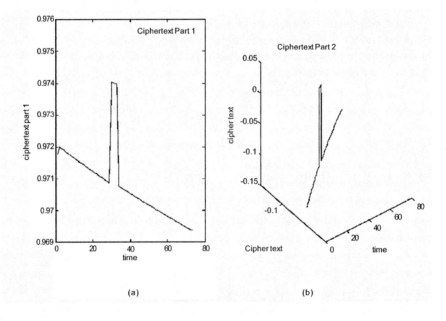

(a)   (b)

Figure 11. Large fixed learning rate effect (Learning rate = 35, learning rate adaptation disabled)

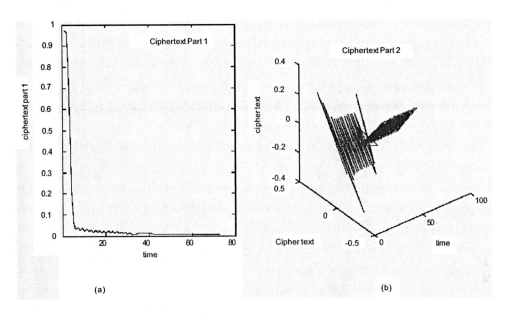

Figure 12. Two parts of the ciphertext output for the third experiment

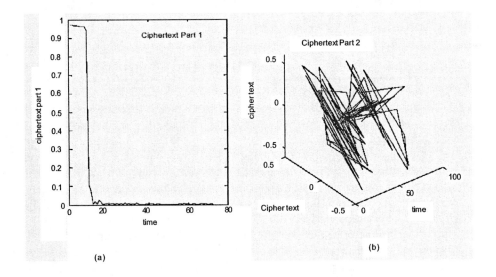

control or predict the gradient, and the state of the system is difficult to determine when the symmetric cipher stops suddenly. There are two possible ways to avoid this problem: (1) place some constraints on the selection of values for the threshold; (2) investigate the possibility of using other learning algorithms than the one proposed in this chapter. This latter alternative requires a comparative study of existing learning and pruning algorithms, in order to determine the best possible choice. The Hebb rule (Sereno and Sereno, 1991) for the back-propagation learning algorithm is a good candidate to address this problem. Also, the proposed symmetric cipher involves many floating-point calculations. It is desirable to avoid floating-point calculation for data encryption purpose.

2.   The proposed symmetric cipher only supports block data encryption. It is desirable to turn this mode into options for stream data encryption, where bits are used rather than blocks of bits. The application of the Hebb rule for data encryption can be used to solve the learning rate selection problem, providing for a way to investigate how finite field operations could be introduced in the framework, in order to avoid floating-point calculations in the future.

3.   Depending on predefined cipher performance metrics, a comparison of the cipher encryption scheme against other well-known encryption schemes (such as DES, RSA, etc.) is desirable, as well as the study of the effect of other cryptanalysis attacks on the proposed cipher design. These studies of particular interest are currently underway. For example, Arvandi (2005) has proposed a possible chosen plaintext attack, as well as a cryptanalysis study of brute-force, differential, and linear attacks against the proposed cipher design. The cipher design is shown to be resistant to these attacks due to the aforementioned cipher's features, referred to as (1) relatively simple architecture; (2) no constraint on the secret key length; and (3) adjustable key size to achieve the desired protection.

Conclusion

In this chapter, a novel symmetric cipher design based on the application of recurrent neural networks in cryptography was described, and its security was analyzed by examining two popular types of attacks. It was found that the proposed cipher encryption can flexibly adjust both the secret key and the message length to accommodate different performance requirements. Furthermore, the inherent parallel computing capability of the symmetric cipher can accommodate high-performance data encryption requirements, such as the secure point-to-point file transfer between gateways, that makes it suitable for wireless Web services security. Simulation results show that the learning procedure of the proposed symmetric cipher can be controlled to provide the secure protection for data by adapting the learning rate. The continued development and refinement of the proposed symmetric cipher design and its self-adaptive learning procedure should remain an important area of research into the foreseeable future.

References

Almeida, L. (1987). A learning rule for asynchronous perceptrons with feedback in a combinatorial environment. In *Proceedings of the 1st EEE International Conference on Neural Networks* (Vol. 2, pp. 105-110).

Arvandi, M. (2005). *Analysis of neural network based ciphers*. MASc thesis. Ryerson University, Department of Electrical and Computer Engineering, Toronto, Canada.

Benitez, J., Castro J. L., & Requena, I. (1997). Are artificial neural networks black boxes? *IEEE Transactions on Neural Networks, 8*(5), 1156-1164.

Cantú-Paz, E. (2003). Pruning neural networks with distribution estimation algorithms. In E. Cantú Paz et al. (Eds.), *Proceedings of Genetic and Evolutionary Computation Conference, GECCO-2003* (pp. 790-800). July 7-16, Chicago, IL.

Coyle, F. P. (2001). *Wireless Web: A manager's guide*. NJ: Addison-Wesley.

Denning, D. (1982). *Cryptography and data security* (1st ed.). Boston: Addison-Wesley.

Haykin, S. (1998). *Neural networks: A comprehensive foundation* (2nd ed.). India: Prentice Hall of India.

Hengartner, U., Bolliger, J., & Gross, T. (2000). TCP Vegas revisited. In *Proceedings of the INFOCOM, 19th Annual Joint Conference of the IEEE Computer and Communications Societies* (Vol. 3, pp. 1546-1555).

IPSec. (2004). *The IPSec architecture*. Retrieved August 18, 2006, from http://www.securitydocs.com/library/2926

Karras, D. A., & Zorkadis, V. (2003). On neural network techniques in the secure management of communication systems through improving and quality assessing pseudorandom stream generators. *Neural Networks, 16*(5-6), 899-905.

Kent, S., & Atkinson, R. (1998). *RFC 2401: Security architecture for the Internet Protocol*. Obsoletes RFC1825. Status: PROPOSED STANDARD.

Kinzel, W., & Kanter, I. (2002). Neural cryptography. *Proceedings of the 9th International Conference on Neural Information Processing (ICONIP'02)* (Vol. 3, pp. 1351-1354).

Klimov, A., Mityaguine, A., & Shamir, A. (2002). Analysis of neural cryptography. In *Proceedings of the AsiaCrypt 2002* (pp. 288-298). Springer Verlag.

Meletiou, G. C., Tasoulis, D. K., & Vrahatis, M.N. (2002). A first study of the neural network approach in the RSA cryptosystem. In *Proc. 7th IASTED International Conference Artificial Intelligence and Soft Computing*, July 17-19, 2002, Banff, Canada.

Meletiou, G. C., Tasoulis, D. K., & Vrahatis, M. N. (2003). Cryptography through interpolation and computational intelligence methods. *Bulletin of the Greek Mathematical Society*, Athens, Greece.

Pointcheval, D. (1994). *Neural networks and their cryptographic applications*. Eurocode '94, Pascale Charpin Ed., INRIA.

Reed, R. (1993). Pruning algorithms: A survey. *IEEE Trans on Neural Networks, 4*(5), 740-747.

Rosen, M., Kanter, I., & Kinzel, W. (2002). *Cryptography based on neural networks: Analytical results*. cond-mat/0202350.

Schneier, B. (1996). *Applied cryptography* (2nd ed.). John Wiley & Sons.

Scott, S., Alvin, L., & Jui-Cheng, Y. (2000). Design and realization of a new chaotic neural encryption/decryption network. In *Proceedings of the IEEE Asia-Pacific Conference on Circuits and Systems* (pp. 335-338).

Sereno, M. I. & Sereno, M. E. (1991). Learning to see rotation and dilation with a Hebb rule. In R. P. Lippmann, J. Moody, & D. S. Touretzky (Eds.), *Advances in Neutral Informal Processing Systems* (Vol. I). San Mateo, CA: Morgan Kaufmann Publishers.

Stallings, W. (2003). *Cryptography and network security: Principles and practices* (3rd ed.). Prentice Hall.

Stubblefield, A., Ioannidis, J., & Rubin, A. D. (August, 2001). Using the Fluhrer, Mantin, and Shamir attack to break WEP, *Technical Report TD04ZCPZZ*. NJ: AT&T Labs.

Su, S., Lin, A., & Yen, J. (2000). Design and realization of a new chaotic neural encryption/decryption network. In *IEEE Asia-Pacific Conference on Circuits and Systems* (pp. 335-338).

Townley, S., Iichmann, A., Weib, M. G., Mcclements, W., Ruiz, A. C., Owens, D. H., & Pratzel-Wolters, D. (2000). Existence and learning of oscillations in recurrent neural networks. *IEEE Trans on Neural Networks, 11*(1), 205-214.

Williams, R. J., & Zipser, D. (1989). A learning algorithm for continually running fully recurrent neural networks. *Neural Computation, 1*, 270-280.

Yee, L., & De Silva, C. (2002). Application of multilayer perceptron networks in public key cryptography. *Proceedings of the 2002 International Joint Conference on Neural Networks* (Vol. 2, pp. 1439-1443).

Chapter III

RFID Systems:
Applications vs. Security and Privacy Implications

Dennis M. L. Wong, Swinburne University of Technology, Malaysia

Raphael C.-W. Phan, Swinburne University of Technology, Malaysia

Abstract

In this chapter, we discuss the business implications, as well as security and privacy issues, of the widespread deployment of radio frequency identification (RFID) systems. We first describe, in more detail, the components that make up an RFID system to facilitate better understanding of the implications of each, and then review the commercial applications of the RFID. We then discuss the security and privacy issues for RFID systems and what mechanisms have been proposed to safeguard these. The topics discussed in this chapter highlight the benefits of using RFIDs for user convenience in ubiquitous and pervasive commercial services and e-businesses, while maintaining the integrity of such systems against malicious attacks on the users' security and privacy. This is vital for a business establishment to coexist with peers and remain competitively attractive to customers.

Introduction

Radio frequency identification (RFID) systems are gaining worldwide popularity for supply-chain management and tracking of goods, as well as for access control in distributed systems, toll systems, car immobilizations, and so forth. There are ongoing research and development (R&D) efforts everywhere in integrating RFID into available technology sectors, including e-business. Some have envisioned that RFID technology will revolutionize the world that we see today, bringing pervasive and ubiquitous systems to the forefront of everyday applications (Stanford, 2003).

Cryptologists and security researchers are also predicting the explosive growth of RFID technology. For instance, Adi Shamir, coinventor of the popular RSA encryption method (Anderson, 2001; Menezes, van Oorschot, & Vanstone, 1996; Stallings, 1999;) commented on the vast potential of RFIDs during his invited talk (Shamir, 2004) at the Asiacrypt 2004 conference attended by security researchers around the world.

With the soon to be widespread use of RFID systems, and their seamless integration into our daily chores, comes the issue of security and privacy. As with other personal data related applications, for example, Smart-Card, Web-based Transaction, and so forth, there are doubts on exactly how safe is an RFID system, from the aspect of information security? To what degree can one entrust his/her personal data, ranging from biodata to financial information, with RFID-based systems? The contactless nature of RFIDs, which is the main advantage of the technology, incidentally, is also the largest vulnerability, where much like the wi-fi technologies, there is no guarantee that the transmission medium cannot be eavesdropped upon.

The idea of automatic identification has been long established in the commercial sector, and the usage of bar-code scanning in the point-of-sale system is probably the most successful example one can openly observe. Consider this scenario: You have decided to purchase some groceries, so you gather them and bring them, in a basket, to the checkout point. The cashier scans through the goods using, probably, an infrared scanner; the price is then automatically displayed in the cash machine. Now, imagine a different scenario: you are carrying a basket with a tiny LCD display; once you put an item into the basket, the LCD screen immediately shows you the price of the item and perhaps a subtotal of your purchase. Once you arrive at the station, you are readily presented with an invoice, where you just need to acknowledge the transaction (say signing), and the bill will be automatically debited from your local bank account. The above scenario might be coming to a local retail branch near you, and the enabling technology behind this vision is the emerging RFID technology.

However, RFID technology is not new, and it has been in existence for decades. Its profile has been raised several folds recently, and there are several factors that account for this change, among which, a major reason is the successful deployment of RFID technology in the commercial sector. In supply-chain management, RFID tags have been envisioned by many to replace the bar-code labeling system, which has been in use since the early 1970s, as the new tool for automatic identification. The latter system is now becoming a bottleneck for big enterprises that have gigantic volumes of transactions. The fact that RFID is contactless enables the technology to be used in a ubiquitous and pervasive environment.

Incidentally, the U.S. Department of Defence (DoD) and Wal-Mart, a key retail giant in the U.S., have recently (ZIH, 2005) required all suppliers to be compliant with RFID technology by January 2005. Other major retail chains, for example, Target and Albertsons, have also mandated the same move. Such requirements imply that if the suppliers are not "RFID compatible," then they will not be getting any contracts from these retailers. Besides the retail sector, local governments have also been playing a key role in the deployment of RFID technologies. In Malaysia, the Malaysian citizens have been using RFID-based technology in their e-passports (Juels, Molnar, & Wagner, 2005) since the end of last century. Although unaware by many, the e-passport contains an identification chip that enables Malaysians to gain easy and quick access at Immigration Control points. In the U.S., the Defense Department is using RFID to administer their military shipments. For local authorities, libraries around the world are also deploying RFID in monitoring the transactions of their collections. Library users would not have to worry about library operation hours: as long as they drop the loaned items in an RFID-enabled collection box before midnight, there will not be an overdue charged.

Apart from logistics and supply-chain management, RFID also found its use in pervasive computing. Although it is still in the "preliminary research" stage, RFIDs have been proposed in robot navigation, in-door positioning, target tracking, and so forth. Other more mature domains where RFIDs are being actively deployed are animal identification and tracking, automotive key and lock, anti-theft systems, airline baggage tracking, motorway tolls collection, and so forth.

The rise of RFIDs has also raised increasing concerns in the actual implementation and deployment of the RFID platform. In particular, in the current generation of RFIDs, security and privacy issues have been seriously overlooked. There are reports of corporations misusing the technology to invade an individual's privacy. The current system also does not offer many security features to avoid leakage of what might be regarded to some as important or personal data. The aim of this chapter is to discuss these issues in RFID systems, and to raise a better level of awareness among the general public on this. Besides, we also want to highlight some recently proposed mechanisms that attempt to safeguard the security and privacy in RFID systems. Though these descriptions are by no means exhaustive, they do serve to reflect the state of the art in RFID security. For a more comprehensive list of references on RFIDs, which gets updated frequently, refer to Avoine (2005).

The rest of this chapter is organized in the following fashion: In the next section, we introduce the key components in a typical RFID system, and currently available standard protocols underlining existing implementations of RFIDs. In the next section, we focus our attention on current concerns about the security and privacy related to RFIDs, discussing recent mechanisms proposed to safeguard the RFID data owner and user. In the next section, we motivate some plausible future directions in RFID-related research and development. Lastly, conclusions are drawn in the final section.

At the end of this chapter, we hope that the reader will have obtained a general perspective of RFIDs and the corresponding security and privacy implications. In particular, the objectives of this chapter include:

- Understanding of the RFID and internal components

- Appreciation of the benefits of RFIDs in providing ubiquitous and pervasive services

- Familiarity with the security and privacy issues and implications of RFID-based systems

- Knowledge of emerging trends and open problems in RFID-based systems

RFID and Applications

RFID Components

In this section, we describe the basic components that make up the RFID system. RFID systems can be classified by using its operating frequency, operating range, as well as its coupling. Depending on its processing system, it could also be classified as a low-end system as electronic article surveillance (EAS) system, midrange system (e.g., system with erasable and programmable memory, most authentication systems fall into this class), and high-end system (e.g., systems equipped with smart-card operating system). However, more generally, an RFID system comprises three standard components, namely, the *transponder*, the *reader*, and the *database* (Figure 1). The database server is connected to the reader, possibly via a PC/workstation based interface. It contains all the vital information (possibly encrypted) about the transponder.

The reader is an active device (equipped with on-board power source). Its main task is to interrogate the existence of transponders in its vicinity, to acquire information borne by the transponder, and relay it onto the database server for further processing. The active range of a reader depends on its operating frequency range and power of transmission.

The transponder, also known as an RFID tag, is at the front end of the RFID system. There are two types of coupling for the transponder, that is, active tags and passive tags. For active tags, the transponder is equipped with a power source, and is capable of communicating with the reader using standard protocols. Quite often, these active tags

Figure 1. Standard RFID components

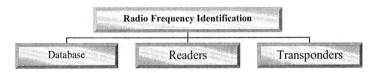

have an on-board sensor system that could acquire certain physical quantities of interest. On the contrary, the passive tags rely on the current induced by the reader's interrogation, and the information is often sent through the backscattered wave of the reader.

There are a few existing ISO standards on the operation and application of RFID systems. The early RFID standard does not take the security of the transponder into consideration. However, the newly proposed Electronic Product Code™ (EPC) standard by MIT's Auto ID Centre (EPC Global, 2004) on second-generation RFID systems has begun to take security and privacy issues into more serious account. EPC provides an identification mechanism for a specific objection in a supply chain, and conveys only that piece of information. With the aid of a firewalled global network, sensitive information related to a specific EPC is only accessible to authorized users. More details on security issues are addressed in the following sections.

We would like to point out here that the technical foundation of RFID technology is built on existing knowledge of telecommunications and electronics that have been well understood for many years. The challenge of RFID development does not focus on new theoretical breakthroughs, but is more geared towards efficient and low-cost implementation of the technology, and on efforts in bringing them to the mass public. An inherent obstacle that the entrepreneurs are facing is the cost of the RFID tags, which could be quite substantial for mass adoption of the technology. However, we are confident that the cost would be lowered to an affordable range within the foreseeable near future, as efforts everywhere are looking into achieving this goal.

The advantages of RFID systems are well summarized in Finkenzeller (2003). In short, such a system offers excellent figures of merit in quality control, data and system integrity, and flexibility, and it also has high immunity toward hostile environmental conditions.

RFID Applications

Smart tags, as RFIDs are often referred to as, find their major, and perhaps most applications, in the retail sector. Unaware of by many, these tags containing implicit data are penetrating into our daily lives. The list (incomplete by all means) to follow shows some applications of RFIDs around us:

Animal identification: An early application of RFID technology is the use of smart tags in identifying animals. The tag is programmed with specific information of the animal, and then attached to (or implanted into) the animal without impacting on the livelihood of the animal. This emerging trend brings revolutionary impacts to animal farming, and has various advantages. For example, we do not need to paint patches of green or red color on our sheep just to identify our herd; the zoologist can monitor the behavior of a precious species without alerting the animals or influencing their natural habitats. Another possibly obvious usage for these smart tags is, of course, stock keeping.

Toll control/Public transport: Toll access control on motorways is yet another early adoption of the RFID technology. A smart tag, containing credits, is purchased by the motorist, to be attached to the vehicle (normally on the windscreen, but not necessarily so, since it is contactless technology). At exits of the motorway, the checkpoint will automatically update the mileage the vehicle has traveled, and fares are automatically debited from the tag.

Another similar application of RFID tags is for public transport, where the traveler in major cities, such as Singapore, could purchase a "Travel Card" that could be used for railways, buses, undergrounds, or taxies when traveling in the city. When the card runs out of credit, the traveler could reload the card at card-vendor machines located at various stations.

The main advantage that RFID provides in this arena is, of course, the decrease of time wasted in passing through tolls; besides, collecting the cash up front would also mean more efficient financial operation for toll operators.

Access authentication: Authentication of personnel in or out of a secure area is often a tedious job for security control. Many are still using manual identification nowadays, and authentication of certain IDs is almost impossible, in some circumstances. To overcome this hurdle, RFID, along with other emerging technologies such as biometrics, is being sought after as a possible solution.

Solutions such as i-Button by Maxim Integrated Products (Maxim, 2005) are used in room access control in replacement of, or in addition to, the conventional key lock mechanism. In the motoring industry, the car manufacturers are making ignition keys with integral transponders, which make simple duplication of the key redundant. RFID technology also enables one to lock or unlock the car simply by pressing a small button on the car, and ignite the engine as long as the RFID-enable key is within access range. Furthermore, in the event that the car is driven away without the RFID-enabled key (e.g., motorway crime), the vehicle would be immobilized after a certain range (RFID are generally short-range compared to other communication protocols) or at an attempt to reignite the car after switching the engine off. These features are value-added features that often please consumers.

Supply-chain management: As aforementioned, the retail sector is seen as the most influential force in pushing the frontier of RFID technology. RFID (also called smart labels) exists in the form of paper strips, and might not look different than the usual conventional barcode label. However, the flexibility in good management and stock checking is far better than their aged counterpart.

The stock could now be tracked from its manufacturing factory to local distribution centers, and then to different department stores, while still remaining wrapped in the container, thanks to the RFID technology.

Positioning and tracking: Indoor positioning and tracking of objects (Ni, Liu, Lau, & Patil, 2003) is often a desirable feature, for example, group visits to public places such as museums and botanic gardens, workers in an access-controlled factory. RFID, being a low-power technology, is useful for automatically collecting information regarding an object's place, time, and transaction (De, Basu, & Das, 2004).

Hospitals could also deploy RFID wristbands for identification of patients, which would facilitate the monitoring of patients, particularly those requiring intensive care. In Smith et al. (Smith, Fishkin, Jiang, Mamishev, Philipose, Rea, Roy, & Sundara-Rajan, 2005),

RFID-based monitoring of human (clinical) activities was demonstrated through two apparatus, namely i-bracelet and wireless identification and sensing platform (WISP). The RFID-based solution is shown to be as accurate as conventional techniques, and with the added advantage of being battery free. Unfortunately, the technique lacks the ability to detect motion, which we believe is a feature to be added eventually.

In large-scale theme parks, RFID-enabled ticketing has provided easy access and monitoring of theme park visitors. Imagine an automated gate authenticating based on the data hidden on your RFID-disguised visitor pass, the waiting time for your favorite roller coaster ride would definitely reduce greatly. Besides, embedded biodata, such as height and age of the visitor, could be useful for authenticating visitors for restricted rides in the theme park. Customized service can also be provided based on information retrieved from the RFID tag.

E-business (instant product information retrieval): There are many potential applications for RFID systems besides those mentioned, including an application for e-business. Poor information availability has been one of the stumbling blocks for firms to interact with their clients. Web-based commerce has managed to improve on that factor quite significantly. However, when shopping in person, we still struggle to find adequate information on certain products. Sometimes, the mall simply lacks the appropriate technical competency to provide such information.

Integrating RFIDs into current mobile telephony systems could enable product comparison and information retrieval at your fingertips (Penttilä, Pere, Soini, Sydänheimo, & Kivikoski, 2005). Current mobile phones have greatly improved processing power, compared with their earlier counterparts. With the appropriate middleware, the mobile device could easily be turned into a reader as well as a gateway to product portals. Information regarding a product could be downloaded for thorough consideration before making a decision to purchase.

In summary, RFID technology offers a wide range of possible integration and service enhancements to current legacy systems. New applications are being appended onto the list every now and then with improved physical specifications and enhanced features. One of the key future research directions, as we mentioned previously, is to enhance the security features on existing RFID technologies. Besides, low-complexity signal processing methods, for example, fixed-point low-resolution algorithms, could further improve the speed and capacity of RFID networks. Hence, this is also a key future area for RFID research.

Security and Privacy Issues

Threats faced by RFID systems — the system data owners and tag users–are generally grouped into two types, namely those by passive attackers and active attackers, respectively (Stallings, 1999).

Passive attackers are those who eavesdrop on or monitor the communications channel, but do not affect or interfere with the communication in any way. Therefore, such attackers are very hard to detect, since you have no straightforward way of knowing when your communication is being monitored.

Considering the case of RFIDs, passive attacks could involve simply tracking the location of a tag. This is possible because of the property of most RFID tags, namely that they are passively powered, nonline-of-sight (non-LoS), and contactless, so anyone nearby with a radio frequency antenna could obtain personal information from a tag, since it is the nature of tags to broadcast their IDs, and so forth. This, of course, intrudes on the privacy of tag users and allows their movements to be tracked.

Active attackers, on the other hand, are those who directly interfere with the communication of messages, either by interrupting, modifying, or fabricating communicated messages. **Interruptions** of messages are direct attacks on the availability of the service, for example, denial of service or detection of RFID tags. Meanwhile, **modifications** are attacks on the integrity of the messages, for example, tampering of tags such that they contain someone else's identity, or swapping expensive tags with inexpensive ones. Finally, **fabrications** are attacks on the authenticity of the messages, for example, forgery of tags to allow access to otherwise restricted systems. All these are serious attacks and should be guarded against.

Compared to passive attacks, an active attacker would be able to mount more devastating attacks on RFIDs. For example, he could modify the messages in transit, causing from the most trivial denial-of-service (DoS) attacks to the more serious impersonations of authorized RFID components.

RFID tags are generally not tamper resistant compared to smart cards, mostly because of their very low costs, typically less than US$0.05. Therefore, some protection mechanisms that ensure security and user privacy are important against attacks that include consumer tracking (intrusion of privacy), forgery of tags (impersonation), and unauthorized access to a tag's memory, which may contain sensitive or private information.

We observe that although RFIDs may be viewed as similar to smart cards, the difference is that the former are not tamper resistant like the latter; thus, they are vulnerable to intense physical attacks. The key is to consider that all threats applicable to smart cards should be considered equally applicable to RFIDs, but furthermore, that even some attacks not applicable to smart cards may be applicable to RFIDs since they are less physically protected. Being contactless and passively-powered may also make it more vulnerable to fault induction (Boneh, DeMillo, & Lipton, 1997) or power attacks (Kocher, Jaffe, & Jun, 1999) than smart cards are.

We emphasize that the main gist is that along with the many enabling technologies that the RFID brings, come new threats to security and privacy that did not exist in conventional systems. This is especially so because the RFID is contactless and nonline-of-sight, thus making it harder to prevent unauthorized communication with it.

Privacy

Tags should not compromise the privacy of their holders. Information within tags must not be leaked to unauthorized readers in order to protect user privacy, nor the locations to be tracked, even in the long-term, in order to protect location privacy. One way is to allow holders to detect and disable (on demand) any tags; another is to ensure that only authorized readers can interrogate the tags.

Among the most counter-intuitive causes of the privacy problem is the diversity of standards (Avoine & Oechslin, 2005) and manufacturers related to the RFID technology. This essentially partitions the RFID tag user space to distinct distinguishable classes that facilitate tracking. Diverse manufacturers also mean different (although slightly, but enough to cause a problem) radio fingerprints (basic technology in mobile devices to detect clones) built into RFID tags; thus again allowing partitioning of classes and hence, tracking. In fact, even devices of the same brand and model may be distinguished from each other due to small differences in the transient behaviour at the beginning of a transmission (Toonstra & Kinsner, 1995).

Hash-Lock Mechanism

One well-known method to safeguard privacy is called the *hash-lock* mechanism (Weis, Sarma, Rivest, & Engels, 2003), and uses a cryptographic one-way hash function, which is basically a function that is easy to compute in one way, but extremely difficult to reverse. To lock a tag, the owner computes a hash output of a random *key* and sends this to the tag as the lock value, *lock = hash(key)*, which the tag stores. Once in locked state, the tag should not reveal private information, but only respond with a meta-ID (pseudonym). To unlock, the owner sends the *key* to the tag, upon which the tag hashes and compares with the stored *lock* value.

One potential privacy problem (Weis et al., 2003) of this is that it still cannot protect against long-term tracking because if the tag always responds with the same meta-ID, then that tag could still be tracked. To overcome this, Weis et al. proposed to tweak the hash-lock scheme such that when locked, the tag answers with the couple <r, y = hash(r Å ID)> where r keeps changing with every session and Å denotes logical exclusive-OR; thus, long-term tracking will no longer be possible.

Yet, the problem (Ohkubo, Suzuki, & Kinoshita, 2003) for this improvement is that it does not provide *forward secrecy*, which means that if the ID is ever revealed at a later stage, the tag owner's identity in past transactions would be revealed. To solve this, they proposed (Figure 2) to use a *hash chain* (Lamport, 1981). The tag stores a secret value s_i. When interrogated by the reader, it would reply with $a_i = hash_1(s_i)$. Further, it would

Figure 2. Providing forward secrecy in the hash lock mechanism

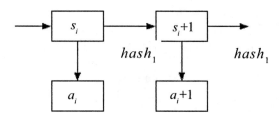

also compute $s_{i+1} = hash_2(s_i)$ for the next transaction's usage. Here, $hash_1$ and $hash_2$ are two different hash functions. Doing so ensures that even if a certain secret s_i is revealed in future, it is not possible to learn secret values prior to that, that is, s_j (for $j < i$); thus, forward secrecy is ensured. We remark that the use of a hash chain for this purpose is quite well known actually.

Although this provides forward secrecy and privacy, it does not provide authentication (Dimitriou, 2005), since an attacker can query the tag and then replay the tag's response to successfully authenticate to a valid reader.

Temporary ID Change

It has been proposed that (Inoue & Yasuura, 2003) a tag be operable in two modes. In the public mode, the tag ID is easily readable, but the tag owner is able (given the control) to change to a protected mode where he supplies a temporary ID that the tag would use in place of the permanent one. We remark that this idea of using a temporary pseudo (not the actual) ID, in place of the actual ID, is commonly used to ensure privacy and anonymity of users. In particular, the tag has two types of memory: a read-only memory (ROM) that stores the permanent actual ID, and a rewriteable, but nonvolatile memory (called RAM) that stores the temporary pseudo ID. The user has a capability to decide when either memory is to be in use, and hence, which ID is to be read from the tag.

Blocker Tags

Juels et al. (Juels, Rivest, & Szydlo, 2003) proposed an elegantly simple method to ensure tag privacy. The idea is for tag users to also carry with them blocker tags that could simultaneously simulate many ordinary (nonblocker) tags, thus confusing RFID readers, and preventing them from being able to scan the ordinary tag carried by the user. This is because of the inherent physical property of readers that are able to only read one tag at a time, that is, it cannot decode radio waves that are reflected by more than one tag simultaneously. This simple concept means it would be quite cheap to implement this technique.

Zero-Knowledge

Engberg et al. (Engberg, Harnig, & Jensen, 2004) have also proposed zero-knowledge based (Menezes et al., 1996; Stallings, 1999) protocols, an established technique used in cryptography, for communication between reader and tag, so that they can authenticate each other without revealing any secrets that may allow them to be tracked, and so forth. In more detail, the tags can operate in either of two modes: EPC and privacy. They are in EPC mode when still in the supply chain, but when they pass on to the consumer, they go into privacy mode, and the consumer controls whether the tag should be totally silent or respond only in certain situation,; and all this without leaking any identifiable information to outsiders.

Universal Encryption Mixnet

Golle et al. (Golle, Jacobson, Jeuls, & Syverson, 2004) proposed an idea based on reencryption mixnets, where to prevent from being tracked, the tag IDs are encrypted and, while in transit, can be further reencrypted by the intermediate communicating networks until the final destination, such that the recipient only needs to perform one decryption to obtain the tag ID, despite it having been encrypted and reencrypted numerous times in transit. While conventional reencryption mixnet schemes require the knowledge of the public keys of previous encryptions in order to do reencryptions, Golle et al.'s universal version eliminates this need and thus, is suitable for the RFID application.

Authentication between Readers and Tags

Besides providing privacy, authentication is also important. Both tags and readers should trust each other, and the protocols specifying how they interact must be analyzed like any security protocol used in computer or network situations.

Mutual authentication can be done via public-key cryptography (Menezes et al., 1996; Stallings, 1999), such as techniques of key exchange, digital signatures, and encryption, but most RFIDs have very low resources, making this impractical.

Juels (2004) describes an authentication scheme based on challenge-response that uses only simple bitwise exclusive-OR operations and no other complicated cryptographic primitives; thus, it would be well suited for the low-computational resources of RFIDs. However, it involves the communication of four messages and frequent updates (Dimitriou, 2005); thus, it may not be desirable in the communications sense.

Hash Function-Based

Henrici and Muller (2004) proposed (Figure 3) an RFID authentication scheme based on hash functions and the challenge-response mechanism.

When the reader requests the tag for identification, the latter replies with $hash(ID)$, $hash(i \oplus ID)$ and Δi, where i is the session number, and Δi is the difference between the current and previous session numbers. Since both the reader and tag are in synchronization on the same i, the reader can verify the freshness of the current session (and hence know it is not a replay by an attacker), and also the tag's ID. It then responds with $hash(r \oplus i \oplus ID)$, where r is a random number. The tag verifies that this is correct; thus, both of them are authenticated to each other.

Avoine and Oechslin (2005) identified some problems with this though. In the first place, the transmitted Δi is not random enough. A tag that has had many sessions with the reader can be distinguished from a tag that has only had a few, thus tracking can still be done. Also, it is possible to tamper with the message $hash(r \oplus i \oplus ID)$ by replacing it with $hash(i \oplus ID)$; thus, even without the reader's involvement, the tag can be fooled into thinking it has successfully authenticated the reader.

Figure 3. Henrici-Muller scheme

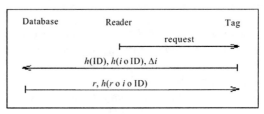

Figure 4. Dimitriou scheme

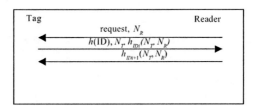

In view of these problems, an improved scheme (Figure 4) was proposed in Dimitriou (2005) that additionally provides forward secrecy. The gist is to use nonces (random numbers that are never reused) by both the reader and tag in their challenges to each other.

Advanced Encryption Standard (AES)-Based

Feldhofer et al. (Feldhofer, Dominikus, & Wolderstorfer, 2004) demonstrated that it is possible to achieve authentication without making use of computationally intensive public-key cryptography, but instead used the advanced encryption standard (AES), which is a symmetric-key (Menezes et al., 1996; Stallings, 1999) technique for encryption. And to further give allowance to slower response time of tags, they proposed to ameliorate over all tags being authenticated by the reader. In particular (Figure 5), the reader sends out a series of challenges C_1, C_2, ... to the tags T_1, T_2, ..., respectively. Upon the reception of its challenge C_i, each tag T_i computes the response $R_i = E_K(C_i)$, but does not immediately send R_i back to the reader. After it has completed sending out the

Figure 5. Interleaving the challenge and response messages among multiple tags

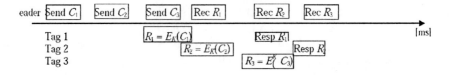

challenges, the reader then sends out requests for the responses R_i. By interleaving the challenge-response messages between the reader with many tags, the reader no longer has to wait for a response from each tag before going on to process another; thus, average communication time between each tag and the reader is significantly reduced.

Pseudo-Random Function (PRF)-Based

More generally, mutual authentication schemes using challenge-response can make use of any pseudo-random function in the computation of responses to challenges, such as that given in Molnar and Wagner (2004). See Figure 6.

The reader sends a random challenge a to the tag, which in turn selects a random number b, and then computes the response $\sigma = ID \oplus f_s(0,a,b)$, where $f_s(\times)$ is a pseudo-random function keyed by a secret s shared between the tag and reader. The reader verifies this response, and further computes $\tau = ID \oplus f_s(1,a,b)$, which the tag verifies.

Nevertheless, Avoine et al. (Avoine, Dysli, & Oechslin, 2005) showed that by tampering one or more tags, an attacker is able to trace other tags with nontrivial probability of success.

Figure 6. Molnar-Wagner scheme

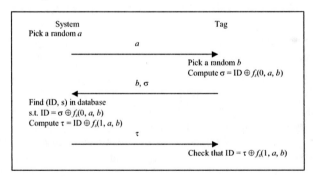

Figure 7. Juels-Weis scheme

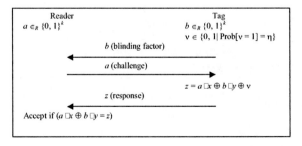

Human Protocol-Based

Juels and Weis (2005) highlighted the interesting analogy between the limitation computational and memory resources of humans and RFIDs, and thus considered the adaptation of human-based protocols to the RFID setting. They adapted the human protocol in Hopper and Blum (2001) and secured it against active attacks. This is shown in Figure 7. The tag first sends a blinding factor b to the reader, which in return sends a challenge a. The tag computes $z = a \times x \oplus b \times y$, where (x,y) are the shared secrets between them. The authentication of the tag to the reader is successful only if the z computed by the reader equals the received z.

This scheme falls to an active attack where the a is manipulated by the attacker (Gilbert et al., 2005) k times, where k is the bit length of a.

Implications

It has become quite vital these days to ensure the security and privacy of users, who are demanding these as one of the basic features offered to them so that they can transact with a peace of mind. Businesses that fail to offer such would not attract many customers, as they would opt to transact with other competing businesses that do.

The need to embed security and privacy-protecting techniques into RFID systems may be viewed by businesses as an extra cost that unnecessarily adds to the already money-constraining cost in developing a nonsecurity-protected version, and secondary to the low-memory, low-power, and low-cost requirements.

However, businesses should realize that the need for providing security and privacy is no longer a secondary requirement, but must be considered one of the indispensable basic requirements, along with low memory, low power, and low cost. Without such satisfactory features, RFID systems will not be attractive to the public market.

In contrast, if this security and privacy feature is embedded into an RFID system, public trust would be gained so that they are no longer wary of using RFIDs, and eventually, RFIDs would become an indispensable part of everyone's daily lives, just as mobile phones are to us in the present day. Once this public distrust is overcome, there will only be increasing demand for RFIDs because of its convenience and ubiquity. The trick is to try as much as possible to eliminate the disadvantages, the most major one being just the security privacy issues. With this gone, the many advantages of RFIDs will become evident, and users will be scrambling to get one of their own.

Future Trends

With the explosion in the popularity of ubiquitous and pervasive devices that includes the widespread use of the RFID, this leads to more information being communicated from one point to another. This includes, at times, confidential information, and also personal information that users would prefer not to disclose to outsiders. Thus, security and privacy issues are abounding. With each new technology trend comes new potential threats against the users; hence, this is an ever-changing field that improves over time and would never remain stagnant.

Current open problems and emerging trends are in the enhancing of the RFID technology to produce more computationally intensive tags and larger memory, while keeping the manufacturing cost to an affordable minimum, including those that would eventually be capable of performing even public-key cryptographic techniques (Menezes et al., 1996; Stallings, 1999) efficiently. The distinction between the physical security of RFIDs and that of the more secure smart cards should become smaller as RFIDs are designed to be more resistant to such physical attacks. And the study of secure RFID authentication protocols amidst adverse RFID conditions (low power, low computation, low memory) would continue to be of interest to the scientific community.

Conclusion

The ability of unique identification of objects without physical or optical contact is a very useful feature and has many commercial applications. This idea is maturing to be a reality with the aid of RFID. From our discussions in the preceding sections, it is evident that the main idea to protect privacy of tag owners is by making tag IDs indistinguishable; hence, hard to track. However, ensuring privacy only is clearly not sufficient; instead, security via mutual authentication of both reader and tag should be provided, so that only authorized RFID parties can access or even query one another.

Only in recent years (21st century) have we seen interesting results by hardcore security researchers on RFID security. Thus, it will take a couple more years for this area to mature, and by then, the scientific community would be comfortable with the level of security offered by such techniques. Past experience has shown the healthy exercise of making and breaking security mechanisms, for example, block ciphers (DES and AES development effort), hash functions (MD5, SHA-1), other security primitives (NESSIE), and authentication and key-exchange protocols (Boyd & Mathuria, 2003). This process can only contribute to the stabilization of security mechanisms.

Finally, we emphasize that nonexistence of an attack does not imply how secure the scheme is, but merely that it appears to resist known attacks. Only time will tell how secure it can be against future human ingenuity.

References

Anderson, R. (2001). *Security engineering: A guide to building dependable distributed systems*. New York: John Wiley & Sons.

Avoine, G. (2004). Privacy issues in RFID banknote protection schemes. In *Proceedings of the International Conference on Smart Card Research & Advanced Applications (CARDIS '04)* (pp. 33-48). Germany: Springer-Verlag

Avoine, G. (2005). *Security and privacy in RFID systems*. Retrieved November 10, 2005, from http://lasecwww.epfl.ch/~gavoine/rfid/

Avoine, G., Dysli, E., & Oechslin, P. (2005). Reducing time complexity in RFID systems. In *Proceedings of the Workshop on Selected Areas in Cryptography (SAC 05)*. To appear.

Avoine, G., & Oechslin, P. (2005). RFID traceability: A multilayer problem. In *Proceedings of the Financial Cryptography Conference (FC 05)* (LNCS 3570, pp. 125-140).

Boneh, D., DeMillo, R. A., & Lipton, R. J. (1997). On the importance of checking cryptographic protocols for faults. In *Proceedings of EUROCRYPT '97* (LNCS 1233, pp. 37-51). Germany: Springer-Verlag.

Boyd, C., & Mathuria, A. (2003). *Protocols for authentication and key establishment*. Germany: Springer-Verlag.

De, P., Basu, K., & Das, S. K. (2004). An ubiquitous architectural framework and protocol for object tracking using RFID tags. In *Proceedings of the International Conference on Mobile & Ubiquitous Systems: Networking & Services (MobiQuitous '05)* (pp. 174-182).

Dimitriou, T. (2005). A lightweight RFID protocol to protect against traceability and cloning attacks. In *Proceedings of the Conference on Security & Privacy for Emerging Areas in Communication Networks (SecureComm 05)*. To appear.

Engberg, S. J., Harning, M. B., & Jensen, C. D. (2004). Zero-knowledge device authentication: Privacy and security enhanced RFID preserving business value and consumer convenience. In *Proceedings of the Conference on Privacy, Security & Trust (PST 04)*, Canada.

EPC Global Inc. (2004) .*The EPCglobal Network™: Overview of design, benefits, and security*. Retrieved September 2004, from http://www.epcglobalinc.org/news/ EPCglobal_Network_Overview_10072004.pdf

Feldhofer, M., Dominikus, S., & Wolkerstorfer, J. (2004). Strong authentication for RFID systems using the AES algorithm. In *Proceedings of the Workshop on Cryptographic Hardware & Embedded Systems (CHES 04)* (LNCS 3156, pp. 357-370). Germany: Springer-Verlag.

Finkenzeller, K. (2003). *RFID handbook* (2nd ed.) Wiley.

Golle, P., Jacobson, M., Juels, A., & Syverson, P. (2004). Universal re-encryption for mixnets. In *Proceedings of the RSA Conference — Cryptographers' Track (CT-RSA 04)* (LNCS 2964, pp. 163-178).Germany: Springer-Verlag.

Henrici, D., & Muller, P. (2004). Hash-based enhancement of location privacy for RFIDs using varying identities. In *Proceedings of the IEEE International Workshop on Pervasive Computing & Communications Security (PerSec 04)* (pp. 149-153). IEEE Press.

Hopper, N., & Blum, M. (2001). Secure human identification protocols. In *Proceedings of ASIACRYPT 01* (LNCS 2248, pp. 52-66). Germany: Springer-Verlag.

Inoue, S., & Yasuura, H. (2003). *RFID privacy using user-controllable uniqueness*. RFID Privacy Workshop, MA.

Juels, A. (2004). Minimalist cryptography for RFID tags. In *Proceedings of the International Conference on Security in Communication Networks (SCN 04)* (LNCS 3352, pp. 149-164). Germany: Springer-Verlag.

Juels, A., Molnar, D., & Wagner, D. (2005). Security and privacy issues in e-passports. In *Proceedings of the Conference on Security and Privacy for Emerging Areas in Communication Networks (SecureComm'05)*. To appear.

Juels, A., & Pappu, R. (2003). Squealing euros: Privacy protection in RFID-enabled banknotes. In *Proceedings of the Financial Cryptography (FC 03)* (LNCS 2742, pp. 103-121). Germany: Springer-Verlag.

Juels, A, Rivest, R., & Szydlo, M. (2003). The blocker tag: Selective blocking of RFID tags for consumer privacy. In *Proceedings of the ACM Conference on Computer and Communications Security (ACM-CCS 03)* (pp. 103-111). ACM Press.

Juels, A., & Weis, S. A. (2005). Authenticating pervasive devices with human protocols. In *Proceedings of CRYPTO 05* (LNCS 3621, pp. 293-308). Germany: Springer-Verlag.

Kocher, P., Jaffe, J., & Jun, B. (1999). Differential power analysis. In *Proceedings of CRYPTO 99* (LNCS 1666, pp. 388-397). Germany: Springer-Verlag.

Lamport, L. (1981). Password authentication with insecure communication. *Communications of the ACM, 24*(11), 770-772.

Maxim Integrated Products. (2005). *iButton: Contact memory, digital temperature data loggers*. Retrieved November 10, 2005, from http://www.maxim-ic.com/products/ibutton/

Menezes, A., van Oorschot, P., & Vanstone, S. (1996). *Handbook of applied cryptography*. CRC Press.

Molnar, D., & Wagner, D. (2004). Privacy and security in library RFID: Issues, practices, and architectures. In *Proceedings of the ACM Conference on Computer & Communications Security (ACM-CCS 04)*. ACM Press.

Ni, L. M., Liu, Y., Lau, Y. C., & Patil, A. P. (2003) LANDMARC: Indoor location sensing using active RFID. In *Proceedings of the IEEE International Conference on Pervasive Computing and Communications* (PerCom 03) (pp. 407-415). IEEE Press.

Ohkubo, M., Suzuki, K., & Kinoshita, S. (2003). *Cryptographic approach to privacy-friendly tags*. RFID Privacy Workshop, MA.

Penttilä, K., Pere, N., Soini, M., Sydänheimo, L., & Kivikoski, M. (2005). Use and interface definition of mobile RFID reader integrated in a smart phone. In *Proceedings of the International Conference on Software Engineering (ISCE'05)*.

Shamir, A. (2004). Stream ciphers: Dead or alive. Keynote address. In *Proceedings of the ASIACRYPT 2004 Conference* (LNCS 3329, p. 78). Germany: Springer-Verlag.

Smith, J. R., Fishkin, K. P., Jiang, B., Mamishev, A., Philipose, M., Rea, A. D., Roy, S., & Sundara-Rajan, K. (2005). RFID-based techniques for human-activity detection. *Communications of the ACM, 48*(9), 39-44.

Stallings, W. (1999). *Cryptography and network security*. Englewood Cliffs, NJ: Prentice-Hall.

Stanford, V. (2003, April/June). Pervasive computing goes the last hundred feet with RFID systems. *IEEE PERVASIVE Computing Magazine*, 9-14.

Toonstra, J., & Kinsner, W. (1995). Transient analysis and genetic algorithms for classification. IEEE WESCANEX 95. *Communications, Power, and Computing, 2*, 454-469.

Weis, S. A. (2003). *Security and privacy in RFID devices*. MSc Thesis, MIT.

Weis, S. A., Sarma, S. E., Rivest, R. L., & Engels, D. W. (2003). Security and privacy aspects of low-cost radio frequency identification systems. In *Proceedings of the International Conference on Security in Pervasive Computing (SPC 03)* (LNCS 2802, pp. 454-469). Springer.

ZIH. (2005). *RFID compliance mandates*. Retrieved November 10, 2005, from http://www.zebra.com/id/zebra/na/en/index/rfid/faqs/compliance_mandates.html

Chapter IV

Mobile Code and Security Issues

E. S. Samundeeswari, Vellalar College for Women, India

F. Mary Magdalene Jane, P. S. G. R. Krishnammal, India

Abstract

Over the years, computer systems have evolved from centralized monolithic computing devices supporting static applications, into client-server environments that allow complex forms of distributed computing. Throughout this evolution, limited forms of code mobility have existed. The explosion in the use of the World Wide Web, coupled with the rapid evolution of the platform-independent programming languages, has promoted the use of mobile code and, at the same time, raised some important security issues. This chapter introduces mobile code technology and discusses the related security issues. The first part of the chapter deals with the need for mobile codes and the various methods of categorising them. One method of categorising the mobile code is based on code mobility. Different forms of code mobility, like code on demand, remote evaluation, *and* mobile agents, *are explained in detail. The other method is based on the type of code distributed. Various types of codes, like* source code, intermediate code, platform-dependent binary code, *and* just-in-time compilation, *are explained. Mobile agents, as autonomously migrating software entities, present great challenges to the design and implementation of security mechanisms. The second part of this chapter deals with the security issues. These issues are broadly divided into code-related issues and host-related issues. Techniques, like sandboxing, code signing, and proof-carrying code, are widely applied to protect the hosts. Execution tracing, mobile cryptography, obfuscated code, and cooperating agents are used to protect the code from harmful agents. The security mechanisms, like language support for safety, OS level security, and safety policies, are discussed in the last section. In order to make the mobile code approach practical, it is essential to understand mobile code technology. Advanced and innovative solutions are to be developed to restrict the operations that mobile code can perform, but without unduly restricting its functionality. It is also necessary to develop formal, extremely easy-to-use safety measures.*

Introduction

Mobile code computation is a new paradigm for structuring distributed systems. Mobile programs migrate from remote sites to a host, and interact with the resources and facilities local to that host. This new mode of distributed computation promises great opportunities for electronic commerce, mobile computing, and information harvesting. There has been a general consensus that security is the key to the success of mobile code computation.

Distributed applications involve the coordination of two or more computers geographically apart and connected by a physical network. Most distributed applications deploy the client/server paradigm. There are certain problems with the client/server paradigm, such as the requirement of a high-network bandwidth and continuous user-computer interactivity. Hence, the mobile code paradigm has been developed as an alternative approach for distributed application design.

In the client/server paradigm, programs cannot move across different machines and must run on the machines they reside on. The mobile-code paradigm, on the other hand, allows programs to be transferred among, and executed on, different computers. By allowing code to move between hosts, programs can interact on the same computer instead of over the network. Therefore, communication cost can be reduced. Besides, one form of mobile code is a program that can be designed to work on behalf of users autonomously. This autonomy allows users to delegate their tasks to the mobile code, and not to stay continuously in front of the computer terminal.

With the growth of distributed computer and telecommunications systems, there have been increasing demands to support the concept of "mobile code," sourced from remote, possibly untrustworthy systems, but executed locally.

Mobile Code

Mobile code consists of small pieces of software obtained from remote systems outside the enclave boundary, transferred across a network, and then downloaded and executed on a local system without explicit installation or execution by the recipient.

The mobile-code paradigm encompasses programs that can be executed on one or several hosts other than the one that they originate from. Mobility of such programs implies some built-in capability for each piece of code to travel smoothly from one host to another. A mobile code is associated with at least two parties: its producer and its consumer, the consumer being the host that runs the code.

Examples of mobile code include a Java script embedded within an HTML page, a visual basic script contained in a WORD document, an HTML help file, an ActiveX Control, a Java applet, a transparent browser plug-in or DLL, a new document viewer installed on demand, an explicitly downloaded executable binary, and so forth. Since mobile code runs in the execution context of the user that downloads the code, it can issue any system calls that the user is allowed to make, including deleting files, modifying configurations or registry entries, ending e-mails, or installing back-door programs in the home directory. The most common type of malicious mobile code is an e-mail attachment.

Mobile-code systems range from simple applets to intelligent software agents. These systems offer several advantages over the more traditional distributed computing approaches, like flexibility in software design beyond the well-established object-oriented paradigm and bandwidth optimization. As usual, increased flexibility comes with a cost, which is increased vulnerability in the face of malicious intrusion scenarios akin to Internet. Possible vulnerabilities with mobile code fall in one of two categories: attacks performed by a mobile program against the remote host on which the program is executed, as with malicious applets or ActiveX programs; and the less-classical category of attacks due to the subversion of the mobile code and its data by the remote execution environment.

Advantages of Mobile Code

Here are some possible advantages of mobile code:

*   Eliminates configuration and installation problems, and reduces software distribution costs of desktop applications
*   The code is potentially portable to many platforms
*   Enhances the scalability of client/server applications
*   Achieves performance advantages
*   Achieves interoperability of distributed applications

Categories of Mobile Code

One method of categorising the mobile code is based on code mobility (Ghezzi & Vigna, 1997). Different forms of code mobility are *code on demand, remote evaluation,* and *mobile agents. Code on demand* is the downloading of executable content in a client environment as the result of a client request to a server. In *remote evaluation,* the code is uploaded to a server, where this code is executed. Multihop migration of code across the network and autonomous execution on many different hosts is termed *mobile agent.*

Code on Demand

In the code on demand paradigm, the client component owns the resources needed for the execution of a service, but lacks the know-how needed to use them in performing the service. The corresponding code component can be retrieved from a remote server component, which acts as a code repository, and subsequently executed, thus providing enhanced flexibility by allowing the server to dynamically change the behavior of the client. This is the scheme typically employed by Web applets, or by the parameter-passing mechanism in Java/RMI.

Remote Evaluation

In the remote-evaluation paradigm, the client component owns the know-how about the service that must be executed, but lacks the resources needed to perform the service, which are owned by the server component. A sort of enhanced client-server interaction takes place, where the client sends a request to the server, but includes also the code component required to perform the service. After the code component is received on the server, the interaction proceeds as in the client-server paradigm, with the code component accessing the resources now colocated with it, and sending the results back to the client. This reduces network traffic by executing a computation close to the resources located at the server's side. A common example is SQL servers performing queries on a remote database.

Mobile Agents

In the mobile-agent paradigm, the mobile components explicitly relocate themselves across the network, preserving their execution state (or part thereof) across migrations. It is, therefore, associated with many security issues needed for "safe" execution. The

Table 1. Summary of mobile code techniques

Type of mobility	Category	Mobility of code	Resources	Processor
Weak	Code on demand	Remote to local (Pull)	Local side	Local side
	Remote evaluation	Local to remote (Push)	Remote side	Remote side
Strong	Mobile agent	Migration	Remote side	Agent's originator

*Where **Resources** represent the information and other resources for code execution*
Processor is the abstract machine that holds the state of computation

mobile agents offer new possibilities for the e-commerce applications, creating new types of electronic ventures from e-shops and e-auctions to virtual enterprises and e-market-places. The agent helps to automate many electronic commerce tasks such as simple information gathering tasks, and all tasks of commercial transactions, namely price negotiation, contract signing, and delivery of (electronic) goods and services. Such agents are developed for diverse business areas, for example, contract negotiations, service brokering, stock trading, and many others. Examples of systems supporting this type of mobility are Telescript (Telescript, 1995), Aglets (IBM Aglets, 2002), and JADE (Java Agent Development Framework, 2005).

The first two forms, code on demand and remote evaluation, can be classified as weak-mobility forms, as they involve the mobility of code only. Since the mobile agent involves the mobility of computation, it is commonly known as strong-mobility form.

The other method of categorizing "mobile code" technologies is based on the type of code distributed (Tennenhouse & Wetherall, 1996):

- Source code
- Intermediate code
- Platform-dependent binary code
- Just-in-time compilation

Source Code

The first approach is based on distributing the source for the "mobile code" used. This source will be parsed and executed by an interpreter on the user's system. The interpreter is responsible for examining the source to ensure it obeys the required syntactic and semantic restrictions of the language; and then for providing a safe execution "sand-box" environment. The safety of this approach relies on the correct specification and implementation of the interpreter.

The main advantages of the source code approach are the distribution of relatively small amounts of code; the fact that since the user has the full source, it is easier to check the code; and that it is easier for the interpreter to contain the execution environment. Disadvantages include the fact that it is slow, since the source must first be parsed; and that it is hard to expand the core functionality, since the interpreter's design limits this. Examples are programmable MUDs, JavaScript, and so forth.

Intermediate Code

A second approach to providing "mobile code" is to have the programs compiled to a platform-independent intermediate code that is then distributed to the user's system. This intermediate code is executed by an interpreter on the user's system. Advantages are that it is faster to interpret than source, since no textual parsing is required, and the intermediate code is semantically much closer to machine code. The interpreter provides a safe execution "sand-box" and again, the safety of the system depends on the interpreter. The code, in general, is quite small, and the user's system can check the code to ensure it obeys the safety restrictions. Disadvantages of this approach are its moderate speed, since an interpreter is still being used, and the fact that less semantic information is available to assist in checking the code than if source was available. Java is a very good example for this category.

Native Binary Code

The third category of code distribution uses native binary code that is then executed on the user's system. This gives the maximum speed, but means that the code is platform-dependent. Safe execution of binary code requires the restricted use of an instruction set and the restricted address space access. Approaches to ensuring this can rely upon

- Traditional heavy address space protection that is costly in terms of system performance and support
- The verified use of a trusted compiler that guarantees to generate safe code that will not violate the security restrictions
- The use of "software fault isolation" technologies that augment the instruction stream, inserting additional checks to ensure safe execution.

A combination of verified use of a trusted compiler and the software fault isolation approach has created considerable interest, especially when used with a just-in-time compiler.

Just-in-Time Compilation

Just-in-time compilation (JIT) is an approach that combines the portability of intermediate or source code with the speed of binary code. The source or intermediate code is distributed, but is then compiled to binary on the user's system before being executed. If source is used, it is slower but easier to check. If intermediate code is used, then it is faster. Another advantage is that users can utilise their own trusted compiler to verify code, and insert the desired software fault isolation run-time checks. Individual procedures are translated on a call-by-call basis. This approach is being used with Java JIT compilers.

Properties of Mobile Code

- Comes in a variety of forms

- Often runs unannounced and unbeknownst to the user

- Runs with the privilege of the user

- Distributed in executable form

- Run in multiple threads

- Can launch other programs

Security Issues of Mobile Code Paradigms

In this section, some possible security attacks to different mobile-code paradigms, and possible mechanisms against these attacks, are discussed.

A security attack is an action that compromises the security requirements of an application. Applications developed using different paradigms are subject to different attacks. In the conventional client/server model, the local computer is usually assumed to be fortress for code and data. Therefore, the sources of security attacks are outsiders of the local machine. The main possible attacks are *masquerading* (pretending the server or the client), *eavesdropping* on the communication channel, and *forging messages* to the client or the server.

The security model of the client/server paradigm also applies to the *remote evaluation* and *code-on-demand* approaches, with the additional concern that the code-receiving side must make sure the code is not harmful to run. In remote evaluation, the code receiving side is the remote side, while it is the local side in code-on-demand. *Mobile agent*, on the other hand, is the most challenging area of mobile-code security, due to the autonomy of agents. Mobile-agent security is usually divided into two aspects: *host security* and *code security*. Host security (Loureiro, Molva, & Roudier, 2000) deals with the protection of hosts against malicious code/agent, whereas code security deals with the protection of code/agents against malicious hosts or other agents.

Host Security Against Malicious Code

In the interconnected world of computers, mobile code generated by a malicious outsider, has become an omnipresent and dangerous threat. Malicious code can infiltrate hosts using a variety of methods, such as attacks against known software flaws, hidden functionality in regular programs, and social engineering.

From the host perspective, a secure execution environment is necessary to protect itself from such types of code. The first step towards a secure environment is to simply limit the functionality of the execution environment in order to limit the vulnerabilities. Techniques for protection of hosts now evolve along two directions (1) executing mobile codes in a restricted environment, (2) a mobile code infrastructure that is enhanced with authentication, data integrity, and access control mechanisms. The following section details both the aspects.

Sandboxing

Sandboxing is a software technique used to protect hosts from malicious mobile code. In an execution environment, local code is executed with full permission, and has access to crucial system resources. On the other hand, mobile code is executed inside a restricted area called a "sandbox" that restricts the code to operating system functionality. A sandboxing mechanism enforces a fixed-security policy for the execution of the mobile code. The policy specifies the rules and restrictions that mobile code should conform to. A mechanism is said to be secure if it properly implements a policy that is free of flaws and inconsistencies.

To contain mobile code within a sandbox, extensive type checking is used. Also, memory accesses and jump addresses are checked at runtime. If these addresses do not fall within the sandbox, then they are redirected to a location within the sandbox. The error, however, is contained within the sandbox, and cannot affect the rest of the system. Sandboxing can also be used for restricting access to file systems, and limiting the ability to open network connections.

The most common implementation of sandboxing is in the Java interpreter inside Java-enabled Web browsers. A Java interpreter contains three main security components: classloader, verifier, and security manager . The classloader converts mobile code into data structures that can be added to the local class hierarchy. Thus, every remote class has a subtype of the classloader class associated with it. Before the mobile code is loaded, the verifier performs a set of security checks on it in order to guarantee that only legitimate

Figure 1. Sandboxing technique

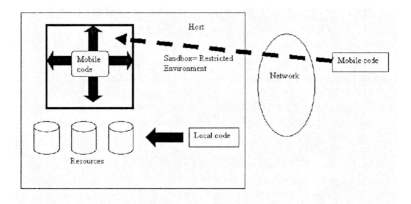

Java code is executed. The mobile code should be a valid virtual machine code, and it should not overflow or underflow the stack, or use registers improperly. Additionally, remote classes cannot overwrite local names, and their operations are checked by the security manager before the execution.

The main problem with the sandbox is that any error in any security component can lead to a violation of the security policy. The sandbox also incurs a high runtime overhead. A downside of the sandboxing technique is that it increases the execution time of legitimate remote code.

Code Signing

In the "code signing" technique, a digitally signed piece of software identifies the producer who created and signed it. It enables the platform to verify that the code has not been modified since it was signed by the creator. Code signing makes use of a digital signature and one-way hash function where a private key is used to sign code, both ensuring transmission integrity and enabling policy defined by trust in the signer. Code signing enables the verification of the code producer's identity, but it does not guarantee that they are trustworthy.

The platform that runs mobile code maintains a list of trusted entities and checks the code against the list. If the code producer is on the list, it is assumed that they are trustworthy and that the code is safe. The code is then treated as local code and is given full privileges; otherwise, the code will not run at all. An example is Microsoft's Authenticode system for ActiveX.

There are two main drawbacks of the code signing approach. First, this technique assumes that all the entities on the trusted list are trustworthy and that they are incorruptible. Mobile code from such a producer is granted full privileges. If the mobile code is malicious, it can use those privileges not only to directly cause harm to the executing platform, but also to open a door for other malicious agents by changing the acceptance policy on the platform. Moreover, the affects of the malicious agent attack may only occur later, which makes it impossible to establish a connection between the attack and the attacker. Such attacks are referred to as "delayed attacks." Secondly, this technique is overly restrictive towards agents that are coming from unrecognized entities, as they do not run at all.

Code Signing and Sandboxing Combined

This technique combines the advantages of both code signing and sandboxing. If the code consumer trusts the signer of the code, then the code will run as if it were local code, that is, with full privileges being granted to it. On the other hand, if the code consumer does not trust the signer of the code, then the code will run inside a sandbox. The main advantage of this approach is that it enables the execution of the mobile code produced by untrustworthy entities. However, this method still suffers from the same drawback as code signing, that is, malicious code that is deemed trustworthy can cause damage and even change the acceptance policy. The security policy is the set of rules for granting

Figure 2. Code signing technique

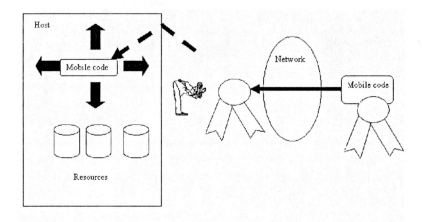

programs permission to access various platform resources. The "black-and-white" policy only allows the platform to label programs as completely trusted or untrusted. The combination of code signing and sandboxing implemented in JDK 1.2 incorporates fine-grained access control where it allows a user to assign any degree of partial trust to a code, rather than just "trusted" and "untrusted."

There is a whole spectrum of privileges that can be granted to the code. In JDK1.2, all code is subjected to the same security policy, regardless of being labelled as local or remote. The run-time system partitions code into individual groups, called protection domains, in such a way that all programs inside the same domain are granted the same set of permissions. The end-user can authorize certain protection domains to access the majority of resources that are available at the executing host, while other protection domains may be restricted to the sandbox environment. In between these two, there are different subsets of privileges that can be granted to different protection domains, based on whether they are local or remote, authorised or not, and even based on the key that is used for the signature.

Proof-Carrying Code

Proof-carrying code (PCC) (Proof-Carrying Code, 2002) strikes an effective balance between security and flexibility. The process, pioneered by Necula and Lee (1998), involves the code producer attaching additional data to a piece of code. This data can be interpreted as proof that a particular property holds for the piece of code.

In this technique, the code producer is required to provide a formal proof that the code complies with the security policy of the code consumer. The code producer sends the code, together with the formal safety proof, sometimes called machine-checkable proof, to the code consumer. Upon receipt, the code consumer checks and verifies the safety proof of the incoming code by using a simple and fast proof checker. Depending on the result of the proof validation process, the code is proclaimed safe, and consequently executed without any further checking, or it is rejected. PCC guarantees the safety of the incoming code, providing that there is no flaw in the verification-condition generator, the logical axioms, the typing rules, and the proof checker.

PCC is considered to be "self-certifying" because no cryptography or trusted-third party is required. It involves low-cost static program checking, after which the program can be executed without any expensive run-time checking. In addition, PCC is considered "tamper-proof," as any modification done to the code or the proof will be detected. Other applications include active networks and extensible operating systems. Proof-carrying code also has some limitations that include the potential size of the proof and the time consumed in the proof-validation process.

Mobile Code Security against Malicious Host

While a mobile agent is roaming among host platforms, it typically carries information such as code, static data, data collected from other hosts that were visited, and the execution state of the mobile agent. The execution state is a dynamic data created during the execution of the agent at each host. Agents may be susceptible to observation of execution or any other information it possesses.

The possible attacks by the host platform on mobile agents are extracting sensitive information such as encryption keys, credit card information, corrupting or modifying the execution state and code information, and denial of service. The data collected by the agent from other hosts or from the host's own database is manipulated to report false information to the user. Similarly, the agent's code and execution sequence is manipulated to learn about the information the user is interested in, and make the agent perform something illegitimately. Denial of service includes terminating the agent without executing it, ignoring the agent's request for services and resources, providing insufficient resources, making it very difficult for the agent to complete execution in a timely fashion, or assigning continuous tasks to the agent so that it will never reach its goal. A malicious agent may assume the identity of another agent in order to gain access to platform resources and services, or simply to cause mischief or even serious damage to the platform. Likewise, a platform can claim the identity of another platform in order to gain access to the mobile agent data. This type of attack is known as masquerading.

It is intrinsically more difficult to protect the agents located on potentially untrusted hosts, since the environment has a total control over the mobile code (otherwise, protecting the host would be impossible). Three categories of solutions exist to protect agents (Chan & Anthony, 1999; Sanders & Tschudin, 1998a; Sanders & Tschudin, 1998b): agent tampering avoidance, detection, and prevention. In avoidance technique, a closed network is established by sending the agents only to trusted hosts, such as intraorganizational applications, or on a third-party-hosted network that is trusted by all parties involved. Such an arrangement is effective but obviously satisfies system openness. The attacks can be detected using techniques such as forward integrity and execution tracing. These techniques are not suitable for very critical actions, for which detection may be too late. The attacks can be prevented either by making the tampering difficult or expensive. This can be achieved either by digitally signing the agent state and the data, or encrypting them with a public key of the targeted host, or by obfuscated code.

In cooperating agents technique, the agent code/state is duplicated to recover from an agent termination attack. These prevention techniques are not well developed and are of current research issue.

Tampering Detection Techniques

Execution tracing (Vigna, 1997) is a technique that enables the detection of any possible misbehaviour by a platform. It is based on cryptographic traces that are collected during an agent's execution at different platforms and attached to the agent itself. Traces are the logs of actions performed by the agent during its lifetime, and can be checked by the agents' owner to see if it contains any unauthorized modifications. This technique has some limitations, such as the potential large size and number of logs to be retained, and the owner has to wait until it obtains suspicious results in order to run the verification process. Tracing is only triggered on suspicion that malicious tampering of an agent has occurred during its itinerary and is too complicated to be used for multithreaded agents. A variation of this technique is by assigning the trace verification process to a trusted third party, the verification server, instead of depending on the agent's owner. These techniques assume that all the involved parties own a public and private key that can be used for digital signatures to identify the involved parties. Another variation of this technique uses a list of secret keys provided by the agent's originator. For each platform in an agent's itinerary, there is an associated secret key. When an agent finishes an execution at a certain platform in its itinerary, it summarizes the results of its execution in a message for the home platform, which could be sent either immediately or later. The agent erases the used secret key of the current visited platform before its migration to the next platform. Destroying the secret key ensures the "forward integrity" of the encapsulation results. Forward integrity guarantees that no platform to be visited in the future is able to modify any results from the previously visited platform.

Tampering Prevention Techniques

Mobile Cryptography

This technique (Sanders & Tschudin, 1998a) is based on executing the agent in its encrypted form. It is not the code that is encrypted, but the function this code executes. The major challenge here is to find encryption schemes for expressing a program of arbitrary functions or login. An approach that uses the mobile cryptography is a time-limited blackbox (Hohl, 1998). It defines the blackbox as an agent that performs the same task as the original agent but has a different structure. The agent has the blackbox property if its code and data cannot be read or modified. The agent holds the blackbox property for a known time interval that should be sufficient to perform the required task. After this time the agent is invalidated, and the attacks have no effect. Various means of code obfuscation and authentication techniques are proposed to achieve this time-limited blackbox.

Obfuscated Code

Obfuscation (Motlekar, 2005) is a technique of enforcing the security policy by applying a behaviour-preserving transformation to the code before it is being despatched to different hosts. It aims to protect the code from being analysed and understood by the host; thereby, making the extraction and corruption of sensitive data, code, or state very difficult. Different obfuscating transformations are layout obfuscation — remove or modify some information in the code such as comments and debugging information; data obfuscation — modifying the data and data structures in the code without modifying the code itself; and control obfuscation — altering the control flow in the code without modifying the computing part of the code. Code mess up is a variation of this approach, where by the code is rendered to look illogically, using irrelevant variable names, having odd data representation, decomposing the variables bit-by-bit and reassembling them into the actual values during execution, adding a small amount of dead code that may appear to be active in the program. It is not sufficient to scramble the code only once, as the code may be reconstituted and comprehended by a malicious observer. The agent must have a new structure for each dispersal from the home origin. Obfuscation concentrates on protecting the code from decompilers and debuggers. It could delay, but not prevent, the attacks on agent via reverse engineering.

Cooperating Agents

This technique distributes critical tasks of a single mobile agent between two cooperating agents. Each of the two cooperating agents executes the tasks in one of two disjoint sets of platforms. The cooperating agents share the same data and exchange information in a secret way. This technique reduces the possibility of the shared data being pilfered by a single host. Each agent records and verifies the route of its cooperating agent. When an agent travels from one platform to another, it uses an authenticated communication channel to pass information about its itinerary to its cooperating agent. The peer agent takes a suitable action when anything goes wrong. The drawbacks of this technique are the cost of setting up the authenticated communication channel for each migration; care should be taken to assign the two agents to disjoint platforms and never assigned to the same malicious host.

Security Mechanisms

Developing sound, reliable security mechanisms is a nontrivial task, and a history of vulnerable and/or incomplete implementations of these mechanisms led to the idea that mobile-code systems are inherently insecure, too complex, and very difficult to deploy. To overcome these problems, the mobile-code system must rely, as much as possible, on the security mechanisms already provided by the language used for developing, and by the underlying operating system. By doing this, it is possible to develop, with reduced effort, security services that rely on well-known, well-understood, and well-tested security mechanisms. Also, by describing the security of the mobile-code system in terms of the language and OS security mechanisms, system administrators can better evaluate the security implications of deploying the system.

Language Support for Safety

The features of the language needed to ensure that various code units do not interfere with each other, and with the system are given next.

*   Heavy address space protection mechanisms

*   Type-safe feature to ensure that arrays stay in bounds, pointers are always valid, and code cannot violate variable typing (such as placing code in a string and then executing it)

*   Designing a modular system, separating interfaces from implementations in programs, and with appropriate layering of libraries and module groups, with particular care being taken at the interfaces between security boundaries.

*   Replace general library routines that could compromise security with more specific, safer ones. For example a general file access routine can be replaced with one that can write files only in a temporary directory.

*   Granting access to resources: Determining exactly which resources a particular code unit is to be granted access to. That is, there is a need for a security policy that determines what type access any "mobile code" unit has. This policy may be:

1. **Fixed for all "mobile code" units:** Very restrictive but easy, and the approach currently is used to handle applet security in Web browsers such as Netscape.

2. **User verifies each security-related access requests:** Relatively easy, but rapidly gets annoying, and eventually is self-defeating when users stop taking notice of the details of the requests. Whilst there is a place for querying the user, it should be used exceedingly sparingly.

3. **Negotiate for each "mobile code" unit:** Much harder, as some basis is needed for negotiation, perhaps based on various profiles, but ultimately this is likely to be the best approach.

OS Level Security

The types of events to be monitored in association with the agent execution are very similar to those audited for the system's users. Moreover, the agents can be easily grouped and differentiated within the system. In addition to extensive authentication and authorization mechanisms, accounting and auditing mechanisms should be implemented.

In a system like "distributed agents on the go" (DAGO) (Felmetsger & Vigna, 2005), a mobile agent is viewed as an ordinary system's user who logs in to the host and uses some of the system's resources for its own needs. Every incoming mobile agent is given an individual account and a unique user identifier (UID) for the duration of its execution on a host. This approach allows the hosting OS to apply to mobile agents the same set of rules and policies that are applied by the OS to all of its users.

In Unix, a number of logging, auditing, and accounting mechanisms are available to monitor the action of its users and the status of its resources. These tools can work at the system call level and can be configured based on different types of events, such as opening and closing of files, reads and writes, programs executed, and so on. They also can allow one to specify groups of system objects to be monitored for certain activities, and can track system usage by recording the statistics about CPU and memory usage, I/O operations, running time, and other forms of system resource usage, along with the user IDs of the processes involved. These tools can be easily leveraged and extended to a multiagent environment.

A variety of customizable tools, such as SNARE — system intrusion analysis and reporting environment (SNARE, 2005), BSM — basic security module provide a greater degree of security assurance. SNARE is a dynamically loadable kernel nodule that can be used as a stand-alone auditing system or as a distributed tool. The tool can be configured to monitor events associated with certain groups of users, filter the monitored events with specific "search expressions," and submit reports in different formats and time frames. The type of events monitored can be either defined by a category (for example, system calls) or by an identifier (such as "denied access").

Safety Policies for Mobile Code Programs

A safety policy is a set of restrictions placed upon locally run untrusted code to ensure that the program does not behave in a manner that is detrimental to the system or to the system security. At the very least, a safety policy should guarantee the following fundamental safety properties (Muller, 2000):

- **Control flow safety:** The program should never jump to and start executing code that lies outside of the program's own code segment. All function calls should be to valid function entry points, and function returns should return to the location from where the function was called.

- **Memory safety:** The program should never be allowed to access random locations in memory. The program should only access memory in its own static data segment, live system heap memory that has been explicitly allocated to it, and valid stack frames.

- **Stack safety:** The program should only be allowed to access the top of the stack. Access to other areas of the stack should be completely restricted.

These three properties, combined, offer the minimum nontrivial level of security for mobile code. More complicated security policies are possible, depending on the application.

Trust

Security is based on the notion of trust. Basically, software can be divided into two categories, namely, software that is trusted and software that is not, separated by an imaginary trust boundary. All software on our side of the trust boundary is trusted and is known as the trusted code base.

All security implementations rely on some trusted code. As a result, a trust model of a particular implementation can be made. The trust model basically specifies which code is to be included in the trusted-code base and which code lies outside of the trust boundary.

At the very least, the trusted-code base should include the local operating system kernel, but can also include other items of trusted software, like trusted compilers or trusted program runtime environments (e.g., the Java interpreter). It is desirable, however, to keep the trusted-code base as small as possible to reduce the security vulnerabilities.

Performance and Security

Unfortunately, as it is in most applications, performance is sacrificed for increased security. It would, however, be profitable to have applications that are both secure and perform well at the same time. For this reason, there is much research concerned with resolving the conflict between these concepts in some way.

Conclusion

The purpose of this chapter is to raise readers' awareness of mobile code and various approaches to addressing security of mobile code and agents. All of the techniques discussed in this chapter offer different approaches to combating malicious mobile code. However, the best approach is probably a combination of security mechanisms. The sandbox and code signing approaches are already hybridized. Combining these with firewalling techniques, such as the playground, gives an extra layer of security. PCC is still very much in the research and development phase at present.

In order to make the mobile code approach practical, it is essential to develop advanced and innovative solutions to restrict the operations that mobile code can perform, but without unduly restricting its functionality. It is also necessary to develop formal, extremely easy–to-use safety languages to specify safety policy.

Organizations relying on the Internet face significant challenges to ensure that their networks operate safely, and that their systems continue to provide critical services, even in the face of attack. Even the strictest of security policies will not be able to prevent security breaches. Educating users in social-engineering attacks based around mobile code is also necessary.

References

Alfalayleh, M., & Brankovic, L. (2004). *An overview of security issues and techniques in mobile agents*. Retrieved from http://sec.isi.salford.ac.uk/cms2004/Program/ CMS2004final/p2a3.pdf

Brown, L. (1996). *Mobile code security* [Electronic version]. Retrieved from http:// www.unsw.adfa.edu.au/~lpb/papers/mcode96.html

Chan, H. W., & Anthony. (1999). *Secure mobile agents: Techniques, modeling and application*. Retrieved from http://www.cse.cuhk.edu.hk/~lyu/student/mphil/ anthony/term3.ppt

Felmetsger, V., & Vigna, G. (2005). *Exploiting OS-level mechanisms to implement mobile code security*. Retrieved from http://www.cs.ucsb.edu/~vigna/pub/ 2005_felmetsger_vigna_ICECCS05.pdf

Ghezzi, C., & Vigna, G. (1997). Mobile code paradigms and technologies: A case study. In K. Rothermet & R. Popescu-Zeletin (Eds.), *Mobile agents, First International Workshop, MA'97, Proceedings* (LNCS 1219, pp. 39-49) Berlin, Germany: Springer.

Hefeeda, M., & Bharat, B. (n.d.) *On mobile code security*. Center of Education and Research in Information Assurance and Security, and Department of Computer Science, Purdue University, West Lafayette, IN. Retrieved from http:// www.cs.sfu.ca/~mhefeeda/Papers/OnMobileCodeSecurity.pdf

Hohl, F. (1997). *An approach to solve the problem of malicious hosts*. Universität Stuttgart, Fakultät Informatik, Fakultätsbericht Nr. 1997/03. Retrieved from http:/ /www.informatik.uni-stuttgart.de/cgi-bin/ncstrl_rep_view.pl?/inf/ftp/pub/library/ ncstrl.ustuttgart_fi/TR-1997-03/TR-1997-03.bib

Hohl, F. (1998). *Time limited blackbox security: Protecting mobile agents from malicious hosts*. Retrieved from http://citeseer.ist.psu.edu/hohl98time.html

Hohl, F. (1998). *Mobile agent security and reliability*. Proceedings of the Ninth International Symposium on Software Reliability Engineering (ISSRE '98).

Hohl, F. (1998). Time limited blackbox security: Protecting mobile agents from malicious hosts. *Mobile Agents and Security, 1419 of LNCS*. Springer-Verlag.

IBM Aglets. (2002). Retrieved from http://www.trl.ibm.com/aglets/

Jansen, W., & Karygiannis, T. (n.d.). *Mobile agent security* (NIST Special Publication 800-19) Retrieved from http://csrc.nist.gov/publications/nistpubs/800-19/sp800- 19.pdf

Java Agent Development Framework. (2005). Retrieved from http://jade.tilab.com/

Karjoth, G., Lange, D. B., & Oshima, M. (1997). A security model for aglets. *IEEE Internet Computing, 1*(4), 68-77. [Electronic version]. Retrieved from http://www.ibm.com/ java/education/aglets/

Loureiro, S., Molva, R., & Roudier, Y. (2000, February). *Mobile code security*. Proceedings of ISYPAR 2000 (4ème Ecole d'Informatique des Systems Parallèles et Répartis), Code Mobile, France. Retrieved from www.eurecom.fr/~nsteam/Papers/mcs5.pdf

Lucco, S., Sharp, O., & Wahbe, R. (1995). Omniware: A universal substrate for mobile code. In Fourth International World Wide Web Conference, MIT. [Electronic version] Retrieved from http://www.w3.org/pub/Conferences/WWW4/Papers/165/

McGraw, G., & Morrisett, G. (2000). *Attacking malicious code*. Retrieved from http://www.cs.cornell.edu/Info/People/jgm/lang-based-security/maliciouscode.pdf

Mobile Code and Mobile Code Security. (2005). Retrieved from http://www.cs.nyu.edu/~yingxu/privacy/0407/main.html

Mobile Code Security. (1996). [Electronic version] Retrieved from http://www.unsw.adfa.edu.au/~lpb/papers/mcode96.html

Mobile Code Security and Computing with Encrypted Functions [Electronic version] Retrieved from http://www.zurich.ibm.com/security/mobile

Motlekar, S. (2005). *Code obfuscation*. Retrieved from http://palisade.paladion.net/issues/2005Aug/code-obfuscation/

Muller, A. (2000). Mobile *code security: Taking the Trojans out of the Trojan horse*. Retrieved from www.cs.uct.ac.za/courses/CS400W/NIS/papers00/amuller/essay1.htm

Necula, G. C., & Lee, P. (1998). Safe, untrusted agents using proof-carrying code. *Lecture Notes in Computer Science*, (1419). Springer-Verlag.

Oppliger, R. (2000). *Security technologies for the World Wide Web*. Computer Security Series. Artech House Publishers.

Proof-Carrying Code. (2002). Retrieved from http://raw.cs.berkeley.edu/pcc.html

Robust Obfuscation. (2005). Retrieved from http://www.cs.arizona.edu/~collberg/Research/Obfuscation/

Roger, A. G. (2001). *Malicious mobile code: Virus protection for Windows* [Electronic version]. O'Reilly & Associates.

Rubin, A. D., & Geer, D. E. (1998). Mobile code security. *IEEE Internet Computing*.

Sander, T., & Tschudin, C. (1998a). *Towards mobile cryptography*. Proceedings of the IEEE Symposium on Security and Privacy.

Sander, T., & Tschudin, C. (1998b). Protecting mobile agents against malicious hosts. [Electronic version] In G. Vigna (Ed.). Mobile agents and security, *Lecture Notes in Computer Science, 1419* (pp. 44-60). Retrieved from http://citeseer.ist.psu.edu/article/sander97protecting.html

SNARE — System iNtrusion Analysis and Reporting Environment (2005). [Electronic version] Retrieved from http://www.intersectalliance.com/projects/Snare

Telescript Language Reference. (1995). Retrieved from http://citeseer.ist.psu.edu/inc95telescript.html

Tennenhouse, D. L., & Wetherall, D. J. (1996) Towards an active network architecture. *Computer Communication Review*. Retrieved from http://www.tns.lcs.mit.edu/publications/ccr96.html

Vigna, G. (1997, June). Protecting mobile agents through tracing. *Proceedings of the 3rd ECOOP Workshop on Mobile Object Systems*, Jyvälskylä, Finland. Retrieved from http://www.cs.ucsb.edu/~vigna/listpub.html

Chapter V

A Survey of Key Generation for Secure Multicast Communication Protocols

Win Aye, Multimedia University, Malaysia

Mohammad Umar Siddiqi, International Islamic University Malaysia, Malaysia

Abstract

Multicast communication demands scalable security solutions for group communication infrastructure. Secure multicast is one such solution that achieves the efficiency of multicast data delivery. Key generation plays an important role in enforcing secure and efficient key distribution. This chapter addresses the issues focused on the area of key generation on key management cryptographic algorithms that support security requirements in multicast group communications. These issues are of importance to application developers wishing to implement security services for their multicast applications. The three main classes, centralized, decentralized, and distributed architectures, are investigated and analyzed here and an insight given to their features and goals. The area of group key generation is then surveyed and proposed solutions are classified according to the efficiency of the cryptographic algorithms and multicast security requirements. We also outline the open problems in this area.

Introduction

Today, e-business applications provide critical links among businesses, customers, and business partners. Web services are rapidly becoming the enabling technology of today's e-business and e-commerce systems, and will soon transform the Web as it is now into a distributed computation and application framework. Web services security is a building block that is used in conjunction with other Web service and application-specific protocols to accommodate a wide variety of security models and encryption technologies. Web services security is flexible and is designed to be used as the basis for the construction of a wide variety of security models including public key infrastructure (PKI).

Companies are turning to unify IP networks to connect employees, customers, vendors, strategic partners, and even competitors. They are creating a digital Web that redefines both business-to-business (B2B) and business-to-customer (B2C) relationships. The emphasis is on real time because the enterprise with the timeliest information has a competitive edge. It can be more responsive to customers, bring products to market faster, and create a value chain that works at Internet speeds.

Specifically, today's enterprises are looking for delivery of real-time information to customers and partners over the Internet, intranets, and extranets. The primary real-time infrastructure products that provide all these required services are publish/subscribe products. Leading publish/subscribe products are looking for most demanding real-time multicast applications such as stock exchanges, financial market data, multimedia content streaming, live news, distance learning, and software distribution.

Key generation is one of the important roles for secure key distribution of content distribution in multicast communication. Group communication can benefit from IP multicast to achieve scalable exchange of messages. Multicast communication as defined in Deering (1989) and Parkhurst (1999) is an efficient means of distributing data to a group of participants depicted in Figure 1. Efficiency is achieved because data packets need to be transmitted once and they traverse any link between two nodes only once, hence saving bandwidth. This contrasts with unicast-based group communications where the sender has to transmit *n copies* of the same packet.

Figure 1. Example of multicast transmission

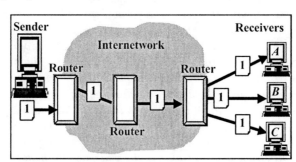

The multicast service currently supported in the Internet (IP multicast) does not have any provisions for restricting delivery of data to a specified set of receivers. Any receiver can join or leave a multicast group (identified by a class D IP address) by sending IGMP (Internet group management protocol) (Fenner, 1997) messages to their local router. Further, any user can send data to a multicast group by addressing the message to the group address. To restrict the flow of multicast data to a specific set of users, it is necessary to use cryptographic mechanisms. Specifically, senders using a session key that is only distributed to members of the group encrypt messages. Ensuring that only members of the group have possession of the session key at any given time restricts participation in a group session. Thus, key creating and distributing session keys to authorized group members are the critical aspects of secure multicast.

Fundamental studies in this chapter are to investigate and analyze each of the group key management architectures categorized into three main classes: centralized, decentralized, and distributed architectures. Next, we address the issues focused on the area of key generation on key management cryptographic algorithms that support security requirements in these group key management architectures. These issues are very important to application developers wishing to implement security services for their multicast applications. The area of group key generation is then surveyed and proposed solutions are classified according to those characteristics.

Salient Characteristics of Group Communication Protocols

The success of the group key management protocol not only depends on the efficiency of the cryptographic algorithms, but also depends on the salient characteristics of multicast security requirements. Hence, we list salient parameters of multicast group (Baugher et al., 2005; Canetti & Pinkas, 2000; Quinn & Almeroth, 2001) that are crucially affecting the security architecture that should be used.

Communication type: There are three general categories of multicast applications. One-to-many (1toM) applications have a single sender and multiple simultaneous receivers. One-to-many multicast applications are scheduled audio/video (a/v) distribution, push media, file distribution, and caching, stock prices. In many-to-many (MtoM) applications, two or more of the receivers also act as senders. In other words, MtoM applications are characterized by two-way multicast communication. Many-to-many applications are multimedia conferencing, distance learning, and multiplayer games. The many-to-one (Mto1) category does not represent a communication mechanism at the IP layer. Mto1 applications have multiple senders and one (or a few) receiver(s), as defined by the application layer.

*   **Collusion**: Evicted members must not be able to work together and share their individual piece of information to regain access to the group key.

*   **Forward access control:** It ensures that departing members cannot get access to future group data.

- **Backward access control:** It ensures that joining members cannot decrypt old group data.

- **Scalability on group size:** For many applications, the group size can vary from several tens of participants in small discussion groups, through thousands in virtual conferences and classes, and up to several millions in large broadcasts. The required communication, storage, and computational resources should not interfere in providing the service as the group size increases.

- **Membership dynamics:** Is the group membership static and known in advance? Otherwise, do members only join, or do members also leave? How frequently does membership change and how fast should changes be updated? Are membership changes bursty?

Key Generation Role

Key generation plays an important role in enforcing cryptographic properties on the group keys and consequently on the group communication. There exist several different ways to achieve key agreement in a group. One solution is to have a single entity that decides upon a key and then distributes it to the group. In this case, the key-generation entity maintains long-term keys with each member of the group in order to enable secure two-party communication used to distribute the key. A flavor of this solution uses a fixed, trusted third party as the key-generation entity. Another solution looks into providing a contributory key where each member of the group adds its own share such that the session key is a function of the individual contributions.

Each of these solutions has advantages and disadvantages. In a centralized key agreement environment, the trust of the whole system is put in the member that generates the key. Moreover, the key-generation responsibility makes this member an attractive target for an attacker. A contributory key generation, in contrast, achieves a better randomness of the key, even if some of the participants lack a good random generator. In general, the computational effect required for a contributory key agreement protocol is much larger. However, in certain cases, when there is no one fixed trusted entity, a centralized key agreement protocol may be more expensive. A good key-agreement protocol needs to provide strong security guarantees such as key independence, key confirmation, perfect forward secrecy, and resistance to known key attacks while being scalable.

Based on these observations, we present and evaluate the following outlines of secure group communication protocols. The evaluation criteria for key-generation area are:

- **Security technology independence:** It is usually possible to provide a given set of security objectives using multiple cryptographic algorithms. The choice of a given cryptographic algorithm is dictated by factors such as security threats, performance concerns, patent issues, and export limitations. Thus, the multicast architecture may assume the availability of standard cryptographic algorithms, but it should not stipulate the use of any specific algorithms.

- **Achieved performance:** Performance is a major concern of multicast security applications. The most immediate costs that should be minimized are the latency and work overhead per sending and receiving data packets, and the bandwidth overhead incurred by inflating the data packets via cryptographic transformations. In particular, key update information transmitted to all receivers needs to be as small as possible. Secure memory requirement (e.g., lengths of keys) is somewhat less important, but should also be minimized.

- **Key length:** In cryptography, the key length (alternatively key size) is a measure of the number of possible keys that can be used in a cipher. Because modern cryptography uses binary keys, the length is usually specified in bits. The length of a key is critical in determining the susceptibility of a cipher to exhaustive search attacks.

In cryptanalysis, a brute-force attack is a method of defeating a cryptographic scheme by trying a large number of possibilities; for example, exhaustively working through all possible keys in order to decrypt a message. In most schemes, the theoretical possibility of a brute-force attack is recognised, but it is set up in such a way that it would be computationally infeasible to carry out. Accordingly, one definition of "breaking" a cryptographic scheme is to find a method faster than a brute-force attack. The selection of an appropriate key length depends on the practical feasibility of performing a brute-force attack.

The key size must be large enough to make a brute-force attack impractical, but small enough for practical encryption and decryption (Stallings, 1999). In practice, the key sizes that have been proposed to make a brute-force attack impractical result in encryption/decryption speeds that are too slow for general-purpose use.

- **Group key secrecy:** It guarantees an adversary does not discover any group key. It is necessary to change the key at regular intervals to safeguard its secrecy. Additional care must be taken when choosing a new key to guarantee the key independence. Each key must be completely independent from any previously used and future keys; otherwise, compromised keys may reveal other keys.

- **Dynamic rekeying:** The keying material shared by the members of the multicast security association should be updated in order to achieve forward secrecy and backward secrecy. When a user joins the group, he should not have access to past keying material (backward secrecy). When a user leaves the group, he should not have access to future keying material (forward secrecy).

- **Computation efficiency:** Setting up the group requires the most computation involved in maintaining the group because all members need to be contacted. Computations for key generation/regeneration needed during group set up and membership changes should be reduced significantly.

- **Execution rounds:** Although multiple rounds offer increasing security for establishing a common root key, the protocol should try to minimize key-generation times among the members to reduce processing and communication requirements.

Contribution of this Chapter

The existing survey papers (Judge & Ammar, 2003; Moyer, Rao, & Rohatgi, 1999) analyze the security issues and key management for group communications. There is no survey paper from a key-generation point of view. In this chapter, we present a survey of various multicast communication protocols in the context of secure key generation and refreshment of keying material. Several protocols are investigated and analyzed, placing them comparatively into three main classes: centralized, decentralized, and distributed architectures that are not only based on the efficiency of the cryptographic algorithms (key generation and key distribution), but also depend on multicast security requirements. In addition, we also outline the open problems in this area.

Survey of Key Generation for Secure Multicast Communication Protocols

In this section, we present the group key-generation solutions proposed in the literature for three main group communication architectures: centralized architectures (Balenson, McGrew, & Sherman, 2000; Chang, Engel, Kandlur, Pendarakis, & Saha, 1999; Harney & Muckenhirn, 1997; Perrig, Song, & Tygar, 2001; Waldvogel, Caronni, Sun, Weiler, & Plattner, 1999; Wallner, Harder, & Agee, 1999; Wong, Gouda, & Lam, 2000), decentralized architectures (Chaddoud, Chrisment, & Schaff, 2001; Dondeti & Mukherjee, 1999; Mittra, 1997; Rafaeli & Hutchison, 2002; Weiler, 2001), and distributed architectures (Dondeti, Mukherjee, & Samal, 2000; Rodeh, Birman, & Dolev, 2000; Yang, Fan, & Shieh, 2001; Yang & Shieh, 2001) focused on group key generation that are designed to efficiently generate the keys to a multicast group.

We also analyze them comparatively within their respective class. There are several cryptographic algorithms used to create the group keys in these multicast architectures. The salient characteristics of the most commonly used cryptographic algorithms for

Table 1. Comparison of secure hash algorithms

Characteristics	MD5	SHA-1	RIPEMD-160
Digest length	128 bits	160 bits	160 bits
Basic unit of processing	512 bits	512 bits	512 bits
Number of steps	64 (4 rounds of 16)	80 (4 rounds of 20)	160 (5 paired rounds of 16)
Maximum message size	□	$2^{64}-1$ bits	$2^{64}-1$ bits
Security against cryptanalysis	Vulnerable	**Invulnerable**	**Invulnerable**
Relative performance (coded in C++ on a 266-MHz Pentium)	**32.4 Mbit/s**	14.4 Mbit/s	13.6 Mbit/s
Speed comparison (written in Assembly on a 90 MHz Pentium)	**136.2 Mbit/s**	54.9 Mbit/s	45.3 Mbit/s

Table 2. Comparison of symmetric key algorithms

Characteristics	DES	IDEA	RC5	Blowfish
Plain text	64 bits	64 bits	Variable (32, 64 or 128 bits)	64 bits
Key length	56 bits	128 bits	Variable (40 to 2040 bits)	Variable (32 to 448 bits)
Block bits	64	64	64	64
Number of rounds	16	8	Variable (0-255)	16
Speed comparison of block ciphers on a Pentium (Clock cycles per round)	18	50	12	**9**
Speed comparison of block ciphers (written in assembly on 90 MHz a Pentium)	16.9 Mbit/s	9.75 Mbit/s	28.9 Mbit/s	**36.5 Mbit/s**
Security properties	Vulnerable to brute-force attack	More resistant to differential cryptanalysis.	**High security**	Variably secure

Table 3. Comparison of asymmetric key algorithms

Characteristics	Diffie-Hellman (DH)	RSA
Key length (bits)	1024 to 4096	512, 768, 1024, 2048, 4096
Digital signature	No	Yes
Speed comparison on 2.1 GHz Pentium 4	**2.002 Sec** (for 1024 bits key agreement)	2.003 Sec (for 1024 bits encryption)
	2.003 Sec (for 1024 bits key agreement)	2.003 Sec (for 1024 bits decryption)
Key exchange	Yes	Yes
Security/Advantages	▪ depends on the difficulty of computing discrete logarithms. ▪ secret keys are created only when needed.	▪ **depends on the difficulty of factorizing the modulus, n.**
Difficulties/Problems	▪ man-in-the-middle attacks. ▪ computational intensity ▪ message expansion	▪ brute-force attack, timing attacks ▪ mathematical attacks ▪ increased processing time ▪ increased key storage requirement ▪ key generation is complex and time consuming ▪ RSA keys are practically more susceptible than DH keys of the same size.

group key management are listed in Tables 1, 2 and 3. A value written in *bold* is the best value of *performance* and *security* for a certain row.

Centralized Architectures

In centralized architectures, only one central controller controls the whole group. It does not rely on any intermediate node such as routers to perform access control and key

Figure 2. Basic centralized architecture

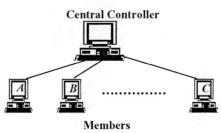

distribution. The successful functioning of the single group controller affects the overall group privacy. If the group controller fails, the group keys are not generated and distributed. Figure 2 illustrates the basic centralized architecture.

Group Key Management Protocol

Harney and Muckenhirn (1997) propose a group key management protocol (GKMP) that allows the creation and maintenance of a group key. Messages between the group controller (GC) and the first member generate two keys for future group actions: the group traffic encryption key (GTEK) and the group key encryption key (GKEK). Messages between the GC and the other members are for the purpose of distributing the keys. The key-generation concept used by GKMP is cooperative generation and allows pairwise keys to be generated between two protocol entities.

Group key generation: GKMP uses two cryptographic algorithms: Diffie-Hellman (DH) and RSA. DH is used to cooperatively generate a shared session key encryption key (SKEK) with members for the transmission of group traffic encryption key (GTEK) and group key encryption key (GKEK).

RSA is used for digital signature operation when messages are transmitted between group controller (GC) and members. In member join operation, GC and all members cooperatively generate a new-shared key (SKEK). GC then sends GTEK and GKEK encrypted with a new SKEK. A single encryption key (GKEK) can update the keys for the whole group and DH effects GKMP with backward secrecy. As all members know the GKEK, GKMP is seriously compromising the forward secrecy since there is no solution for rekeying the group after a member has left.

Logical Key Hierarchy

Wallner et al. (1999) and Wong et al. (2000) propose the use of a logical key hierarchy (LKH) to efficiently update the session key if a member joins or leaves the group. Keys exist only at the server and at the users. There are no keys at the intermediate nodes (logical nodes).

Group key generation: In LKH, DH effects only to cooperatively generate a unique pairwise key (KEK) with each member. Once each user has a KEK known to the server, the server generates a key for each intermediate node in the tree. Key server then encrypts the intermediate node keys and a common root key with its KEK. LKH achieves forward secrecy, backward secrecy, and is robust against collusion of excluded users with generating fresh keys and sending them to members securely.

One-Way Function Tree

Balenson et al. (2000) propose the one-way function tree (OFT), which is an improvement in the hierarchical binary tree approach. Each leaf is associated with a member of the group. Each internal node of the tree has exactly two children. For a binary tree, each member stores $\log_2(n+1)$ keys, where n is total number of group members.

Group key generation: The group manager randomly chooses a secret key shared with each member. Each member is able to generate all keys along the path from its leaf up to the root. SHA-1 is used to compute the node's blinded key. Blowfish for encryption and XOR function is used to compute intermediate node key (KEK) from two input values of SHA-1. OFT depends on SHA-1 and XOR functions rather than Blowfish.

Efficient Large Group Key

Perrig et al. (2001) introduce the efficient large group key (ELK) protocol, an efficient, scalable, and secure method for distributing group keys. It uses a hierarchical tree in which a parent node key is generated from its children keys.

Group key generation: ELK uses pseudorandom functions (PRFs) to build and manipulate the keys in the hierarchical tree. A PRF uses a key K on input M of length m to generate output of length n represented by the following notation: $PRF_K^{m-->n}(M)$. ELK also addresses reliability by using short hint messages to data packets to enable key recovery in case the key update message is lost. The only function of ELK that is relevant to the hint computation is the speed of PRF, because PRF is the only function that is used repeatedly to derive the lost key in the exhaustive search.

Centralized Flat Table

Instead of organizing the bits of the ID in a hierarchical tree-based fashion for a flat table (FT) and distributing the keys accordingly, Waldvogel et al. (1999) assign the bits of the ID in a flat fashion. This has the advantage of greatly reducing storage requirements, and it obviates the group manager from the need of keeping all participants in memory.

Group key generation: There are two types of keys: traffic encryption key (TEK) is given by the local key manager to the appropriate unit, and key encryption keys (KEKs) used to encrypt the control traffic in the key control group, ultimately containing the TEK. FT requires an establishment of a shared secret key (KEK) using DH agreement. IDEA is used for encryption/decryption, and MD5 is used to update the keying material when a member joins or leaves the multicast group. However, this scheme is vulnerable to collusion attacks. Evicted members with complementary ID bits may reveal a valid set of keys; hence, they are able to have unauthorized access to group communication.

Summary of Centralized Architectures

In this section, we summarize the comparative analysis of centralized architectures with their salient comparison criteria shown in Tables 4 and 5. A value written in bold is the best value for a certain column. One-to-many multicast applications are available for these architectures.

Among them, the protocol GKMP (Harney & Muckenhirn, 1997) achieves better results for storage on both KDC and member. However, GKMP is seriously compromising the

Table 4. Comparison of key management algorithms in centralized architectures

Centralized Architectures (Ctrl-As)	Cryptographic Algorithms (CAs)	Key Independence	Ctrl-As depend on CAs?	Storage	
				Group Controller	Member
GKMP [10]	RSA (512 bits) DH (512 bits)	N	N	$2K_s$	$2K_s$
LKH [27]	DES (56 bits) DH (512 bits)	Y	N	$(2n-1)K_s$	$(h+1)K_s$
OFT [1]	Blowfish (128 bits) SHA-1 (160 bits) XOR (160 bits)	Y	Y	$(2n-1)K_s$	$(h+1)K_s$
ELK [16]	PRFs (64 bits) RC5 (64 bits)	Y	Y	$(2n-1)K_s$	$(h+1)K_s$
FT [22]	DH (512 bits)	N	Y	$(2b+1)K_s$	$(b+1)K_s$

K_s: size of a symmetric key in bits n: no. of members in the group
b : no. of bits in member ID h: height of a key tree

Table 5. Multicast security requirements

Centralized Architectures	BS	FS	SAC	Membership dynamics	Communication Type	Expected Group Size
GKMP [10]	Y	N	Y	Every time	1 to M	Small
LKH [27]	Y	Y	Y	Every time	1 to M	Medium
OFT [1]	Y	Y	Y	Bursty	1 to M	Medium
ELK [16]	Y	Y	Y	Expedient leave & join	1 to M	**Large**
FT [22]	Y	Y	N	Expedient leave & join	1 to M	**Large**

Small   : up to several tens of participants   *SAC: Secure Against Collusion*
Medium : up to thousands of participants   *FS: Forward Secrecy*
Large   : up to several millions of participants   *BS: Backward Secrecy*

forward secrecy since there is no solution for rekeying the group after a member has left. Furthermore, it is suitable for small group size since encryption overhead and number of key distribution overhead increases with group members.

LKH and OFT achieve forward secrecy, backward secrecy, and robust against collusion of excluded users with generating fresh keys and sending them to members securely. They use logical hierarchical trees and do not trust intermediate nodes. However, they both suffer from one–affects-all scalability problem in managing dynamic multicast groups. ELK (Perrig et al., 2001) uses pseudorandom functions (PRFs) to build and manipulate the keys in the hierarchical tree because PRF is used repeatedly to derive the lost key in the exhaustive search. Instead of organizing the bits of the ID in a hierarchical tree, flat table (FT) (Waldvogel et al., 1999) assigns the bits of the ID in a flat fashion. This approach has the advantage of greatly reducing storage requirements on the group manager; however, this scheme is susceptible to collusion attacks.

Decentralized Architectures

In decentralized architectures, the large group is divided into a hierarchy of small subgroups to address scalability. Each subgroup is managed by a subgroup manager to assist group access control as well as key distribution. Figure 3 depicts the decentralized architecture.

Iolus

Mittra (1997) addresses the problems of efficient key updates and reliable data transmission by dividing a multicast group into a hierarchy of subgroups, each with relatively few members and its own multicast address. The architecture uses a secure distribution tree that is composed of group security agents (GSAs), trusted entities that coordinate packet routing and manage security for the group. The GSA at the root of the tree is called the group security controller (GSC), and the other GSAs are called group security interme-

Figure 3. Decentralized architecture

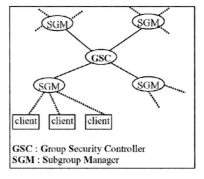

diaries (GSIs). Each group has its own cryptographic keys. The GSI is in charge of a subgroup.

Group key generation: GSI generates the local subgroup key K_{SGRP} that is used to encrypt the group data. GSI uses DH to generate a shared secret key K_{GR} with each member. This key is used to encrypt the new local subgroup key $K\!\!\not\!{}_{SGRP}$ when a new member leaves the group. Iolus utilizes DES for encryption, keyed MD5 for MAC computation, and DH with authenticated public values for mutual authentication with key exchange.

Dual Encryption Protocol

Dondeti and Mukherjee (1999) propose the dual encryption protocol (DEP), which uses hierarchical subgrouping to address scalability, but it does not trust the internal nodes of a key distribution tree. Each subgroup is managed by a subgroup manager (SGM), which assists in key distribution as well as group access control.

Group key generation: DEP uses public key and symmetric key encryption schemes for *securely distributing* the top level key encryption key (KEK) *and the subgroup keys*. The sender incurs key-generation costs for data encryption key (DEK), top-level key KEK, local subgroup key LS, its private and public keys. Additionally, the sender generates a key distribution packet and sends it to its children. Subgroup managers incur key-generation cost for its public, private, and local subgroup keys. Members need to generate public and private keys. RSA is used for digital signature operation. DEP also uses anonymous conventional encryption and decryption algorithms. RSA affects DEP to enforce group access control and securely distribute the top level KEKs and the subgroup keys.

Baal

Chaddoud et al. (2001) present the protocol *Baal* that is based on decentralized group key management with only one symmetric key shared among group members. *Baal* defines three entities: group controller (GC), local controller (LC), and group member.

Group key generation: GC creates the session key and distributes it to group members via LC. The GC delegates LC, per subnetwork. It receives the session key and distributes it to group members in its own subnetwork. At any time of the group life, an LC can play the role of the group controller if there is any change in its subnetwork. It can create and distribute a new session key, accept or refuse a new member in the group, and notify any change in the group to the other group controller. The cryptographic algorithms used in Baal are RSA for signature operation and DES-CBC for encryption/decryption. RSA affects Baal to enforce group access control.

SEMSOMM

Weiler (2001) proposes the protocol SEMSOMM, which has similar properties to those of DEP; however, it uses the dual-encryption technique to encrypt the group communication rather than the group data encryption key (session key). SEMSOMM relies on two main ideas: First, intermediate nodes of the multicast distribution tree are used as untrusted relaying nodes in order to overcome the need to rekey the entire group upon each membership change.

Second, the session key is periodically renewed and redistributed to legitimate group members, thus inhibiting any collusion attack.

Group key generation: In initial key generation, the key distributor generates the secret key known only to the receiver. The sender is responsible for generating session key (SR) known only to receiver and encryption key (SN) known only to intermediate nodes. The intermediate node also generates encrypting key (N_iR) used between intermediate node N_i and its adjacent receivers. For performance reasons, SEMSOMM mainly uses symmetric algorithms and one-way hash function.

Hydra

Rafaeli and Hutchison (2002) present a decentralized architecture, called Hydra, to create and distribute the symmetric cryptographic keys to large multicast-based groups. The large group is split into smaller subgroups and a hydra server manages each subgroup.

Group key generation: This architecture does not use a central entity to generate the session key. When a member joins or leaves the group, a subgroup hydra server generates the session key and sends this key to the other hydra servers involved in that session. Then, it relays the session key to their respective subgroup members. Hydra employs a public key infrastructure (PKI) model to authenticate all parties in the system. The public key is used to encrypt a randomly generated encryption key that encrypts the message.

Summary of Decentralized Architectures

In this section, we summarize the comparative analysis of decentralized architectures with their salient comparison criteria shown in Tables 6 and 7. A value written in bold is the best value for a certain column. One-to-many multicast applications are available for these architectures. In the decentralized architectures, the large group is split into small subgroups. Different controllers are used to manage each subgroup, avoiding the single point of failure. Among them, *Iolus and SEMSOMM* achieve good overall results without compromising any aspects of security. *DEP* uses a timed rekey that makes happening delays to update the local subgroup key during membership changes. Thus, leave

Table 6. Comparison of key management algorithms in decentralized architectures

Decentralized Architectures (DAs)	Cryptographic Algorithms (CAs)	DAs depend on CAs?	1 affects n scalability	Storage		
				Group controller	Local controller	Member
Iolus [12]	DH(512 bits)	N	Y	$2K_s$	$2(K_s+K_p)$	$3K_s$
	DES (56 bits)					
	MD5 (128 bits)					
DEP [6]	RSA (512 bits)	Y	Y	$K_s(C+2)$	$3K_s+2K_p$	$2(K_s+K_p)$
	Symmetric key					
Baal [9]	RSA (512 bits)	Y	N	CK_p+K_s	$2K_p$	$2K_p$
	DES (512 bits)					
SEMSOMM [24]	-symmetric key -hash function	Y	Y	$(n+2)K_s$	$2K_s$	$3K_s$
Hydra [18]	PKI model	Y	N	$3K_s$	$3K_s$	$2K_s$

K_p : Size of a public key in bits K_s: size of a symmetric key in bits
C : Size of the sender's subgroup   n: no. of members in the group

Table 7. Multicast security requirements

Decentralized Architectures	BS	FS	SAC	Membership dynamics	Communication Type	Expected Group Size
Iolus [12]	Y	Y	Y	Timed rekey	M to M	Large
DEP [6]	Y	Y	Y	Timed rekey	1 to M	Large
Baal [9]	Y	Y	Y	Timed rekey	1 to M	Medium
SEMSOMM [24]	Y	Y	Y	Expedient leave & join	1 to M	Large
Hydra [18]	Y	Y	Y	Timed rekey	1 to M	Large

Small : up to several tens of participants   **SAC**: Secure Against Collusion
Medium : up to thousands of participants   **FS**: Forward Secrecy
Large : up to several millions of participants   **BS**: Backward Secrecy

member can still access the group data during that period of time. *Hydra* achieves better storage result on member, but it suffers from one-affects-all scalability.

Distributed Architectures

In a distributed architecture, there is no group controller. The session key can be either generated in a contributory fashion or generated by one member. In a contributory fashion, all participants collaboratively establish the session key. This avoids the issues with centralized trust, single point of failure, and provides strong security properties such as forward secrecy, backward secrecy, and key independence.

A Secure Multicast Protocol

Yang et al. (2001) propose a scalable and secure multicast protocol (SMP) that is suitable for multicast backbone (MBone). In this protocol, group members are divided into local subgroups. Each subgroup belongs to an island that is physically a subnetwork on MBone. This protocol employs a distributed method to achieve key agreement without the participation of a key distribution center. The key-renewing process is confined to local islands when users join and leave. This property reduces the cost of key-renewing operations significantly, and scalability is also achieved. SMP employs RSA to efficiently generate the encryption key with only group members. SMP strongly depends on RSA for his efficient key-generation process.

Secure Key Agreement Protocol

Yang et al. (2001) propose a secure key agreement protocol (SKA) where all participants collaboratively establish the session key. The concept of ID-based schemes is used in this protocol for mutual authentication and key establishment between two members; hence, key agreement can be efficiently achieved without the aid of a trusted third party or the exchange of members' public information. This protocol employs identity-based scheme and symmetric cryptographic technique for better performance. MD5 is also used to compute the extended identity. This protocol strongly depends on ID-based cryptosystems.

Distributed Logical Key Hierarchy

Rodeh et al. (2000) propose a distributed approach based on the logical key hierarchy (DLKH). This approach uses no centralized server and members play symmetric roles. This protocol uses the notion of subtrees agreeing on a mutual key, which means that two group leaders from left and right subtree securely agree on a mutual encryption key. DLKH utilizes the symmetric cryptographic technique for mutual key agreement.

Distributed Framework

Dondeti et al. (2000) propose a distributed framework (DISEC) that supports scalable and secure many-to-many communication. This framework assigns binary IDs to members, and defines a key association for each member based on its ID. DISEC delegates group control responsibilities and key distribution tasks evenly to all members.

Each member generates a unique secret key, the unblinded keys of the internal nodes of the tree in its path to the root, and the root key. The root key is used for group data encryption. For each secret key there is a blinded version that is computed by applying a given one-way function to the secret key. DISEC employs binary IDs, MD5, and XOR functions. MD5 is used to compute the node's blinded key, and XOR function is used to compute the intermediate node key from two input values of MD5. DISEC depends on MD5 and XOR functions.

Summary of Distributed Architectures

In this section, we summarize the comparative analysis of distributed architectures with their salient comparison criteria shown in Tables 8 and 9. A value written in bold is the

Table 8. Comparison of key management algorithms in distributed architectures

Distributed Architectures (DAs)	Cryptographic Algorithms (CAs)	No. of execution rounds	DAs depend on CAs?	Computation at Group Creation	
				Leader	Member
SMP	RSA (512 bits)	2	Y	4P+S+Ex	0
SKA	MD5 (128 bits)	$\log_2 n$	Y	-	h(2Ex+D+E)
	Identity-based				
DLKH	Secret key	$\log_2 n$	N	$(\log_2 n)E$	$(\log_2 n)D$
DISEC	Binary IDs	$\log_2 n$	Y	-	h(M+H)+S

P: prime number S: secret information Ex: exponentiation D: decryption h: the height of a key tree
E: encryption   M: mixing operation   H: hash function   n: no. of members in the group

Table 9. Multicast security requirements

Distributed Architectures	BS	FS	Membership dynamics	Communication Type	Expected Group Size
SMP [25]	Y	Y	Timed rekey	M to M	Large
SKA [26]	Y	Y	Expedient leave & join	M to M	Medium
DLKH [20]	Y	Y	Expedient leave & join	M to M	Small
DISEC [7]	Y	Y	Expedient leave & join	M to M	Large

best value for a certain column. Many-to-many multicast applications are available for these architectures.

In a distributed architecture, there is no group controller. The session key can be either generated in a contributory fashion or generated by one member. All members compute the session key at the final round. *SMP* has a fixed number of rounds, which means that number of iterations among the members is independent of group members. Both *SKA* and *DISEC* do not have a leader; all participants collaboratively establish the session key, and key distribution overhead is distributed evenly among all the senders. *DLKH* achieves low latency in the case of membership changes, but it can handle a small group size up to 100 members.

Future Trends

In this research area, new techniques will surely evolve over time to supplement those that currently exist. However, there remain *open problems* in this area that must be resolved to help secure multicast applications.

*   **Security for application-specific constraints**: Primarily, the usage of key-generation mechanism for secure group communication should be made transparent to the

user. The best solution for a particular application may not be the best for another; hence, it is important to fully understand the requirements of the application before selecting a security solution focused on key-generation algorithms.

- **Independence from specific key-generation algorithms**: Most of the multicast architectures depend on a specific cryptographic algorithm for their performance and security reasons. Instead, an ideal solution is they would choose the best components from each of the requirements outlined and combine them as appropriate.

- **Key-renewing operation**: When a member joins or leaves the group, the keys associated with joining and leaving members must be changed in order to achieve forward secrecy and backward secrecy. The computational overhead on key generation should incur a little computational overhead on key-renewing operation during membership changes and group creation.

- **Periodic batch rekeying**: It consists of key distribution algorithms when join and leave requests are collected in a batch and treated in a subsequent interval. This kind of algorithm will periodically process all joining and leaving requests produced since the last rekeying process at once. Batch rekeying algorithms are efficient if and only if the multicast tree is balanced. Periodic batch rekeying is also essential to alleviate the out-of-synchronization phase. However, new users may have to wait for a batch rekey to get their key, and old users may be able to stay in the group longer than they should be.

Conclusion

In this chapter, we present a survey of various multicast communication protocols in the context of secure key generation and refreshment of keying material. Several protocols are investigated and analyzed, placing them into three main classes: centralized, decentralized, and distributed architectures. Although the centralized architectures are easy to implement, they incur key-generation overhead on group controller. They suffer one-affects-all scalability problem. In addition, the single group controller affects the overall group privacy. In decentralized schemes, the large group is split into a hierarchy of small groups to address scalability. Each subgroup is managed by a subgroup manager to assist group access control as well as key distribution. They are harder to implement, but they localize the effect of group membership changes to one subgroup. Distributed architectures do not rely on a group leader during group set up, and they delegate key-generation overhead evenly among all members of the group. They avoid the single point of failure and provide strong security properties. However, these schemes would be vulnerable to security attacks from inside the group because of trusting all group members.

The success of the group key management protocol not only depends on the efficiency of the cryptographic algorithms (key generation and key distribution), but also depends on multicast security requirements. Primarily, the usage of key-generation mechanism for secure group communication should be made transparent to the user, and it should also work well with other protocols. A best solution for secure group communication should complement a multicast application requirement rather than drive its implementation.

References

Balenson, D., McGrew, D., & Sherman, A. (2000). *Key management for large dynamic groups: One-way function trees and amortized initialization.* Internet draft, (draft-irtf-smug-groupkeymgmt-oft-00.txt).

Baugher, M., Canetti, R., Dondeti, L., & Lindholm, F. (2004). *MSEC group key management architecture.* Internet Draft IETF MSEC WG.

Baugher, M., Canetti, R., Dondeti, L., & Lindholm, F. (2005). Multicast Security (MSEC) Group Key Management Architecture. (Request for Comments — 4046), IETF Network Working Group.

Canetti, R., & Pinkas, B. (2000). *A taxonomy of multicast security issues.* (draft-irtf-smug-taxonomy-01.txt), IBM Research.

Chaddoud, G., Chrisment, I., & Schaff, A. (2001). Dynamic group communication security. In *Proceedings of the Sixth IEEE Symposium on Computers and Communications, ISCC'01*, Hammanet, Tunisia (pp. 49-56).

Chang, I., Engel, R., Kandlur D., Pendarakis, D., & Saha, D. (1999). Key management for secure Internet multicast using Boolean function minimization techniques. In *INFOCOM, 2*, 689-698.

Deering, S. (1989). *Host extensions for IP multicasting.* (Request for Comments: 1112).

Dondeti, L. R., & Mukherjee, S. (1999). A dual encryption protocol for scalable secure multicasting. In *The Fourth IEEE Symposium on Computers and Communications*, Red Sea, Egypt (pp. 2-8).

Dondeti, L. R., Mukherjee, S., & Samal, A. (2000). DISEC: A distributed framework for scalable secure many-to-many communication. In *Proceedings of the Fifth IEEE Symposium on Computers and Communications* (pp. 693-698).

Fenner, W. (1997). *Internet group management protocol, version 2.* (Request For Comments: 2236).

Harney, H., & Muckenhirn, C. (1997). *Group key management protocol (GKMP) specification/architecture.* (Request For Comments- 2093 and 2094).

Judge, P., & Ammar, M. (2003). Security issues and solutions in multicast content distribution: A Survey. *IEEE Network*, 2-8.

Mittra, S. (1997). Iolus: A framework for scalable secure multicasting. In *Proceedings of the ACM SIGCOMM*, Cannes, France, *27*(4), 277-288.

Moyer, M. J., Rao, J. R., & Rohatgi, P. (1999). A survey of security issues in multicast communications. *IEEE Network, 13*(6), 12-23.

Parkhurst, W. R. (1999). *Cisco Multicast Routing and Switching*. New York: McGraw Hill.

Perrig, A., Song, D., & Tygar, J. D. (2001, May). ELK, a new protocol for efficient large-group key distribution. In *Proceedings of the IEEE Symposium on Security and Privacy* (pp. 1-15). Oakland, CA.

Quinn, B., & Almeroth, K. (2001). *IP multicast applications: Challenges and solutions.* (Request for Comments: 3170), IETF Network Working Group.

Rafaeli, S., & Hutchison, D. (2002). Hydra: A decentralized group key management. In *Proceedings of the Eleventh IEEE International Workshops on Enabling Technologies: Infrastructure for Collaborative Enterprises*, IEEE Computer Society Press, Los Alamitos, CA, (pp. 62-67).

Rescorla, E. (1999). *Diffie-Hellman key agreement method. Network Working Group*, (Request For Comments- 2631).

Rodeh, O., Birman, K., & Dolev, D. (2000). Optimized group rekey for group communication systems. In *Symposium on network and Distributed System Security (NDSS'00),* San Diego, CA (pp. 39-48).

Stallings, W. (1999). *Cryptography and network security, principles and practice* (2nd ed.). NJ: Prentice Hall.

Waldvogel, M., Caronni, G., Sun, D., Weiler, N., & Plattner, B. (1999). The VersaKey framework: Versatile group key management. *IEEE Journal on Selected Areas in Communications*, *17*(9), 1614-1631.

Wallner, D., Harder, E., & Agee, R. (1999). *Key management for multicast: Issues and architectures.* (Request For Comments 2627).

Weiler, N. (2001). SEMSOMM- A scalable multiple encryption scheme for one-to-many multicast. In *Proceedings of the 10th International Workshops on Enabling Technologies: Infrastructure for Collaborative Enterprises (WET ICE' 01)* (pp. 231-236). IEEE.

Wong, C. K., Gouda, M. G., & Lam, S. S. (2000). Secure group communications using key graphs. *IEEE/ACM Transactions on Networking (TON)*, *8*(1), 16-29.

Yang, W.-H., Fan, K.-W., & Shieh, S.-P. (2001). A secure multicast protocol for the Internet's multicast backbone. *International Journal of Network Management*, *11*(2), 129-136.

Yang, W.-H., & Shieh, S.-P. (2001). Secure key agreement for group communications. *International Journal of Network Management*, *11*(6), 365-374.

Chapter VI

Security in Mobile Agent Systems

Chua Fang Fang, Multimedia University, Malaysia

G. Radhamani, Multimedia University, Malaysia

Abstract

Agent technologies have grown rapidly in recent years as Internet usage has increased tremendously. Despite its numerous practical benefits and promises to provide an efficient way of mitigating complex distributed problems, mobile agent technology still lacks effective security measures, which severely restricts its scope of applicability. This chapter analyzes and synthesizes the different security threats and attacks that can possibly be imposed to mobile agent systems. The security solutions to resolve the problems and the research challenges in this field are presented.

Introduction

Software agent is a very generic term for a piece of software that can operate autonomously and that helps facilitate a certain task. Software agents can communicate and be intelligent in the way that they have the attributes of proactive/reactive, and have learning capabilities. In agent-based systems, humans delegate some of their decision-making processes to programs that are intelligent, mobile, or both (Harrison, Chess, & Kershenbaum, 1995). Software agents may be either stationary or mobile, such that stationary agents remain resident at a single platform while mobile agents are capable of suspending activity on one platform and moving to another, where they resume execution (Jansen, 2000). In most mobile intelligent agent systems, the software agent travels autonomously within the agent-enabled networks, executes itself in the agent execution environment, gathers related information, and makes its own decision on behalf of its owner.

Scope

Currently, distributed systems employ models in which processes are statically attached to hosts and communicate by asynchronous messages or synchronous remote procedure calls; mobile agent technology extends this model by including mobile processes (Farmer, Guttman, & Swarup, 1996a). Compared to the client/server model, the mobile agent paradigm offers great opportunities for performing various attacks because mobile agent systems provide a distributed computing infrastructure where applications belonging to different users can execute concurrently (Bellavista, Corradi, Federici, Montanari, & Tibaldi, 2003).

A mobile agent is an object that can migrate autonomously in a distributed system to perform tasks on behalf of its creator. It has the ability to move computations across the nodes of a wide-area network, which helps to achieve the deployment of services and applications in a more flexible, dynamic, and customizable way than the traditional client-server paradigm. For instance, if one needs to perform a specialized search of a large free-text database, it may be more efficient to move the program to the database server than to move large amounts of data to the client program. Security issues in regard to the protection of host resources, as well as the agent themselves, are extremely critical in such an environment. Apart from that, there is a greater chance for abuse or misuse, and it is difficult to identify a particular mobile process with a particular known principal and to depend on the reference monitor approach to enforce the security policy (Varadharajan, 2000).

Problem Statement

The general lack of security measures in existing mobile intelligent agent systems restricts their scope of applicability. According to Bellavista et al. (2003), the widespread acceptance and adoption of the mobile agent technology is currently delayed by several complex security problems that still need to be completely solved. Harrison et al. (1995) identifies security as a severe concern and regards it as the primary obstacle in adopting the mobile agent systems. Full-scale adoption of mobile agent technology in untrustworthy network environments, for example Internet, has been delayed by several security complexities. The security risks that can be encountered in mobile agent environments include malicious hosts, malicious agents, and malicious network entities. Without an appropriate security level for agents, mobile agent applications could only execute in trusted environments, and could not be deployed in the Internet scenario.

To illustrate the security requirements and issues raised by the mobile agent technology (Bellavista et al., 2003), consider the case of a shopping mobile agent that has to find the most convenient offer for a flight ticket. Suppose that Babu accesses a flight-ticket booking service (FBS) to search for and book the cheapest Rome-to-London flight ticket. Before starting an FBS provisioning session, the client requires Babu to authenticate. After a successful authentication, a middleware mobile proxy called Alfred is instantiated to represent Babu over the fixed network and to support Babu's shopping operations. A trusting relationship should be established between Babu and Alfred now that Alfred generates a shopping mobile agent and delegates it the flight searching and booking operations. The shopping agent could migrate among the various air-travel agencies' nodes to locally operate on needed resources. Once its tasks are completed, the shopping agent should be granted the same rights and submitted to the same restrictions as Alfred. In this scenario, several security issues arise and several attacks such as user-agent trust, interagent security, agent-node security, and so forth, are possible, as Figure 1 shows.

Figure 1. Security threats in mobile agent systems

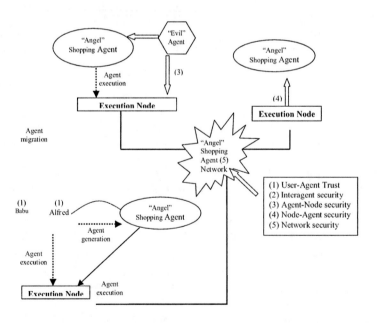

Malicious Host

A malicious hosting node can launch several types of security attacks on the mobile agent and divert its intended execution towards a malicious goal, or alter its data or other information in order to benefit from the agent's mission (Sander & Tschudin, 1998). According to Jansen (2001), a receiving-agent platform can easily isolate and capture an agent and may attack it by extracting information, corrupting or modifying its code or state, denying requested services, or simply terminating it completely. An agent is very susceptible to the agent platform and may be corrupted merely by the platform responding falsely to requests for information or service, altering external communications, or delaying the agent until its task is no longer relevant.

In the case of the shopping agent scenario as mentioned (Mitchell, 2004), a malicious host could try to

- **Erase** all information previously collected by the agent so that the host is guaranteed at least to have the best current offer.

- **Change** the agent's route so that airlines with more favorable offers are not visited.

- **Terminate** the agent to ensure that no competitor gets the business either.

- Make the agent execute its commitment function, ensuring that the agent is committing to the offer given by the malicious host. Besides this, the agent might be carrying information that needs to be kept secret from the airline (e.g., maximum price).

Integrity Attacks

Integrity of the mobile agent has been violated when tampering with the agent's code, state, or data. There are two subclasses of integrity attacks, namely **integrity interference** and **information modification** (Bierman & Cloete, 2002). Integrity interference occurs when the executing host interferes with the mobile agent's execution mission but does not alter any information related to the agent, whereas information modification includes several actions that the executing host can take against a mobile agent in an unauthorized way such as altering, manipulating, deleting the agent's code, data, status, and control flow. Modification of the agent by the platform is a particularly insidious form of attack, since it can radically change the agent's behavior or the accuracy of the computation (Jansen, 2001).

Availability Refusals

Availability refusal occurs when an authorized mobile agent is prevented from accessing objects or resources to which it should have legitimate access. It is a deliberate action performed by the executing nodes in order to obstruct the agent. There are three subclasses of availability refusal, namely **denial-of-service**, **delay-of-service**, and **transmission-refusal**.

- **Denial of service** occurs when the requested resources that the agent needs to accomplish its mission are denied. Nevertheless, it is also possible for a malicious host to bombard the agent with too much irrelevant information, so that the agent finds it impossible to complete its goals.

- **Delay of service** occurs when the host lets the mobile agent wait for the service and only provides the service or access to the required resources after a certain amount of time. This delay can have a negative effect on the actual purpose of the mobile agent.

- **Transmission refusal** occurs when a host with malicious intentions disregards the itinerary of the mobile agent and refuses to transmit the agent to the next host that is specified in the agent's itinerary.

Confidentiality Attacks

The privacy of the mobile agent is intruded when the assets of the mobile agent are illegally accessed or disposed by its host. The confidentiality attacks include **theft**, **eavesdropping,** and **reverse engineering** (Bierman & Cloete, 2002).

- **Eavesdropping** is an invasion of privacy that mostly occurs when the host spies on the agent and gathers information about the mobile agent's information or about the telecommunication between agents.

- **Theft** means that besides spying on the agent, the malicious host also removes the information from the agent. The malicious host may also "steal" the agent itself and use it for its own purposes, or simply kill it.

- **Reverse engineering** occurs when the malicious host captures the mobile agent and analyzes its data and state in order to manipulate future or existing agents. This kind of attack enables the host to construct its own similar agents, or update the profile of information to which the agent gets access.

Authentication Risks

The host may jeopardize the intended goal for the mobile agent by hiding its own identity or refusal to present its own credentials, for example, **masquerading** and **cloning**. Masquerading occurs if an executing host masks itself as one of the hosts on the agent's itinerary when, in fact, it is not. Cloning happens when each agent carries its own credentials in order to gain authorized access to the services of its executing hosts.

Nonrepudiation

Interaction between the hosts can be very ad hoc due to the mobile agent's capability in moving autonomously in the network. The malicious host can deny the previous commitments or actions and cause dispute.

Malicious Agents

According to Schoeman and Cloete (2003), a host is faced with two potential threats from mobile agents, namely, a malicious agent that might be a virus or Trojan Horse vandalizing the host or a benign agent that might simply abuse the host's local resources. In an uncontrolled environment, mobile agents can potentially run indefinitely and consume the system level resources such as files, disk storage, I/O devices, and so forth, in their execution environment. An agent can interfere with other agents so that they cannot perform their tasks completely. Besides that, servers are exposed to the risk of system penetration by malicious agents, which may leak sensitive information. Agents may mount "denial-of-service" attacks on servers, whereby they hog server resources and prevent other agents from progressing. An attack made by a mobile agent is pretty annoying because the user may never know if the mobile agent has visited the host computer and (Ylitalo, 2000) has presented seven types of potential malicious agent attacks:

- **Damage and system modification** means a mobile agent can destroy or change resources and services by reconfiguring, modifying, or erasing them from memory or disk. Consequently, it inadvertently destroys all the other mobile agents executing there at the time.

- **Denial of service** means impeding the computer services to some resources or services. Executing mobile agent can overload a resource or service, for example, by constantly consuming network connections or blocking another process by overloading its buffers to create deadlock.

- **Breach and invasion of privacy or theft** means remove the data from the host or mobile agent illegally. A mobile agent may access and steal private information and uses covert channels to transmit data in a hidden way that violates a host's security policy.

- **Harassment and antagonism** means repeating the attacks to irritate people.

- **Social engineering** means using misinformation or coercion to manipulate people, hosts, or mobile agents.

- **Logic bomb** goes off when code, concealed within an apparently peaceful mobile agent, is triggered by a specific event, such as time, location, or the arrival of a specific person (Trojan horse program).

- **Compound attack** means using cooperating techniques whereby mobile agents can collaborate with each other in order to commit a series of attacks.

Malicious Network Entities

The network layer is responsible for the final encoding of the encrypted serialized agent object so that it can be transported by the underlying network to its next host (Schoeman & Cloete, 2003) and the network communication on the Internet is always insecure. Network entities outside the hosting node can launch attacks against a mobile agent in transit, interrupt it, and steal the encryption key and thus corrupt its integrity. Other entities both outside and inside the agent framework may attempt actions to disrupt, harm, or subvert the agent systems even when the locally active agents and the agent platform are well behaved. The obvious methods involve attacking the interagent and interplatform communications through masquerade or intercept. An attacking entity may also intercept agents or messages in transit and modify their contents, substitute other contents, or simply replay the transmission dialogue at a later time in an attempt to disrupt the synchronization or integrity of the agent framework (Jansen, 2001).

Security Goals/Solutions

The security infrastructure should have the ability to flexibly and dynamically offer different solutions to achieve different qualities of security service depending on application requirements. The mobile agent system must provide several types of security mechanisms for detecting and foiling the potential attacks that include confidentiality mechanisms, authentication mechanisms, and authorization mechanisms. Four types of countermeasures, namely measures based on trust, recording and tracking, cryptography, and time techniques to address malicious host problems were presented by Bierman and Cloete (2002).

Host's Security Mechanism (Protecting Host)

Yang et al. (Yang, Guo, & Liu, 2000) have suggested employing a number of security methods to ensure that an agent is suitable for execution. The suggestions are as follows:

Authentication

Authentication involves checking that the agent was sent from a trustworthy site. This can involve asking for the authentication details to be sent from the site where the mobile agent was launched or the site from which the agent last migrated. A mobile agent that fails authentication can be rejected from the site or can be allowed to execute as an anonymous agent within a very restricted environment. For authenticating incoming agents, agent principals can be associated with personal public/private keys and can be forced to digitally sign agents to ensure the correct identification of their responsible party. The public key-based **authentication** process safely verifies the correspondence between principal identities and keys and most authentication solutions based on public key cryptography delegate key lifecycle management to public key infrastructures (Bellavista et al., 2003).

Verification

Verification entails checking the code of a mobile agent to ensure that it does not perform any prohibited action. In order to protect the hosts, some formal techniques that can be used to develop the provably secure code are:

- **Proof carrying code:** Proof carrying code that forces agent code producer to formally prove that the mobile code has the safety properties required by the hosting-agent platform. The proof of the code correct behavior is transmitted to the hosting node that can validate the received node (Necula, 1997).
- **Path history logs:** Path history logs can be exploited to allow hosting platforms to decide whether to execute an incoming agent (Chess, Grosof, Harrison, Levine, Parris, & Tsudik, 1995). The authenticable record of the prior platforms visited by the agent is maintained so that a newly visited platform can determine whether to process the agent and the type of constraints to apply. Computing a path history requires each agent platform to add a signed entry to the agent path, indicating its identity and the identity of the next platform to visit, and to supply the complete path history to the next platform.
- **State appraisal:** Another technique for detecting malicious agent logic uses a state appraisal function that becomes part of the agent code and guarantees that the agent state has not been tampered by malicious entities (Farmer, Guttman, & Swarup, 199b). The agent author produces the state appraisal function and it is signed together with the rest of the agent. The visited platform uses this function to verify that the agent is in a correct state and to determine the type of privileges to grant to the agent.

Authorization

After the authentication of an agent, some proper authorization must be realized (Vuong & Fu, 2001). **Authorization** determines the mobile agent's access permissions to the host resources. This indicates the amount of times a resource can be accessed or how much of a resource can be used, and the type of access the agent can perform (Yang et al., 2000). With an **authorization** language, a complete security policy can be implemented on a host, specifying which agents are allowed to do the operations and for resource usage control. Access control mechanisms can enforce the control of agent behavior at run time and can limit access to resources. For example, agents should run in a sandbox environment in which they have limited privileges, in which they are safely interpreted (Claessens, Preneel, & Vandewalle, 2003; Volpano & Smith, 1998). It is also ideally suited for situations where most of the code falls into one domain that is trusted, since modules in trusted domains incur no execution overhead.

Allocation

Allocation should prevent agents from flooding hosts and denying resources to other agents. A host has to allocate the available resources to the competing mobile agents and for some resources types, it may be possible to schedule requests in time such that all resources requests of authorized mobile agents can be satisfied eventually (Tshudin, 2000).

Payment for Services

Payment for services determines the mobile agent's ability or willingness to pay for services (Yang et al., 2000). This includes ensuring that a mobile agent can actually pay, that payment is effected correctly, and that the service paid for is satisfactory to the payee. Since the agent is consuming at least computational resources at the server and may in fact be performing transactions for goods, its liability must be limited, and this can also be done by the mechanism of payment for services.

Security Mechanism of Mobile Agents (Protecting Mobile Agents)

Bierman and Cloete (2002) presented four types of countermeasures to address the problem of malicious hosts in protecting the mobile agents. The first type of countermeasure refers to **trust-based computing,** where a trusted network environment is created in which a mobile agent roams freely and fearlessly without being threatened by a possible malicious host. A second type of countermeasure includes methods of **recording and tracking** that make use of the itinerary information of a mobile agent, either by manipulating the migration history or by keeping it hidden. The third type of solution includes **cryptographic** techniques that utilize encryption/decryption algorithms, private and public keys, digital signatures, digital timestamps, and hash functions to address different threat aspects. The forth type of countermeasure is based on **time techniques** to add restrictions on the lifetime of the mobile agent. On the other hand, similarly, Bellavista et al. (2003) explains that the main issues to be addressed to protect agents against malicious hosts are agent **execution, secrecy,** and **integrity**.

Trust-Based Computing

Creating a trusted environment in which a mobile agent roams freely and fearlessly without being threatened by a possible malicious host can possibly alleviate most of the classes of threats. Protecting agent execution requires ensuring that agents are not hijacked to untrusted destinations that may present agents with a false environment, thus causing them to execute incorrectly, do not commit to unwilling actions, and do not suffer from premature termination or starvation due to unfair administrator's policies that fail to provide necessary system resources.

- **Tamper-resistant hardware:** Installing tamper-resistant hardware is a method well suited to implement the notion of trust in agent-to-host relationships. This method uses the concept of a secure coprocessor model, where physically secure hardware is added to conventional computing systems.
- **Trusted nodes:** Sensitive information can be prevented from being sent to untrusted hosts and certain misbehaviors of malicious hosts can be traced by introducing trusted nodes into the infrastructure to which mobile agents can migrate when required (Mitchell, 2004).
- **Detection objects:** Detection objects, such as dummy data items or attributes accompanying the mobile agent, are used to see if the host in question can be trusted. If the detection objects have not been modified, then reasonable confidence exists that legitimate data has not been corrupted also. Apparently, it is necessary that hosts are not aware of the inserted detection objects (Meadows, 1997).

Recording and Tracking

This type of countermeasure makes use of the itinerary information of a mobile agent, either by manipulating the migration history or by keeping it hidden.

- **Execution tracing:** To address the malicious host attacks, an **execution-tracing** mechanism is used. A host platform executing an agent creates a trace of an agent's execution that contains precisely the lines of code that were executed by the mobile agent and the external values that were read by the mobile agents (Tan & Moreau, 2002). When the mobile agent requests to move, a hash of this trace and of the agent's intermediate state are signed by the host platform. This guarantees nonrepudiation by providing evidence that a specific state of execution was achieved on the host platform prior to migration.
- **Path histories:** A record of all prior platforms visited by a mobile agent is maintained in this method. The computation of a path history requires that each host add a signed entry to the itinerary carried by the mobile agent. Ordille (1996) explains that this signed entry includes the identity of the host and the identity of

the next host to be visited. A path history is a countermeasure that is strongly used in the malicious agent problem, where it is needed to maintain record of the agent's travels that can be substantiated.

Cryptographic

Techniques under this type of countermeasure, titled encryption/decryption algorithms, private and public keys, digital signatures, digital timestamps and hash functions, are used to address different threat aspects. Protecting agent integrity requires the identification of agent tampering, either of its code or of its state, by malicious execution hosts (Bellavista et al., 2003).

- **Digital signature:** Yi et al. (Yi, Siew, & Syed, 2000) proposed a **digital signature** scheme in which users have a long-term key pair, but in which a message-dependent virtually certified one-time key pair is generated for each message that has to be signed. A private key that can only be used once would be an ideal solution for a mobile agent. The private key in this system is unfortunately message-related, which makes it unusable for a mobile agent that does not know the message to be signed in advance. According to Mitchell (2004), the simplest solution to tackle the malicious host problem is to use contractual means. Operators of agent platforms guarantee, via contractual agreements, to operate their environments securely and not to violate the privacy or the integrity of the agent, its data, and its computation.

- **Environmental key generation:** With environmental security measures, the execution of an agent is actually not kept private, but it is only performed when certain environmental conditions are met. **Environmental key generation** (Riordan & Schneier, 1998) is a concept in which cryptographic keys are constructed from certain environmental data. For example, an agent or part of it could be encrypted with such a key in order that it would only be decrypted and executed if this environmental data were present at the host. In theory, this could prevent agents from being executed on a malicious host; provided that the environmental conditions that identify whether a host is malicious can be defined.

- **Sliding encryption:** Young and Yung (1997) presented a special implementation of encryption, sliding encryption, that encrypts the mobile agent piecewise, which in turn yields small pieces of cipher text. The encryption is performed so that it is intractable to recover the plain text without the appropriate private key. Extra measures are employed so that it is extremely difficult to correlate the resulting cipher texts, thus making it possible to have mobile agents that are not easy to trace.

- **Proxy certificates:** Romao and Silva (1999) proposed **proxy certificates** in which instead of giving the mobile agent direct access to the user's private digital signature key, a new key pair is generated for the mobile agent. The key pair is certified by the user, thereby binding the user to that key pair; hence, proxy certificate, and as such to the transactions that the mobile agent will perform. The lifetime of the certificate is short and therefore revocation is not needed. It should be difficult for a malicious host to discover the private key before the certificate expires. Besides that, the proxy certificate can contain constraints that prevent the private key from being used for arbitrary transactions.

- **Blinded-key signature using RSA:** There are two encryption algorithms that are often used (Yang et al., 2000): secure key and public key. In secure key encryption algorithm (single key method), a common secure key used for encrypting/decrypting is shared by both sender and receiver. The typical algorithm of secure-key encryption methods is DES. In public key encryption algorithm, both parties create two particular keys, one public and the other secure. Sender encrypts the data using the public key of receiver, while receiver decrypts the very data using the secure key of its own. The typical algorithm of public-key encryption methods is RSA. It is obvious that RSA is more suitable for mobile agents, which run in an open environment.

Ferreira and Dahab (2002) presented an idea in which the private signature key is blinded. A blinded signature can be produced using this blinded-signature key. The blinding is claimed to be performed in such a way that only the resulting signature can be unblinded, but not the key. Mobile agents carry the blinded-signature key and a signed policy that defines the restrictions under which the signature key may be used. The blinding factor can be given to a third party or to the mobile agent. In the first case, the private key is cryptographically protected, as opposed to merely being obfuscated or distributed over multiple agents. The second case corresponds to the regular proxy certificate situation, where the host is able to obtain signatures on any message, but the signed policy will still determine which signatures should be considered valid.

Network Entities Security (Protecting Communication)

Security mechanisms can be included in the agent's transport protocols (Schoeman & Cloete, 2003). Secure socket layer (SSL) and transport layer security (TLS), although a bit heavyweight, can be used for securing transmission of data between two hosts. On the other hand, the key exchange protocol (KEP) offers a lightweight transport security mechanism that suits the notion of small transferable objects better. Protecting the communication can be achieved by setting up secure channels between the hosts. SSL is the most widely used protocol for secure network nowadays, which provides authentication and encryption services for TCP connections (Vuong & Fu, 2001). SSL provides encrypted communication so that eavesdropping attacks can be prevented. SSL also provides mutual authentication of both sides of the connection so that man-in-middle attacks can be prevented. SSL can be plugged into applications at the socket layer and the application does not need any special security knowledge or security-related code about SSL.

Related Work (Security Architecture)

Secure Actigen System (SAS)

Many mobile agent systems have been built for both academic research and commercial purposes in recent years. The security system proposed by Vuong and Fu (2001), **secure actigen system (SAS)** uses a rich-security model that provides an identification capability to each principal and supports system resource access control to a very fine level of granularity. It offers some methods to detect if the behavior or data of an actigen agent is tampered.

Verifiable Distributed Oblivious Transfer (VDOT)

In mobile agent security, oblivious transfer (OT) from a trusted party can be used to protect the agent's privacy and the hosts' privacy. Zhong and Yang (2003) introduce a new cryptographic primitive called **verifiable distributed oblivious transfer (VDOT)** that allows the replacement of a single trusted party with a group of threshold-trusted servers. This design of VDOT uses two novel techniques: consistency verification of encrypted secret shares and consistency verification through rerandomization. CDOT protects the privacy of both the sender and the receiver against malicious attacks of the servers.

Concordia System

The agent platform protection is achieved through agent authentication and resource access control in the **Concordia system** (Wong, Paciorek, Walsh, Dicelie, Young, & Peet, 1997). Any Concordia agent has a unique identity associated with the identity of the user that has launched it, and the resource control is based on the Java 1.1 security model and relies on simple access control lists that allow or deny access to resources on the basis only of agent identities.

Aglets System

The **aglets system** provides an aglet security manager to implement own security policies (Lange & Oshima, 1998). The behavior of the security manager cannot be changed directly, but via a GUI tool or directly editing policy files. In the aglet security model, agents can access resources depending on their associated principles.

Ajanta

The Ajanta security manager proposed by Tripathi (1999) is used only for mediating access to system-level resources. **Ajanta** protects hosting resources through an ad hoc security manager that uses identity-based access control lists to grant or deny agent access. For all application-defined resources, Ajanta uses a proxy-based mechanism where a proxy intercepts agent requests and denies or grants access based on its own security policy and on the agent's credentials.

The Secure and Open Mobile Agent (SOMA)

The secure and open mobile agent (Corradi, Montanari, & Stefanelli, 2001) developed at the University of Bologna, is another mobile agent system implemented in Java. A **SOMA** agent (a Java program) executes in an environment (the agent platform) called SOMA place, which represents physical machines, and the SOMA places can be grouped into domains that represent LANs. Places and domains provide two layers of abstraction that represent the Internet. SOMA takes security into consideration at a very early stage of its design; therefore, it provides a relatively rich and comprehensive solution for security problems. It uses a location-independent naming scheme for mobile agents' identities, which can be verified by the agent owner's digital signatures. The public keys of the agent owners are distributed by using X.509 certification infrastructure. Only the agents from the untrusted domains are subject to authentication checks and the agents from trusted domains will be trusted automatically.

Research Challenges

The design challenges for interagent communication mechanisms arise due to the mobility of agents. There are several design choices such as connection-oriented communication such as TCP/IP, connectionless communication such as RPC or indirect communication. Security is an important concern in providing remote communication facilities to visiting agents, which provides a good research opportunity. Security and fault tolerance remain to be the most challenging problems in this field.

Most current security frameworks lack a clear separation between policies and security mechanisms and provide monolithic security solutions where applications cannot choose their suitable trade-off between security, scalability, and performance. A wider diffusion of the mobile agent technology is limited by the lack of an integrated and flexible security framework that is able to protect both execution sites and agents and that is capable of balancing application performance and security requirements. The interactions between the different entities in the framework need to be formalized so that specific security properties can be identified and maintained.

According to Montanari et al. (Montanari, Stefanelli, & Naranker, 2001), an approach that can provide the requested degree of flexibility and dynamicity in mobile agent-based applications is to integrate within mobile agent systems the solutions already proposed in the field of policy-driven management (Sloman, 1994). A primary advantage of this approach is the possibility of fully separating the control of agent behavior from implementation details: policies are completely uncoupled from the automated managers in charge of their interpretation. Investigation needs to be carried out with regards to the other types of security techniques that can be employed in conjunction with execution tracing and the manner in which they can be integrated into the framework (Tan & Moreau, 2002).

Security policies may prohibit communication between two agents while any one of them is located at some untrusted host. The issue of the support that is needed for mutual authentication of mobile agents needs to be taken up in a wider context (Tripathi, Ahmed, & Karnik, 2000). There is a lack of experience with large-scale mobile agent-based applications. Most of the existing mobile agent applications are generally "small" in size, requiring at most a few tens of agents. Good program development and debugging tools can be an interesting line of research.

Conclusion

The revolution of the Internet enhances the rapid development of mobile agent technology, and mobile agent is potentially playing an important role in the future communication systems. There are a number of agent-based application domains for which basic and conventional security techniques should prove adequate (Jansen, 2001). Full-scale adoption of mobile agent technology in the Internet and standards definition for security in mobile agent frameworks can be achieved by effective and improved security mechanisms and strategies.

References

Bellavista, P., Corradi, A., Federici, C., Montanari, R., & Tibaldi, D. (2003). *Security for mobile agents: Issues and challenges.* Retrieved April 20, 2005, from http://zeus.elet.polimi.it/is-manet/Documenti/pap-deis-10.pdf

Bierman, E., & Cloete, E. (2002). Classification of malicious host threats in mobile agent computing. In *Proceedings of SAICSIT* (pp. 141-148).

Chess, D., Grosof, B., Harrison, C., Levine, D., Parris, C., & Tsudik, G. (1995). Itinerant agents for mobile computing. *IEEE Personal Communications, 2*(5), 34-49.

Claessens, J., Preneel, B., & Vandewalle, J. (2003). (How) Can mobile agents do secure electronic transactions on untrusted hosts? A survey of the security issues and the current solutions. *ACM Transactions on Internet Technology, 3*(1), 28-48.

Corradi, A., Montanari, R., & Stefanelli, C. (2001). Security of mobile agents on the Internet. *Internet Research: Electronic Networking Applications and Policy, 11*(1), 84-95.

Farmer, W., Guttman, J., & Swarup, V. (1996a). Security for mobile agents: Issues and requirements. In *Proceedings of the 19th National Information Systems Security Conference*, Baltimore (pp. 591-597).

Farmer, W., Guttman, J., & Swarup, V. (1996b). Security for mobile agents: Authentication and state appraisal. In *4th European Symposium on Research in Computer Security*, Rome, Italy (pp. 118-130).

Ferreira, L., & Dahab, R. (2002). Blinded-key signatures: Securing private keys embedded in mobile agents. In *Proceedings of the 2002 ACM symposium on Applied Computing* (pp. 82-86).

Harrison, C. G., Chess, D. M., & Kershenbaum, A. (1995). *Mobile agents: Are they a good idea?* Technical Report, IBM Research Report, IBM Research Division, T.J. Watson Research Center, Yorktown Heights, NY. Retrieved June 23, 2004, from http://www.research.ibm.com/massive

Jansen, W. (2000). Countermeasures for mobile agent security. *Computer Communications: Special Issue on Advances in Research and Application of Network Security* (pp.1667-1676).

Lange, D., & Oshima, M. (1998). *Programming and deploying Java mobile agents with aglets*. Menlo Park, CA: Addison Wesley.

Meadows, C. (1997). *Detecting attacks on mobile agents*. Foundations for Secure Mobile Code Workshop. Centre for High Assurance Computing Systems. Montery, CA: DARA.

Mitchell, C. J. (2004). Cryptography for mobile security. Chapter 1 of *Security for Mobility* (pp. 3-10).

Montanari, R., Stefanelli, C., & Naranker, D. (2001). Flexible security policies for mobile agent systems. *Microprocessors and Microsystems* (pp. 93-99).

Necula, G. (1997). Proof carrying code. In *24th ACM Symposium on Principle of Programming Languages*. Paris: ACM Press.

Ordille, J. J. (1996). When agents roam, who can you trust? In *Proceedings of the First Conference on Emerging Technologies and Applications in Communications*, Portland, OR.

Riordan, J., & Schneier, B. (1998). Environmental key generation towards clueless agents. In G. Vigna (Ed.), *Mobile agents and security, Lecture Notes in Computer Science, 1419* (pp. 15-24). New York: Springer-Verlag.

Romao, A., & Silva, M. M. (1999). Proxy certificates: A mechanism for delegating digital signature power to mobile agents. In *Proceedings of the Workshop on Agents in Electronic Commerce* (pp. 131-140).

Sander, T., & Tschudin, C. (1998). Protecting mobile agents against malicious hosts. In *Mobile agents and security, Lecture Notes in Computer Science, 1419* (pp. 44-60). New York: Springer-Verlag.

Schoeman, M., & Cloete, E. (2003). Architectural components for the efficient design of mobile agent systems. In *Proceedings of the 2003 Annual Research Conference of the South African Institute of Computer Scientists and Information Technologists on Enablement through Technology* (pp. 48-58).

Sloman, M. (1994). Policy driven management for distributed systems. *Plenum Press Journal of Network and Systems Management, 2*(4), 333-360.

Tan, H. K., & Moreau, L. (2002). Certificates for mobile code security. In *Proceedings of the 2002 ACM Symposium on Applied Computing* (pp. 76-81).

Tripathi, A. (1999). *Mobile agent programming in Ajanta.* 19th IEEE International Conference on Distributed Computing Systems Workshop (ICDCS'99), IEEE Computer Society Press, Austin, TX.

Tripathi, A., Ahmed, T., & Karnik, N. M. (2000). *Experiences and future challenges in mobile agent programming. Microprocessor and Microsystems.* Retrieved July 26, 2004, from http://www.cs.umn.edu/Ajanta/publications.html

Tshudin, C. (2000). Mobile agent security. In Matthias Klusch (Ed.), *Intelligent information agents: Agent based discovery and management on the internet* (pp. 431-446). Springer Verlag.

Varadharajan, V. (2000). Security enhanced mobile agents. In *Proceedings of the 7th ACM Conference on Computer and Communications Security* (pp. 200-209).

Volpano, D., & Smith, G. (1998). Language issues in mobile program security. In G. Vigna (Ed.), *Mobile Agents and Security, Lecture Notes in Computer Science, 1419* (pp. 25-43). New York: Springer-Verlag.

Vuong, S., & Fu, P. (2001). A security architecture and design for mobile intelligent agent systems. *ACM SIGAPP Applied Computing Review, 9*(3), 21-30.

Wong, D., Paciorek, N., Walsh, T., Dicelie, J., Young, M., & Peet, B. (1997). Concordia: An infrastructure for collaborating mobile agents. *First International Workshop on Mobile Agents, LNCS 1219* (pp. 86-97). Berlin: Springer-Verlag.

Yang, K., Guo, X., & Liu, D. (2000). *Security in mobile agent systems: Problems and approaches, 34*(1), 21-28.

Yi, X., Siew, C. K., & Syed, M.R. (2000). Digital signature with one-time pair of keys. *Electron. Lett., 36,* 130-131.

Ylitalo, J. (2000). *Secure platforms for mobile agents.* Retrieved January 22, 2005, from http://www.hut.fi/~jylitalo/seminar99/

Young, A., & Yung, M. (1997). Sliding encryption: A cryptographic tool for mobile agents. In *Proceedings of the 4th International Workshop on Fast Software Encryption* (pp. 230-241).

Zhong, S., & Yang, R. (2003). Verifiable distributed oblivious transfer and mobile agent security. In *Proceedings of the 2003 Joint Workshop on Foundations of Mobile Computing* (pp. 12-21).

Chapter VII

Intrusion Detection System:
A Brief Study

Robin Salim, Multimedia University, Malaysia

G. S. V. Radha Krishna Rao, Multimedia University, Malaysia

Abstract

This chapter introduces the intrusion detection system (IDS). It starts with a brief explanation of the history of IDS and proceeds with generic components of IDS. Besides highlighting current advances in IDS, the chapter describes recent challenges to the system. The authors hope that this chapter sheds a light for readers who are unfamiliar with this domain.

Introduction to
Intrusion Detection System

Intrusion detection is the process of monitoring events occurring in a computer system or network and analyzing them for signs of security problems. The intrusion detection system itself is a system to realize such a process. Early work on the IDS involves military and governmental agencies. Among the reasons was that an increasing number of agencies were using computers for daily operations. Hence, it was deemed necessary to assure the system was secured.

In the realm of information technology, IDS works by observing a computer system for any sign of intrusion through anomalous event or misuse signature. The primary goal of IDS is detecting any security breaches, preferably in real time. The intrusion detection system is an important security tool that complements various computer security products. It acts as the burglar alarm for information systems, ringing alerts and sending notifications on the occurrence of a computer security incident. Not to be confused with a prevention system, IDS does not in anyway modify the current environment setting besides alerting the responsible party.

Many times information security is related to confidentiality, availability, and integrity of information. From this perspective, one can infer that intrusions are the act that breaches any of confidentiality, availability, and integrity. The intrusion detection goal is to detect those incidents. By detecting them in time, appropriate actions can be taken either by the security officer or handled by the system itself.

As it advances, the computer system domain has become more sophisticated. In order to fulfill infinite human needs, the computer has become faster, processing more data, and as a result has become more complex. With that in mind, in order to detect attacks, IDS faces even greater challenges. In order to deliver response in near real time, the observer must perform faster than the object being observed. There are more applications and services deployed. In order to meet real-life scenarios, more network protocols have been deployed. As a result, the attack vector has increased. In order to recognize attacks, IDS needs to understand the object being monitored. For example, in network-based IDS, deep-packet inspection could help in analyzing network attacks.

The intrusion prevention system (IPS) is the logical evolution of IDS. Besides sending alerts, it also tries to prevent further damages. For instance, it reconfigures the firewall automatically, modifies the access control list (ACL) at network gateway to block suspicious conversation or even reroute a suspicious packet through. By saying that, we are actually witnessing the combination of functions from various networking nodes. Besides that, in order to support its task, there needs to be communication among IDS in the network.

History and Background
of Intrusion Detection

During the 1980s, computer systems had already been equipped with audit capability. With such a component, the operating system could gather system-wide attributes. As events gathered were increasing, and analysis being done by humans was tedious, there needed to be an automated method of correlating audit data to produce important information. This automated tool was the root of IDS. IDS originates from the information audit field.

Among the first IDS was Denning and Neumann's intrusion detection expert system (IDES) (Denning, 1986). The research, funded under the U.S. Navy's Space and Naval Warfare, proposed the use of profiles in monitoring subjects of interest. It used statistical metrics and models to determine anomalous events. These events were correlated to misuse of the system monitored. The research spanned from 1984 to 1986. Collecting statistical data for inferring system profiles and usage patterns was a popular choice during the 1980s for IDS research.

Another system using statistical methods was Steve Smaha's Haystack intrusion detection system (Smaha, 1988). U.S. Air Force Cryptologic Support Center sponsored the project to assist security officers to detect intrusion in Air Force multiuser computer system. By characterizing audit trail data into features and utilizing statistical models to analyze it, Haystack was able to reduce enormous quantities of audit data by delivering summaries of user behavior for analysis by security officers. Haystack was written in ANSI C and SQL, implemented on Oracle database.

Besides that, there were a few similar systems operated in batch-mode and utilizing statistical analysis aided with expert systems to deduce anomalous events. For example, Multics Intrusion Detection and Alerting System (MIDAS) from National Computer Security Center (NCSC) (Sebring, Shellhouse, Hanna, & Whitehurst, 1988), Discovery (Tener, 1986), Network Audit Director and Intrusion Reporter (NADIR) (Hochberg, Jackson, Stallings, McClary, DuBois, & Ford, 1993), and so forth. With the exception of NADIR, other systems took audit logs from monitored hosts as their source of data. NADIR monitored a computer network node for trail from network activities.

The early 1990s marked the start of network intrusion detection. Heberlein and team introduced the notion of a network intrusion detection system in their paper (Heberlein, 1990). The paper described their study on developing IDS in a broadcast network environment: Ethernet. By collecting data from local area networks, they could hierarchically develop profiles on usage of network resources. These profiles were used as patterns to identify security violations.

Commercial IDS did not take off until around the 1990s with Haystack Labs, stemmed from Haystack research, developing host-based Stalker product. The intrusion detection market was not gaining popularity until the later half of the decade. Prominently, Internet Security System (ISS) launched its network intrusion detection system, RealSecure. Besides that, there was Cisco participating in the market with its product of NetRanger. NetRanger was the direct result of Cisco acquiring Wheel Group. Entering the new millennia, Sourcefire jumped into the foray by bringing the popularity of Snort. Sourcefire founder Martin Roesch developed Snort (Roesch, 1999). Snort is one of the many open source products specializing in network intrusion detection. As the paper describes, Snort utilizes a pattern-matching algorithm to perform misuse detection on network data packets.

Computer Security Principle and its Relation with IDS

Secure computer system is a trusted and reliable system such that it behaves as it is intended to. Formally, information technology security is often analyzed in terms of confidentiality, integrity, and availability. Confidentiality requires that access to information be granted only to those who are authorized. An example of such a system is a banking system, where you would expect only relevant parties and yourself to have access to your banking information. Integrity describes the information state is guaranteed to be intact, protected from unexpected changes. Online transactions require a high degree of integrity during data transfer. Imagine that somehow your online shopping experience got corrupted. The transaction you did online could possibly cost you more than it should be. Availability requires computer systems to be able to serve resources and to provide access at the time expected. This concept is critical toward computer networks, as users expect no more (and no less) than fast and secured delivery of data.

From the concepts, we clearly observe that intrusion detection system is very much relevant. IDS is a tool that provides services of guaranteeing confidentiality, integrity, and availability for computer infrastructure. Its main function is detecting any security breaches in the information system. Because of its critical role, IDS itself is considered an important system worth protecting from any tampering.

Components of IDS

To effectively carry out its task, IDS is often separated into three logical modules, namely, its information sources, detection method, and response mechanism. By dividing into these logical modules, it makes it easier for various interested parties to understand IDS. Besides that, researchers could work on a particular module for further optimization. Practically, it is also possible to configure different architectures according to these modules. In an enterprise, NIDS can have multiple remote sensors deployed into various network segments for data-gathering purposes. Sensors submit data to a centralized engine for the purpose of detection analysis. Nevertheless, the division is not clear-cut for implementation. Many detection systems, especially host based, accumulate these modules into one.

Information Sources

Basically, the sources are divided into three categories. The first category is grouping input data accumulated from an individual system (host-based). Second is data originated from a network (network-based), and the last one is data produced by other sources. Some system strictly adheres to this division, whereas some others are hybrids of such.

First research on IDS focused on individual hosts. Among the first system was intrusion detection expert system (IDES) by Denning (1986). One of the significant data sources for any intrusion detection is an operating system audit trail. This data is generated by a dedicated subsystem designed to churn out trails from events carried out by users. In many operating systems, current audit-trail requirement comes from urgency to meet prerequisite of trusted product evaluation program. Among the criteria is trusted computer system evaluation criteria (TCSEC), known as "Orange Book." It evaluates commercial operating systems into "trust level" to benchmark a system's trustworthiness.

Audit trail is an important source because it offers the finest level of detail regarding events occurring in the operating system. Besides that, the operating system always gives a higher level of protection toward audit trail records, making it less probable to be corrupted. On the other hand, because of its finer detail, IDS needs to do more to process audit trails into relevant information. Sometimes there is a need to correlate multiple records of audit trails to acquire more important information.

Network-based intrusion detection system monitors a particular network. Network data packets are its information source. Many current NIDS gather data by employing network tap. By sniffing in the gateway of certain network segments, it is possible for NIDS to observe all conversation in and out of the network. Sniffing is the act of gathering those data. Normally, data are not analyzed straight away. NIDS needs to decode data following protocol layer. Hence, by detecting what protocol was used in the transfer, the decoder extracts relevant data for analysis.

The last data source could be various out-of-band data. This includes data coming from the physical attempt to break the system, attack signatures created by system administrator, and so forth. This sort of data comes from human intervention. As many other systems, IDS works better with some human interventions.

Source data reduction and correlation is all too important for detection system. With too fine-grain information, the analysis engine might be faced with a sea of uncategorized information. Hence, a reduction technique is employed in IDS systems. For example, in an NIDS system monitoring a network, the data collection component might employ a filtering technique to just gather relevant data to the monitored network. Data that does not flow into or out of the monitored network could be ignored. For an enterprise network, normally the system administrator deploys more than one sensor in various locations. Hence, data coming from these sensors need to be correlated for further processing by an analysis engine. This implies that the correlation technique is considered important also.

Recently, there are systems called intrusion prevention system (IPS). Not only do they detect attacks, but they also block those attacks. Some of the host-based IPS monitors the operating system itself. By monitoring the application binary interface (ABI), the system could cancel instructions that deemed dangerous (Amarasinghe, 2005).

Analysis Method

In the context of intrusion detection, analysis is the core mechanism. In fact, it is the component that determines whether a particular event is an attack. Besides the main purpose of identifying suspicious events, an analyzer should be designed to collect relevant information pertinent to the attack. It is important for an analyzer to identify possible intrusions and collect their supporting evidence and traces. Most of the time, human interventions are needed for the sake of traces and logs verification. For a more advanced system, those evidence and traces could be accountable in court.

Due to the operating environment, it is quite impossible to generically summarize all requirements for any intrusion detection system. There are various trade-offs and priorities. Nevertheless, among the preferred requirements are accountability and real-time intrusion detection. Accountability depends on system capability to collect context-relevant information pertaining to suspicious events. As mentioned previously, these data could be used in a legal framework. Real-time intrusion detection implies that the time period between incident and notification is narrow. Hence, it almost immediately raises an alarm for any security officer. Such a system is preferable because it alerts officers when an incident is occurring, instead of after the incident, where the full damage might have occurred. Early detection allows security officers to respond accordingly, like preventing further damage or even tracing down the culprit.

Many models for intrusion detection exist. Most detection methods, ranging from simple string detection to an advanced system utilizing artificial intelligence (AI) technique, fall into two mostly generic categories, namely misuse detection and anomaly detection. Misuse detection categorizes events as intrusion based on its previous knowledge of such a known intrusion. Anomaly detection stores what is considered to be normal behavior in its system and considered any events out of normal behavior as intrusions.

Depending on its detection algorithm, analyzer is normally divided into phases of operation. The first phase involves constructing the analyzer. In this phase, preprocessing of available data is taking place. For misuse detection, this involves gathering information for known attack to assemble an attack signature. For an anomaly-based system, it gathers normal user behavior from a live system. Available inputs are preprocessed into a suitable format for later usage in analysis. Sometimes this format is referred to as a canonical format. The format is a unified format for the system. Hence, porting the system to another platform only involves interpretation of input information and conversion of the input information into a canonical format. For example, in NIDS, data packets coming into the system must be reassembled to form complete transmission control protocol (TCP) protocol data unit (PDU). Based on preprocessed data, the system could build an analyzer engine depending on its algorithm.

Operating analysis is the second phase of the analyzer. Having constructing its model, an analyzer can take input data to observe any possible intrusions. For some details, the input events could be preprocessed first, for optimal system performance. This involves filtering out irrelevant input data and taking a particular parameter of interest. From the analysis phase, there could be a feedback phase into this analyzer itself. This phase is more into maintenance and adaptability purposes.

Researchers have observed various techniques for intrusion detection. It is easier if we observe it based on either a misuse-based or anomaly-based category. A misused-detection scheme involves many pattern-matching techniques against a given signature. For example, Snort is one of them where its detection engine utilizes the Boyer-Moore (1977) famous string-pattern matching and enhanced with Aho-Corasick (1975) in a newer version. Besides normal pattern matching, there are systems that employ state-transition approaches.

Anomaly detection is based on the system capability to store what is called as normal behavior. Among others is a neural network approach used by Debar, Becker, and Siboni (1992). Besides that, various statistical-based approaches have been observed. Probably among the most popular method is using threshold method. The system determines how many suspicious events are considered as deviation from normal. By crossing a certain threshold in a particular time interval, it triggers alerts. IDES system utilizes statistical profile based on certain user. It stores knowledge of a user and its history for duration of interaction with the system. Hence, if for any particular time a user logged into the system and does tasks that are very much out of past behavior, the IDS might alert for possible intrusion (Javitz & Valdes, 1991). Tripwire utilizes checksum calculation of important system objects to determine whether they have been corrupted or not.

Response Mechanism

After analysis is done, the system has found an intrusion and need to alert security officers. This component is called a response mechanism. Obviously, its role is to convey notifications and messages regarding suspicious activities under its radar. The message is not necessarily targeted to a human directly, but sometimes it is passed to another system. Hence, the design of the response mechanism depends very much on receivers.

Generally, IDS responses might be passive or active. Active responses take actions against intruders. This means the system could trace down the attacker and execute retaliations against it. Even though it seems appropriate to retaliate, it has its own weaknesses. The attacker could possibly hijack another vulnerable host to perform the intrusion. Hence, the retaliation against such a host is actually being performed on an innocent party. Spoofing an address is feasible in the current Internet set up. The attacker might masquerade as someone else, so any retaliation seems to be against an innocent party. Another kind of active response could be blocking intrusions or attacks from continuing. For example, the system could further block a network connection from an attacker. This has to be done carefully as to not drop a valid connection.

Passive responses are done through alerting administrators; letting them take appropriate action. The alerts could be in many forms, for example, e-mail message, logging message, or pop-up in the screen. Passive responses might be act of sending message to another host. This could be a centralized monitoring host. For example, the system could incorporate simple network management protocol (SNMP). If there is a need to communicate the message to a remote host, the system should pay close attention to message transport security.

Requirements for a response mechanism depend on various factors. While an IDS used by a simple home user are expected to show notifications in a visual and simple manner, systems that are used by proficient operators should display more verbose data. IDS that are deployed in a time-critical environment should not degrade the overall system performance. Apart from technical issues, some enterprises require IDS to have responses according to company policy. An IDS requires collecting as much attack evidence as possible without violating privacy policy.

Not only communicating with humans, the response component is in charge of communicating with other systems such as management systems or even other intrusion detection systems. Intrusion Detection Exchange Format Working Group (IDWG) is set up for developing standards in governing message exchange, because of the urgency for various IDS products to communicate with each other. IDWG has defined an extensible markup language (XML)-based message format. According to the working group, XML was chosen because of its flexibility in allowing extension of exchange language. Besides that, it allows vendor-specific extension in standard fashion. Specifically for IDS, XML allows definition of a special language to accommodate communication of data between IDS products. IDWG has released three documents, namely Intrusion Detection Message Exchange Requirement, The Intrusion Detection Message Exchange Format, and The Intrusion Detection Message Exchange Protocol (IDXP).

Criteria for Evaluating Intrusion Detection System

Selecting and implementing an intrusion detection system (IDS) is a challenging task. It should be noted that any party interested in deploying IDS in their system might have their own environment, constraint, urgency, need, and requirement. For instance, staff availability, staff's skill capability, funding, deployment constraint, system being monitored, size of information system, and so forth. Hence, it is suggested that the company that wishes to employ IDS gathers that information from within itself.

This section provides information on some of those criteria that should be observed for an IDS product. Even though it might not cover all criteria exhaustively, but this section provides a starting point. One obvious criterion for IDS is its capability to detect attacks according to its purpose. According to the computer system being monitored, a security officer would like the IDS to be able to identify attacks that really bring threat to the system. A system having features such as threat severity level is a nice proposition. For example, network port scan takes place very often. Hence, in comparison to denial of service (DOS) attack (which is more severe), DOS-related attacks should be alerted of higher importance. DOS is a kind of network attack where an attacker tries to deprive a valid system's patronage from using the system in convenient manner. For instance, an attacker tries to suffocate networking bandwidth of the system.

Being able to identify attack, a system having a low false positive is preferable. False positive is the situation where the identified intrusion is actually a normal behavior of the system that is not dangerous. Since a security officer must attend every alert carefully, wasting resources on something that is not dangerous does not look good. On the other hand, false negative is an attack that takes place but goes unidentified. These are dangerous. A system having high degree of such symptoms is as good as not having it.

The next criterion is whether the system is capable of identifying a new attack. As new attack methods are identified daily, a system that has the capability to identify an unknown pattern of attack is recommended.

An IDS monitoring a system should understand the system being monitored and be able to identify relevant attacks. An attack purported on a UNIX host might not apply on a monitored Windows host. Hence, the said events must be logged, but at the same time, be put on lower-severity level because it really does not threaten the system being monitored.

IDS must be able to run reliably in all circumstances. For example, the system should be running for years without memory leakage. Since its logged data and alerts are crucial, in case of abrupt shut down, IDS must preserve its data consistency. Preferably, given the same event source, several IDS should be able to identify an attack with the same result. Hence, a security officer that has deployed various IDS from vendors does not have to deal more in term of alert inconsistencies. For NIDS, this standard might be linked to a vulnerability database such as common vulnerabilities and exposure (CVE).

Because IDS is an important component of computer system infrastructure, very often it becomes an attack target. Hence, IDS must be secured enough to withstand attacks. Its operating system should be hardened and unnecessary services are shut off.

An advanced IDS user might analyze alerts generated. For example, intrusion and forensic expert might want to verify whether an attack is really taking place. Hence, IDS must be able to interface nicely with such a scenario.

IDS needs to provide relevant information. This includes source and target of attacks, log and traces, time of incidents, duration and period breaches, and even the reason why this is categorized as active attack. These are all evident to prove the attack. Besides that, validity of data is important if any legal actions will be taken.

From a manageability point of view, an IDS with ease of configuration is preferable. One of the examples is configuring what kind of system being monitored like Web server, e-mail server, and so forth. Besides that, there should be different options to configure for a suitable environment. A complex configuration interface should be avoided.

The next pressing criterion is scalability. As a computer network grows, the system administrator will deploy more IDS to new segments. Hence, IDS interoperability is important. With many IDS deployed in the network, the capability of a centralized-monitoring system is preferable. Alerts correlation from various network segments might increase the likelihood of attack detection.

Contemporary System for Intrusion Detection

Tripwire is one of many popular host-based IDS. It monitors a set of files for any changes. The system tries to solve the problem of monitoring file integrity and detecting alterations. Of course the simplest course of action could be keeping the entire original file intact in backup storage to be compared with the current file. This method might work well with a small file, but could possibly be a problem in dealing with larger files. By duplicating the original file, we are actually consuming extra spaces, not to mention processing power needed if we were to monitor remote files.

Tripwire proposes a solution by using a message-digest algorithm. The basic idea is to use an integrity checksum algorithm to generate a signature/fingerprint of important files. This checksum is kept in a database to be later verified for any file alteration (Kim & Spafford, 1994). Message-digest algorithm is a one-way hash function where one could easily compute a digest signature of any file efficiently. On the other hand, reversing the process of creating an original file from the signature is known to be hard and consuming many resources. Because of the nature of the algorithm, it is suitable for usage in keeping a file's fingerprint.

During its time, there was a lack of a dedicated file integrity-checking tool. Tripwire brought forward a notable idea of keeping important file's checksum in a database. Among its strengths was its capability to monitor a remote system by putting configuration and database files on a separate system. Hence, it reduces the risk of direct tampering with a checking mechanism. Initially, Tripwire supported up to 10 slots of signature algorithm. In its first distribution, it came with MD5, MD4, MD2 (all three are from RSA Data Security Inc. Message-Digest Algorithm), 4-pass Snefru (Xerox Secure Hash Function), 128-bit HAVAL, and SIIA (NIST Secure Hash Algorithm). By having 6 out of 10 slots filled in, the system allows administrators to code in their favorite algorithm. The interface of adding a new algorithm was made easy, to support flexibility. Tripwire was initially available as freeware, but later on offered as paid services from Tripwire Inc.

Snort is a network-based IDS. It is a signature-based network intrusion detection system that utilizes a pattern-matching algorithm to detect malicious network packets by analyzing content (Roesch, 1999). Snort operates by monitoring network packets in a local area network (LAN). For every packet of interest, Snort applies a string pattern-matching algorithm based on its predefined signature. Because of its importance, its pattern-matching algorithm has always been improved. Currently, it is using a modified version of Boyer-Moore (1977) fast string-matching algorithm.

Snort has been a popular NIDS because of its flexibility of allowing signature updates. Currently, Snort rules are available from its Web site and being developed actively as newer attacks appear. Some of the signature development is done by the community through a mailing list and support forum. Deployment of Snort is relatively simple. Snort needs to be able to take packets from a computer network. It means it needs to sniff those data that are not only purported to its system, but also purported to other systems under the same network. As long as the running setup satisfies this setting, Snort has no problem in decoding the packet. Snort has the capability of decoding various link-layer protocols, such as Ethernet, 802.11, token ring, and point-to-point protocol (PPP). Upper layer protocols, like Internet protocol (IP) and transport control protocol (TCP), are decoded in order to support attack detection. Hence, Snort is a suitable IDS for an Ethernet environment. In contrast with Tripwire, Snort has been and still is a freeware available under GNU general public license. Its source code is free and available for download.

Recently, there is proactive solution based on open-source tools, such as Snort and Nmap, for attack detection that automatically blocks malicious internal nodes (Cox, 2005). University of Indianapolis IT staffers developed and named it "Shelob." The system operates by monitoring internal traffic for suspicious personal computers (PC). Those PCs infected by virus, spyware, and adware are "trapped" into a virtual LAN, constraining its connection. Users are automatically rerouted onto a Web page notifying such event, and required to act to solve the situation. Not strictly categorized as IDS, this system actually delivers a proactive solution against real-world scenarios. As more adwares, worms, and viruses infiltrate into our PCs, such a solution shows that an IDS solution makes sense. If deployed and used appropriately, it could mitigate those attacks.

Recent Challenges of Intrusion Detection System

As computer technology advances, IDS needs to keep up in order to function at its best. Computer systems have enhanced to be more complex for processing advanced requirements. Its speed has increased; data processing and transferring have been leaping tremendously. For IDS to function in real time, it faces challenges to understand complex systems and must be able to extract meaningful data from a pool of data sources. Not only extracting data, but it also needs to extract and analyze it fast. This stands in contrast with batch-mode IDS, where data processing is not necessarily done in real time.

Up on the networking-protocol stack, there are more protocols formed to keep up with business needs. For example, Web services have used several XML-based protocols like SOAP protocol. In order to extract any meaningful data, the system must be able to interpret a protocol data unit by inspecting packets all the way up to the upper layer protocol. This is another enormous challenge.

In addition, threats of viruses, worms, and other malicious programs have brought additional challenges to IDS. Those programs have become a constant threat. Not only are they getting sophisticated in distribution and attack mechanism, but they are also spreading fast. According to previous work, flash worm could saturate one million hosts in around 30-seconds time (Staniford, Paxson, & Weaver, 2002). For such a fast spreading mechanism, misuse detection might not be very effective. On the other hand, anomaly detection might perform better for its capability to remember what good behavior is. Inherently, such a system could derive a new vector of attacks.

Signature-based intrusion detection system has been around for sometime. Its operation depends very much on human intervention to supply an accurate signature for attack detection. Its incapability to observe new attacks has been a great disadvantage, especially against zero-day exploit. For that reason, anomaly-based IDS might come to help. Having said that, it does not mean that traditional IDS is dead. On the other hand, it has evolved and integrated into a hybrid of both signature based and anomaly based. For other, IDS has been easily integrated with firewall and other network infrastructure to form what is knows as intrusion prevention system (IPS).

As more people have access to networks, security officers face more obstacles in determining incidents. IDS's role in detecting attack suffers from false positives and false negatives. False positive signifies symptoms detected by IDS but they are not real attacks. False negative implies certain valid attacks go undetected. With increasingly more events occurring on computer systems, IDS is facing heavy trial to help security staffers in detecting intrusions effectively and efficiently. Lower false positives and capability to detect more attacks have been urgent for IDS like never before.

Conclusion

Intrusion detection system, as security officers' eyes on a computer system, has been an integrated and important infrastructure for digital information security. From its inception rooted from audit systems, IDS has been able to answer challenges in detecting intrusion. With the initial research trend based on anomaly detection and later on misused schemes, we are now witnessing products that try to apply a hybrid approach in detecting attacks. Signature-based detection has been important for its effectiveness and lower false positives. On the other hand, to answer challenges from newer threats (zero-day attack) that spread fast, anomaly detection could help more. Hence, a hybrid-type of IDS becomes relevant.

To predict that IDS is dead might be a little overboard. Even though declining in general usage, IDS has been functionally merged with other networking nodes. Besides that, its important value of gathering traces to be analyzed by forensics is paramount. For now, IDS has evolved into a more sophisticated system: intrusion prevention system (IPS). Its effectiveness is still being observed.

For the time being, researchers have adequately identified a method of detecting attack that has a common pattern. But the next challenge is to secure a computer system in a way that it is resistant against not only old attacks, but also newer attack vectors.

References

Aho, A.V., & Corasick, M.J. Efficient String Matching: An aid to bibligraphic search. *Communications of ACM, 18*(6), 33-340.

Amarasinghe, S. (2005). *Host-based IPS guards endpoints*. Retrieved January 22, 2005, from http://www.networkworld.com/news/tech/2005/072505techupdate.html?fsrc=rss-intrusion

Boyer, R. S., & Moore, J. S. (1977). A fast string searching algorithm. *Communications of ACM, 20*(10), 762-772.

Cox, J. (2005). *School nixes malware with open source*. Retrieved from http://ungoliant.sourceforge.net/

Debar, H., Becker, M., & Siboni, D. (4-6 May, 1992). A neural network component for an intrusion detection system. In *Proceedings of the IEEE Symposium on Security and Privacy* (pp. 240-250), 1992.

Denning, D. E. (7-9 May, 1986). An intrusion detection model. In *Proceedings of the Seventh IEEE Symposium of Security and Privacy*, (pp. 118-131).

Heberlein, L. T. (1990). A network security monitor. In *Proceedings of the IEEE Symposium on Research in Security and Privacy* (pp. 296-304).

Hochberg, J., Jackson, K., Stallings, C., McClary, J. F., DuBois, D., & Ford, J. (1993). NADIR: An automated system for detecting network intrusion and misuse. *Computers and Security, 12*(3), 235-248.

Javitz, H. S., & Valdes, A. (1991). The SRI IDES statistical anomaly detector. In *Proceedings IEEE Symposium on Security and Privacy*.

Kim, G. H., & Spafford, E. H. (1994). The design and implementation of Tripwire: A file system integrity checker. In *Proceedings of the 2ⁿᵈ ACM Conference on Computer and Communication Security* (pp. 18-29).

Roesch, M. (1999). Snort — Lightweight intrusion detection for networks. In *Proceedings of the 13ᵗʰ USENIX LISA Conference*, USENIX Association (pp. 229-238).

Sebring, M., Shellhouse, E., Hanna, M. E., & Whitehurst, R. A. (October, 1988). Expert systems in intrusion detection: A case study. In *Proceedings of the Eleventh National Computer Security Conference*, Baltimore, MD (pp. 74-81).

Smaha, S. E. (12-16 Dec, 1988). Haystack: An intrusion detection system. In *Proceedings of the Fourth Aerospace Computer Security Applications Conference,* Orlando, FL (pp. 37-44).

Staniford, S., Paxson, V., & Weaver, N. (August 2002) How to own the Internet in your spare time. In *Proceedings of the 11ᵗʰ USENIX Security Symposium*, San Francisco, CA (149-167).

Tener, W. T. (1986). Discovery: An expert system in the commercial data security environment. In *Proceedings of the IFIP Security Conference*, Monte Carlo.

Chapter VIII

Node Authentication in Networks Using Zero-Knowledge Proofs

Richard S. Norville, Wichita State University, USA

Kamesh Namuduri, Wichita State University, USA

Ravi Pendse, Wichita State University, USA

Abstract

Zero-knowledge proof (ZKP) based authentication protocols provide a smart way to prove an identity of a node without giving away any information about the secret of that identity. There are many advantages as well as disadvantages to using this protocol over other authentication schemes, and challenges to overcome in order to make it practical for general use. This chapter examines the viability of ZKPs for use in authentication protocols in networks. It is concluded that nodes in a network can achieve a desired level of security by trading off key size, interactivity, and other parameters of the authentication protocol. This chapter also provides data analysis that can be useful in determining expected authentication times based on device capabilities. Pseudocode is provided for implementing a graph-based ZKP on small or limited processing devices.

Introduction

The concept of zero-knowledge proof was introduced by Goldwasser, Micali, and Rackoff (1991). Node authentication methods based on ZKPs were investigated in the past. However, their suitability for small computing devices, as well their implementation mechanisms, received less attention (Aronsson, 1995). With the advent of small wireless computing devices such as PDAs and smart sensors, the importance of authentication schemes that can provide high levels of confidence with less computational power has tremendously increased. This chapter contributes to this field of research by investigating the suitability of ZKP-based authentication schemes for small computing devices and provides their complexity analysis. It also provides implementation details needed for a practitioner.

Several authentication protocols are available in the literature. Examples include timed efficient stream loss-tolerant authentication (TESLA) (Perrig, Canetti, Song, & Tygar, 2001), authentication schemes based on polynomial rings (Hoffstein, Lieman, & Silverman, 1999), and elliptic curve cryptography (ECC) (Aydos, Sunar, & Koc, 1998) among several others. The reader is referred to text books on cryptography (Menezes, Oorschot, & Vanstone, 1997; Stinson, 2002) for a survey of authentication protocols based on hash functions and symmetric encryption algorithms.

ZKP-based authentication protocols provide a smart way to prove an identity of a node without giving away any information on the secret of that identity. There are many advantages as well as disadvantages in using this protocol over other authentication schemes such as challenges to overcome in order to make it practical for general use.

One advantage of ZKPs is that their computational requirements can be minimized based on the nature of the underlying problem. This makes them appealing for devices that are limited by processor speed.

The most noteworthy benefit in using a ZKP is that during the entire authentication process, no hints about the secret are ever given. This is important when one considers how effective hackers have been at infiltrating and stealing personal information from databases. Since keys are usually publicly available there is no need to store secrets.

Networks can also benefit from the ZKP protocol for two reasons. The transactions that take place during the authentication process are relatively light. Trust is gained through repeated interaction, not necessarily by the key size alone. The main benefit to network users is that no secure channel or encryption is needed to authenticate. Hackers listening in during the exchange of information gain no knowledge that they could not have already gathered on their own.

Challenges to overcome include the high memory requirements needed for ZKPs. Since the protocol uses public keys, they must be large enough to be difficult to solve in a timely manner. Also the amount of traffic generated by ZKPs is larger than other authentication schemes due to its interactive nature.

Motivation and Problem Statement

Analysis of the ZKP provides the information necessary to estimate the level of trust, memory requirements, and possible traffic in the network based on parameters such as the key size, and time spent on authentication. Authentication protocols based on ZKP can be made less computational (or memory) intensive based on the nature of the underlying problem on which the authentication scheme is designed. In this chapter, ZKP-based authentication scheme is analyzed for its viability in networks.

Contributions of this Chapter

This chapter makes three main contributions to the field of node authentication in networks. One is the implementation of a graph isomorphism-based ZKP detailed in section 4. Much has been written about ZKP protocols in theory, but not so much practical implementations or viability analysis is available in the literature (Schilcher, 2004). In order to evaluate the viability of this authentication scheme, the proposed scheme has been implemented with the intent of making it computationally lightweight through the use of simple functions. Pseudocode is provided, which can be easily implemented on small devices.

The other two contributions are in the form of data collection and analysis as outlined in Section 5. Data has been collected from running several experiments utilizing the ZKP protocol. The key size and the amount of interactivity used during the authentication are varied for these experiments. Large sets of samples are collected to provide accurate and meaningful analysis and comparisons. Authentication time and memory requirements for implementing ZKP-based protocols are estimated, analyzed, and discussed in detail; confidence (trust) levels estimated in terms of interactivity and time. Finally, it has been shown that the level of trust increases exponentially as a function of number of nodes in the graph, whereas the corresponding authentication time only increases linearly.

Organization of the Chapter

The organization of the rest of the chapter is as follows. Section 2 provides an overview of ZKP including its properties, and related research. This is followed by an overview of graph theory in Section 3 that explains the ZKP method based on graph isomorphism (GI). Pseudocode for various functions for GI-based ZKP, their descriptions and run times are given in Section 4. Experiments are conducted for analysis, and the results of experiments are presented in Section 5. Section 6 concludes the chapter with a summary and suggestions for future work.

Background and Related Work

This section gives a detailed overview of what a zero-knowledge proof is, how it is constructed, and how it is used in authentication schemes.

Simple Example of ZKP

A simple example of a ZKP can be pictured using a maze (RSA Security). Assume that there is a complex maze and you have a view of the entrance and exit, but the interior may be obscured from view. There is only one correct path from start to finish of this maze and only *Alex* knows the secret. Now *Alex* wants to prove to *Bob* that he knows the secret to this maze without disclosing that secret itself.

Alex can prove to *Bob* that he knows the correct path by obscuring the maze and walking to any random spot within it. *Alex* then reveals his position in the maze and *Bob* proceeds by asking *Alex* to either walk to the exit or to the entrance. Let us assume *Bob* picked the entrance, so *Alex* would cover the maze and arrive at the entrance. At this moment *Bob* would only be 50% certain that *Alex* knows the secret because *Alex* could have picked the random spot by traveling from the entrance in the first place. On the next trial *Bob* might pick the exit, but even after this interaction *Bob* may still not trust *Alex*. *Alex* may have anticipated this choice and selected the spot in the maze by traveling from the exit. So *Alex* and *Bob* repeat this procedure as many times as it takes for *Bob* to trust *Alex*, since surely *Alex* cannot guess *Bob*'s choices indefinitely. Notice that during the whole process, no hints are ever given about the secret itself since the maze is always covered. ZKPs in practice are more complex.

A typical interactive zero-knowledge proof round consists of a prover sending an "assertion" message to the verifier. The verifier then sends back a challenge to the prover. The prover then responds to the challenge and this round is then repeated several times. When the verifier is satisfied with the responses, the verifier then accepts the proof. Goldreich, Micali, and Wigderson showed (1991) that all problems in NP have zero-knowledge proofs assuming the existence of secure encryption functions.

ZKPs are constructed using problems in NP-complete. This is because no polynomial algorithm for an NP-complete problem has ever been found (Cormen, Leiserson, Rivest, & Stein, 2001). Classic examples of ZKPs include graph isomorphism, discrete logarithms, factoring the product of large primes, graph coloring, and Hamilton paths.

Properties of Zero Knowledge Proofs

In cryptographic applications, the following properties are useful for interactive proofs (RSA):

- **Completeness (RSA):** Both the prover and the verifier follow the protocol and the verifier always accepts the proof if it is true.

- **Soundness (RSA):** As long as the verifier follows the protocol, the verifier will always reject the proof if the fact is false.

- **Zero knowledge (RSA):** As long as the prover follows the protocol, the verifier learns nothing about the fact being proved, except that it is true, even if the verifier does not follow the protocol. In a ZKP, even if the exchange is recorded, the verifier cannot later prove the fact to anyone else.

Related Work

The following sections discuss research relating to ZKP. The first section describes a Fiat-Shamir-based ZKP and the following section discusses resource-bounded ZKPs.

Zero Knowledge Proof Based on Fiat-Shamir's Factoring Scheme

One of the most well-known protocols using interactive zero knowledge is presented in Feige, Fiat, and Shamir (1998). Fiat and Shamir introduced an identification scheme that would enable any user to prove his identity to any other user without shared keys. They claim that if factoring is difficult, the schemes are provably secure against any known message attack. In Fiat and Shamir (1986), the authors bring into play a scenario that contains a facility (i.e., a trusted third party) through which smart cards would be issued. A high level of security can be achieved in their model. A confidence level of $1-(1/2^{20})$ required an average of 14 modular multiplications to verify the proof of identity. They pointed out that with enough ROM, larger keys could be stored to reduce the number of multiplications while maintaining similar confidence levels. The RSA-based scheme (RSA) can trade off the time to authenticate, space needed to store keys, and amount of data that needs to be transmitted between the two participating nodes. Guillou and Quisquater (1988) further improved Fiat-Shamir's protocol in terms of memory requirements and number of rounds.

Modular multiplication is heavily used in current cryptographic systems (Bunimov & Schimmler, 2003) such as RSA, Diffie-Hellman key exchange, and elliptic curve cryptography. Given a word length of n bits, an n-bit integer M, called the modulus, and two n-bit operands X and Y, the problem is the computation of $X*Y \bmod M$. Smaller computing devices have strict limitations in chip area and power consumption, will not be able to implement modular multiplications in real time, given that the typical problem size n is rather large (e.g., $n=1024$). Hence, ZKP protocols, which are based on the designs that require modular multiplication, may not be suitable for small devices. The verification model used in this chapter uses bit comparisons and matrix indexing to significantly reduce computation complexity.

Timed Zero-Knowledge Proof

One type of a resource-bounded ZKP design makes use of time limits to verify a prover. The timed-ZK (Goldreich, 2004) uses the idea that ZKPs are based on problems in NP, and thus the prover can expect a hacker's response time to be greater than the time taken by a legitimate prover. The verifier, in effect, limits the resources available to the prover by requiring him/her to respond within a certain amount of time. The motivation for using a timed-ZK is to reduce the number of rounds required to verify the prover, and thereby reducing the amount of traffic exchanged.

Another variant of timed-ZK is to strictly limit the number of computations. The verifier limits the prover by a fixed number of computational steps (where this number is a fixed polynomial in the length of the common input). In this case, the prover's actual running time is monitored by the verifier rather than time duration. In Dwork, Shaltiel, Smith, and Trevisan (2004) the number of rounds is reduced to two by limiting time and device (the amount of pre-computed information).

These approaches may not be practical for network devices. The amount of delay and jitter introduced in a network environment may cause some provers to be falsely denied authentication. In the stricter version of timed-ZK, it is difficult to monitor run time of devices several hops away.

Overview of a Graph Isomorphism-Based ZKP

This section gives a brief overview of graph theory, and a detailed presentation of how graph isomorphism can be used to construct zero-knowledge proof based on reference (Goldreich et al., 1991), in which it has been shown that graph isomorphism can be used as a perfect zero-knowledge proof system.

Graph Theory and Definitions

Definition 1. A graph G consists of two entities a set of vertices, and a set of edges between the vertices. Typically written $G = (V, E)$, the elements of V are the *vertices* of G, and the elements of E are its *edges* (Figure 1). When more than one graph is under consideration, it may be useful to write V(G) and E(G) for its vertex and edge sets, respectively (Merris, 2000).

Definition 2. If $e = \{u, v\}$ in E(G), vertices u and v are said to be *adjacent* (to each other) and incident to e. Two edges are *adjacent* if they have exactly one common vertex: that is, if their set-theoretic intersection has cardinality 1 (Merris, 2000).

Figure 1. Elements of a simple graph

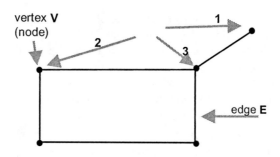

Definition 3. The simple graphs $G_1 = (V_1, E_1)$ and $G_2 = (V_2, E_2)$ are isomorphic if there is a one-to-one and onto function f from V_1 to V_2 with the property that u and v are adjacent in G_1 if and only if f(u) and f(v) are adjacent in G_2, for all u and v in V_1. Such a function is called an isomorphism (Rosen, 1998).

Graph Representation

A graph can be represented using an adjacency matrix. Each row and column of the adjacency matrix shown in Figure 2a represents a vertex in the graph H1 shown in Figure 2b. If there is an edge between two vertices, then it is represented by a bit "1." For example, in Figure 2b, there is no edge between vertex 1 and vertices 2 and 3, but there is an edge between vertex 1 and vertices 4 through 7. This is represented in the adjacency matrix by choosing row 1 and entering "0" bit for the two columns representing vertices 2 and 3, and "1" bit for the four columns representing vertices 4 through 7.

Graph Isomorphism

The following sections describe graph isomorphism as the basis in the construction of a ZKP based on reference (Goldreich et al., 1991). Graph isomorphism has been chosen for two reasons. It is relatively easy to implement ZKP based on GI on most small devices and, although it is difficult to determine if two graphs are isomorphic, it is simple to verify when given the solution permutation.

GI in NP-Complete

It is still unknown if graph isomorphism is an NP-complete problem (Cormen et al., 2001; Garey & Johnson, 1979). Some mathematicians speculate that graph isomorphism lies somewhere in between P and NP-complete. In other words, it is a hard problem, but not

Figure 2a. Adjacency matrix: Representation of Graph H1

	1	2	3	4	5	6	7	8	9	10
1	0	0	0	1	1	1	1	0	1	0
2	0	0	0	0	1	0	1	1	0	0
3	0	0	0	0	1	1	1	1	0	1
4	1	0	0	0	0	1	1	0	0	0
5	1	1	1	0	0	1	0	0	1	0
6	1	0	1	1	1	0	1	1	1	1
7	1	1	1	1	0	1	0	0	0	1
8	0	1	1	0	0	1	0	0	0	1
9	1	0	0	0	1	1	0	0	0	0
10	0	0	1	0	0	1	1	1	0	0

Figure 2b. Graph H1: Vertices labeled

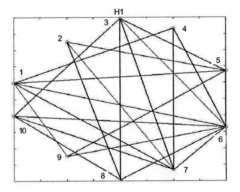

NP hard. Many programs have been developed to determine if two graphs are isomorphic (Foggia, Sansone, & Vento, 2001), and it has been a subject of research for decades.

Some find a solution faster than others by focusing on special types of graphs, such as planar graphs in which no edge intersects with another. Even though these programs continue to get faster, none of them have a polynomial worst-case time for all graphs.

GI-Based ZKP Authentication

The following sections present how a GI-based ZKP is constructed and implemented as an authentication scheme. In the first section, the protocol is given and one round of interactivity is shown. The following section shows in detail the information exchanged during 10 rounds of ZKP. The two graphs G1 and G2, shown in Figure 3, are used to explain this protocol.

Figure 3. The two graphs (G1 and G2) used to illustrate the Gi-based ZKP protocol functionality

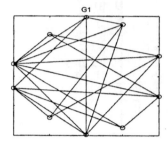 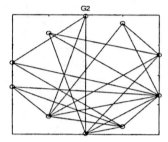

Figure 4. Graph H obtained by applying **r** *to* G_2

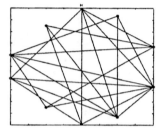

GI-Based ZKP Protocol

A protocol for graph isomorphism in a zero-knowledge proof consists of the following steps (Goldreich et al., 1991).

- Prior to starting the ZKP, Paula the prover creates a random graph G_1 and then randomly permutes the vertices to create a second graph G_2. These two graphs are the public keys, and the random permutation that created G_2 from G_1 will be the secret (Π).

- (P ➜ V) Paula generates a random permutation (ρ). She then randomly selects between G_1 and G_2 and permutes that graph according to ρ. This new random graph H (shown in Figure 4) is sent to Vince the verifier.

- (P ⬅ V) Vince tells Paula to show him an isomorphism between graph H and G_1 or G_2 that he randomly selects.

- (P ➜ V) Paula replies with the solution σ. Vince verifies the solution by applying σ to random graph H.

This completes one ZKP round. After one round of the ZKP, Vince is only 50% certain that Paula knows the isomorphism between G_1 and G_2. This is because Paula could have guessed Vince would challenge her to make an isomorphism to G_1 and could therefore create graph H, which is already isomorphic to G_1. When Vince challenges for the solution between H and G_1, Paula can reply with the permutation even if she does not know the secret. However, if Vince instead challenges Paula to make H isomorphic to G_2, then she must know the secret or be able to solve the challenge, in order to reply. Since a ZKP is ideally composed of problems in NP-complete, the challenge is difficult to solve.

One Round of GI-Based ZKP

This section presents a detailed explanation of how one round of a ZKP is accomplished, including how public keys and the secret is formed, what information is transmitted, and how the challenges and answers are determined.

The graph G_2 is generated from G_1 using secret permutation Π: $(5, 1, 9, 0, 7, 4, 3, 6, 2, 8)$. This means we relabeled G_1's vertices according to Π. When the vertices are then rearranged sequentially, while preserving the edges, we get G_2.

Table 1. Information exchanged during a 10-round ZKP authentication protocol

Round 1
→ $H1 = \rho(G_2)$
← 1
→ $(5, 8, 9, 7, 4, 0, 3, 2, 1, 6) = \sigma = \rho(\Pi^{-1})$
Round 2
→ $H2 = \rho(G_2)$
← 1
→ $(3, 8, 2, 7, 0, 5, 4, 9, 6, 1) = \sigma = \rho(\Pi^{-1})$
Round 3
→ $H3 = \rho(G_1)$
← 1
→ $(3, 4, 6, 0, 1, 9, 2, 7, 5, 8) = \sigma = \rho$
Round 4
→ $H4 = \rho(G_1)$
← 1
→ $(8, 3, 7, 1, 5, 2, 6, 4, 0, 9) = \sigma = \rho$
Round 5
→ $H5 = \rho(G_2)$
← 2
→ $(0, 4, 3, 2, 1, 5, 7, 9, 8, 6) = \sigma = \rho$
Round 6
→ $H6 = \rho(G_2)$
← 1
→ $(3, 5, 4, 9, 2, 8, 6, 0, 7, 1) = \sigma = \rho(\Pi^{-1})$
Round 7
→ $H7 = \rho(G_2)$
← 1
→ $(7, 5, 6, 1, 8, 2, 3, 0, 9, 4) = \sigma = \rho(\Pi^{-1})$
Round 8
→ $H8 = \rho(G_1)$
← 2
→ $(5, 4, 6, 3, 1, 2, 7, 8, 9, 0) = \sigma = \rho(\Pi)$
Round 9
→ $H9 = \rho(G_2)$
← 2
→ $(6, 5, 1, 9, 7, 0, 3, 2, 4, 8) = \sigma = \rho(\Pi)$
Round 10
→ $H10 = \rho(G_1)$
← 1
→ $(0, 3, 2, 8, 5, 7, 4, 9, 6, 1) = \sigma = \rho$

Paula randomly selects G_2 to create random graph H to send to Vince. She creates a random permutation ρ (7, 8, 1, 3, 0, 5, 2, 4, 6, 9). After applying ρ to G_2 she obtains H.

The protocol then proceeds as follows: Paula sends H to Vince. Vince randomly selects G_1 and challenges Paula for the solution. Paula must then provide σ, the permutation to turn H into G_1. Since she created H from G_2, she must use Π and ρ to create σ. In this case σ is (5, 8, 9, 7, 4, 0, 3, 2, 1, 6). There are three cases for which σ are calculated.

Case 1: If Paula picks the same graph as Vince, then Paula simply replies with $\sigma = \rho$. This is because Vince chose the same graph that Paula made the random graph H from.

Case 2: If Paula created H from G_1 and Vince chose G_2, then Paula will reply with $\sigma = \rho\ (\mathbf{P})$.

Case 3: If Paula created H from G_2 and Vince chose G_1, then Paula will reply with $\sigma = \rho\ (\mathbf{P^{-1}})$.

In this example we have case 3. To calculate σ, we select the indices of ρ by the vertices from Π. To get the first number of σ, we look at the first number of Π, which is 5. We then go to **r** and search through the indices proceeding from 0 through 5. The number at index 5 happens to be 5. This is repeated for each vertex in Π. Figure 3.5 demonstrates how σ is created from ρ and Π.

Authentication Using a 10-Round ZKP

Table 1 shows the information exchanged between Paula and Vince during a 10-round ZKP authentication using the same example. First, a random graph is sent, a random challenge is sent back, and finally a solution is given to permute the random graph into one that is isomorphic to the public key.

An eavesdropper cannot gain any knowledge from the exchanged messages pertaining to the secret Π: (5, 1, 9, 0, 7, 4, 3, 6, 2, 8). This is because the answer is nothing more than a random selection of Π from ρ or the random permutation **r** itself.

Figure 5. Pseudocode for generating isomorphic graph. Note that r is written as "ro" readability purposes

```
function makeIsomorphic(Ga[n][n], ro)
1  for i ← 1 to n
2    for j ← 1 to n
3      H[ro[i]][ro[j]] = Ga[i][j]
4  return H
```

Complexity Analysis

This section starts off showing that the computational complexity is lightweight for this graph isomorphism-based ZKP protocol, as seen by examining the functions in sections 4.1.1 and 4.1.2. Section 4.2 explains the memory requirements based on key complexity. Level of trust analysis is presented in section 4.3 with some examples.

Time Complexity Analysis

The functions needed to implement the authentication protocol based on ZKPs are presented from the perspective of the prover and the verifier. Notice that these functions are comprised of simple *for* loops and matrix indexing. Small computing devices can benefit from such lightweight code when considering processor power.

Prover-Time Complexity

In the first exchange of the ZKP round, Paula must send a random graph H to Vince. The function *makeIsomorphic*( ), shown in Figure 5, takes in the chosen graph G_a represented by an $n \times n$ adjacency matrix, and the random permutation ρ. It returns a random graph H that is isomorphic to G_a. It has a running time of $\Theta(n^2)$ where n is the number of vertices in G_a.

In the third exchange, Paula, the prover, must respond with a solution to the challenge from Vince, the verifier. The pseudocode *createSigma*( ), shown in Figure 6, takes in the bit "*a*" from Paula's original random choice, the bit "*b*" from Vince's challenge, the secret permutation Π, and the random permutation ρ. The bit "*a*" corresponds to G_1 or G_2 from which Paula created a random graph. The bit "*b*" corresponds to which graph Vince wants to see a solution permutation.

Figure 6. Pseudocode for CreateSigma() function used by the prover

```
function createSigma(a, b, pi, ro)
1  if( ( a = 0 AND b = 0) OR ( a = 1 AND b = 1)
2     do for i ← 1 to length(ro)
3        sigma[i] ← ro[i]
4  else if( a = 1 AND b = 0)
5     do for i ← 1 to length(ro)
6        sigma[i] ← ro[pi[i]]
7  else
8     do for i ← 1 to length(ro)
9        sigma[pi[i]] ← ro[i]
10 return sigma
```

Figure 7. Functions used by the verifier

```
function applyPermutation(Gb[n][n], sigm
1  for i ← 1 to n
2    for j ←1 to n
3      A[i][j] ← Gb[sigma[i]][sigma[j]]
4  return A[n][n]
```

```
function checkGraphs( Gb[n][n], A[n][n])
1  for i ← 1 to n
2    for j ← 1 to n
3      if( Gb[i][j] != A[i][j] )
4        return FALSE
5  return TRUE
```

There are three cases. Case 1: both bits are the same, that is, $0 - 0$ or $1 - 1$. Case 2: $a = 0$ and $b = 1$. Case 3: $b = 1$ and $a = 0$. The function returns a solution permutation, and has a running time of $\Theta(n)$ where n is the number of vertices in Ga.

Verifier-Time Complexity

In order for Vince to verify the solution, he has to apply the solution from Paula to random graph H. If successful, random graph H will be transformed into G_b where G_b represents either $\mathbf{G_1}$ or $\mathbf{G_2}$; the graph Vince has randomly selected. This is done by calling two functions *applyPermutation* ( ) and *checkGraphs* ( ).

The function *applyPermutation*( ) is very similar to *makeIsomorphic*( ), except that it reverses the process. It accepts the adjacency graph G_b and the solution sigma, sent from Paula, and returns an answer graph A. Function *checkGraphs*( ) simply does a bit–by–bit comparison to verify if the answer graph A is identical to graph G_b. It returns TRUE if they are and FALSE if not. Both run in $\Theta(n^2)$, where n is the number of vertices in G_b.

All of the functions described are simple enough to implement on most programmable small devices. They consist of nothing more than *for* loops, *if* statements, and bit comparisons.

Memory Requirements

The following sections determine the memory needed to store the public keys and secret keys. The last section discusses how more memory can help to increase confidence levels by having a larger pool of keys to choose from.

Memory Requirements for Public Key

The memory requirement for key storage is very high, like most authentication schemes. For each public key graph, it is required to store n^2 bits for n vertices when using an adjacency matrix. Since undirected graphs are symmetric about the diagonal, memory can be conserved by representing the graph with $(n^2 - n)/2$ bits. Each client must store both public key graphs in order to create random graph H. Each verifier must store both keys for each client it wants to authenticate.

Memory Requirement for Secret Key

Each client must store the secret permutation Π. For graphs with less than $2^{16}-1$ or 65,535 vertices, the memory requirement for Π is $n \times 2$ bytes where n is the number of vertices in a public key.

Level of Trust Provided by ZKP

The level of trust that one can have after n rounds of ZKP is $1-(1/2^n)$. For example, the probability to hack a ZKP protocol at 10 rounds is $1/(2^{10})$ or 0.097%. This corresponds to a confidence level of 99.9023%. The level of trust increases exponentially by adding more rounds of interaction.

The confidence level can also be raised without increasing the amount of interactivity. In order to do this, we must have more than two options to choose from. If we have, say, k choices instead of two, then the probability that a hacker can cheat the ZKP is $1/k^n$. Thus the confidence level rises to $1-(1/k^n)$. This is useful if the amount of interactivity during the authentication process is undesirable and memory requirements are less of a concern.

Experiments and Analysis

This section starts with an overview of how the experiment was implemented and conducted. The data collected is presented using histograms. Lastly, the analysis of the data is presented.

Experimental Setup

The ZKP protocol was implemented on a Pentium III system. The tests measure performance of this protocol for keys of varying length using 10 rounds of interactivity. We then ran the same tests with an increased interactivity of 20 rounds. Each scenario was run 1,000 times. The public keys were created using high-density graphs, since denser graphs have no effect on authentication time but are more difficult for cheaters to guess (Foggia et al., 2001). The graphs used have a density of 50%, which means for each vertex, the random generator had 50% chance of creating an edge to another vertex.

Results and Discussion

The plots in Figures 8 through 13 depict the authentication times obtained by simulating a 10-round ZKP-based authentication protocol as a function of the key size. Figures 14 through 19 depict the authentication times obtained from a 20-round ZKP-based protocol

Figure 8. Authentication time in seconds for 10 rounds of ZKP – 10-node key

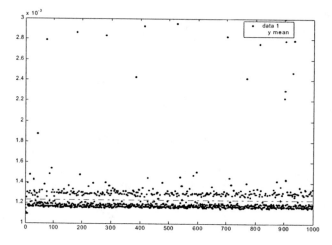

Figure 9. Authentication time in seconds for 10 rounds of ZKP – 50-node key

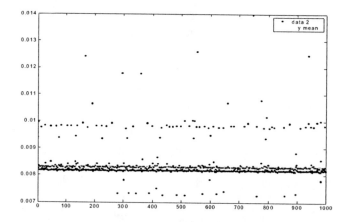

Figure 10. Authentication time in seconds for 10 rounds of ZKP – 100-node key

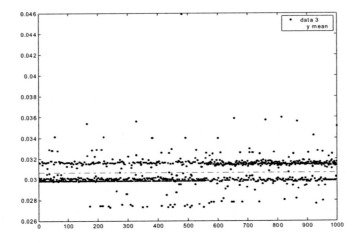

Figure 11. Authentication time in seconds for 10 rounds of ZKP – 150-node key

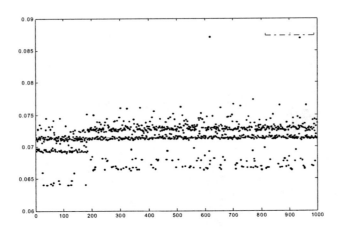

as a function of the key size. The x-axis represents the trial number and the y-axis represents the total time needed to authenticate.

The average authentication times needed to authenticate for Figures 8 through 13 are 0.0012, 0.0083, 0.0306, 0.0715, 0.1236, and 0.2141 seconds respectively. In Figures 14 through 19, the number of rounds is doubled and the average authentication times are increased to 0.0022, 0.0163, 0.0608, 0.1422, 0.2474, and 0.3999 seconds, respectively. The maximum authentication times for Figures 8 through 13 are 0.0030, 0.0140, 0.0459, 0.0871,

Figure 12. Authentication time in seconds for 10 rounds of ZKP – 200-node key

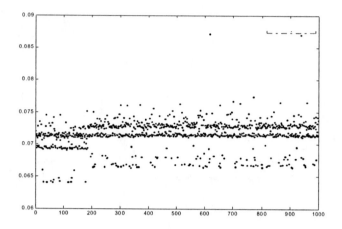

Figure 13. Authentication time in seconds for 10 rounds of ZKP – 250-node key

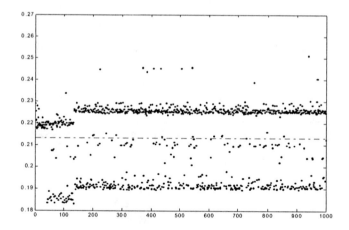

0.1477, 0.2512 seconds, respectively. In Figures 14 through 19, the authentication time is increased to 0.0039, 0.0318, 0.0768, 0.1579, 0.2662, and 0.4258 seconds, respectively.

Analysis

Figures 20 and 21 show the mean authentication times for 10 and 20 rounds of ZKP. From these figures, this protocol has a worse-case running time $\Theta(n^2)$ where n is the number

Figure 14. Authentication time in seconds for 20 rounds of ZKP – 10-node key

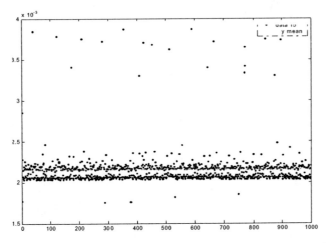

Figure 15. Authentication time in seconds for 20 rounds of ZKP – 50-node key

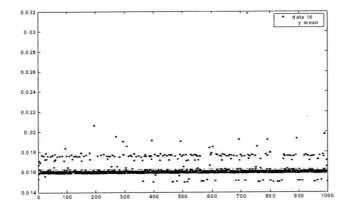

of vertices in the graph. The two plots indicate that as the nodes per key increases, the authentication time increases by a factor of $C * V^2$ where C is a constant determined by the device capabilities and V is the number of nodes in the key. C, in this case, was approximately 3.5×10^{-6} for a Pentium III system.

The probability that a hacker can hack a ZKP protocol at 10 rounds is $1/(2^{10})$ or 0.097%. This corresponds to a confidence level of $1-(1/2^{10})$ or 99.9023%. When the number of

Figure 16. Authentication time in seconds for 20 rounds of ZKP – 100-node key

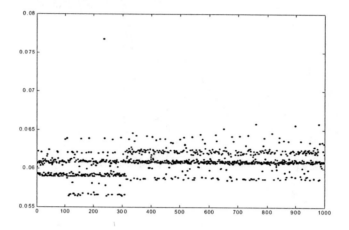

Figure 17. Authentication time in seconds for 20 rounds of ZKP – 200-node key

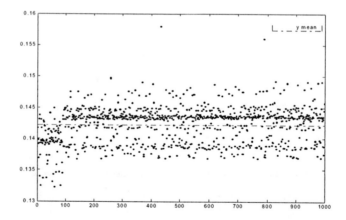

rounds is doubled from 10 to 20, we virtually double the authentication time, which is clear after comparing Figure 13 to Figure 14. However, we decrease the chance of hacking the ZKP enormously. The probability of hacking this protocol at 20 rounds decreases to $1/(2^{20})$ or 0.000095%. This corresponds to an increased confidence level of $1-(1/2^{20})$ or 99.9999%.

Figure 18. Authentication time in seconds for 20 rounds of ZKP – 200-node key

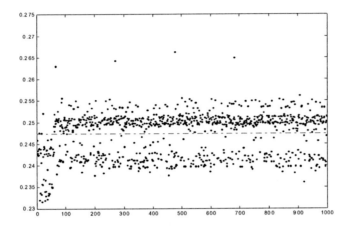

Figure 19. Authenticate time in seconds for 20 rounds of ZKP – 250-node key

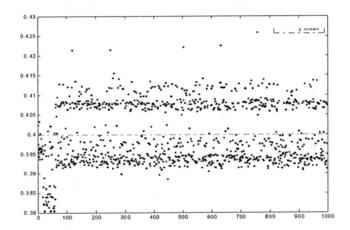

Figure 20. Mean authentication time for 10 rounds of ZKP with varied key size

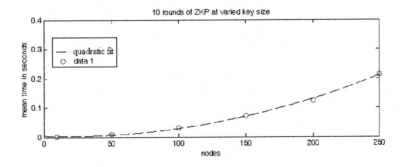

Figure 21. Mean authentication time for 20 rounds of ZKP with varied key size

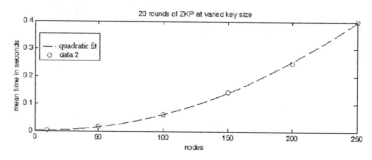

Conclusion and Future Work

Zero-knowledge proofs provide a computationally lightweight method for node authentication. Small devices that could not implement security due to the resource requirements of traditional authentication schemes may be able to afford a level of security using ZKP authentication schemes.

Some tradeoffs have to be considered when using ZKPs. As the level of confidence increases the amount of interactivity (traffic) will increase. The memory requirements are similar to other authentication schemes since keys need to be large enough to be difficult to solve. ZKPs are based on problems for which efficient algorithms are not known to exist. Therefore, one must base a ZKP on a problem that can be easily verified by the device, but is several orders of magnitude more difficult to solve by an eavesdropper.

Memory requirements and the amount of traffic generated by ZKPs are obstacles that have to be overcome to make them an attractive solution for small devices. Traffic may be reduced by passing several keys at once by using a hash function and the verifier randomly choosing a challenge for each key. However, this might cause a loss of the zero-knowledge properties. Traffic may also be reduced by using provers that are resource-bounded. For example, by using the data collected in this chapter, the prover would be required to respond in less than 5 msecs for a 250-node key. If the node takes longer than 5 msecs, it can be deduced that the device is trying to hack the problem and therefore is cheating.

ZKPs have two major advantages over traditional authentication schemes. The computational complexity is lightweight and therefore appealing to small devices. The biggest advantage is that no information about the secret is ever given during the authentication process.

Acknowledgments

The authors would like to acknowledge the support from the following grants: NSF DUE Grant #0313827, and Kansas NSF EPSCoR Grant #NSF32223/KAN32224.

References

Aronsson, H. (1995). *Zero knowledge protocols and small systems*. Department of Computer Science, University of Helsinki. Retrieved from http://www.tml.hut.fi/Opinnot/Tik-110.501/1995/zeroknowledge.html#zintro

Aydos, M., Sunar, B., & Koc, C. K. (1998). *An elliptic curve cryptography based authentication and key agreement protocol for wireless communication*. International Workshop on Discrete Algorithms and Methods for Mobile Computing and Communications.

Bunimov, V., & Schimmler, M. (2003). *Area and time efficient modular multiplication of large integers*. The IEEE International Conference on Application-Specific Systems, Architectures, and Processors (ASAP'03).

Cormen, T., Leiserson, C., Rivest, R., & Stein, C. (2001). *Introduction to algorithms* (2nd ed.). Cambridge, MA: MIT Press and McGraw-Hill.

Dwork, C., Shaltiel, R., Smith, A., & Trevisan, L. (2004). *List-decoding of linear functions and analysis of a two-round zerokKnowledge argument*. Retrieved from http://citeseer.ist.psu.edu/676524.html

Feige, U., Fiat, A., & Shamir, A. (1988). Zero knowledge proofs of identity. *Journal of Cryptology, 1*, 77-94.

Fiat, A., & Shamir, A. (1986). *How to prove yourself: Practical solutions to identification and signature problems*. Advances in Cryptology CRYPTO'86 (pp. 186-194). Springer-Verlag.

Foggia, P., Sansone, C., & Vento, M. (2001). A performance comparison of five algorithms for graph isomorphism. In *Proc. of the 3rd IAPR TC-15 Workshop on Graph-based Representations in Pattern Recognition* (pp. 188-199).

Garey, M. R., & Johnson, D. S. (1979). *Computers and intractability; A guide to the theory of NP-completeness*. Freeman.

Goldreich, O. (2001). *Foundations of cryptography: Basic tools*. Cambridge University Press.

Goldreich, O. (2004). *Zero-knowledge twenty years after its invention*. Rehovot, Israel: Weizmann Institute of Science.

Goldwasser, S., Micali, S., & Rackoff, C. (1991). The knowledge complexity of interactive proof systems. *SIAM Journal on Computing, 18*(1), 186-208.

Goldreich, O., Micali, S., & Wigderson, A. (1991). Proofs that yield nothing but their validity or all languages. In NP Have Zero-knowledge Proof Systems. *Journal of the ACM, 38*(1), 691-729.

Goldreich, O., & Oren, Y. (1994). Definitions and properties of zero-knowledge proof systems. *Journal of Cryptology, 7*(1), 1-32.

Guillou, L. C., & Quisquater, J. J. (1988). A practical zero-knowledge protocol fitted to security microprocessor minimizing both transmission and memory. *Advances in Cryptology — Eurocrypt '88* (pp. 123-128). Springer-Verlag.

Hoffstein, J., Lieman. D., & Silverman, J. H. (1999). NTRU: Polynomial rings and efficient public key authentication. In *Proc. of International workshop on Cryptographic techniques and E Commerce* (pp. 7-19).

Menezes, A., Oorschot, P. V., & Vanstone, S. (1997). *Handbook of applied cryptography.* CRC Press.

Merris, R. (2000). *Graph theory.* John Wiley & Sons.

Perrig, A., Canetti, R., Song, D., & Tygar, J. D. (2001). Efficient and secure source authentication for multicast. In *Proc. of IEEE Symposium on Network and Distributed System Security (NDSS)* (pp. 35-46).

Rosen, K. H. (1998). *Discrete mathematics and its applications.* McGraw-Hill Higher Education.

RSA Security. Retrieved from http://www.rsasecurity.com/rsalabs/faq/2-1-8.html

Schilcher, F. (2004). *Key management and distribution for threshold cryptography schemes.* Retrieved from http://www13.informatik.tu-muenchen.de/lehre/seminare/WS0304/UB-hs/Fabian Schilcher_KeyManagement_report.pdf

Stinson, D. (2002). *Cryptography: Theory and practice.* CRC Press.

Chapter IX

Web Services Security in E-Business:
Attacks and Countermeasures

Wei-Chuen Yau, Multimedia University, Malaysia

G. S. V. Radha Krishna Rao, Multimedia University, Malaysia

Abstract

Web services enable the communication of application-to-application in a heterogeneous network and computing environment. The powerful functionality of Web services has given benefits to enterprise companies, such as rapid integrating between heterogeneous e-business systems, easy implementation of e-business systems, and reusability of e-business services. While providing the flexibility for e-business, Web services tend to be vulnerable to a number of attacks. Core components of Web services such as simple object access protocol (SOAP), Web services description language (WSDL), and universal description, discovery, and integration (UDDI) can be exploited by malicious attacks due to lack of proper security protections. These attacks will increase the risk of e-business that employs Web services. This chapter aims to provide a state-of-the-art view of Web services attacks and countermeasures. We examine various vulnerabilities in Web services and then followed by the analysis of respective attacking methods. We also discuss preventive countermeasures against such attacks to protect Web services deployments in e-business. Finally, we address future trends in this research area.

Introduction

As the use of the Internet and the World Wide Web (WWW) is expanding rapidly, more and more companies are implementing e-business using Web technologies to replace the traditional business model. Conventional Web application is human-centric, which relies on lots of time-consuming human intervention. The development of Web services technology has changed this computing paradigm to application-centric.

A Web service is any piece of software that supports interoperable program-to-program interaction over a network (Booth, Haas, McCabe, Newcomer, Champion, Ferris, et al., 2004). This technology is not tied to any specific operating systems and programming languages. Thus, it enables the communication of application-to-application in a heterogeneous network and computing environment. This allows enterprise companies to implement and integrate their e-business systems rapidly. Also, reusability of e-business services becomes easy. All of these benefits are a great attraction for enterprise companies to adopt Web services in their e-business environment.

While Web services provide the flexibility for e-business, they introduce security issues that are less known in the e-business communities. The objective of this chapter is to address security challenges presented in Web services and explain which types of solutions are plausible for countering Web services attacks. In the following sections, we review current Web services technology, present different attacks against Web services, discuss some of the security countermeasures, suggest directions for future research, and present a conclusion of this chapter.

Web Services Architecture

A Web services architecture (Booth et al., 2004) is a set of systems and protocols that facilitate application-to-application communication over a network. There are many technologies that are related to the Web services architecture. The main building blocks (Figure 1) that we describe here are extensible markup language (XML) (Bray, Paoli, Sperberg-McQueen, Maler, & Yergeau, 2004), simple object access protocol (SOAP) (Gudgin, Hadley, Mendelsohn, Moreau, & Nielsen, 2003a, 2003b; Mitra, 2003), Web services description language (WSDL) (Booth, & Liu, 2005; Chinnici, Haas, Lewis, Moreau, Orchard, & Weerawarana, 2005; Chinnici, Moreau, Ryman, & Weerawarana, 2005), and universal description, discovery, and integration (UDDI) (Clement, Hately, Riegen, & Rogers, 2004).

Figure 1. Main building blocks of Web services (Source: W3C)

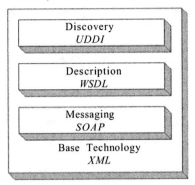

XML

XML defines documents in a structured format (Bray et al., 2004). This format can represent the data to be exchanged as well as the metadata of the data contents. An XML file contains labels of different parts of the document. These labels are specified in a tag format. For example, Listing 1 shows an XML document that contains the address of Multimedia University. The document has a root element <address>. Each piece of data is described by a pair of tags, such as <> and </>, that identify the start and end of the data. The nature of XML documents enable exchange of information between application to application becomes easy. It is the foundation for Web services building blocks. Other Web services components are encoded in the XML format.

SOAP

SOAP describes how XML messages exchange in a decentralized, distributed environment (Mitra, 2003). SOAP provides a stateless and one-way message exchange framework that can be extended to request/response, request/multiple responses, and other

Listing 1. A simple XML document

```
<?xml version="1.0" encoding="UTF-8" ?>
<address>
    <name>Multimedia University</name>
    <street>Jalan Multimedia</street>
    <city>Cyberjaya</city>
    <state>Selangor Darul Ehsan</state>
    <postcode>63100</postcode>
</address>
```

more complex message exchange ways. SOAP messages can be carried by various network protocols, such as HTTP (hypertext transfer protocol), SMTP (simple mail transfer protocol), and raw TCP/IP (transmission control protocol/Internet protocol). SOAP messaging framework is independent of any particular programming language or platform. The basic structure of a SOAP message contains the following four parts (Figure 2):

- **Envelope**: The SOAP envelope is the root element of the soap message. It contains an optional header element and a mandatory body element.

- **Header**: The SOAP header is an optional element that contains additional application requirements for processing the message in the message path, such as security credentials, routing instructions, and transaction management.

- **Body**: This element contains the actual application data or an optional fault message.

- **Fault**: A fault message is generated by an intermediary or an ultimate receiver of the SOAP message to describe any occurrence of exceptional situation.

Listing 2 shows a simple SOAP request message for a Web service that performs addition for two numbers. The request asks the service to add the numbers 2 and 3. Listing 3 shows the response message with the result of the addition (i.e., 5).

Figure 2. Basic structure of a SOAP message (Source: W3C)

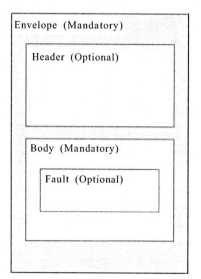

Listing 2. Simple SOAP request message

```
<?xml version="1.0" encoding="utf-8"?>
<env:Envelope xmlns:env="http://www.w3.org/2003/05/soap-envelope">
    <env:Body>
        <m:Add xmlns:m="http://example.org/addition">
            <m:FirstNum>2</m:FirstNum>
            <m:SecondNum>3</m:SecondNum>
        </m:Add>
    </env:Body>
</env:Envelope>
```

Listing 3. Simple SOAP response message

```
<?xml version="1.0" encoding="utf-8"?>
<env:Envelope xmlns:env="http://www.w3.org/2003/05/soap-envelope">
    <env:Body>
        <m:AddResponse xmlns:m="http://example.org/addition">
            <m:AddResult>5</m:AddResult>
        </m:AddResponse>
    </env:Body>
</env:Envelope>
```

WSDL

WSDL is an XML format that describes Web services (Booth, & Liu, 2005). A WSDL document tells us what a service does, how a service is accessed, and where a service is located. A Web service is defined using seven major elements:

- **Description:** This is the root element of a WSDL document.
- **Types:** This element describes data types that are used for the exchanged messages.
- **Interface:** This element defines the abstract interface of the Web service.
- **Operation:** This element describes operations supported by the Web services and also specifies the types of messages that the service can send or receive.
- **Binding:** The binding element specifies concrete protocol and encoding style for the operations and messages.
- **Service**: This element defines the name of the service.

Listing 4. Sample WSDL document (Source: W3C)

```xml
<?xml version="1.0" encoding="utf-8" ?>
<description xmlns="http://www.w3.org/2005/08/wsdl"
  targetNamespace= "http://greath.example.com/2004/wsdl/resSvc"
  xmlns:tns= "http://greath.example.com/2004/wsdl/resSvc"
  xmlns:ghns = "http://greath.example.com/2004/schemas/resSvc"
  xmlns:wsoap= "http://www.w3.org/2005/08/wsdl/soap"
  xmlns:soap="http://www.w3.org/2003/05/soap-envelope"
  xmlns:wsdlx= "http://www.w3.org/2005/08/wsdl-extensions">

  <types>
      <xs:schema xmlns:xs="http://www.w3.org/2001/XMLSchema"
        targetNamespace=http://greath.example.com/2004/schemas/resSvc
        xmlns="http://greath.example.com/2004/schemas/resSvc">
      <xs:element name="checkAvailability" type="tCheckAvailability"/>
        <xs:complexType name="tCheckAvailability">
        <xs:sequence>
         <xs:element name="checkInDate" type="xs:date"/>
         <xs:element name="checkOutDate" type="xs:date"/>
         <xs:element name="roomType" type="xs:string"/>
        </xs:sequence>
        </xs:complexType>
        <xs:element name="checkAvailabilityResponse" type="xs:double"/>
        <xs:element name="invalidDataError" type="xs:string"/>
      </xs:schema>
  </types>

  <interface name = "reservationInterface" >
      <fault name = "invalidDataFault" element = "ghns:invalidDataError"/>

      <operation name="opCheckAvailability" pattern="http://www.w3.org/2005/08/wsdl/in-out"
          style="http://www.w3.org/2005/08/wsdl/style/iri" wsdlx:safe = "true">
        <input messageLabel="In" element="ghns:checkAvailability" />
        <output messageLabel="Out" element="ghns:checkAvailabilityResponse" />
        <outfault ref="tns:invalidDataFault" messageLabel="Out"/>
      </operation>

  </interface>

  <binding name="reservationSOAPBinding" interface="tns:reservationInterface"
    type="http://www.w3.org/2005/08/wsdl/soap"
    wsoap:protocol="http://www.w3.org/2003/05/soap/bindings/HTTP">
      <fault ref="tns:invalidDataFault" wsoap:code="soap:Sender"/>
      <operation ref="tns:opCheckAvailability"
         wsoap:mep="http://www.w3.org/2003/05/soap/mep/soap-response"/>
  </binding>

  <service name="reservationService" interface="tns:reservationInterface">
      <endpoint name="reservationEndpoint" binding="tns:reservationSOAPBinding"
        address ="http://greath.example.com/2004/reservation"/>
  </service>

</description>
```

- **Endpoint:** This element defines an endpoint for the service and specifies the address to access the service using previously specified binding.

Listing 4 shows an example of a WSDL document. The document describes a Web service that can check the availability of a room for hotel GreatH (Booth & Liu, 2005).

UDDI

UDDI provides a mechanism for publishing and finding Web services (Clement et al., 2004). A UDDI registry is like an electronic phone book that provides the classification and catalog of Web services. Web services providers can register their business or Web services to a UDDI server. A user of the Web service can search a specific Web service using the UDDI registry. The following core data structures of UDDI are used for describing an organization, the available Web services, and technical requirements for access to those services:

- **businessEntity:** Describes a business or organization that provides Web services.
- **businessService:** Describes a single or group of related Web services offered by an organization.
- **bindingTemplate:** Describes the technical information to access a particular Web service.
- **tModel:** Describes a technical model that enable the user to identify the technical specifications of Web services.

Basic Roles and Operations

A simple Web service system consists of three participants: a service requester, a service provider, and a service registry. Figure 3 shows their basic roles and operations in a Web service architecture. The service provider provides the interface and implementation of a Web service. The Web service description is specified in WSDL. The provider can publish the Web service in the registry. The service requester or the consumer can find the Web service and its description in the registry. The requester can then communicate with the provider using SOAP messages based on the service description in the WSDL.

Attacks in Web Services

Web services are vulnerable to a wide range of attacks. Various studies (Lindstrom, 2004; Negm, 2004; Wilson, 2003) have shown conceptual attacks that are most likely to be used

Figure 3. Basic roles and operations in a Web service architecture

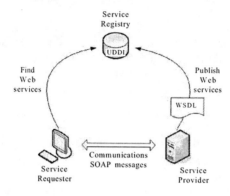

for compromising Web services architectures. This section discusses in detail how malicious attackers launch a number of these attacks against Web services.

Information Gathering

This is the preparation stage for attackers before launching any attacks. Attackers try to gather information that is related to a targeted-service provider. This information includes organization or business description, available Web services, technical access requirement, and so on. Such information can be found from a UDDI registry.

WSDL Scanning

Since a WSDL file provides a clear view of how to interact with a specific Web service, the initial step for launching an attack is to obtain a copy of the WSDL file. An attacker can scan through the WSDL document to get information such as the available operations, and the expected parameters or types of the messages. After this, the attacker may proceed by sending various manipulated SOAP messages in order to discover weaknesses of the Web service. For example, the attacker may guess what operations are supported but unpublished in the WSDL file. This can be achieved by sending different message request patterns with various operation string combinations. The reason for such an attack to be successful is because of poor programming practices.

Parameter Tampering

After scanning through a WSDL file for a specific Web service, an attacker can further test if the Web service application is performing any type of input validation. If the application does not sanitize invalid client inputs, then it is susceptible to parameter tampering attack. An attacker can submit different parameter patterns in order to crash the application or gain further access to unauthorized information. For example, if a Web service application expects an input with an integer type parameter, then an attacker may try to submit an input with type of string or float. This may cause a denial-of-service attack if the application does not know how to process the unexpected content.

SQL (Structure Query Language) Injection

SQL injection is an attack that uses parameter tampering. This attack exploits Web service application that does not perform proper validation check of client-supplied input in SQL queries. An attacker can submit some special characters (e.g., a single quotation or a semicolon) to the input string. If the application accepts and passes the data to an SQL statement, the attacker may bypass the authentication procedure (e.g., a form-based login) to retrieve unauthorized information in the database. The attacker may attack further by modifying the record in the database or perform remote command execution. Faust (2003) has demonstrated this attack against a test Web service that simulates a simple product inventory system.

Coercive Parsing

An XML parser reads through or parses an XML document into its component parts. Not all XML parsers handle consistently with peculiar XML documents that have a format that differs from what is expected. A coercive parsing attack exploits this weakness to overwhelm the processing capabilities of the system. Examples of this attack include recursive payloads, oversized payloads, and SOAP messages flooding.

Figure 4. An XML document with massive nested elements

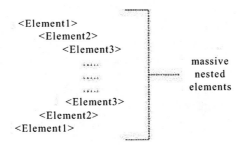

Figure 5. SOAP messages flooding

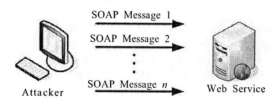

Recursive Payloads

XML allows nested elements within a document to describe complex relationships among elements. An attacker can create a deeply nested document to test the capability of XML parser. For example, the attacker can create an XML document that has 100,000 levels of nested elements (Figure 4). This may overload the processor when it parses the document.

Oversized Payloads

Performance of an XML parser is affected when parsing a large size of XML documents. An attacker can send an extremely large payload in order to degrade the performance of an XML parser. This may result a denial-of-service attack if the parser cannot handle the oversized payload.

SOAP Messages Flooding

The goal of this attack is to overload a Web service by sending SOAP message requests repeatedly (Figure 5). The SOAP message itself is valid but the XML processor may not be able to process excessive SOAP messages in a short period of time. Thus, this may deter the Web service application from receiving other nonmalicious SOAP message requests.

Schema Poisoning

XML schema (Byron & Malhotra, 2004; Thompson, Beech, Maloney, & Mendelsohn, 2004) describes the structure of an XML document. A valid XML document must conform to its schema. A parser reads an XML document and compares it to its schema to check

Figure 6. A SOAP message routes via an intermediary

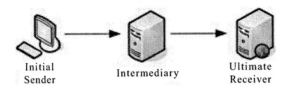

Initial
Sender

Intermediary

Ultimate
Receiver

Figure 7. Compromised intermediary route a SOAP message to a malicious location

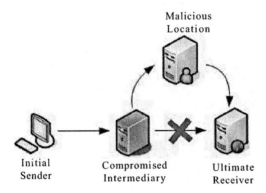

Malicious
Location

Initial
Sender

Compromised
Intermediary

Ultimate
Receiver

the validity of the document. Attackers can perform a schema poisoning by first compromising a node that stores the schema. Then, they replace the original schema with a modified one. As such, any incoming SOAP messages will be determined as invalid by the parser since they do not conform to the modified schema. Consequently, a denial-of-service attack is achieved.

External Entity Attacks

External entities enable XML to build a document dynamically by referring to an external content. They get this content by referencing it via a specified URL (universal resource locator). An attacker may replace the third-party content with a malicious content. Parsing an XML document from this malicious source may result the Web service application to open arbitrary files or network connections.

Routing Detours

A SOAP message may route through some intermediary nodes when it travels from the initial sender to the ultimate receiver (Figure 6). If one of these intermediaries is

Figure 8. Compromised intermediary route a SOAP message to a nonexistent destination

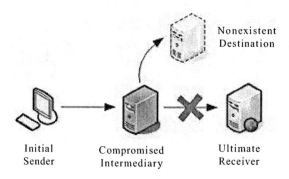

compromised and controlled by an attacker, then either one of the following bogus routing instructions may be inserted:

- Route the message to a malicious location (Figure 7): This may result the critical information stolen by the attacker. However, the attacker may still forward the SOAP message to the original destination after stripping out the additional malicious instructions.

- Route the message to a nonexistent destination (Figure 8): This may cause a denial-of-service attack since the message will never be routed to the intended destination.

Malicious Contents

This attack is related to binary attachments of SOAP messages. Attackers may modify binary attachments such as executable files in order to cause exception within the Web service applications. Attached malicious programs such as viruses, worms, or Trojan horse programs may be transmitted via SOAP messages across the Web service architecture.

Countermeasures against Web Services Attacks

There are many challenges for implementing secure Web services. As valuable business transaction data and sensitive customer information are transmitted or stored within the Web services architecture, compromising of any nodes in the architecture may result in

Listing 5. Simple payment information (Source: W3C)

```
<?xml version='1.0'?>
<PaymentInfo xmlns='http://example.org/paymentv2'>
    <Name>John Smith</Name>
    <CreditCard Limit='5,000' Currency='USD'>
        <Number>4019 2445 0277 5567</Number>
        <Issuer>Example Bank</Issuer>
        <Expiration>04/02</Expiration>
    </CreditCard>
</PaymentInfo>
```

Listing 6. Encrypting an XML element (Source: W3C)

```
<?xml version='1.0'?>
<PaymentInfo xmlns='http://example.org/paymentv2'>
    <Name>John Smith</Name>
      <EncryptedData xmlns='http://www.w3.org/2001/04/xmlenc#'
      Type='http://www.w3.org/2001/04/xmlenc#Element'/>
      <EncryptionMethod Algorithm='http://www.w3.org/2001/04/xmlenc#tripledes-cbc'/>
      <ds:KeyInfo xmlns:ds='http://www.w3.org/2000/09/xmldsig#'>
          <ds:KeyName>John Smith</ds:KeyName>
      </ds:KeyInfo>
      <CipherData><CipherValue>DEADBEEF</CipherValue></CipherData>
      </EncryptedData>
</PaymentInfo>
```

a leakage of sensitive information to an unauthorized third party. In addition, disruption of any Web services may cost a great amount of loss to an organization. It is crucial to protect the Web services from various attacks, as mentioned in the previous section. Therefore, we need robust security schemes that take into consideration the susceptible nature of the Web services architecture. In this section, we discuss some security countermeasures and specifications that have been proposed to safeguard the security of the Web services architecture (Beznosov, Flinn, Kawamoto, & Hartman, 2005; Geuer-Pollmann & Claessens, 2005; Gutiérrez, Fernández-Medina, & Piattini, 2004; Naedele, 2003).

Confidentiality and Integrity

Confidentiality deals with the security requirement on keeping secrecy of information. As e-business applications exchange SOAP messages that contain sensitive information such as customer data and business transaction, it is important to protect the data from the threat of interception.

Listing 7. An example of XML signature (Source: W3C)

```
<Signature Id="MyFirstSignature" xmlns="http://www.w3.org/2000/09/xmldsig#">
    <SignedInfo>
        <CanonicalizationMethod
        Algorithm="http://www.w3.org/TR/2001/REC-xml-c14n-20010315"/>
        <SignatureMethod Algorithm="http://www.w3.org/2000/09/xmldsig#dsa-sha1"/>
        <Reference URI="http://www.w3.org/TR/2000/REC-xhtml1-20000126/">
            <Transforms>
                <Transform Algorithm="http://www.w3.org/TR/2001/REC-xml-c14n-20010315"/>
            </Transforms>
            <DigestMethod Algorithm="http://www.w3.org/2000/09/xmldsig#sha1"/>
            <DigestValue>j6lwx3rvEPO0vKtMup4NbeVu8nk=</DigestValue>
        </Reference>
    </SignedInfo>
    <SignatureValue>MC0CFFrVLtRlk=...</SignatureValue>
    <KeyInfo>
        <KeyValue>
            <DSAKeyValue>
                <P>...</P><Q>...</Q><G>...</G><Y>...</Y>
            </DSAKeyValue>
        </KeyValue>
    </KeyInfo>
</Signature>
```

Ensuring the completeness and accuracy of data is the security goal of integrity. Soap messages sending from a source may travel through some intermediaries before reaching to an ultimate destination. It is required to provide a mechanism for the message recipient to verify that the message has not been altered or modified during transmission.

World Wide Web Consortium (W3C) has developed two specifications, namely XML encryption (Eastlake & Reagle, 2002) and XML signature (Eastlake, Reagle, & Solo, 2002), to address the issue of data confidentiality and integrity respectively. However, these two specifications do not specify implementation issues of SOAP messages integrity and confidentiality. This part is covered by additional standard that has been defined in Nadalin, Kaler, Hallam-Baker, and Monzillo (2004). The detail of each specification is described as follows:

- **XML encryption:** The XML encryption syntax and processing specification describes the processing rules for encrypting/decrypting data (Eastlake & Reagle, 2002). This specification also defines the syntax that represents the encrypted data in XML format. XML encryption supports the encryption of arbitrary data (including an XML document), an XML element, or XML element content. The following example illustrates how to keep sensitive information confidential by encrypting an XML element (Eastlake & Reagle, 2002). Listing 5 shows the payment information that contains credit card number in clear text format, while Listing 6 shows the entire *CreditCard* element is encrypted from its start to end tags. An eavesdropper does not know any sensitive information contained in this XML document. The *CreditCard* element is encrypted using TripleDES algorithm in cipher block chaining (CBC) mode, which is specified by the *EncryptionMethod* element. The resulting encrypted data is contained in the *CipherValue* element.

- **XML signature:** The XML-signature syntax and processing specification provides the security services in terms of data integrity, message authentication, and/ or signer authentication (Eastlake et al., 2002). This specification defines the processing rules for creating and verifying XML signatures. It also includes the syntax for representing the resulting signature information. Listing 7 is an example of XML signature (Eastlake et al., 2002). The signature algorithm for signing the document is DSA, which is specified in the *SignatureMethod* element, while the *DigestMethod* element specifies the digest algorithm (i.e., SHA-1 in this case) applied to the signed object. The resulting digital signature value and digest value are encoded using base64 and specified in the *SignatureValue* element and the *DigestValue* element respectively.

- **Web service security: SOAP message security:** This is a specification developed by the Organization for the Advancement of Structured Information Standards (OASIS). This specification defines a set of SOAP extensions to provide the support of message integrity and confidentiality (Nadalin et al., 2004). The specification is flexible and can be accommodated to various security models such as PKI, Kerberos, and SSL.

Authentication and Authorization

Authentication in e-business is the process to validate the identities of business entities, while authorization is a process to determine an authenticated party can access what sort of resources or perform what kind of actions. For example, only specific authenticated business partners should be able to access sensitive information. In general, access control rules are created to apply the restriction to specific contents or application functionality. The following specifications should be applied in the Web service architecture to ensure these security goals.

- **Security assertion markup language (SAML):** This specification defines a framework for exchanging authentication and authorization information between e-business partners (Cantor, Kemp, Philpott, & Maler, 2005). SAML supports single sign-on (SSO) for affiliated sites. Basic SAML components include assertions, protocols, bindings, and profiles. There are three types of assertions: authentication, attribute, and authorization. The authentication statements contain authenticated related information of a user. The attribute statements describe specific details about the user, while the authorization statements identify what the user is permitted to do. There is a set of request/response protocols for obtaining assertions. The bindings define how SAML protocols map onto the transport protocol, such as HTTP, while the profiles define how SAML assertions, protocols, and bindings are combined for a particular use case.

- **XML access control markup language (XACML):** This specification provides a common language for expressing access control policies in XML vocabulary (Moses, 2005). It defines the mechanism for creating the rules and policy sets that determine what users can access over a network.

- **Access control for SOAP messages**: It is important to apply a security mechanism such as access control to SOAP messages. Damiani, De Capitani di Vimercati, Paraboschi, and Samarati (2001, 2002) have proposed a work on fine-grained access control for SOAP e-services. The authorization model enforces access restrictions to SOAP invocations. There is an authorization filter to intercept every SOAP message and evaluates it against the specified access control rules. Based on the policies, each soap message may (1) be rejected; (2) be allowed; or (3) be filtered and executed in a modified form.

Audit Trails

Audit trails are also an important security requirement in Web services architecture (Booth, et. al., 2004). They can audit the activities for the Web services architecture such as changes in any configuration. On the other hand, they may provide audit on a business level. All the Web service transactions can be recorded as a proof of the business transaction occurred. In addition, they can support, for tracing, user access and behavior when there is any security breach. The audit trails may also provide as data sources for an intrusion detection system in the Web services environment.

Intrusion Detection and Prevention

Almost every organization allows network traffic pass through port 80 or 443 to access Web applications. As such, traditional network firewalls do not block most of the SOAP messages that transport via HTTP (port 80) or HTTPS (port 443). In addition, they do not check if there are any malicious contents in the SOAP messages. As attackers generally manipulate SOAP messages for attacking Web services, it is inadequate for traditional network firewalls to protect the existing Web service architecture.

Web service-based intrusion detection and prevention systems may address this issue. They can monitor SOAP traffic and inspect the SOAP contents for anomaly behaviors or intrusion patterns. Malicious SOAP traffic, such as parameter tampering and SQL injection, should be denied before they travel to a critical system. In addition, they should validate syntax of SOAP messages and filter those with improper syntax such as oversized payloads. The systems may also provide access control based on different roles, groups, and responsibilities for preventing unauthorized use of Web services. For example, only authenticated business partners are allowed to view some of the restricted WSDL documents for critical Web services.

Future Trends

It is expected that new specifications and protocols will be defined as Web services technology evolve. Also, new applications related to Web services will be developed gradually. All these new technologies may introduce new vulnerabilities to the Web services architecture. It is required to examine every security aspect of the new Web services technologies. The study and analysis of potential attacks and their countermeasures is important in this issue. Automated testing or benchmarking tools may be developed for evaluating the security of the Web services.

Malicious codes such as viruses and worms spread across the existing network infrastructure, and result in a great deal of business loss. It may foresee that the Web services architecture will be another new avenue for the propagation of the malicious codes. Antivirus scanners should ensure that they have the ability to recognize malicious codes that embedded in XML documents as well as to control the propagation of malicious software within the Web services architecture (Negm, 2005).

Gutiérrez et al. (2004) stated that an XML vocabulary for expressing audit data and protocol for distributed audit processes may be defined as an extension to some existing security specifications. They also proposed that contingency protocols, security alerts management, and countermeasures need to be developed in the future. All these researches will be essential for building efficient intrusion detection and prevention systems in the Web services architecture.

Conclusion

Web services provide a framework for intersystem communication that enables flexible implementation and integration of e-business systems. However, there are risks for adopting Web services by enterprises if they do not address security challenges in the Web services architecture. Therefore, it is crucial for the developers and users to understand the security issues in Web services. This chapter is meant to provide a state-of-the-art view of security attacks and preventive countermeasures in Web services. We presented core components of Web services such as SOAP, WSDL, and UDDI. In addition, we briefly discussed their roles and operations. The inherently insecure nature of the Web services architecture is susceptible to numerous attacks. We also discussed these attacks and examined how attackers exploit vulnerabilities in the Web services architecture. Proper security schemes should be applied to counter these attacks. We presented these security countermeasures and specifications to protect Web services deployments in e-business. We also discussed some security issues to be addressed for future directions of Web services technology.

References

Beznosov, K., Flinn, D. J., Kawamoto, S., & Hartman, B. (2005). Introduction to Web services and their security. *Information Security Technical Report, 10*, 2-14.

Booth, D., Haas, H., McCabe, F., Newcomer, E., Champion, M., Ferris, C., et al. (Eds.). (2004). *Web services architecture* (W3C Working Group Note). Retrieved April 18, 2005, from http://www.w3.org/TR/2004/NOTE-ws-arch-20040211/

Booth, D., & Liu, C. K. (Eds.). (2005). *Web services description language (WSDL) version 2.0 part 0: Primer* (W3C Working Draft). Retrieved August 14, 2005, from http://www.w3.org/TR/2005/WD-wsdl20-primer-20050803

Bray, T., Paoli, J., Sperberg-McQueen, C. M., Maler, E., & Yergeau, F. (Eds.). (2004). *Extensible markup language (XML) 1.0 (Third Edition)* (W3C Recommendation). Retrieved May 16, 2005, from http://www.w3.org/TR/2004/REC-xml-20040204/

Byron, P., & Malhotra, A. (Eds.). (2004). *XML schema part 2: Datatypes* (W3C Recommendation). Retrieved April 18, 2005, from http://www.w3.org/TR/2004/REC-xmlschema-2-20041028

Cantor, S., Kemp, J., Philpott, R., & Maler, E. (Eds.). (2005). *Assertions and protocols for the OASIS security assertion markup language (SAML) V2.0* (OASIS Standard). Retrieved August 4, 2005, from http://docs.oasis-open.org/security/saml/v2.0/saml-core-2.0-os.pdf

Chinnici, R., Haas, H., Lewis, A., Moreau, J.-J., Orchard, D., & Weerawarana, S. (Eds.). (2005). *Web services description language (WSDL) version 2.0 part 2: Adjuncts* (W3C Working Draft). Retrieved August 14, 2005, from http://www.w3.org/TR/2005/WD-wsdl20-adjuncts-20050803

Chinnici, R., Moreau, J.-J., Ryman, A., & Weerawarana, S. (Eds.). (2005). *Web services description language (WSDL) version 2.0 part 1: Core language (W3C Working Draft)*. Retrieved August 14, 2005, from http://www.w3.org/TR/2005/WD-wsdl20-20050803

Clement, L., Hately, A., Riegen, C. von, & Rogers, T. (Eds.) (2004). *UDDI version 3.0.2* (UDDI Spec Technical Committee Draft). Retrieved May 16, 2005, from http://uddi.org/pubs/uddi-v3.0.2-20041019.htm

Damiani, E., De Capitani di Vimercati, S., Paraboschi, S., & Samarati, P. (2001, May 1-5). Fine grained access control for SOAP e-services. In V. Y. Shen, N. Saito, M. R. Lyu, & M. E. Zurko (Chair), *Proceedings of the 10th International Conference on World Wide Web* (pp. 504-513). Hong Kong, China. New York: ACM Press.

Damiani, E., De Capitani di Vimercati, S., Paraboschi, S., & Samarati, P. (2002). Securing SOAP e-services. *International Journal of Information Security, 1*(2), 100-115.

Eastlake, D., & Reagle, J. (Eds.). (2002). *XML encryption syntax and processing* (W3C Recommendation). Retrieved August 4, 2005, from http://www.w3.org/TR/2002/REC-xmlenc-core-20021210/

Eastlake, D., Reagle, J., & Solo, D. (Eds.). (2002). *XML-signature syntax and processing* (W3C Recommendation). Retrieved August 4, 2005, from http://www.w3.org/TR/2002/REC-xmldsig-core-20020212/

Faust, S. (2003). *SOAP Web services attack — Part 1: Introduction and simple injection.* Retrieved May 10, 2005, from http://www.spidynamics.com/whitepapers/ SOAP_Web_Security.pdf

Geuer-Pollmann, C., & Claessens, J. (2005). Web services and Web service security standards. *Information Security Technical Report, 10,* 15-24.

Gudgin, M., Hadley, M., Mendelsohn, N., Moreau, J.-J., & Nielsen, H. F. (Eds.). (2003a). *SOAP version 1.2 — Part 1: Messaging framework* (W3C Recommendation). Retrieved May 16, 2005, from http://www.w3.org/TR/2003/REC-soap12-part1-20030624/

Gudgin, M., Hadley, M., Mendelsohn, N., Moreau, J.-J., & Nielsen, H. F. (Eds.). (2003b). *SOAP version 1.2 part 2: Adjuncts* (W3C Recommendation). Retrieved May 16, 2005, from http://www.w3.org/TR/2003/REC-soap12-part2-20030624/

Gutiérrez, C., Fernández-Medina, E., & Piattini, M. (2004, May 14-17). A survey of Web services Security. In A. Laganà et al. (Eds.), *Computational science and its applications — ICCSA 2004, Proceedings of the International Conference on Computational Science and Its Applications — ICCSA 2004,* Assisi, Italy (LNCS 3043, pp. 968-977). Berlin: Springer.

Lindstrom, P. (2004). *Attacking and defending Web services.* Retrieved April 7, 2005, from http://forumsystems.com/papers/Attacking_and_Defending_WS.pdf

Mitra, N. (Ed.). (2003). *SOAP version 1.2 Part 0: Primer* (W3C Recommendation). Retrieved May 16, 2005, from http://www.w3.org/TR/2003/REC-soap12-part0-20030624/

Moses, T. (Ed.). (2005). *eXtensible access control markup language (XACML) version 2.0* (OASIS Standard). Retrieved August 4, 2005, from http://docs.oasis-open.org/ xacml/2.0/access_control-xacml-2.0-core-spec-os.pdf

Nadalin, A., Kaler, C., Hallam-Baker, P., & Monzillo, R. (Eds.). (2004). *Web services security: SOAP message security 1.0 (WS-Security 2004)* (OASIS Standard). Retrieved August 4, 2005, from http://docs.oasis-open.org/wss/2004/01/oasis-200401-wss-soap-message-security-1.0.pdf

Naedele, M. (2003). Standards for XML and Web services security. *IEEE Computer, 36*(4), 96-98.

Negm, W. (2004). *Anatomy of a Web services attack.* Retrieved April 26, 2005, from http://forumsystems.com/papers/Anatomy_of_Attack_wp.pdf

Negm, W. (2005). *XML malware: Controlling the propagation of malicious software within service oriented architectures.* Retrieved July 15, 2005, from http://forumsystems.com/papers/Forum_XML_Malware_wp_summer_05.pdf

Thompson, H., Beech, D., Maloney, M., & Mendelsohn, N. (Eds.). (2004). *XML schema part 1: Structures* (W3C Recommendation). Retrieved April 18, 2005, from http://www.w3.org/TR/2004/REC-xmlschema-1-20041028

Wilson, P. (2003). Web services security. *Network Security, 2003*(5), 14-16.

Chapter X

Verifiable Encryption of Digital Signatures Using Elliptic Curve Digital Signature Algorithm and its Implementation Issues

R. Anitha, PSG College of Technology, India

R. S. Sankarasubramanian, PSG College of Technology, India

Abstract

This chapter presents a new simple scheme for verifiable encryption of elliptic curve digital signature algorithm (ECDSA). The protocol we present is an adjudicated protocol, that is, the trusted third party (TTP) takes part in the protocol only when there is a dispute. This scheme can be used to build efficient fair exchanges and certified e-mail protocols. In this paper we also present the implementation issues. We present a new algorithm for multiplying two $2n$ bits palindromic polynomials modulo x^p-1 for prime $p = 2n + 1$ for the concept defined in Blake, Roth, and Seroussi (1998), and it is compared with the Sunar-Koc parallel multiplier given in Sunar and Koc (2001).

Finally, we conclude that the proposed multiplication algorithm requires $(2n^2 - n + 1)$ *XOR gates, which is 34% approximately extra as compared to* $1.5(n^2 - n)$ *XOR gates required by the Sunar-Koc parallel multiplier and 50% lesser than the speculated result* $4n^2$ *XOR gates given by Sunar and Koc (2001). Moreover, the proposed multiplication algorithm requires* $(2n^2 - n)$ *AND gates, as compared to* n^2 *AND gates, which is doubled that of the Sunar-Koc method.*

Introduction

This chapter provides a solution to the existing problems that occur in the Internet such as fair exchange problem, lack of e-mail certification and so forth. It in turn designs a new protocol that can be used to ensure e-mail certification and fairness. The protocol makes use of the upcoming systems that have been used for cryptography such as elliptic curve cryptosystems along with ECDSA — elliptic curve digital signatures. Hence, whenever the message is sent, an assurance is provided that the message has been properly delivered to the intended recipient. This is done through a three-pass key agreement protocol called ECMQV. The session key is obtained through this protocol. Domain parameters and shared secret key are transferred through protocol header between Alice and Bob. Once the signature is verified, message is transferred and the receipt is sent to Alice, after Bob receives the message. The main advantage of the protocol designed is it makes use of the trusted third party (TTP) only when there is a dispute. Hence, if Bob does not send the receipt, then Alice contacts the trusted entity. The TTP, after verification, sent a receipt to Alice in spite of Bob and pass this information to Bob. In this protocol Alice cannot retrieve a receipt from the TTP without revealing the message to Bob. The protocol fairness is built around the assumption that the sender Alice can verify that the verifiable encryption indeed contains a valid receipt. Only the trusted third party can recover the verifiable encryption. The scope of this protocol lies in the need of certified e-mail protocol. A fair exchange of digital signatures can be provided via verifiable encryption schemes. Whenever a message is sent over the Internet, there is no assurance that it will be delivered to the intended recipient. Even if the message has been delivered, the recipient may claim otherwise. This may be unpleasant, particularly in today's society where networked computers are increasingly being used to exchange items between distrusted parties.

In the real world, some form of simultaneity can be achieved. For instance, two parties can sign a contract *simultaneously* by holding the contract itself: One party will continue to hold the contract until the other party pays the cash. Similarly, when we buy an item from a store, the merchant could hold the item until we pay the amount. Unfortunately, physical proximity cannot be exploited in the digital world and exchanging items over the Internet is considered as a difficult problem, called the *fair exchange problem*. There have been several approaches to solve the fair exchange problem that are based on different definitions of fairness. Fairness is interpreted as *equal computational effort* by Even, et al. in 1985. In this paper, it is assumed that two parties, Alice and Bob, have equal computational power and they exchange their items bit by bit by taking turns. This approach does not require the intervention of a trusted third party but it involves many rounds of interactions. A probabilistic approach was adopted by Ben-Or, et al. in 1990, and in this paper, the probability of successfully completing the protocol is gradually increased after every round of interaction. Asokan et al. (Asokan, Shoup, & Waidner, 1998) introduced the *optimistic* approach. It relies on the existence of a trusted third party that is invoked only in case of an exception. As long as the two parties follow the exchange protocol, there is no need for the trusted party's intervention, but if one deviates from the protocol then the trusted party can easily restore fairness. This approach results in particularly efficient fair exchange protocols for generic items. Asokan et al. and Bao et al. in 1998 have built fair exchange protocols by means of *verifiable encryption* of digital signatures (i.e., a way of encrypting a signature under a designated public key and subsequently proving that the resulting ciphertext indeed contains such a signature). Camenisch and Damgard in 2000 generalized the schemes given by Asokan et al. (1998) so to achieve more efficient schemes that can be proved secure without relying on random oracles. In this paper we present a new simple scheme for verifiable encryption of elliptic curve digital signature algorithm (ECDSA).

Elliptic Curves

Elliptic curves as algebraic/geometric entities have been studied extensively for the past 150 years, and these studies contributed a rich and deep theory. Elliptic curve systems, as applied to cryptography, were first proposed in 1985 independently by Neal Koblitz from the University of Washington, and Victor Miller, who was then at IBM, Yorktown Heights.

Many cryptosystems often require the use of algebraic groups. Elliptic curves may be used to form elliptic curve groups. A group is a set of elements with custom-defined arithmetic operations on those elements satisfying some conditions. For elliptic curve groups, these specific operations are defined geometrically. Introducing more stringent properties to the elements of a group, such as limiting the number of points on such a curve, creates an underlying field for an elliptic curve group. Elliptic curves are first examined over real numbers in order to illustrate the geometrical properties of elliptic curve groups. Thereafter, elliptic curve groups are examined with the underlying fields of F_p (where p is a prime) and F_2m (a binary representation with 2^m elements).

Elliptic Curve Groups Over Real Numbers

An elliptic curve over real numbers may be defined as the set of points (x,y) that satisfy an elliptic curve equation of the form: $y^2 = x^3 + ax + b$, where x, y, a, and b are real numbers. Each choice of the numbers a and b yields a different elliptic curve. For example, a = -4 and b = 0.67 gives the elliptic curve with equation $y^2 = x^3 - 4x + 0.67$; the graph of this curve is shown in Figure 1. If $x^3 + ax + b$ contains no repeated factors, or equivalently if $4a^3 + 27b^2 \neq 0$, then the elliptic curve $y^2 = x^3 + ax + b$ can be used to form a group. An elliptic curve group over real numbers consists of the points on the corresponding elliptic curve, together with a special point O called the point at infinity.

Elliptic Curve Addition: A Geometric Approach

Elliptic curve groups are additive groups; that is, their basic operation is addition. The addition of two points in an elliptic curve is defined geometrically. The negative of a point $P = (xP, yP)$ is its reflection on the x-axis: the point -P is (xP,-yP). We can see that for each point P on an elliptic curve, the point -P is also on the curve under modular arithmetic.

Adding Distinct Points P and Q

Suppose that P and Q are two distinct points on an elliptic curve, and P is not -Q. To add the points P and Q, a line is drawn through the two points. This line will intersect the elliptic curve at another point, called -R. The reflection of the point -R on the x-axis is the point R. The law for addition in an elliptic curve group is $P + Q = R$, which is illustrated in Figure 2.

Adding the Points P and –P

The line through P and -P is a vertical line that does not intersect the elliptic curve at a third point; thus the points P and -P cannot be added as previously. It is for this reason that the elliptic curve group includes the point at infinity O, and $P + (-P) = O$ shown in Figure 3. As a result of this equation, $P + O = P$ in the elliptic curve group. O is called the additive identity of the elliptic curve group; all elliptic curves have an additive identity.

Figure 1.

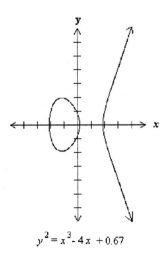

$$y^2 = x^3 - 4x + 0.67$$

Figure 2.

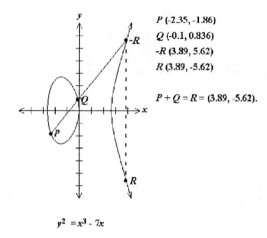

$$y^2 = x^3 - 7x$$

Doubling the Point P

To add a point P to itself, a tangent line to the curve is drawn at the point P. If

$yP \neq 0$, then the tangent line intersects the elliptic curve at exactly one other point, $-R$. $-R$ is reflected on the x-axis to R. The law for doubling a point on an elliptic curve group is defined by: $P + P = 2P = R$, which is shown in Figure 4.

If a point P is such that $yP = 0$, then the tangent line to the elliptic curve at P is vertical and does not intersect the elliptic curve at any other point. By definition, $2P = O$ for such a point P. If one wanted to find 3P in this situation, one can add $2P + P$. This becomes $P + O = P$. Thus $3P = P$. $4P = O$, $5P = P$, $6P = O$, $7P = P$, and so forth. Refer to Figure 5.

Figure 3.

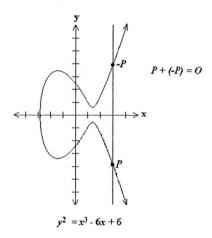

$$y^2 = x^3 - 6x + 6$$

Figure 4.

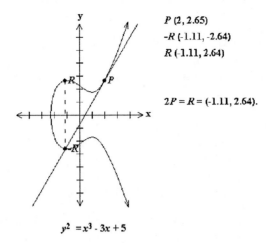

$P\ (2, 2.65)$

$-R\ (-1.11,\ -2.64)$

$R\ (-1.11,\ 2.64)$

$2P = R = (-1.11,\ 2.64).$

$y^2 = x^3 - 3x + 5$

Elliptic Curve Groups Over F_p

Calculations over the real numbers are slow and inaccurate due to round-off error. Cryptographic applications require fast and precise arithmetic; thus elliptic curve groups over the finite fields of F_p and F_2m are used in practice. We know that the field F_p uses the numbers from 0 to p - 1, and computations end by taking the remainder on division by p. An elliptic curve with the underlying field Fp can be formed by choosing the variables a and b within the field F_p. The elliptic curve includes all points (x,y) that satisfy the elliptic curve equation modulo p (where x and y are numbers in F_p).

Figure 5.

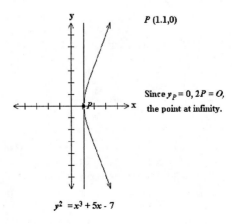

$P\ (1.1, 0)$

Since $y_P = 0, 2P = O,$
the point at infinity.

$y^2 = x^3 + 5x - 7$

Example

Consider an elliptic curve over the field F_{23} with a = 1 and b = 0. The elliptic curve equation is $y^2 = x^3 + x$. The point (9,5) satisfies this equation since: $y^2 \bmod 23 = x^3 + x \bmod 23 = 2$. The 23 points that satisfy this equation are: (0,0) (1,5) (1,18) (9,5) (9,18) (11,10) (11,13) (13,5) (13,18) (15,3) (15,20) (16,8) (16,15) (17,10) (17,13) (18,10) (18,13) (19,1) (19,22) (20,4) (20,19) (21,6) (21,17).

Arithmetic in an Elliptic Curve Group over F_p

There are several major differences between elliptic curve groups over F_p and over real numbers. Elliptic curve groups over F_p have a finite number of points, which is a desirable property for cryptographic purposes. The geometry used in elliptic curve groups over real numbers cannot be used for elliptic curve groups over F_p. However, the algebraic rules for the arithmetic can be adopted for elliptic curves over F_p. Unlike elliptic curves over real numbers, computations over the field of F_p involve no round-off error, which is an essential property required for a cryptosystem.

Adding Distinct Points P and Q

The negative of the point $P = (x_p, y_p)$ is the point $-P = (x_p, -y_p \bmod p)$. If P and $Q = (x_Q, y_Q)$ are distinct points such that P '•-Q, then $P + Q = R = (x_R, y_R)$:

$$x_R = s^2 - x_P - x_Q \bmod p \text{ and } y_R = -y_P + s(x_P - x_R) \bmod p$$

where $s = (y_P - y_Q) / (x_P - x_Q) \bmod p$ is the slope of the tangent PQ.

Doubling the Point P

Provided that $y_P \neq 0$, $2P = R = (x_R, y_R)$; $x_R = s^2 - 2x_P \bmod p$ and $y_R = -y_P + s(x_P - x_R) \bmod p$ where $s = (3x_P^2 + a) / (2y_P) \bmod p$ is the slope of the line through P and Q.

Elliptic Curve Groups over F_2m

Elements of the field F_2m are m-bit strings. The rules for arithmetic in F_2m can be defined by either polynomial representation or by optimal normal basis representation. Since F_2m operates on bit strings, computers can perform arithmetic in this field very efficiently. An elliptic curve with the underlying field F_2m is formed by choosing the elements a and b within F_2m (the only condition is that b ≠ 0). As a result of the field F_2m having a characteristic 2, the elliptic curve equation is slightly adjusted for binary representation: $y^2 + xy = x^3 + ax^2 + b$. The elliptic curve includes all points (x,y) that satisfy the elliptic curve equation over F_2m (where x and y are elements of F_2m). An elliptic curve group over F_2m consists of the points on the corresponding elliptic curve, together with a point at infinity O.

Example

As a very small example, consider the field F_24, defined by using polynomial representation with the irreducible polynomial $f(x) = x^4 + x + 1$. The element g = (0010) is a generator for the field. The powers of g are:

$g^0 = (0001)$, $g^1 = (0010)$, $g^2 = (0100)$, $g^3 = (1000)$, $g^4 = (0011)$, $g^5 = (0110)$, $g^6 = (1100)$, $g^7 = (1011)$, $g^8 = (0101)$, $g^9 = (1010)$, $g^{10} = (0111)$, $g^{11} = (1110)$, $g^{12} = (1111)$, $g^{13} = (1101)$, $g^{14} = (1001)$ and $g^{15} = (0001)$.

In a true cryptographic application, the parameter m must be large enough to preclude the efficient generation of such a table; otherwise the cryptosystem can be broken. In today's practice, m = 160 is a suitable choice. The table allows the use of generator notation (g^e) rather than bit string notation, as used in the following example. Also, generator notation allows multiplication without reference to the irreducible polynomial Consider the elliptic curve $y^2 + xy = x^3 + g^4x^2 + 1$. Here $a = g^4$ and $b = g^0 = 1$. The point (g^5, g^3) satisfies this equation over F_2m as:

$(g^3)^2 + g^5g^3 = (g^5)^3 + g^4g^{10} + 1$ i.e., $g^6 + g^8 = g^{15} + g^{14} + 1$ i.e., $(1100) + (0101) = (0001) + (1001) + (0001)$ and we get $(1001) = (1001)$.

The 15 points that satisfy this equation are:

$(1, g^{13}) (g^3, g^{13}) (g^5, g^{11}) (g^6, g^{14}) (g^9, g^{13}) (g^{10}, g^8) (g^{12}, g^{12}) (1, g^6) (g^3, g^8) (g^5, g^3) (g^6, g^8) (g^9, g^{10}) (g^{10}, g) (g^{12}, 0) (0, 1)$.

Arithmetic in an Elliptic Curve Group over F_2m

Elliptic curve groups over F_2m have a finite number of points, and their arithmetic involves no round-off error. This combined with the binary nature of the field F_2m, arithmetic can be performed very efficiently by a computer. The following algebraic rules are applied for arithmetic over F_2m.

Adding Distinct Points P and Q

The negative of the point $P = (xP, yP)$ is the point $-P = (xP, xP + yP)$. If P and $Q = (x_Q, y_Q)$ are distinct points such that P is not -Q, then $P + Q = R = (xR, yR)$

$xR = s^2 + s + xP + xQ + a$ and $yR = s(xP + xR) + xR + yP$

where $s = (yP - yQ) / (xP + xQ)$.

Doubling the Point P

If $xP = 0$, then $2P = O$, provided that $xP \neq 0$, $2P = R = (xR, yR)$ $xR = s^2 + s + a$ and $yR = xP^2 + (s + 1) * xR$ where $s = xP + yP / xP$.

Elliptic Curve Groups and the Discrete Logarithm Problem

At the foundation of every cryptosystem there is a hard mathematical problem that is computationally infeasible to solve. The discrete logarithm problem is the basis for the security of many cryptosystems including the elliptic curve cryptosystem. More specifically, the ECC relies upon the difficulty of the elliptic curve discrete logarithm problem (ECDLP). We examined two geometrically defined operations point additions and point doubling over certain elliptic curve groups. By selecting a point in an elliptic curve group, one can double it to obtain the point 2P. After that, one can add the point P to the point 2P to obtain the point 3P. The determination of a point nP in this manner is referred to as scalar multiplication of a point. The ECDLP is based upon the intractability of scalar multiplication.

In the multiplicative group Zp*, the discrete logarithm problem is, given elements r and q of the group, find a number k such that $r = qk \mod p$. If the elliptic curve group is described using multiplicative notation, then the elliptic curve discrete logarithm problem can be stated as shown in the example; given points P and Q in the group, find a number k such that $kP = Q$; k is called the discrete logarithm of Q to the base P.

Example

In the elliptic curve group defined by $y^2 = x^3 + 9x + 17$ over F_{23}, the discrete logarithm k of $Q = (4,5)$ to the base $P = (16,5)$ can be obtained as follows:

One way to find k is to compute multiples of P until Q is found. The first few multiples of P are P = (16,5), 2P = (20,20), 3P = (14,14), 4P = (19,20), 5P = (13,10), 6P = (7,3), 7P = (8,7), 8P = (12,17), 9P = (4,5). Since 9P = (4,5) = Q, the discrete logarithm of Q to the base P is k = 9. In a real application, k would be large enough such that it would be infeasible to determine k in this manner.

In any cryptosystem, authentication ensures the origin of the message or electronic document is correctly identified, with an assurance that the identity is not false. In elliptic curve cryptosystem, to provide authentication we use elliptic curve digital signature algorithm (ECDSA).

ECDSA Domain Parameters

1. a field size q, where either $q = p$, an odd prime, or $q = 2^m$;

2. an indication FR (field representation) of the representation used for the element of F_q;

3. (optional) a bit string *seedE* of length at least 160 bits, if the elliptic curve was generated verifiably at random;

4. two field elements a and b in F_q that define the equation of the elliptic curve E over F_q (i.e., $y^2 = x^3 + ax + b$ when $p > 3$, and $y^2 + xy = x^3 + ax^2 + b$ when $p = 2$);

5. two field elements x_G and y_G in F_q that define a finite point $G = (x_G, y_G)$ of prime order in $E(F_q)$;

6. the order n of the point G, with $n > 2^{160}$ and $n > 4\sqrt{q}$; and

7. the cofactor $h = \#E(F_q)/n$.

ECDSA Signature Generation and Verification

To sign a message m, an entity A with domain parameters $D = (q, FR, a, b, G, n, h)$ and associated key pair (d, Q) does the following:

1. Select a random or pseudorandom integer k, $1 \leq k \leq n-1$.

2. Compute $kG = (x_1, y_1)$ and $r = x_1 \mod n$. If $r = 0$ then go to step 1.

3. Compute $k^{-1} \mod n$.

4. Compute $e = SHA - 1(m)$ .//Secure Hash Algorithm//

5. Compute $s = k^{-1}(e + dr) \bmod n$. If $s = 0$ go to step 1.

6. A's signature for the message m is (r, s).

To verify A's signature (r, s) on m, B obtain an authentic copy of A's domain parameters $D = (q, FR, a, b, G, n, h)$ and associated public-key Q. B then does the following:

1. Verify that r and s are integers in the interval $[1, n-1]$.

2. Compute $e = SHA - 1(m)$.

3. Compute $w = s^{-1} \bmod n$.

4. Compute $u_1 = ew \bmod n$ and $u_2 = rw \bmod n$.

5. Compute $X = u_1 G + u_2 Q$. If $X = \infty$, then reject the signature, else compute $v = x_1 \bmod n$ where $X = (x_1, y_1)$.

6. Accept the signature if and only if $v = r$.

The following proof proves that the signature verification works correctly. If a signature (r, s) on a message m was indeed generated by A, then n. Rearranging gives n.

Thus, $u_1 G + u_2 Q = (u_1 + u_2 d)G = kG$ and so $v = r$ as required.

Verifiable Encryption using ECDSA

We will assume that the communication is carried over private and authenticated channels. The protocol provides fairness; specifically, it ensures that the sender receives the receipt if and only if the recipient will have the message in his mailbox within a finite period of time. Even in our protocol the TTP is invoked only in case of dispute. As long as both Alice and Bob follow the protocol steps, there is no need to involve the trusted entity in the protocol. This represents an improvement over the approach employed by online protocols, where a trusted entity is needed for each transaction. Moreover, the protocol is designed to make sure that Alice cannot misbehave. Only Bob is allowed to cheat by not sending the receipt in the last step. Since the sender initiates the exchange

Figure 6. Initialization phase

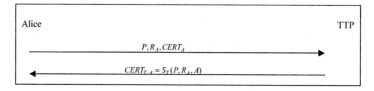

process, it appears natural to desire that the recipient of the message be relieved by any burden caused by malicious senders.

Whenever a message is sent to Bob, Alice will go for Initialization phase. In this phase, Alice sends her certificate along with the base point P and $R_A = k_A P$ to the TTP. The TTP sends its certificate $CERT_{T:A}$ to Alice. This certificate may be included as a proof when there is a dispute between Alice and Bob.

After the initialization phase, Alice undergoes the following protocol:

Procedure ECMQV – Goal: Alice and Bob establish a shared secret key.

- **Step 1:** Alice→Bob: A, R_A

  1.1   Alice selects $k_A \in R[1, n-1]$, computes $R_A = k_A P$, and sends A, R_A to Bob

- **Step 2:** Alice→Bob: $B, R_B, t_B = MAC_{k_1}(2, B, A, R_B, R_A)$

  Bob does the following:

  2.1   Perform an embedded public key validation of R_A

  2.2   Select $k_B \in R[1, n-1]$ and compute $R_B = k_B P$

  2.3   Compute7 $S_B = (k_B + \overline{R}_B d_B) \bmod n$ and $Z = hS_B(R_A + \overline{R}_A Q_A)$ where $\overline{R}_B$ is the x-coordinate of R_B and verify that $Z \neq \infty$.

  2.4 $(k_1, k_2) \leftarrow KDF(x_Z)$, where x_Z is the x-co-ordinate of Z. //KDF is a key derivation function that is constructed from a hash function H. If a key of l bits is required, then KDF(S) is defined to be the concatenation of the hash values H(S,i), where i is a counter that is incremented for each hash function evaluation until l bits of hash values have been generated.//

  2.5   Compute $t_B = MAC_{k_1}(2, B, A, R_B, R_A)$.

  2.6   Send B, R_B, t_B to Alice

- **Step 3:** Alice→Bob: $t_A = MAC_{k_1}(3, A, B, R_A, R_B)$

  Alice does the following:

  3.1   Perform an embedded public key validation of R_B.

  3.2   Compute $S_A = (k_A + \overline{R}_A d_A) \bmod n$ and $Z = hS_A(R_B + \overline{R}_B Q_B)$, and verify that $Z \neq \infty$

  3.3 $(k_1, k_2) \leftarrow KDF(x_Z)$,

  3.4   Compute $t = MAC_{k_1}(2, B, A, R_B, R_A)$ and verify that $t = t_B$

3.5   Compute $t_A = MAC_{k_1}(3, A, B, R_A, R_B)$ and send t_A to B.

Bob computes $t = MAC_{k_1}(3, A, B, R_A, R_B)$ and verifies that $t = t_A$. The session key is k_2.

Procedure transmitting the message — Goal: Alice transmits her message to Bob

- **Step 4:** Alice encrypts the message using the shared secret session key k_2 and signs the message using Alice secret key and sends it to Bob.
- **Step 5:** Alice sends a copy to TTP, which will never validate any thing until there is any dispute.
- **Step 6:** Bob verifies the signature using Alice's public key and decrypts the message using the shared secret key. Here a strong symmetric encryption algorithm should be used. On receiving the message, Bob should send a receipt to Alice.

If Bob denies that he has received any message from Alice, then Step 7 and Step 8 are required.

- **Step 7:** Alice and TTP establish a session key k using ECMQV and Alice encrypts $k_1, k_2, t_A, CERT_{T:A}$ using k and sends it to TTP. The TTP verifies and sends the receipt on behalf of Bob for that message.
- **Step 8:** Intimation will be passed to Bob stating that the receipt has been sent to Alice on behalf of Bob.

Figure 7. Verifiable encryption of an ECDSA signature

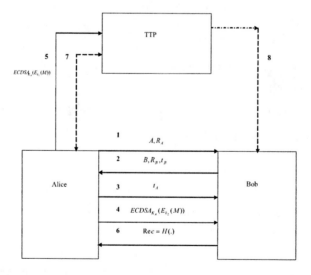

Explanation

ECMQV key agreement is a three-pass key agreement protocol that has been standard-ized in ANSI X9.63, IEEE 1363-2000, and ISO/IEC 15946-3. $D = (q, FR, S, a, b, P, n, h)$ are elliptic curve domain parameters, KDF is a key derivation function, and MAC is a message authentication code algorithm. If R is an elliptic curve point, then $\overline{R}$ is defined to be the integer $(\overline{x} \bmod 2^{\frac{f}{2}}) + 2^{\frac{f}{2}}$ where $\overline{x}$ is the integer representation of the x-coordinates of R, and $f = \log_2 n + 1$ is the bit length of n. The protocol can be viewed as an extension of the ordinary Diffie-Hellman key agreement protocol. The quantity $S_A = (k_A + \overline{R}_A d_A) \bmod n$ as an implicit signature for A's ephemeral public key R_A. It is a signature in the sense that the only person who can compute S_A is A, and is "implicit" in the sense that B indirectly verifies its validity by using $S_A P = R_A + \overline{R}_A Q_A$ when deriving the shared secret Z. Similarly, S_B is an implicit signature for B's ephemeral public key R_B. The shared secret is $Z = h S_A S_B P$ rather than $K_A K_B P$, as would be the case with ordinary Diffie-Hellman. Multiplication by h and the check $Z \neq \infty$ ensures that Z has order n and therefore is in $<P>$. We can note that Z is derived using the ephemeral public keys (R_A and R_B) as well as the long term public keys (Q_A and Q_B) of the two entities. The strings "2" and "3" are included in the MAC input in order to distinguish authentication tags created by the initiator A and responder B.

Successful verification of the authentication tags t_A and t_B convinces each entity that the other entity has indeed computed the shared secret Z (since computing the tags requires knowledge of k_1 and therefore also of Z), that the communications have not been tampered with (assuming that the MAC is secure), and that the other entity knows the identity of the entity with which it is communicating (since the identities are included in the message that are MAC ed.)

Comparison

We compare our work with Giuseppe and Atheniese (2004). They present a scheme for verifiable encryption of digital signature that uses RSA algorithm for their frame work. In their scheme, in case of dispute the TTP computes $H(m)^d$ from $\alpha = H(m)^{2d}$ by using the Euclidean algorithm, which is indeed an extra effort to give the judgment. Our protocol uses a session key by ECMQV that is proved to be a secure exchange. In case of dispute, Alice sends $k_1, k_2, t_A, CERT_{T:A}$ to TTP and the judgment is purely based on the verification of the parameters rather than calculations; hence, our scheme is simple and secure.

Implementation Issues

Arithmetic operations in the Galois field $GF(2^n)$ (i.e., addition, subtraction, multiplication, and inversion) have several applications in coding theory, computer algebra, and cryptography. In these applications, time-and area-efficient algorithms and hardware structures are desired for addition, multiplication, squaring, and exponentiation operations. The performance of these operations is closely related to the representation of the field elements. The finite field $GF(2^n)$ is a vector space of dimension n over binary field $GF(2)$. As such, it can be represented using any basis of n linearly independent elements of $GF(2^n)$ over $GF(2)$. Therefore, elements of $GF(2^n)$ are represented by binary vectors of length n. Field arithmetic is realized in all bases by a bit wise exclusive OR (XOR) operation, whereas the structure of field multiplication is determined by the choice of basis for the representation. There are many different bases of $GF(2^n)$ over $GF(2)$. Some bases lead to more efficient software or hardware implementations of the arithmetic in $GF(2^n)$ than other bases. ANSI X9.62 permits two kinds of bases: polynomial bases and normal bases. In Blake et al. (1998), they proposed a new type of representation of field elements called palindromic representation, but they have not given any explicit algorithm for multiplication of two palindromic polynomials. We present a new algorithm for that and compare the results with the existing one given in Sunar and Koc (2001).

Polynomial Basis Representations

The basis elements have the form $\{1, \omega, \omega^2, ...\omega^{n-1}\}$ where ω is a root in $GF(2^n)$ of an irreducible polynomial $P(x)$ of degree n over $GF(2)$. In an equivalent interpretation of this representation, the elements of $GF(2^n)$ are polynomials of degree at most n-1 over $GF(2)$, and arithmetic is carried out modulo an irreducible polynomial or otherwise called reduction polynomial $P(x)$ degree n over $GF(2)$. ANSI X9.62 specifies the following rules for selecting the reduction polynomial for representing the elements of $GF(2^n)$. If there exists an irreducible trinomial (a polynomial of the form $x^n + x^K + 1$ where $1 \leq k \leq n-1$) of degree n over $GF(2)$, then the reduction polynomial $P(x)$ must be an irreducible trinomial of degree n over $GF(2)$. To maximize the chances for interoperability, ANSI X9.62 recommends that the trinomials used should be $x^n + x^k + 1$ for the smallest possible k. If there does not exist an irreducible trinomial of degree n over $GF(2)$, then the reduction polynomial $P(x)$ must be an irreducible pentanomial (a polynomial of the form $x^n + x^c + x^b + x^a + 1$ where $1 \leq a \leq b < c \leq n-1$). To maximize the chances for interoperability, ANSI X9.62 recommends that the pentanomial used should be $x^n + x^c + x^b + x^a + 1$ chosen accordingly to the criteria c is as small as possible, for this particular value of c, b is as small as possible, and for these particular values of c and b, a is as small as possible.

Normal Basis Representations

The basis elements have the form $\{\alpha, \alpha^2, \alpha^{2^2}, ...\alpha^{2^{n-1}}\}$ for a certain element $\alpha \in GF(2^n)$. Normal basis representations have the computational advantages that squaring an element can be done very efficiently. Multiplying distinct elements, on the other hand, can be cumbersome in general. For this reason, ANSI X9.62 specifies that Gaussian normal bases (GNB) be used, for which multiplication is both simpler and more efficient. The type of a GNB is a positive integer T measuring the complexity of the multiplication operation with respect to that basis. Generally speaking, the smaller the type, the more efficient the multiplication. For a given n and T, the field $GF(2^n)$ can have at most one GNB of type T. A GNB exists whenever n is not divisible by 8. Let n be a positive integer not divisible by 8, and let T be a positive integer. Then a type T GNB for $GF(2^n)$ exists if and only if $p = Tn + 1$ is prime and $\gcd(Tn / k, m) = 1$, where k is the multiplicative order of 2 modulo p.

Optimal Normal Basis (ONB) Representations

The normal basis elements have the form $\{\alpha, \alpha^2, \alpha^{2^2}, .. \alpha^{2^{n-1}}\}$ for a certain element $\alpha \in GF(2^n)$. In addition, if for all $0 \le i_1 \ne i_2 \le n-1$ there exists j_1, j_2 such that $\alpha^{2^{j_1}+2^{j_2}} = \alpha^{2^{j_1}+2^{j_2}}$ the basis is called optimal. The element α is called the generator of the basis. Optimal normal basis exists for an infinite subset of values of n. The standard representation lends itself to efficient software implementation of the field arithmetic. In particular, multiplication can be made very efficient if the polynomial $P(x)$ is sparse, and inversion can be realized using the extended Euclidean algorithm. On the other hand, the ONB representation allows for efficient hardware implementation of field arithmetic. Inversion, however, remains a difficult operation in this case.

Palindromic Representation of Field Elements

In Blake et al. (1998), palindromic representation has been introduced. Let $p = 2n + 1$ be a prime and either 2 is primitive modulo p or $p \equiv 3 \pmod 4$ and the multiplicative order of 2 modulo p is n hold. For such values of n, let γ be a pth root of unity in $GF(2^{2n})$. Let ϕ denote vector space of all polynomials over $GF(2)$ of the form $a(x) = \sum_{i-1}^{n} a_i x^i$ where $a_i = a_{p-i}$ for $i = 1, 2 ... n$, such polynomials are called palindromic polynomials. In palindromic representation, of $GF(2^n)$, each element is represented as a palindromic polynomial. Addition is defined as the ordinary polynomial addition of elements in ϕ and the product of two palindromic polynomials $a(x), b(x) \in \phi$ is the unique polynomial $c(x) \in \phi$ such that $c(x) \equiv a(x).b(x) \mod(x^p - 1)$. As for inversion, the palindromic representation allows the use of the extended Euclidean algorithm to find the inverse of the palindromic polynomial $a(x) \mod x^p - 1$, from which the inverse in ONB representation is easily derived. The Euclidean algorithm admits efficient implementation in both hardware and software.

We prose the following multiplication algorithm to multiply two $2n$ bits palindromic polynomials modulo $x^p - 1$ for prime $p = 2n + 1$ for the concept defined in Blake et al. (1998).

Multiplication algorithm: $GF(2^n) = \{(a_1 a_2 ... a_n) : a_i \in \{0,1\}\}$

$$GF(2^{2n}) = \{(a_1 a_2 ... a_n a_{n+1} ... a_{2n}) : a_i \in \{0,1\}\} \text{ where } a_i = \begin{cases} a_i; 1 \le i \le n \\ a_{2n+1-i}; n+1 \le i \le 2n \end{cases}$$

We represent any element $A, B \in GF(2^n)$ of n bits as a $2n$ bit in $GF(2^{2n})$

Let $A, B \in GF(2^{2n})$ $A = (a_1 a_2 ... a_{2n})$, $B = (b_1 b_2 .. b_{2n})$

- **Step 1:** Compute $C_j = \sum_{i=1}^{j-1} a_i b_{j-i}$ where $j = 2...2n$ and $C = (0 c_2 c_3 ... c_{2n})$

- **Step 2:** Compute C' the reverse of C, i.e., $C' = (c_{2n} ... c_3 c_2 0)$

- **Step 3:** Compute $C' \oplus C$ which is the product AB

Analysis

The number of XOR gates in Step 1 is $1 + 2 + ... + (2n - 2) = 2n^2 - 3n + 1$

The number of XOR gates in Step 3 is $2n$

Therefore, the total number of XOR gates is $2n^2 - n + 1$

The number of AND gates in this procedure is yielded by $1 + 2 + ... + (2n - 1) = 2n^2 - n$

Example

Consider the case $n = 6$ so that $p = 2n + 1 = 13$, which is prime.

We represent any element $A, B \in GF(2^n)$ of n bits as a $2n$ bit in $GF(2^{2n})$; therefore,

the formed closure set $GF(2^{2(6)}) = :\{000000000000, 000001100000, 000010010000,$
000011110000, 000100001000, 000101101000, 000110011000, 000111111000, 001000000100,
001001100100, 001010010100, 001011110100, 001100001100, 001101101100, 001110011100,
001111111100, 010000000010, 010001100010, 010010010010, 010011110010, 010100001010,
010101101010, 010110011010, 010111111010, 011000000110, 011001100110, 011010010110,
011011110110, 011100001110, 011101101110, 011110011110, 011111111110, 100000000001,
100001100001, 100010010001, 100011110001, 100100001001, 100101101001, 100110011001,
100111111001, 101000000101, 101001100101, 101010010101, 101011110101, 101100001101,
101101101101, 101110011101, 101111111101, 110000000011, 110001100011, 110010010011,

110011110011, 110100001011, 110101101011, 110110011011, 110111111011, 111000000111, 111001100111, 111010010111, 111011110111, 111100001111, 111101101111, 111110011111, 111111111111}

Let $A = (010101101010)$ and $B = (011011110110)$

Step 1: Compute $C_j = \sum_{i=1}^{j-1} a_i b_{j-i}$ where $j = 2...2n$ and $C = (0c_2c_3...c_{2n})$

$C_2 = a_1b_1 = 0.0 = 0$
$C_3 = a_1b_2 + a_2b_1 = 0.1 + 1.0 = 0$
$C_4 = a_1b_3 + a_2b_2 + a_3b_1 = 0.1 + 1.1 + 0.0 = 1$
$C_5 = a_1b_4 + a_2b_3 + a_3b_2 + a_4b_1 = 0.0 + 1.1 + 0.1 + 1.0 = 1$
$C_6 = a_1b_5 + a_2b_4 + a_3b_3 + a_4b_2 + a_5b_1 = 0.1 + 1.0 + 0.1 + 1.1 + 0.0 = 1$
$C_7 = a_1b_6 + a_2b_5 + a_3b_4 + a_4b_3 + a_5b_2 + a_6b_1 = 0.1 + 1.1 + 0.0 + 1.1 + 0.1 + 1.0 = 0$
$C_8 = a_1b_7 + a_2b_6 + a_3b_5 + a_4b_4 + a_5b_3 + a_6b_2 + a_7b_1 = 0.1 + 1.1 + 0.1 + 1.0 + 0.1 + 1.1 + 1.0 = 0$
$C_9 = a_1b_8 + a_2b_7 + a_3b_6 + a_4b_5 + a_5b_4 + a_6b_3 + a_7b_2 + a_8b_1 = 0.1 + 1.1 + 0.1 + 1.1 + 0.0 + 1.1 + 1.1 + 0.0 = 0$
$C_{10} = a_1b_9 + a_2b_8 + a_3b_7 + a_4b_6 + a_5b_5 + a_6b_4 + a_7b_3 + a_8b_2 + a_9b_1 = 0.0 + 1.1 + 0.1 + 1.1 + 0.1 + 1.0 + 1.1 + 0.1 + 1.0 = 1$
$C_{11} = a_1b_{10} + a_2b_9 + a_3b_8 + a_4b_7 + a_5b_6 + a_6b_5 + a_7b_4 + a_8b_3 + a_9b_2 + a_{10}b_1 = 1$
$C_{12} = a_1b_{11} + a_2b_{10} + a_3b_9 + a_4b_8 + a_5b_7 + a_6b_6 + a_7b_5 + a_8b_4 + a_9b_3 + a_{10}b_2 + a_{11}b_1 = 1$

$C = (000111000111)$

Step 2: Compute C^1 the reverse of C i.e. $C^1 = (c_{2n}...c_3c_20)$

$C^1 = (111000111000)$

Step 3: Compute $C^1 \oplus C$, which is the product AB

Product of $010101101010 * 011011110110 = 111111111111$

No of XOR gates $= 2(6*6)-6+1 = 67$

No of AND gates $= 2(6*6)-6 = 66$

Comparisons

Let $fx(n) = 2n^2 - n + 1$ and $gx(n) = 1.5 n^2 - n$ denote the number of XOR gates required using our proposed multiplication algorithm and Sunar-Koc parallel multiplier algorithm respectively. The comparison shows that the proposed multiplication algorithm requires 34% approximately extra XOR gates when compared to Sunar-Koc algorithm. Let $fa(n) = 2 n^2 - n$ and $ga(n) = n^2$ denote the number of AND gates required using our proposed multiplication algorithm and Sunar-Koc parallel multiplier algorithm respectively. The comparison shows that the proposed multiplication algorithm requires twice the number of extra XOR gates when compared to Sunar-Koc algorithm. The graph for these comparisons is shown in Figure 8.

Moreover, in Sunar and Koc (2001), the speculated results are given as $4 n^2$, we made a comparison with the proposed result and the speculated result and found that our

Figure 8. XOR and AND gates comparisons

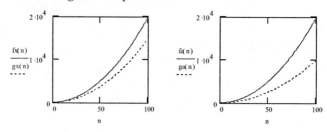

Figure 9. XOR Gates comparisons proposed result and speculated result

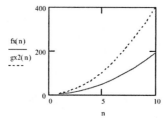

Figure 10. XOR Gates comparisons proposed result and Sunar-Koc

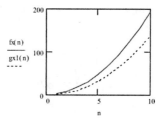

algorithm requires 50% lesser XOR gates than the speculated results. The graph for these comparisons is shown in Figure 9.

Conclusion

This chapter presented simple and particularly very efficient verifiable encryption protocols designed for digital signatures. These protocols can be used as building blocks in the design of efficient fair exchange of digital signatures and certified e-mail protocols. We have presented an explicit algorithm for multiplying two 2m-length polynomials modulo $x^p - 1$. We compare this algorithm to the one presented by Sunar and Koc (2001). The proposed multiplication algorithm requires $(2n^2 - n + 1)$ XOR gates, which is approximately 34% extra as compared to $1.5(n^2 - n)$ XOR gates required by the Sunar-Koc parallel multiplier and 50% lesser than the speculated result $4n^2$ given by Sunar and Koc (2001). Moreover, our multiplication algorithm requires $(2n^2 - n)$ AND gates, as compared to n^2 AND gates, which is doubled that of Sunar-Koc method. The result shows that representing the field elements in palindromic form is very costly. The XOR gates are increased approximately to 34% and AND gates are doubled.

References

Asokan, N., Shoup, V., & Waidner, M. (1998). Optimistic fair exchange of digital signatures. *IEEE on Selected Areas in Communications, 18*(4), 593-610.

Bao, R., Deng, R. H., & Mao. W. (1998). Efficient and practical fair exchange protocol with off-line TTP. In *IEEE on Symposium on Security and Privacy*. Oakland, CA: IEEE.

Ben-Or, M., Goldreich, O., Micali, S., & Riverst, R. (1990). A fair protocol for signing contracts. *IEEE Transactions of Information Theory IT-36, 1*, 40-46.

Blake, I. F., Roth, R. M., & Seroussi, G. (1998). *Efficient arithmetic in GF(2ⁿ) through palindromic representation*. Hewlett-Packard, HPL-98-134.

Camenisch, J., & Damgard, I.B. (2000). Verifiable encryption group encryption, and their applications to separable group signatures and signature sharing schemes. In *Advances in Cryptology — ASIACRYPT'00*. Lecture notes in Computer Science, 1976, 331-335. Berlin: Springer-Verlag.

Camenisch, J., & Michels, M. (1999*)*. Separability and efficiency for generic group signature schemes. In *Advances in Cryptology — Crypto'99*.

Even, S., Goldreich, O., & Lempel, A. (1985). A randomized protocol for signing contracts. *Communications of the ACM 28, 6*, 637-647.

Giuseppe & Atheniese. (2004). Verifiable encryption of digital signatures and applications. *ACM Transactions of Information and System Security, 7*(1), 1-20.

Lidl, R., & Niederreiter, H. (1983). Finite fields. In G. C. Rota (Ed.), *Encyclopedia of Mathematics and its Applications*. Addison-Wesley.

Menezes, A. J. (Ed.) Blake, I. F., Gao, X., Mullin, R. C. Vanstone, S. A., & Yaghoobian, T. (1993). *Applications of finite fields*. Boston: Kluwer.

Naccache, D., & Stern, J. (1998). A new public key cryptosystem based on higher residues. *Fifth ACM Conference on Computer and Communications Security* (pp. 59-66). ACM Press.

Schnorr, C. P. (1991). Efficient signature generation by smart-cards. *Journal of Cryptology, 4*(3), 161-174.

Sunar, B., & Koc, C. K. (2001). An efficient optimal normal basis Type II multiplier. *IEEE Transactions on Computers, 50*(1), 83-87.

Chapter XI

An Introductory Study on Business Intelligence Security

Chan Gaik Yee, Multimedia University, Malaysia

G. S. V. Radha Krishna Rao, Multimedia University, Malaysia

Abstract

Firstly, the fact that business intelligence (BI) applications are growing in importance, and secondly, the growing and more sophisticated attacks launched by hackers, the concern of how to protect the knowledge capital or databases that come along with BI or in another words, BI security, has thus arisen. In this chapter, the BI environment with its security features is explored, followed by a discussion on intrusion detection (ID) and intrusion prevention (IP) techniques. It is understood through a Web-service case study that it is feasible to have ID and IP as countermeasures to the security threats; thus further enhancing the security of the BI environment or architecture.

Introduction

Over the years, business intelligence (BI) has evolved to become sets of technically sophisticated but user-friendly tools for efficiently extracting useful and intelligent information from huge volumes of data. This consequently has enabled users who are not so technically inclined to have easy access to the data, analyze them, and draw useful conclusions from them. Basically, what a BI system does is to query a data source (the data source may be from sales and marketing, customers, partners, suppliers, or even competitor related), use data mining techniques to analyze the extracted information, report the results of analysis, and thus enable the users to make timely and accurate decisions. With the rise of e-commerce, more users have become encouraged to utilize BI in the real-time, Web-based world. For instance, an online retailer could make use of BI to analyze data in real time to determine whether customer purchasing patterns or market conditions have changed For example, if a customer buys more than a certain amount of a product alerted by the BI system, then the online retailer could immediately offer a quantity-based discount to encourage further big purchases.

As BI databases can be centralized in a shared server, it is therefore cost-effective to let hundreds and thousands of users (including mobile users) access the BI database without geographical boundaries. Consequently, more and more organizations see the benefits of utilizing BI and the importance of BI, which is a process of turning data into information and then into knowledge about the customers, competitors, conditions, and economics in the industry, technology, and cultural trends. As a result of this, focus on BI has to be shifted from enhancing the data-warehousing and data-mining techniques such as OLAP (online analytical processing), OLAM (online analytical mining), multi-dimensional modeling, design methodologies, optimization, indexing, and clustering techniques (Golfarelli, Rizzi, & Cella, 2004; Hu & Cercone, 2002), to how to securely protect these knowledge capitals from being tampered with by unauthorized use.

Another reason why a BI system has to have maximum security is due to the various security threats and malicious attacks that hackers can launch nowadays. Security threats such as denial of service, malicious or virus attack, "Sniffer" attack, "Evil Twins" attack, dictionary attack, and buffer overflow attack, just to name a few, are impossible to be eliminated completely as these attacks can be launched from the interface/perimeter, network, host, or even the application.

Take for example, denial of service attack. It is launched through overwhelming the network connections with massive traffic, usually in the form of fake IP addresses. When the server is full and has reached the maximum capacity with fake connections, the real and authorized users are denied service or access to the network or system.

Attack from another aspect, for example malicious or virus attack, could cripple the computer or operating system by generating malicious programs and at the same time, destroying, deleting, altering files and databases, and so on.

For wired networks, a hacker could make use of a "sniffer," a tool to wiretap or eavesdrop on a computer network; thus grabbing information off the communication line. Even for the wireless, "Evil Twins" could disguise as hot spots; thus stealing important information such as user ID and password directly from the wireless system.

In dictionary attack, invaders make use of common usernames and passwords to try to get entry into systems. Common passwords or combinations of characters are encrypted into a dictionary. These encrypted words are then used to compare with those in the system under attack until a match is found. Although this may take weeks or months to be successful, the vulnerability is there for it to become a brute force attack, in which case spam e-mails may be generated while the mail server is opened for such attack.

A fault in the program or application that leads to buffer overflow may create an opportunity for a hacker to overwrite the original code. This kind of buffer overflow attack can cause files to be altered, data to be lost, or even the server to be disabled entirely.

Although measures such as frequently updating security software and applying security patches for operating systems, using antivirus software to block out viruses and worms, firewalls to keep out of the untrusted sites, have more security features for the Web browser, and so on, just to name a few, are in place, but they are not sufficient and safe enough to protect BI, the knowledge capital of an organization, against these security vulnerabilities.

Knowing the fact that BI is too precious to be tampered with by unauthorized use, and too invaluable to be lost or destroyed through security threats, an enhanced BI security framework is, indeed, urgently called for.

Literature Summary

Before any recommendations for an enhanced security framework for BI could be put forward, let us examine first the existing BI environment and its security. After discussing the feasibilities of using intrusion detection and intrusion protection for BI, an enhanced BI security framework based on a Web-service case study is then proposed.

BI Environment and Security

Currently, as depicted in Diagram 1, the BI environment as mentioned in Gangadharan and Swami (2004) Xie et al. (Xie, Xu, Sha, Li, & Liu, 2001), Spil et al. (Spil, Stegwee, & Teitink, 2002), and Soper (2005), could be built up from several layers, namely

- **Business domain layer:** This layer consists of legacy, OLTP (online transaction processing) systems, and so on.
- **Source data layer:** This layer consists of data gathered, extracted, and updated from business domain layer.
- **Data warehouse (data mart) layer:** This layer consists of cleaned, filtered, integrated, transformed data (information) stored and loaded in various data marts.
- **Knowledge capital layer:** This layer consists of BI applications such as:
  - HRM (human resource management)
  - ERP (enterprise resource planning)
  - CRM (customer relationship management)
  - SCM (supply chain management)
  - DSS (decision support system)
  - E-commerce (e.g., B2B, B2C)
- **Users layer:** This layer consists of internal and external users such as employees, customers, partners, suppliers, and the general public accessing the knowledge capital layer through LAN/WAN/WWW/WIRELESS.

Figure 1. BI environment

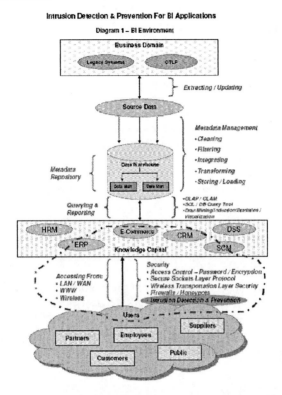

As can be seen from the diagram, users have several channels of accessing or reaching the knowledge capital of the organization. Although currently, as mentioned in Ortiz (2002), security approaches such as the use of password authentication and encryption, the secure sockets layer protocol for Web transactions, and wireless transportation layer security for wireless application protocol are in place, but there is a great need to ensure the knowledge capital is secure and deterred from being unduly accessed. Thus, another layer, the security layer, is to be included between the knowledge capital and user layer. Currently, this security layer encompasses existing security approaches categorized into five protective shields namely physical, system, application/DBMS, Web server, and network, as seen in information builders (2002). To further enhance this security layer, another protective shield coupled with intrusion detection and prevention techniques is required to protect the knowledge capital of the organization.

An Enhanced Security Framework for BI

After exploring what the existing environment and security framework could offer for BI, it was found that there is a feasibility of incorporating a security layer coupled with intrusion detection and prevention shield for enhancing the existing BI security framework.

The proposed enhanced security layer should therefore consist of six protective shields, namely, the physical shield, system shield, application/DBMS shield, Web server shield, network shield, intrusion detection and prevention (ID & IP) shield.

Physical Shield

This protective shield represents a physical barrier between the users and the network and system resources. These barriers could be in the form of biometrics, for example, finger print, hand signature, facial features, voice, or actual physical object such as a smart card. They are used to authenticate and verify the authorized access to the organization's network and system.

System Shield

Security measures at this layer are provided at the operating system level and enforced at the user's entry point into local or shared resources (example, using user id and password for authentication). It can also be enforced on a system where application services are being requested (for example, allowing a certain user group to gain access to a particular domain or application).

Application/DBMS shield

After passing through the physical and system shields for authentication, as mentioned previously, this application/DBMS shield should provide protection for data integrity. Data from data warehouse could be stored in an encrypted form, and encryption and decryption is done using asymmetric keys as described in Spil et al. (2002), where private keys are for decryption and public keys for encryption. Besides encryption, and to further ensure data integrity, protection should incorporate control over access to these data by the following levels of protection as mentioned in Pilot Software (2002):

- **Data-level** protects data from unauthorized access to tables, columns, and values.
- **Report-level** assigns multiple users or groups to a single or multiple Domain(s) so as to limit the access privileges of the users to within their domain(s) for viewing/ querying reports, and so on.
- **Role-level** access privileges are based on the role of users within their domain or group.
- **Functional-level** grants or limits the ability of the users or groups to utilize certain functional features or capabilities.

Web Server Shield

The Web server shield could make use of secure socket layer (SSL) features such as digital signatures to verify the identity of the client and the server, and encryption of data to prevent eavesdropping and to protect the integrity of the data. For example, to ensure secure communication or connection, all content indexing or querying should be encrypted using secure socket layer (SSL) coupled with HTTP or S-HTTP authentication. This can be augmented by using LDAP (lightweight directory access protocol), whereby user authentication information is located in a central directory; thus providing a useful route for single sign-on.

Network Shield

Firewalls could be used to implement a security policy between networks so as to create a secure boundary between untrusted external networks and trusted internal networks. Firewalls could be complimented with packet filters that operate on the IP level, scanning the headers of each IP packet crossing the firewalls and comparing its characteristics to a fixed set of rules.

However, traditional firewalls can only filter on the packet level, not on the content level. In order to filter on the content level, XML firewalls are to be used. XML firewalls will examine SOAP (simple object access protocol) headers and XML tags, and based on what they find, block any dangerous or unauthorized content or services from getting inside the enterprise.

Intrusion Detection and Prevention (ID & IP) Shield

Intrusion detection systems (IDS) mainly set off an alarm when an intrusion is detected, while intrusion prevention systems (IPS) shall prevent the attack before it happens. Thus, these protective shields shall ensure that whatever is passing through the security layer is genuine and authorized user's access, and unauthorized usage of the system shall be barred.

These shields should work to compliment each other, for example, as mentioned in Baroudi et al. (Baroudi, Ziade, & Mounla, 2004), to exchange secure data over the Internet, we can implement secure protocols like IPsec, SSL, and IPv6. To authenticate authorized users, password and encryption can be used. The use of firewalls could reduce the amount of bad traffic that can reach IDS and IPS; hence reducing false alarms and suspicious data. Honeypot could be used to gather as much information as possible for IDS and IPS, and to divert hackers from productive system.

A Survey on ID and IP Techniques

In order to have the best ID and IP techniques to be incorporated in the enhanced BI security framework, continuous research in this area is ongoing. And, before embarking on the ID and IP research bandwagon, a survey of the existing ID and IP techniques for its feasibility to be incorporated into existing BI security framework is firstly being carried out.

Currently, commercial tools do exist and provide intrusion detection capabilities such as using an alerting mechanism that notifies administrators that the system is potentially under attack. One of the features, as in Entrust (2003), for example, is setting the threshold value for failed login within a certain time period; if these threshold values are exceeded, the account will be locked out. However, more efficient and effective intrusion detection and prevention techniques are required to counter the ever-changing, sophisticated attacks launched by the hackers.

Intrusion Detection Techniques

Generally, there are two approaches for intrusion detection, namely signature based and anomaly based. Signature-based or misuse detection employs pattern matching to match attack signatures with observed data, making it ideal for detecting known attacks. However, its disadvantage is that it is not able to detect truly new or innovative attacks.

Anomaly-based detection uses machine-learning techniques to create a profile of normal system behavior and uses this profile to detect deviations from the normal behavior (Joglekar & Tate, 2004). Contrary to misuse detection, anomaly detection can detect new intrusions without prior knowledge. However, this also causes a high false-positive rate. Moreover, these approaches are difficult to establish, require intensive resources, cause data overload, create high false-positive rate or negative rates (Yin, Li, Ma, & Sun, 2004), and so on. Although prevention mechanisms such as distributed certificate authorities using threshold cryptography, message authentication code to ensure integrity of route request packets, using hash chains to authenticate routing updates sent by a distance-vector protocol (Deng, Zeng, & Agrawal, 2003) are in place, however, there is no perfect or close to perfect IDS and IPS yet to counter against intrusion!

Basically, the main areas for research and improvement on techniques revolve around data collection, data analysis, response/pattern matching, machine-learning/retrain data, network protocol (wired/ wireless), encryption/cryptography, and authentication

For example in Joglekar and Tate (2004), it was mentioned that a new approach, specification-based detection, has been applied to address the problem of high false positives. In this approach, manually developed specifications are used to characterize the legitimate system behavior, rather than relying on machine-learning techniques to learn the normal behavior, thus eliminating false positives caused by legitimate but previously unseen behavior.

In another study by a researcher mentioned in Joglekar and Tate (2004), dynamic analysis of security protocols, rather than a static analysis, enables detection of a certain class of attacks on cryptographic protocols. This technique is based on protocol-oriented state-based attack detection that reconstructs protocol sessions in terms of state models and matches these with previously generated attack state models to detect attacks.

A step further for researchers, Joglekar and Tate (2004) introduce another approach that detects attacks on protocols embedded in encrypted sessions by integrating monitoring into processes taking part in the protocols. This approach provides the ability to move data collection and analysis off the host to a central protocol monitor process to make it possible to correlate alerts in order to further reduce the false alarm rate and to detect network-wide attack patterns in encrypted packets. Embedding the monitoring into the protocol processes also helps to eliminate the need for inspection at the network level.

The use of protocol specifications in this approach enables manual characterization of legitimate behavior rather than learning the normal behavior by observing data over a period of time, thus eliminating false positives caused by behavior that are legitimate but absent in the training data.

In an attempt to eliminate problems of high false alarms rate, data overload, and intensive use of resources, researchers in Yin et al. (2004) have introduced a honeypot port-scan detection technique to lure hackers into attacking a seemingly vulnerable but well observed system so as to learn and capture more information about the tactics and tools used by the hackers. Under this detection scheme, an unused IP is assigned to the honeypot; when the attacker accesses it, the honeypot reacts like normal but is actually recording and transferring packets into a scan plug-in devise. The plug-in then uses a predefined algorithm to analyze the properties of the packets. If it is identified as an attack, alerts will be sent to the console and the malicious packet is logged in the local machine as well as the remote server immediately. It was recorded that this technique can detect scan activity with high veracity and less time.

It has been a fact that wireless ad hoc networks are more vulnerable to attacks than conventional wired networks due to their characteristics of being open medium and dynamic topology. In view of this, researchers in Deng et al. (2003) have introduced a real-time intrusion detection system suitable for ad hoc wireless networks. In this approach, there are two models: the distributed hierarchical system model, and the completely distributed system model. For the distributed hierarchical model, the entire network is logically divided into several clusters, each consisting of cluster head and cluster members. Since the cluster members do not have the multihop routing capabilities, they will route the packets via the cluster head nodes, which collects detection results from other clusters. Final decision is then based on a predefined cooperative rule. For the completely distributed system model, every node takes part in the intrusion detection process. Each node is responsible for detecting intrusion locally and independently based on the data collected. When a malicious node is found by the local detector, it is broadcasted to the entire network. Each node also makes a final decision based on the detection reports from other nodes. Once a malicious node is confirmed to be detected, an alarm is propagated in the whole network. Simulation results using these two models have shown a higher detection accuracy.

In Manganaris et al. (Manganaris, Christensen, Zerkle, & Hermiz, 1999) and Huang et al. (Huang, Kao, Hun, Jai, & Lin, 2005), data-mining techniques are employed to screen and analyze alerts of attacks. Experiments conducted using data-mining techniques in analysis of alarms showed results that perform very well on attack-detection rate and false-alarm rate. Basically in this approach, a data-mining tool is used to classify records by analyzing historical data and feedback from incident resolutions. From this constantly updated knowledge base, once an attack is recognized, a decision engine or rule tuner will run automatically according to a machine-learning algorithm and tune or adjust the parameters or thresholds to block the attack from the source.

Intrusion Prevention Techniques

As intrusion prevention techniques mainly concentrate on authentication, there are four major approaches for code security that have emerged as mentioned in Drinic and Kirovski (2004): code signing, sandboxes, firewall, and proof-carrying code.

- **Code signing:** Signing a program binary for authentication purposes is conceptually the simplest code security technique. In this case, authentication is done according to standardized authentication protocols.

- **Sandbox:** Sandbox is designed at the security layer to protect the application against malicious users and the host from malicious applications.

- **Firewall:** Firewalling technique is used for code security to conduct comprehensive examination of the provided program at the very point where it enters the respective domain.

- **Proof carrying code:** This is a mechanism by which the host system can determine with certainty that it is safe to execute a program provided by a distrusted source. This is accomplished by requesting that the source provides a security proof that attests to the code's adherence to a host-defined security policy.

Performance results based on these approaches are not satisfactory for overcoming buffer overflow exploit; therefore, researchers in Drinic and Kirovski (2004) provided a hardware-assisted intrusion prevention platform that makes use of overlapping of program execution and MAC (message authentication code) verification. This platform partitions a program binary into blocks of instructions. Each block is signed using a keyed MAC that is attached to the footer of the block. When the control flow reaches a particular block, its instructions are speculatively executed, while dedicated hardware verifies the attached MAC at run-time. In the case that the integrity check fails, the current process will be aborted by the processor. Together with a software optimization technique that aims at reducing the performance overhead incurred due to run-time MAC verification, this platform had shown an overhead reduction of up to 90% from experimental results.

As mentioned in Reynolds et al. (Reynolds, Just, Clough, & Maglich, 2003), security related faults such as in design, programs, and configuration could propagate from machine to machine and are likely to be repeatable in time; thus, demanding more innovative and improved fault diagnosis, machine learning, and system adaptation techniques for intrusion prevention. The approach used in Reynolds et al. (2003), therefore, is to augment the standard fault-tolerant techniques such as failure detection, failfast semantics, redundancy, and failover with active defenses and design diversity. Using this approach, repeatable errors are prevented by an out-of-band control system that modifies the system security posture in response to detected errors.

In short, the approach is built with hardware and software setups that compliment each other. The hardware is configured in such a way that there is no direct communication possible between the primary and backup. The potential for propagation from the primary to the out-of-band (OOB) machine is limited by constraining and monitoring the services and protocols by which OOB communicates with the primary. Failover is controlled by the mediator/adapter/controller (MAC) on the OOB machine. When failure occurs, possibly caused by intrusion, continued service to the end user is provided by promoting the backup to be the new primary.

As for the software architecture, it consists of the following components:

- **Web server protective wrapper:** This wrapper monitors calls to dynamic link libraries (DLLs) for file access, process execution, memory protection changes, and other potentially malicious functions. When it detects a violation of specified behavior, it will alert, disallow, or modify the call, depending on set policies.

- **Application monitor:** This application monitor implements specification-based behavior, monitoring critical applications accordingly.

- **Host monitor:** This host monitor communicates with MAC and sends alerts. It has the capability to restore a failed primary to a healthy backup and is responsible for continual repair.

- **Forensic agent:** This agent analyzes a "log" that contains recent requests to determine which request(s) may have caused the failure.

- **Sandbox:** This sandbox consists of an exact duplicate of the machine and application that failed. If a suspicious request received from Forensic Agent causes the same conditions in the Sandbox that resulted in failover of the primary or backup, then it is identified as a "Bad Request."

- **Content filter:** This filter consists of a list of "Bad Requests." It generalizes bad requests identified by Forensic Agent so that simple variants are also blocked; hence, previously unknown attacks are automatically and immediately prevented from repeatedly causing failover.

Other techniques that are discussed in Reynolds et al. (2003) also involve:

- **Diversity:** This has two different Web servers operating on the primary and backup based on the assumption that an exploit against one product of a type of software will seldom work against another product of the same type; thus, although the exploit succeeded on one, it should not propagate to the other.

- **Random rejuvenation:** This is a countermeasure for an intrusion that may become part of a legitimate process over time (e.g., malign threads that "live" within a process, "sleep" for an indefinite length of time, then "wake up" to do damage) by randomly initiating a failover with the average internal between random failovers.

- **Continual repairs:** This is to detect unauthorized file accesses due to wrapped failure or other unknown vulnerabilities to accelerate recovery; detect, and correct continuously.

Weaknesses of ID and IP Techniques/Models

Although it is feasible to integrate ID and IP techniques into a BI system security framework, the weak points of these techniques must not be ignored as well. Bearing in mind the downsides of the techniques could enable future research to improve further on them for best performances. This section shall thus review the weaknesses of the models that employ ID, IP, or some other security techniques.

As mentioned earlier, a signature-based intrusion detection technique is ideal for detecting known attacks but not able to detect new attacks. Anomaly-based technique, on the other hand, is able to detect new attacks but at the same time causes a high false positive rate. Intrusion-prevention techniques using authentication and code security are not ideal also. Authentication using user id and encrypted password or encrypted database requires a good and secure cryptographic algorithm! As mentioned in Drinic and Kirovski (2004), security code approaches using a firewall, code signing, or sandbox do not provide satisfactory performance results for overcoming buffer overflow exploits.

A study in Botha et al. (Botha, Solms, Perry, Loubser, & Yamoyany, 2002) proposed to improve the intrusion-monitoring functionality in an intrusion detection system based on the assumption that the intruders' behaviours could be grouped into common generic phases, and that all users' actions on the system could be monitored in terms of these phases. However, when the underlying assumption changes, which is most likely overtime, as intruders' behaviours change, so the intrusion phases have to change as well. This shall render the model lacking in consistency.

In a study on security modelling in Brennan et al. (Brennan, Rudell, Faatz, & Zimmerman, 2004), the researchers provided a specification for modelling security designs in graphical representation. And, to model system and security administration, it shall require building separate administration diagrams as the security requirements and controls are different. As a result, the model lacks the consistency, efficiency, and not being optimized to model security designs across different platforms.

In another security modeling study in Collins et al. (Collins, Ford, & Thuraisingham, 1991), security-constraint processing is used to secure database query and update based on the assumption that security administration would generate an initial set of security constraints. As it is difficult to generate a consistent initial set of security constraints, it is even more difficult to verify the completeness of this initial list of security constraints. Consequently, the model lacks consistency and completeness.

Business Intelligence Security: A Web Service Case Study

As concluded in Reynolds et al. (2003), these fault-tolerant techniques can indeed provide a means for detecting and preventing online cyberattacks. However, future works are still required for extending these techniques in more complex real-world applications. This opens up a feasible opportunity for ID and IP to be integrated into a BI system — a complex real-world application, be it a business performance management (BPM) system, customer relationship management (CRM) system, supplier chain management (SCM) system, or e-commerce!

As mentioned in Ortiz (2002), the trend in BI application is going to be Web services enabled. As Web services are platform-neutral designed to ease and deliver BI results

Figure 2. Web-service case study set-up

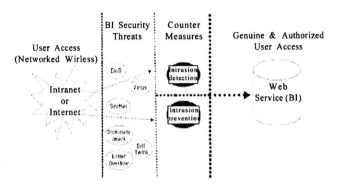

across platforms over the intranets and Internet, be it wired or wireless, real time and ad hoc, companies can make use of these technologies to access and analyze data in multiple locations, including information stored by partners and suppliers. Due to the fact that BI applications are going to be mainly Web services enabled in the future, users accessing through the Internet in real time, whether wired or wireless, the knowledge capital and data warehouse that are stored in centralized servers, are going to increase in numbers. Consequently, BI applications are still susceptible to all the common security threats such as denial of service, virus attack, "sniffer" attack, "evil twins" attack, dictionary attack, and buffer overflow exploit mentioned in an earlier section. As a result, a tighter security framework that includes ID and IPs is definitely required to be integrated into the BI enterprise architecture.

Subsequently, further study on BI security can be started off with a Web-service case study. In this case study, as shown in Figure 2 — Web-service case study set up, various security threats significant to the BI environment to check unauthorized access are to be simulated and identified. Countermeasures using ID and IP mechanisms are then designed and constructed. This prototype design consisting of ID and IP security method is then incorporated into existing security framework as an enhanced security framework for BI as mentioned in the previous section. Unauthorized user access with security threats through the intranet/Internet, be it networked or wireless, are filtered using intrusion detection and intrusion prevention techniques. This framework shall ensure that only genuine and authorized user accesses are allowed.

Conclusion

However, due to the fact that weaknesses do exist in models employing ID and IP techniques, more innovative researches have to continue to be carried out to improve both the signature-based and anomaly-based intrusion detection techniques.

In general, for example, better and more innovative data-mining techniques could be employed in data collection and data analysis so as to reduce the overloading of unnecessary data and subsequently reducing the false positive/negative alarm rates. Better algorithms for response/pattern matching of intrusions data, for machine learning and retraining of data should also be explored extensively. As for intrusion prevention, improvement on network/communication protocols for both wired and wireless should also jump onto this bandwagon for innovative research of ID and IP. In addition, using biometrics for authentication should be set as a future norm in parallel with improved cryptographic algorithms. Firewall, honeypot, and code security shall continue to be used perhaps with greater ingenuity and innovation for continuous improved performance.

In particular, more innovative researches should be carried out in the area of wireless and mobile ad hoc networks, for example in Zhang et al. (Zhang, Lee, & Huang, 2003), the researchers had examined the vulnerabilities of wireless networks and argue that intrusion detection must be included in the security architecture for mobile computing environment. They have thus developed such security architecture with distributed and cooperative features catering for anomaly detection for mobile ad hoc networks. Although experimental results from this research had also shown good performance and effectiveness, but as these researchers mentioned, new techniques must continue to be developed to make intrusion detection and prevention work better for the ever-evolving wireless networks.

All in all, it can be concluded, as shown in the Web-service case study, that intrusion detection and prevention is feasible and must be included in BI's security architecture. This shall ensure a tighter security, subsequently protecting the knowledge base or assets of the enterprise from being unduly tampered with or used in an unauthorized manner since the knowledge base is, indeed, too valuable to allow for exploitation!

References

Baroudi, S., Ziade, H., & Mounla, B. (2004). Are we really protected against hackers? In *Proceedings of 2004 International Conference on Information and Communication Technologies: From Theory to Applications* (pp. 621-622).

Botha, M., Solms, R. V., Perry, K., Loubser, E., & Yamoyany, G. (2002). The utilization of artificial intelligence in a hybrid intrusion detection system. In *ACM International Conference Proceeding, Proceedings of the 2002 Annual Research Conference of The South African Institutes of Computer Scientists and Information Technologists on Enablement Through Technology* (pp. 149-155).

Brennan, J. J., Rudell, M., Faatz, D., & Zimmerman, C. (2004). Visualizing enterprise-wide security (VIEWS). In *20th Annual Computer Security Applications Conference* (pp. 71-79).

Collins, M., Ford, W., & Thuraisingham, B. (1991). Security constraint processing during the update operation in a multilevel secure database management system. In *The Seventh Annual Proceedings of the Computer Security Applications Conference* (pp. 23-32).

Deng, H., Zeng, Q.-A., & Agrawal, D. P. (2003). SVM-based intrusion detection system for wireless ad hoc networks. In *Vehicular Technology Conference, 2003. VTC 2003-Fall. 2003 IEEE 58th 3* (pp. 2147-2151).

Drinic, M., & Kirovski, D. (2004). A hardware-software platform for intrusion prevention. In *Proceedings of the 37th International Symposium on Microarchitecture. (MICRO-37'04)* (pp. 233-242). IEEE.

Entrust® GetAccess™. (2003). *Secure identity and access management, technical overview* (pp. 1-28).

Gangadharan, G. R., & Swami, S. N. (2004). Business intelligence systems: Design and implementation strategies. In *26ᵗʰ International Conference on Information Technology Interfaces* (Vol. 1, pp. 139-144).

Golfarelli, M., Rizzi, S., & Cella, I. (2004). Beyond data warehousing: What's next in business intelligence? In *Proceedings of the 7ᵗʰ ACM International Workshop on Data Warehousing and OLAP* (pp. 1-6).

Hu, X., & Cercone, N. (2002). An OLAM framework for Web usage mining and business intelligence reporting. In *Proceedings of the 2002 IEEE International Conference on Fuzzy Systems, FUZZ-IEEE'02* (pp. 950-955).

Huang, N.-F., Kao, C.-N., Hun, H.-W., Jai, G.-Y., & Lin, C.-L. (2005). Apply data mining to defense-in-depth network security system. In *Proceedings of the 19ᵗʰ International Conference on Advanced Information Networking and Applications (AINA'05)* (pp. 1-4).

Information Builders. (2002). *A roadmap for implementing business intelligence solutions. Best practices in information delivery* (pp. 1-33).

Joglekar, S. P., & Tate, S. R. (2004). ProtoMon: Embedded monitors for cryptographic protocol intrusion detection and prevention. In *Proceedings of ITCC 2004. International Conference on Information Technology: Coding and Computing* (Vol. 1, pp. 81-88).

Manganaris, S., Christensen, M., Zerkle, D., & Hermiz, K. (1999). A data mining analysis of RTID alarms (pp. 1-11). IBM.

Ortiz, S., Jr. (2002). Is business intelligence a smart move? *Computer, 35*(7), 11-14.

Pilot Software Acquisition Corp. (2002). *Scaling to support very large user communities. Web-based business intelligence* (pp. 1-9).

Reynolds, J. C., Just, J., Clough, L., & Maglich, R. (2003). Online intrusion detection and attack prevention using diversity, generate-and-test, and generalization. In *Proceedings of the 36ᵗʰ Annual Hawaii International Conference on System Sciences* (p. 8).

Soper, D. S. (2005). A framework for automated Web business intelligence systems. In *Proceedings of the 38ᵗʰ Annual Hawaii International Conference on System Sciences, 2005, HICSS'05* (p. 217a).

Spil, T. A. M., Stegwee, R. A., & Teitink, C. J. A. (2002). Business intelligence in healthcare organizations. In *Proceedings of the 35ᵗʰ Annual Hawaii International Conference on System Sciences, 2002, HICSS* (p. 9).

Xie, W., Xu, X., Sha, L., Li, Q., & Liu, H. (2001). Business intelligence based group decision support system. In *International Conferences on Info-tech and Info-net, 2001, Proceedings ICII 2001*, Beijing (Vol. 5, pp. 295-300).

Yin, C., Li, M., Ma, J., & Sun, J. (2004). Honeypot and scan detection in intrusion detection system. In *Canadian Conference on Electrical and Computer Engineering* (Vol. 2, pp. 1107-1110).

Zhang, Y., Lee, W., & Huang, Y.-A. (2003). Intrusion detection techniques for mobile wireless networks. *Wireless Networks, 9*(5), 545-556.

Chapter XII

Secure Trust Transfer Using Chain Signatures

Amitabh Saxena, La Trobe University, Australia

Ben Soh, La Trobe University, Australia

Abstract

In this chapter, we discuss the concept of "trust transfer" using chain signatures. Informally, transferring trust involves creating a trust (or liability) relationship between two entities such that both parties are liable in the event of a dispute. If such a relationship involves more than two users, we say they are connected in a chained trust relationship. The members of a chained trust relationship are simultaneously bound to an agreement with the property that additional members can be added to the chain but once added, members cannot be removed thereafter. This allows members to be incrementally and noninteractively added to the chain. We coin the term "chained signatures" to denote signatures created in this incremental way. An important application of chained signatures is in e-commerce transactions involving many users. We present a practical construction of such a scheme that is secure under the Diffie-Hellman assumption in bilinear groups.

Introduction

An *aggregate signature* [introduced by Boneh, Gentry, Lynn, & Shacham (2003) in Eurocrypt'03)] is a novel cryptographic primitive constructed using bilinear maps based on the hardness of the Computational Diffie-Hellman problem (CDHP). In addition to the necessary properties of *signature aggregation* and *batch verification*, the aggregate signatures of Boneh et al. (2003) possess another interesting property, namely; the *inability to extract* any individual signatures just from the aggregation. This was demonstrated in Boneh et al. (2003) using the example of *verifiably encrypted signatures* (VES). The security of the VES scheme relies on the hardness of the k-element aggregate extraction problem (k-EAEP). It was shown in Coron and Naccache (2003) that the k-EAEP is as hard as the CDHP.

In this chapter, we introduce the idea of chain signatures as another novel application of the k-EAEP. At the conclusion of this chapter, it will be evident that a chain signature is a more general case of the VES scheme of Boneh et al. (2003). The rest of the chapter is organized as follows. We give an overview of the problems addressed by our chapter in section 2 and formalize the notion of chain signatures in section 3. We give a brief overview of bilinear pairings (the cryptographic primitives of the scheme) in section 4. Finally, in section 5 we present the scheme and show, as an application, a novel method to prevent spam in section 8. Our intention is to summarize the work of Saxena and Soh (2005c).

Motivation

Before going into the details of chain signatures, we give some motivation for the need of such a definition. A real-life example will only be given in section 8 (spammer tracing). For now, we assume a hypothetical contract-signing scenario between n distinct users $ID_1, ID_2, ..., ID_n$ such that any user ID_i wants to commit to a contract only if the $(i-1)$ users $ID_1, ID_2, ..., ID_{i-1}$ have committed. At the same time, ID_i does not want to be liable for (or is unaware of) the rest of the $n-i$ users $ID_{i+1}, ID_{i+2}, ..., ID_n$.[1]

As a second requirement, once ID_i commits to the contract, he/she wants to ensure that the next (unknown) user ID_{i+1} cannot convince a court of ID_i's commitment independent of the commitments of the rest of the users $ID_1, ID_2, ..., ID_{i-1}$. That is, it must not be possible to remove any user ID_j's commitment ($1 \leq j \leq i$) without removing the rest of the $(i-1)$ commitments assuming that users cannot interact.

To make this scenario meaningful, we additionally require that each user ID_i cannot interact (or collude) with any of the past users $ID_1, ID_2, ..., ID_{i-1}$ once they have committed to the contact. If two or more users collude, then we require that at least one member from the coalition is in this chain.

We propose a model to address this type of issue. Essentially, the aim of our model is to be able to arbitrarily connect many entities in a nonrepudiable chained trust relationship. Using our commitment scheme, trust (and liability) can be *sequentially transferred* from user ID_i to ID_n via the chain of users. Although chain signatures resemble accountable-subgroup multisignatures (ASM) of Micali et al. (Micali, Ohta, & Reyzin, 2001) in many ways, they are different. We elaborate the major differences between chain signatures and accountable-subgroup multisignatures.

1. **Accountable-subgroup multisignatures:** An accountable-subgroup multisignature of a subgroup of signers S for a message m provides, without any trusted managers or third parties, a self-contained and universally verifiable proof of (1) the composition of S and (2) the fact that each member of S stood behind m (Micali et al., 2001). Thus, an ASM is a one-time signature and in most cases requires three or more rounds of interaction between the subgroup of signers.

2. **Chain signatures:** A chain signature (CS) of a subgroup of signers S for a message m provides, without any trusted manager or third parties, a self-contained and universally verifiable proof of (1) the *noninteractive* and *incremental* composition of S (with the order) and (2) the fact that each member of S stood behind m. In our definition, two properties stand out from ASM: (a) The process of composition is completely *noninteractive* and (b) It is possible to add more commitments to the composition such that once added, removing any one commitment is infeasible without access to the original commitment itself.

Formal Definition: Chained Signatures

First we give some notation. A sequence is similar to a set except that the order of its elements matters. We require that the elements of a sequence must be distinct. The elements of a sequence are written in order and enclosed within the $\langle$ and $\rangle$ symbols. For instance, $\langle y_1, y_2, y_3 \rangle$ and $\langle y_1, y_3, y_2 \rangle$ are two different sequences. Let $L_1 = \langle y_1, y_2, ..., y_k \rangle$ be some sequence. For any other sequence L_2, we say that $L_2 \in L_1$ if and only if $L_2 = \langle y_1, y_2, ..., y_i \rangle$ and $0 \le i < k$.

Since all elements of a sequence are distinct, any sequence can also be considered as a set (by ignoring the order). We define the operations $\cup$, $\cap$ for sequences to have same meaning as for sets. That is, for any two sequences L_a, L_b, the symbol $L_a \cup L_b$ denotes the set of elements that belong to at least one of $\{L_a, L_b\}$. Similarly $L_a \cap L_b$ denotes the set of elements that belong to both L_a and L_b. It is important to note that the result of the $\cup$ and $\cap$ operations is a set (and not a sequence). The symbol $\varnothing$ denotes the empty sequence (i.e., a sequence with zero elements) and the symbol e denotes the empty string (i.e., a string of zero length).

We define a chain signature scheme using three algorithms *KeyGen*, *ChainSign*, *ChainVerify* with the following properties. It is convenient to describe *ChainVerify* before *ChainSign*.

1. *KeyGen*: (Key Generation) This algorithm takes as input some fixed parameters and outputs a randomly selected key-pair (x, y) such that x is the private key and y is the public key. We write $(x_i, y_i) \leftarrow KeyGen$ to denote that (x_i, y_i) is the output of the

algorithm on the ith run. The algorithm is expected to output different pairs on each run.

2.   *ChainVerify*: (Verification) This algorithm takes as input a tuple (m, σ_i, L_i). Here L_i is some sequence of i public keys $\langle y_1, y_2, ..., y_i \rangle$ and the pair (σ_i, L_i) is a purported chain signature on message m. The algorithm works as follows:

   a.   If $L_i = \varnothing$ and $\sigma_i = \varepsilon$ the algorithm outputs VALID and terminates.

   b.   If $L_i = \varnothing$ and $\sigma_i \neq \varepsilon$ the algorithm outputs INVALID and terminates.

   c.   If this step is executed then $L_i \neq \varnothing$. The algorithm uses a deterministic poly-time procedure after which it outputs either VALID or INVALID and terminates.

3.   *ChainSign*: (Signing) The *ChainSign* procedure takes as input a tuple $(x_i, y_i, m, \sigma_j, L_j)$. Here (xi, yi) is a valid private-public key-pair (generated using the *KeyGen* algorithm), the pair (σ_j, L_j) is a purported chain signature on message m, and L_j is some sequence of j public keys $\langle y_1, y_2, ..., y_j \rangle$ such that $y_i \notin \{y_1, y_2, ..., y_j\}$. The algorithm works as follows:

   a.   If any of the input conditions (as described above) are violated, the algorithm outputs ERROR and terminates.

   b.   The algorithm invokes *ChainVerify* with (m, sj, Lj) as input (i.e. it checks whether (sj, Lj) is a valid chain signature on m or not). If (sj, Lj) is not a valid chain signature on message m, the algorithm outputs ERROR and terminates.

   c.   If this step is executed then no input conditions are violated and (σ_j, L_j) is a valid chain signature on m. In this case this algorithm uses the private key xi to compute a new valid chain signature (σ_i, L_i) on message m such that $L_i = \langle y_1, y_2, ..., y_j, y_i \rangle$.

The *ChainVerify* and *ChainSign* algorithms must satisfy the standard consistency constraint of signatures. That is, if the input (m, σ_i, L_i) to the *ChainVerify* is the output of the *ChainSign* algorithm then the *ChainVerify* algorithm must output VALID.

Security of Chain Signatures

We define adaptive security of a chain signature scheme using the following game. For simplicity, we assume that the adversary is not allowed to use a chosen private key. The adversary is, however, allowed to extract private keys of choice. In this respect, our model is similar to an identity-based system. We call this *adaptive security under known key and chosen message attack*.

The reader should note that this is a weaker requirement than *adaptive security under chosen key and chosen message attack* used in the aggregate signatures of Boneh et al. (2003). We feel, however, that our notation is more suitable in modeling the requirements of chain signatures (which are slightly different from aggregate signatures).

Game 1

1. **Setup:** First the adversary chooses the parameter n. The challenger then generates n key-pairs $\{(x_1,y_1),(x_2,y_2),...(x_n,y_n)\} \xleftarrow{R} KeyGen$ and gives the set $Y=\{y_1,y_2,...y_n\}$ of public keys to the adversary. Denote by L, the set of all sequences with elements from Y.

2. **Queries:** Working adaptively, the adversary A issues at most q_s chain-sign queries and q_e private-key extract queries as follows:

    a. *Chain sign queries*: For each chain sign query i on distinct pairs (m_i,L_i) for $1 \le i \le q_s$ where $m_i \in \Sigma^*$ and $L_i \subsetneq L$, the challenger responds with a valid chain signature (σ_i,L_i) on m_i. This signature is computed using the *ChainSign* algorithm.

    b. *Extract queries*: For each extract query j on public key y_j for $1 \le j \le q_e$, the challenger responds with the private key x_j corresponding to y_j.

3. Output: Finally A outputs a valid message-chain signature pair $\langle m_A,(\sigma_A,L_A)\rangle$ and wins the game if both conditions hold:

    a. No sign query has been issued on (m_A,L_A); $|L_A| \ge 1$ and there is at least one public key in LA on which an extract query has not been issued.

    b. If $m_A=m_j$ for any j such that a sign query has been issued on (m_j,L_j) and $L_j \in L_A$ or $L_A \in L_j$, then there is at least one public key in $(L_j \cup L_A)\backslash(L_j \cap L_A)$ on which an extract query has not been issued.

Additionally, we model any hash functions as random oracles. Thus, the adversary can also make q_h hash queries to the random oracle.

Definition 1: We say that a chain signature scheme is $(n, t, q_s, e_e, q_h, \mu)$-secure against existential forgery under an adaptive known key and chosen message attack if for any n given public keys, there is no adversary A such that; A runs for at most time t; A makes at most q_s signature queries; A makes at most q_e extract queries; A makes at most q_h hash queries; and A wins game 1 with probability at least μ. Alternatively, if such an adversary exists then we say that A $(n, t, q_s, e_e, q_h, \mu)$-wins game 1.

Bilinear Pairings

Pairing-based cryptography is based on the existence of efficiently computable nondegenerate bilinear maps (or "pairings") that can be abstractly described as follows:

Let $\mathbf{G}_1$ be a cyclic additive group of prime order q and $\mathbf{G}_2$ be a cyclic multiplicative group of the same order. Assume that computing the discrete logarithm in both $\mathbf{G}_1$ and $\mathbf{G}_2$ is hard. A bilinear pairing is a map e: $\mathbf{G}_1 \times \mathbf{G}_1 \to \mathbf{G}_2$ that satisfies the following properties (Boneh & Franklin, 2001; Boneh, Lynn, & Shacham, 2001):

1. *Bilinearity*: $e(aP, bQ) = e(P, Q)^{ab}$ $P, Q \in \mathbf{G}_1$ and $a, b \in \mathbb{Z}_q$

2. *Nondegeneracy*: $P \neq 0 \Rightarrow e(P, P) \neq 1$

3. *Computability*: e is efficiently computable

The above properties also imply:

$$e(P+Q,R) = e(P,R) \cdot e(Q,R)   P,Q,R \in \mathbf{G}_1$$

$$e(P,Q+R) = e(P,Q) \cdot e(P,R)   P,Q,R \in \mathbf{G}_1$$

Additionally, we assume that it is easy to *sample* elements from $\mathbf{G}_1$. Typically, the map e will be derived from either the modified Weil pairing or the Tate pairing on an elliptic curve over a finite field (Barreto, Kim, Lynn, & Scott, 2002; Boneh & Franklin, 2001; Boneh et al., 2001). Without going into the details of generating suitable curves (since the same parameters of Boneh et al. (2003) will suffice[2]), we assume that $q \approx 2^{171}$ so that the fastest algorithms for computing discrete logarithms in $\mathbf{G}_1$ take ≈ 285 iterations. For the rest of this discussion, we fix $P \neq 0$ as any uniformly chosen generator of $\mathbf{G}_1$. Define the following problems in $\mathbf{G}_1$:

1. **Computational Diffie-Hellman problem (CDHP):** Given $P, xP, yP \in \mathbf{G}_1$ for unknowns $x, y \in \mathbb{Z}q^*$, output $xyP \in \mathbf{G}_1$.

2. **k-element aggregate extraction problem (k-EAEP):** Let $k \geq 2$. Given the $2k+2$ elements

$$(P, x_1 P, x_2 P, \ldots x_k P, y_1 P, y_2 P, \ldots y_k P, \sum_{i=1}^{k} x_i y_i P) \in \mathbf{G}_1^{2k+2}$$

for unknowns $x_i, y_i \in \mathbb{Z}q^*$, output

$$\sum_{j=1}^{h} x_{u_j} y_{u_j} P \in \mathbf{G}_1$$

such that $\{u_1, u_2, \ldots u_h\} \subsetneq \{1, 2, \ldots k\}$.

Theorem 1. (Coron & Naccache, 2003) k-EAEP $\Leftrightarrow$ CDHP. In other words, the k-EAEP is hard if and only if the CDHP is hard.

Proof. It is known that k-EAEP $\Leftrightarrow$ CDHP with a tight reduction in either direction. We refer the reader to Coron and Naccache (2003) for the proof.

The security of the chain signature scheme described next depends on the following assumption.

Diffie-Hellman Assumption: The CDHP is Intractable

On the other hand, it is well known that the decisional Diffie-Hellman problem (DDHP), which requires given $P, xP, yP, R \in \mathbf{G}_1$ deciding if $R=xyP$, is easy in bilinear maps due to the following observation: $R = xyP$ if and only if $e(R, P)=e(xP, yP)$.

Chained Signatures using Bilinear Pairings

We now describe our chained signature scheme using bilinear pairings as an extension of aggregate signatures. We refer the reader to Boneh et al. (2003) for details on aggregate signatures. A preliminary setup is necessary where a public directory is created. This preliminary setup is carried out by a trusted authority (TA) as follows.

Preliminary Setup

1. The TA selects a security parameter l and uses the *BDH parameter generator* of Boneh et al. (2001), which we will call **Params**, to set the system parameters as follows. It generates $\{e, q, \mathbf{G}_1, \mathbf{G}_2\} \xleftarrow{R} \mathbf{Params}(1^l)$ where $\mathbf{G}_1, \mathbf{G}_2$ are group descriptions for two groups each of prime order $q > 2l$ and $e: \mathbf{G}_1 \times \mathbf{G}_1 \rightarrow \mathbf{G}_2$ is a bilinear mapping as defined in section 4. The TA then defines a cryptographic hash function $H: \mathrm{S}^{*}\,2^{G_1} \rightarrow \mathbf{G}_1$. This hash function can be constructed using the *MapToGroup* mapping described in Boneh et al. (2001). Finally, the TA generates $P \xleftarrow{R} \mathbf{G}_1$. If $P^l \neq 0$, then P is a generator of $\mathbf{G}_1$. The system parameters are $\langle e, q, l, \mathbf{G}_1, \mathbf{G}_2, H, P \rangle$.

2. Each participant ID_i generates $x_i \xleftarrow{R} \mathbb{Z}q$ as the private key. The corresponding public key is $Y_i = x_i P \in \mathbf{G}_1$. Each user also obtains a certificate from a certification authority (CA) linking the identity ID_i and the public key Y_i.

Chain Signature Protocol

In this scenario, there are n ordered distinct participants $\langle ID_1, ID_2, ..., ID_n \rangle$ and $m \in \Sigma^*$ is the contract to be signed. The original signer of the message m is ID_1. The message is passed from ID_i to ID_{i+1} along with a chain-signature, as described next.

On receiving the message from ID_{i-1} $(i>1)$, user ID_i first performs the verification process. Before passing the message to ID_{i+1}, user ID_i performs the signing process. The first user,

ID_1 only performs the signing process.

1. **Signing:** Let $L_r = \langle Y_1, Y_2, \ldots Y_r \rangle$ for $r \geq 1$. Define $Z_0 = 0 \in \mathbf{G}_1$. Define recursively,
   $Z_i = x_i H(m, L_i) + Z_{i-1} \in \mathbf{G}_1$ for $i \geq 1$

The chain-signature of IDi on the message m is $\langle Z_i, L_i \rangle$.

2. **Verification:** An arbitrary user ID_{i+1} accepts the chain signature $\langle Z_i, L_i \rangle$ of ID_i on m as valid if the following check passes

$$e(Z_i, P) \stackrel{?}{=} \prod_{r=1}^{i} e(H(m, L_r), Y_r)$$

The correctness of the verification process follows directly from the property of bilinear maps:

$$LHS = e(Z_i, P) = e(\sum_{r=1}^{i} x_r H(m, L_r), P) = \prod_{r=1}^{i} e(H(m, L_r), x_r P) = RHS$$

The benchmarks of Ateniese, Fu, Green, and Hohenberger (2005) indicate that each pairing operation using these parameters takes » 8.6ms and each elliptic curve point exponentiation takes » 1.5 ms. These results were obtained on a desktop PC with an AMD Athlon 2100+ 1.8 GHz, 1 GB RAM and an IBM 7200 RPM, 40 GB, Ultra ATA/100 hard drive (Ateniese et al., 2005). Using these values and neglecting the faster operations, we obtain the following performance estimates of this protocol (assuming n users in the chain):

1. **Signing:** one exponentiation in $\mathbf{G}_1$, one addition in $\mathbf{G}_1$, one computation of H (total <2ms).
2. **Verification:** n pairing computations and multiplications in $\mathbf{G}_2$, and n computations of H (giving <1 second for $n=100$).

The reader may note that our construction of chain signatures is identical to Boneh et al.'s construction of aggregate signatures (2003) with two minor modifications: (a) Each user signs the same message m and (b) The aggregate signature is created *incrementally*. Due to this, the security of our scheme follows more or less from Boneh et al. (2003). The difference is that *extractability* of individual signatures is not a problem with aggregate signatures. However, this property renders chain signatures completely insecure. The hardness of the k-EAEP ensures that such extraction is not possible.

Security of the Scheme

We use definition 1 of section 3 to prove adaptive security of the chain signature scheme. The security of the scheme follows from the following theorem. We only give a sketch of the proof. First we define the security of aggregate signatures under an *adaptive chosen message and chosen key attack* using the following game. We refer the reader to Boneh et al. (2003) for more details on this.

Game 2

1. **Setup:** The challenger generates a key pair $(x,y) \xleftarrow{R} KeyGen$ and gives y, the challenge public key to the adversary.

2. **Queries:** Working adaptively, the adversary A issues at most q_s' sign queries and q_h' hash queries as follows:

    a. **Sign queries:** For each sign query i on distinct messages mi for $1 \leq i \leq q_s'$, the challenger responds with a valid *individual* signature σ_i on m_i under the private key x using the BLS scheme of Boneh et al. (2001).

    b. **Hash queries:** For each hash query j on distinct messages m_j for $1 \leq j \leq q_h'$, the challenger responds with $H(m_j)$.

3. **Output:** Finally, A outputs an aggregate signature σ_A of N distinct public keys (on some set of chosen messages) such that m_A is the message signed under the challenged public key y while the other N-1 public keys are chosen by the adversary. We say that A wins the game if (a) σ_A is a valid aggregate signature, (b) No sign query has been previously been issued on m_A and (c) Each message in the aggregate signature σ_A is *distinct*.

Definition 2: We say that the aggregate signature scheme of Boneh et al. (2003) is (N', t', q_s', q_h', μ')-secure against existential forgery under an adaptive chosen key and chosen message attack if there is no adversary A, that runs for at most time t'; makes at most q_s' signature queries; makes at most q_h' hash queries; outputs an aggregate signature of size N and wins game 1 with probability at least μ'.

We state the following theorem that shows that chain signature scheme is secure in the random oracle model assuming that CDHP is hard.

Theorem 2. If there exists an algorithm A_1 that (n, t, q_s, q_e, q_h, μ)-wins game 1, than there exists an algorithm A_2 that (N, t', q_s', q_h', μ')-wins game 2 where; t'=t+cq$_s$; q'$_s$ ≤ q$_s$; q'$_h$ = q$_h$; N ≤ q$_e$; and μ' = $\Theta((n-q_e)/n^2)$. Here c is a constant.

For a proof, the reader is referred to Saxena et al. (2005c).

Forward and Backward Chain Signatures

The protocol of Section 5 demonstrates a type of chaining that we call *backward* chaining because the receiver of the message "adds" a link to the chain. Likewise, we also define *forward* chaining, where this addition is instead done by the sender. We enumerate the major differences between the two:

Forward Chain Signatures

1. In a forward chaining scheme, each sender must be aware of the next receiver. Referring to the definitions of section 3, in a forward chaining scheme each user ID_i is liable for the knowledge (of involvement) of the *presumed* user ID_{i+1} who has not yet committed to the contract.

2. Forward chaining has the advantage that the order of participants can be strictly specified by senders. However, such a scheme also increases the liability of each sender and restricts the scalability of the entire system; a message will have to be signed multiple times if it is sent to many receivers in parallel (see next section, applications).

3. The backward chaining protocol of section 5 can be converted to a forward chaining one simply by redefining Lj in section 5.2 as follows: $L_0 = \langle Y_1 \rangle$ and $L_i = \langle L_{i-1}, Y_{i+1} \rangle$ if $i > 0$. This variant is much more efficient than the example given with signature size $O(1)$.

Backward Chain Signatures

1. In a backward chaining scheme, the sender ID_i is only liable for the knowledge of users who have already committed to the contract. Thus, in effect, the receiver can choose to be completely anonymous from the sender.

2. In a backward chaining scheme, multiple senders within a "trust zone" can use a single signing gateway without revealing the identity of the recipients.

3. It is possible that there are no trivial constructions for backward chaining schemes without pairings. This may be considered as a disadvantage.

Applications of Backward Chain Signatures

In this section, we present some applications of backward chain signatures. The use of backward chain signatures in higher-layer Internet protocols gives rise to some unique and interesting features.

Spammer Tracing

We present a novel method to prevent spam (or unsolicited e-mail). Our approach to spam prevention involves path authentication of any received mail. Since it is impossible to completely stop spam, we propose a combination of proactive and reactive measures. Using the previous notation, the ordered list of mail relays is $\langle ID_1, ID_2,...ID_n \rangle$. We do not involve the senders or recipients simply because we feel that this process should be completely transparent to the end users. The only time when a recipient is involved is when an e-mail is to be reported as spam. Our approach is based on the following assumptions:

1.   We first assume that spam (and all other mail) can be classified according to the path of relays it follows to reach a recipient. In other words, the path of any received mail can be accurately determined.

2.   Due to assumption 1, the *first* relay mentioned in the path of relays for a spam mail is automatically considered responsible unless it is able to delegate this liability to a different relay.

3.   A successful mail will be accepted for forwarding if, and only if, it is accompanied by a valid *backward chain signature* (as described in section 5 keeping *m* as the mail message).

4.   The above assumption ensures that even if some relay accepts a message without a valid signature (a) either the message will be rejected by the next relay that validates the signature or (b) if this relay includes its own valid signature, it will automatically become liable for spam according to assumption 2.

5.   The use of a chain signature ensures that intermediate names in the list cannot be deleted unless *all* names are deleted. In this case, the relay that deletes the names will automatically become liable according to assumption 2.

6.   Two or more relays can collude and remove names of intermediate nodes. However, even in this case, at least one member from the coalition will always be liable.

7.   Reactive measures (like blacklisting) can be taken against a relay continuously generating spam.

8.   To ensure smooth integration to the existing e-mail infrastructure, the sender of an e-mail need not worry about the signing process. Only the relays would be responsible for the entire authentication process. It is the duty of each relay to sign only those e-mails originating from its local users. Otherwise, it will automatically become liable according to assumption 2.

We believe that this approach to classifying, enforcing, and blacklisting relays using backward chain signatures will efficiently reduce spam to an acceptable level. The use of backward chaining ensures that the same message destined for multiple recipients (and having branching paths) need only be signed once at each node. We observe that the verification process involves many (computationally intensive) pairing computations.

However, typically the number of relays involved for a mail delivery is very small (usually two to three). This ensures that only a few pairing computations are carried out during verification.

Summary

In this chapter, we introduced the notion of chain signatures as an extension of Boneh et al.'s aggregate and verifiably encrypted signatures (2003). Although chain signatures arise naturally from the aggregate signatures, the security requirements of chain signatures is significantly different, as demonstrated in sections 2 and 3. We note that chain signatures without using bilinear maps were independently proposed in Saxena and Soh (2005a, 2005b) in which the authors used hypothetical primitives called *strong associative one-way functions* (SAOWFs3) and coined the term "additive zero-knowledge" to refer to the underlying properties.

The protocol presented here uses a standard certificate-based PKI. However, it is possible to construct identity based chained signatures (IBCS) because of the observation that the identity based signature (IBS) schemes of Cha and Cheon (2003) and Libert and Quisquater (2004) support signature aggregation with the property that, once aggregated, individual signatures cannot be extracted.

Considering that chained signatures enable us to correctly validate the path of any received message and provide nonrepudiation, we can consider several applications: mobile agent authentication (Saxena & Soh, 2005a, 2005b), electronic auctions, relaying, and token-based authentication. As a practical demonstration of applications, we presented a novel method for spam prevention.

References

Ateniese, G., Fu, K., Green, M., & Hohenberger, S. (2005). *Improved proxy reencryption schemes with applications to secure distributed storage* (Cryptology ePrint Archive, Rep. No. 2005/028) [online]. IACR.

Barreto, P. S. L. M., Kim, H. Y., Lynn, B., & Scott, M. (2002). Efficient algorithms for pairing-based cryptosystems. *Crypto '02: Proceedings of the 22nd annual international cryptology conference on advances in cryptology* (pp. 354-368). London: Springer-Verlag.

Boneh, D., & Franklin, M. K. (2001). Identity-based encryption from the weil pairing. *Crypto '01: Proceedings of the 21st Annual International Cryptology Conference on Advances in Cryptology* (pp. 213-229). Springer.

Boneh, D., Gentry, C., Lynn, B., & Shacham, H. (2003). Aggregate and verifiably encrypted signatures from bilinear maps. In E. Biham (Ed.), *Eurocrypt, 2656* (pp. 416-432). Springer.

Boneh, D., Lynn, B., & Shacham, H. (2001). Short signatures from the weil pairing. *Asiacrypt '01: Proceedings of the 7th International Conference on the Theory and Application of Cryptology and Information Security* (pp. 514-532). London: Springer-Verlag.

Cha, J. C., & Cheon, J. H. (2003). An identity-based signature from gap diffie-hellman groups. In Y. Desmedt (Ed.), *Public key cryptography, 2567* (pp. 18-30). Springer.

Coron, J.-S., & Naccache, D. (2003). Boneh et al.'s k-element aggregate extraction assumption is equivalent to the diffie-hellman assumption. In C.-S. Laih (Ed.), *Asiacrypt, 2894* (pp. 392-397). Springer.

Libert, B., & Quisquater, J. (2004). *The exact security of an identity based signature and its applications* (Cryptology ePrint Archive Rep. No. 2004/102) [online]. IACR.

Micali, S., Ohta, K., & Reyzin, L. (2001). Accountable-subgroup multisignatures: Extended abstract. *Ccs '01: Proceedings of the 8th ACM Conference on Computer and Communications Security* (pp. 245-254). New York: ACM Press.

Saxena, A., & Soh, B. (2005a). Authenticating mobile agent platforms using signature chaining without trusted third parties. *Proceedings of the 2005 IEEE International Conference on e-Technology, E-Commerce and E-Service (eee-05)* (pp. 282-285). Hong Kong: IEEE Computer Press.

Saxena, A., & Soh, B. (2005b). A novel method for authenticating mobile agents with one-way signature chaining. *Proceedings of the 7th International Symposium on Autonomous Decentralized Systems (isads 05)* (pp. 187-193). China: IEEE Computer Society.

Saxena, A., & Soh, B. (2005c). *One way signature chaining: A new paradigm for group cryptosystems and e-commerce* (Cryptology ePrint Archive Rep. No. 2005/335) [online]. IACR.

Endnotes

[1]   As noted in section 7, the solution becomes trivial when each user is made aware of the next.

[2]   The aggregate signature scheme of Boneh et al. (2003) uses a bilinear map $G_0 \times G_1 \rightarrow G_2$ such that an efficiently computable isomorphism $\psi: G_1 \rightarrow G_0$ exists. Their construction can be directly adapted to our's by setting $G_0 = G_1$.

[3]   SAOWFs exhibit properties similar to multilinear maps.

Chapter XIII

Distributed Intrusion Detection Systems:
An Overview

Rosalind Deena Kumari, Multimedia University, Malaysia

G. Radhamani, Multimedia University, Malaysia

Abstract

The recent tremendous increase in the malicious usage of the network has made it necessary that an IDS should encapsulate the entire network rather than at a system. This was the inspiration for the birth of a distributed intrusion detection system (DIDS). Different configurations of DIDSs have been actively used and are also rapidly evolving due to the changes in the types of threats. This chapter will give the readers an overview of DIDS and the system architecture. It also highlights on the various agents that are involved in DIDS and the benefits of the system. Finally, directions for future research work are discussed.

Introduction

Intrusion detection (ID) is a term that is used for an automated security system that can identify attempts made to violate security of the system. The main objective of this system is to detect unusual activity such as a large number of unsuccessful login attempts from one point or several attempts made to access the password of a file. The method is based on statistical analysis or rule-based expert systems. Intrusion detection is a powerful security tool because of its ability to counter attacks from insiders who misuse their privileges, and attacks resulting from such events as lost or stolen passwords or cryptographic keys.

Different ID systems have differing classifications of "intrusions"; a system attempting to detect attacks against Web servers might consider only malicious HTTP requests, while a system intended to monitor dynamic routing protocols might only consider RIP spoofing (Ford, 1994). A security system cannot be complete without intrusion detection and an ID system complements other security technologies. The ID system provides information to the site administration regarding detection of attacks that are handled by other systems, as well as about new attacks unforeseen by other security components. It also provides information that is useful to track the origin of the attack. This helps in restricting attackers, as their identity would be revealed. But an IDS is limited to individual machines, which does not secure an entire network of machines.

Intrusion detection approaches can be divided into two categories:

- **Anomaly detection model:** Anomaly detection uses the method of modeling normal behavior. Any instances of violation of this model are considered to be of concern and suspicious. For example, a normally inactive public Web server attempting to open connections to a large number of addresses may be indication of a worm infection.

- **Misuse detection model:** Misuse detection tends to model abnormal behavior, any occurrence of such behavior clearly indicates system abuse. For example, an HTTP request referring to the cmd.exe file may indicate an attack.

Anomaly detection is bugged from accuracy problems, whereas misuse detection can reach high levels of accuracy. The major problem in misuse detection is creation of compact models of attacks. Since these two methods are complementary in nature, many systems tend to combine both of these techniques (Du, Wang, & Pang, 2004)

A DIDS consists of multiple intrusion detection systems (IDS) covering a large network, and all the IDSs communicate with each other, or with a central server that provides advanced network monitoring, incident analysis, and instant attack data. As these cooperative agents are distributed across a network, incident analysts, network operations personnel, and security personnel will be able to get a broader view of the occurrences on their network as a whole. A DIDS enables a company to efficiently manage its incident analysis resources with a centralized database of its attack records, and by giving the analyst a quick and easy way to identify new trends and patterns and to pinpoint threats on the network across multiple network segments (Zhang, Xiong, & Wang, 2005).

Scope

The DIDS architecture combines distributed monitoring and data reduction with centralized data analysis. Basically, it consists of a central analysis server (CAS) and a cooperative agent network. This server would ideally consist of a database and Web server. This allows the interactive querying of attack data for analysis as well as a useful Web interface to allow the administrator to see the current attack status of the network.

The agent network is one of the most important components of a DIDS. An agent is a piece of software that reports attack information to the central analysis server. The use of multiple agents across the network allows the incident analysis team a broader view of the network than can be achieved with a single IDS system. The agent might be a simple firewall on a home user's dial-up machine, or a commercial IDS on a company's network perimeter, or a host-based IDS on a network inside an educational institution. Ideally, these agents will be located on separate network segments and geographical locations. They can also be distributed across multiple physical locations, allowing for a single incident analysis team to view attack data across multiple corporate locations.

The DIDS is a system that works on the principle of data aggregation and incident analysis. Incident analysis is the core of DIDS. The whole system's power lies in this analysis. Data from different geographical locations need to be collected and analyzed efficiently so that an attack can be detected and a response is sent to protect the related systems. In order to do data aggregation, different components of the network are used. They are IP addresses, destination port of the data, the agent used (agent ID), date, time, protocol, or attack type. Their properties are as follows:

- Collection of data based on IP address of the intruder will help the analyst to view the steps of an attacker's attempt from start to finish across the various network segments.

- Accumulating data by destination port allows an analyst to view new trends in attack types, and to be able to identify new attack methods or exploits being used.

- Aggregating by agent ID allows an analyst to see what variety of attacks have made attempts on the specific network segment the agent is on. Consequently, the analyst can determine if there are multiple attackers working in conjunction, or if there are network segments that are of more interest to attackers than others, thereby giving the security team a list of common targets to work on. Aggregating by date and time allows the analyst to view new attack patterns, and to potentially identify new worms or viruses that are only triggered at certain times.

- Aggregating by protocol helps in a purely statistical manner that could allow an analyst to identify new attacks in particular protocols, or identify protocols on a network segment that should, under no circumstances, be there anyhow (Einwechter, 2001).

All these aggregation methods will enable the analyst to view data from different sources and to correlate against other attacks. It can also be used to detect coordinated distributed attacks, attacks from within the network, and other related malicious activities of the hacking community. The connection of all individual networks and intranets forms the Internet. Similarly, host-based IDS and network-based IDS can be combined to create a DIDS (Robbins, 2002).

Literature Summary

Various forms of DIDS are being designed and tested for performance, scalability, and other parameters. All of these systems try to overcome problems faced in the initially designed DIDS or to improve on certain factors. Snapp et al. (Snapp, Brentano, Dias, Goan, Grance, Heberlein, et al., 1991) proposed an architecture of a DIDS in which the network security monitor was introduced and the prototype implementation was discussed in accordance with a heterogeneous network of computers. Barrus and Rowe (1998) proposed a distributed architecture with autonomous agents to monitor security-related activity within a network.

Du et al. (2004) have designed an independent agents-based DIDS (IADIDS). In this system, an application is composed of a series of interconnected elements or entities. These entities are called "agents" that can make a response to behavior (activity). Addition of categorized agents to corresponding entity models enabled users to append new function through distributed application, while the other main parts need not be changed. Agents for an application may be distributed on different network nodes. Thus the task of this application may be operated distributed. By this way, network bottleneck of data transmission problem can be solved, and the real-time character and dependability are strengthened. Gopalakrishna and Spafford (2001) discussed DIDS using interest-driven cooperating agents.

High-speed, large-scale networks present new challenges to IDS. These challenges include the volume of data that must be analyzed, and the high-speed data stream that the IDS must deal with. To adapt to these new demands, architecture for large-scale DIDS was proposed (Chu, Li, & Yang, 2005). The current trend of application of DIDS is for mobile/wireless networks. It is called distributed intrusion detection system using mobile agents (DIDMA). It addresses some of the issues with centralized ID models (Kannadiga & Zulkernine, 2005).

A network-based preemptive distributed intrusion detection system using mobile agents is proposed by Chan and Wei (2002). Packets are diverted to various types of agents strategically placed over the network. Burroughs et al. (Burroughs, Wilson, & Cybenko, 2002) proposed an approach that involves the application of Bayesian methods to data being gathered from distributed IDS. Increase in the network speed by leaps and bounds (from megabytes to gigabytes) has changed the concept of DIDS configuration. Instead of using always a master/slave concept, a peer to peer DIDS architecture using high-speed networks has been proposed by Song et al. (Song, Ye, & Li, 2003)

Agents Involved in DIDS

DIDS have grown in versatility in terms of function, and they have evolved into a powerful and complex system. The new generation agents of DIDS use previous generation agents as data sources, applying better-sophisticated detection algorithms to determine even more targeted responses. Usually, one or more IDS and management systems may be employed by an organization within its own network, without any regard to their neighbors or the global Internet. There are five types of agents involved in the DIDS as discussed by Chan and Wei (2002): they are as follows:

- **Gateway agent:** A gateway agent is an agent that resides in the gateway between the internal network and the external network. In order to detect distribution intrusion, several controller agents would join together to form a cluster for the information exchanges.

- **Controller agent or mobile agent:** A controller agent is an agent residing in computers in the internal network. This is a mobile agent and hence when the host is overloaded, the controller agent will move to another host to continue its detection work.

- **Detection agent:** Each detection agent is responsible for detecting certain types of intrusions. This makes it easier for updating when a new type of intrusion is found or new types of detection methods are invented

- **Home agent:** Receiving the incoming packets and sending the outgoing packets to the controller agent is the responsibility of the home agent.

- **Policy agent:** A policy agent is an agent responsible for what action a home agent or a gateway agent should take when an intrusion is found.

Organizations that Implement and Support DIDS

There are various organizations that implement DIDS, namely, Internet storm center, Dshield.Org., MyNetWatchman, DeScan.net, and so forth. Basically all these organizations form a network of security sites, and there is a coordination team that supports to disseminate information and to decide an appropriate action or response. A few of these organizations are described next.

- **Internet storm center (ISC):** This is one of the more popular DIDS centers globally. Its main aim is to provide global Internet security, in a sense that, impending security breaches or storms can be detected early and appropriate action can be recommended. This is possible because the ISC has a network of information support from the SysAdmin, Audit, Networking and Security (SANS) institute and from various other bodies like the U.S. government Internet monitoring and analysis agencies, security service providers, and large corporations. The ISC provides free service with regards to information on new and existing attacks from all over the world. It has a coordination center that coordinates any requests or new developments in the form of attacks. It has the support of a group of intrusion detection analysts that help to identify the severity of an attack and decide on the most appropriate action that can be taken. The ISC also maintains a record of the top 10 attacks, and this information is accessible through its Web site.

- **Dshield.Org:** The implementation of DIDS by this organization is governed by the principle of free service and focuses on firewall users. It has a database of registered users to whom it provides information regarding the top 10 attacks and the ports that are widely attacked. A user (registered) may request regarding an abnormal behavior or intrusion, this information is processed through its database and the responsible ISP is informed. The user also obtains a copy of the information. Here information from only registered users is provided. This DIDS links with the ISC for wider access, resources, and information. It also has links with a few other security sites. One unique feature is the ability to search Dshield's database for records based on the source IP, data, and source or destination port (Robbins, 2002)

Benefits and Future Research Challenges

Concerning the future research work, there is an abundance of research opportunities since DIDS provides a large area of network coverage. The DIDS wins over the IDS in two aspects, namely, one, it has the ability to detect attack patterns across a very large area, overcoming all boundaries of countries or time zones as well. This will be beneficial, as an organized attack can be detected early and security provided to those targeted. It also helps in the prevention of an Internet worm from winding its way into the corporate network. This indirectly reduces financial losses, which may occur in the corporate world. Secondly, it minimizes the number of personnel required if IDS was implemented. In DIDS, a single team can cover different locations whereas for IDS, every location will require their own analysis team. Also, these teams will have to communicate to exchange information. Some information may be viewed as not important for a particular location, but when viewed as a whole for all locations of a corporation, it may be significant. This can be done only by DIDS. DIDS also aides in tracking down malicious employees within the corporation, tracking what they were attempting to do as well as providing evidence against them.

All these benefits are only possible if information is shared between IDSs. The corporate agent network should be able to access reports of abnormal activity at individual IDSs. Hence, DIDSs provide certain services to contributing agents. These include client software-it enables a firewall or router ,and so forth, to act as an agent; private Web site — owners of agents can examine reports of collected analysis, information on types of recent attacks, and the response (if any) given. It also provides reports on source of attacks and how it progressed. It also provides a kind of database on previous attacks in and around other systems. Information related to emergency response teams, visualization tools for attacks, top attacking IP addresses, and so forth, are provided (Robbins, 2002).

Participating and contributing to a DIDS of global scope needs to be taken up in a wider context. When agents are used, more traffic inside the internal network is introduced. The solution to load balancing is an interesting area of research. As attacks become more sophisticated, more coordinated, and more distributed, the strength that DIDS can bring to attack discovery, countermeasures, and resolution will continue to increase in the future.

Conclusion

DIDS can be implemented with existing IDS facilities. It is a network-based system that covers large geographical areas without boundaries. It overcomes the limitations of IDS, which is restricted by location. The DIDS helps to identify coordinated attacks by aggregating data from different source IDSs or network segments. Financially, it is a better option as DIDS uses a single team of analysts, thereby reducing the cost of maintenance. Our next step to do in the near future includes a study on the implementation of the DIDS with agents deployed at different levels in the architecture.

References

Barrus, J., & Rowe, N. C. (1998). A distributed autonomous-agent network-intrusion detection and response system. In *Proceedings of Command and Control Research and Technology Symposium, Monterey* (pp. 8-10).

Burroughs, J. D., Wilson, L. F., & Cybenko, G. V. (2002). Analysis of distributed intrusion detection systems using Bayesian methods. In *IEEE International conference on Performance, Computing and Communications Conference* (pp. 329-334).

Chan, P. C., & Wei, V. K. (2002). Preemptive distributed intrusion detection using mobile agents. In *Proceedings of WETICE '02* (pp. 103-108).

Chu, Y., Li, J., & Yang, Y. (2005). The architecture of the large-scale distributed intrusion detection system. In *Sixth International Conference on PDCAT* (pp. 130-133).

Du, Y., Wang, H.-Q., & Pang, Y.-G. (2004). Design of a distributed intrusion detection system based on independent agents. In *Intelligent Sensing and Information Processing, Proceedings of International Conference* (pp. 254-257).

Einwechter, N. (2002). *An introduction to distributed intrusion detection systems.* Retrieved December 1, 2005, from http://online.securityfocus.com/infocus/1532

Ford, W. (2001). *Computer communications security: Principles, standard protocols and techniques.* Englewood Cliffs, NJ: Prentice Hall.

Gopalakrishna, R., & Spafford, E. H. (2001). *A framework for distributed intrusion detection using interest driven cooperating agents.* Purdue University. Retrieved December 15, 2005, from www.homes.cerias.purdue.edu/~rgk/papers/2001-44.pdf

Kannadiga, P., & Zulkernine, M. (2005). DIDMA: A distributed intrusion detection system using mobile agents. In *Proceedings of the Sixth International Conference on SNPD/SAWN* (pp. 238- 245).

Robbins, R. (2002). *Distributed intrusion detection systems: An introduction and review.* GSEC Practical assignment, version 1.4b. Retrieved December 20, 2005, from www.sans.org/reading_room/whitepapers/detection/897

Snapp, S. R., Brentano, J., Dias, G. V., Goan, T. L., Grance, T., Heberlein, L. T., et al. (1991). A system for distributed intrusion detection. In *IEEE, Compcon '91* (pp. 170-176).

Song, B., Ye, M., & Li, J. (2003). Intrusion detection technology research based high-speed network. In *PDCAT* (pp. 206-210).

Zhang, Y. U, Xiong, Z. Y, & Wang, X. Q. (2005). Distributed intrusion detection based on clustering. In *Proceedings of the Fourth International Conference on Machine Learning and Cybernetics* (pp. 2379-2383).

Chapter XIV

Subtle Interactions:
Security Protocols and Cipher Modes of Operation

Raphael C.-W. Phan, Swinburne University of Technology, Malaysia

Bok-Min Goi, Multimedia University, Malaysia

Abstract

In this chapter, we show how security protocols can be attacked by exploiting the underlying block cipher modes of operation. We first present a comprehensive treatment of the properties and weaknesses of standard modes of operation. We then show why all modes of operation should not be used with public-key ciphers in public-key security protocols. This includes the cipher block chaining (CBC) mode when there is no integrity protection of the initialisation vector (IV). In particular, we show that it is possible in such instances to replace a block at the beginning, middle, or end of a CBC-encrypted message. We further demonstrate that the security of single-block encryptions can be reduced to the security of the electronic codebook (ECB) mode, and show that in the absence of integrity, one could exploit this to aid in known- and chosen-IV attacks. Finally, we present chosen-IV slide attacks on counter (CTR) and output feedback (OFB) modes of operation. Our results show that protocol implementers should carefully select modes of operation, be aware of the pitfalls in each of these modes, and incorporate countermeasures in their protocols to overcome them. It is also important to realize that modes of operation only provide confidentiality, and that when used in the context of security protocols, these modes should be combined with authentication and integrity protection techniques.

Introduction

It is necessary in a distributed computer system that two agents can be assured of each other's identity. They would really wish to talk to each other rather than to a third-party impostor. This is achieved with an *authentication protocol* (Boyd, 1997; Boyd & Park, 1998; Lowe, 1995, 1996; Mao & Boyd, 1993, 1994, 1994a, 1995, 1995a; Park, Boyd, & Dawson, 2000). Often, they also need to exchange a shared secret key to guarantee the confidentiality of the messages that they communicate. This is achieved with a *key-exchange protocol* (Boyd & Mathuria, 1997).

In this chapter, we consider how the security of authentication and key exchange protocols can be compromised by exploiting the underlying modes of operation.[1] Reminders have been made in the past as to the careful use of the underlying modes of operation, and that they should be used in conjunction with integrity protection (Bellovin, 1996; Bellovin & Blaze 2001). We strive to strengthen this by further presenting new attacks on security protocols based on the exploitation of the modes of operation used. Our first main contribution is in showing why even the popular CBC mode is insecure when used in the absence of *IV* integrity protection in public-key security protocols. Our second contribution is to reduce the security of single-block encryptions to that of the ECB mode, and further presenting chosen *IV* slide attacks on the two stream cipher modes of operation.

This chapter is organized as follows: In Section 2, we describe the five standard modes of operation, and then in Section 3, comprehensively treat the properties and weaknesses of these modes. In Section 4, we show why modes of operation should not be used with public-key protocols, concentrating particularly on the CBC mode. In Section 5, we relate the security of single-block encryptions to the ECB mode security, and hence show that single-block encryptions cause known and chosen-*IV* attacks to be practical. Finally, we show that by abusing the *IV*s, one could mount chosen-*IV* slide attacks on the CTR and OFB modes. We conclude in Section 6.

Modes of Operation

We will briefly describe, in this section, the standard modes of operation used when encrypting messages longer than the block size of a block cipher. One main observation is that though the term "block cipher" is often taken to mean secret-key block ciphers, there are also public-key block cipher versions. The most popular example is the public-key RSA cipher, which encrypts messages one block at a time.

When plaintext, P, to be encrypted by a block cipher is longer than the block size, n, the plaintext is divided into several n-bit blocks, P_i, and each one is encrypted at a time using a block cipher mode of operation that could either be the electronic code book (ECB), cipher block chaining (CBC), cipher feedback (CFB), output feedback (OFB) or counter (CTR) modes.

- **ECB:** The ECB mode is the simplest, where each plaintext block, P_i, is independently encrypted to a corresponding ciphertext block, C_i:

$$C_i = E_K(P_i)$$

- **CBC:** The CBC mode uses the previous ciphertext block, C_{i-1}, as the feedback component that is XORed to the current plaintext block, P_i, before the resulting XOR is encrypted to obtain the current ciphertext block, C_i:

$$C_i = E_K(P_i \oplus C_{i-1})$$

where C_o = initialisation vector (*IV*).

- **CFB:** The CFB mode also uses the previous ciphertext block, C_{i-1}, as feedback, which is encrypted and then XORed to the current plaintext block, P_i, to obtain the current ciphertext block, C_i:

$$C_i = P_i \oplus E_K(C_{i-1})$$

where C_o = initialisation vector (*IV*). The CFB mode can also viewed as a stream cipher mode by treating $X_i = E_K(C_{i-1})$ as a keystream that is XORed to the plaintext, P_i, to obtain the ciphertext, C_i.

- **OFB:** The OFB mode is similar to the CFB in that a keystream is also generated to be XORed to the current plaintext block, P_i, to obtain the current ciphertext block, C_i. The difference lies in that the keystream is not a function of the previous ciphertext block, C_{i-1}, but is the previously encrypted feedback component, X_i:

$$X_i = E_K(X_{i-1})$$
$$C_i = P_i \oplus E_K(X_i)$$

where X_o = initialisation vector (*IV*). Note that the keystream is independent of previous plaintext and ciphertext blocks.

- **CTR:** Finally, the CTR mode (Lipmaa, Rogaway, & Wagner, 2000; McGrew 2002) can be considered a variant of the OFB in that the keystream is also independent of previous plaintext and ciphertext blocks. The input to this keystream is a counter, CTR_i, that is distinct for all blocks, and is a function of the previous counter, CTR_{i-1}, via the counter update function, U:

Figure 1. Standard block modes of operation

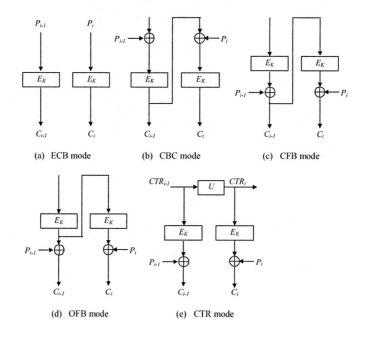

(a) ECB mode   (b) CBC mode   (c) CFB mode

(d) OFB mode   (e) CTR mode

$$CTR_i = U(CTR_{i-1})$$
$$C_i = P_i \oplus E_K(CTR_i)$$

where CTR_1 = initialisation vector (*IV*).

All 5 modes are depicted in Figure 1, (a) to (e) respectively.

Properties of the Standard Modes of Operation

In this section, we review past reported properties and often weaknesses of the standard modes of operation, as summarized in Table 1. Almost all of these properties can be exploited by an attacker to attack security protocols, be they for authentication, key exchange, or others. This will serve as a reminder to protocol designers and implementers on the importance of carefully choosing the modes that best suit their purpose and to ensure the suggested safeguards when using a certain mode.

Table 1. Properties of the standard modes of operation

Property	ECB	CBC	CFB	OFB	CTR
Distinct-block	×				
Cut-and-paste	×	×	×		
Collision	×	×	×		
Non-collision	×	×	×		×
Complementation			×	×	×
IV-Collision				×	

ECB mode

The ECB mode as outlined in Section 2 is the simplest, and the only mode where each block is encrypted independent of any other. This fact means that when two plaintext blocks are the same, they would be encrypted to the same ciphertext blocks. We call this the **distinct-block property**.

Property 1 (ECB) (Schneier, 2000): Distinct block

If $\qquad\qquad C_i = C_j \qquad$ for $i \neq j$

then $\qquad\qquad P_i = P_j.$

An attacker who observes two identical ciphertext blocks would know that the plaintext blocks are identical, therefore leaking information (Ferguson & Schneier, 2003) about the plaintexts. Also, if an attacker knows several plaintexts and corresponding ciphertexts, he could compile them in a **code book** so that he could observe all ciphertext blocks and wait until he sees a match, immediately allowing him to know what the plaintext block is. This has also been described as a matching ciphertext attack (Coppersmith et al., 1996) or as a birthday attack (Knudsen, 2000). Based on the birthday paradox, when we have collected $2^{n/2}$ blocks, where n is the block size, then we would expect to get two ciphertext blocks, C_i and C_j ($i \neq j$), that are equal.

By exploiting this property, Schneier (2000) also reports a **block replay attack**[2] on the ECB mode first discussed in 1978. In this attack, an attacker does not even have to know what the block cipher or the secret key is. Having obtained the ciphertext blocks corresponding to plaintext blocks that are advantageous to him/her, he/she simply replaces other ciphertext blocks with these ciphertext blocks.

An example of how an attacker could exploit this to his/her advantage is in the case of a bank transaction. If an account holder issues an instruction to the bank saying "Transfer $1,000 from my account to B's account," and if this whole instruction is encrypted in ECB mode, then an attacker C could replace the block encryption of "*B*" word with "*C*" so the money is transferred to C instead of B. Or even B could replace the block encryption of the "$1,000" with "$1,000,000" to change the amount transferred.

This problem is due to the fact that the ECB mode only guarantees confidentiality but not integrity. Since this weakness has been reported fairly early, it is known, at least among the security research community, that though the ECB mode does provide confidentiality, the ECB mode is not recommended for encrypting messages of multiple blocks. Instead, the ECB mode should strictly be limited to the encryption of single-block messages, that is, messages whose length is equal to the block size. As a further concrete example, we present in the Appendix an attack on the well-known wide-mouthed-frog protocol that exploits the distinct-block property of the ECB mode.

CBC Mode

The CBC mode is the most popular mode of operation and is recommended by many standards as their mode of choice. The CBC mode, however, exhibits what is called the **cut-and-paste** property, as has been reported in (Bellovin, 1996) as follows:

Property 2 (CBC) (Biham & Knudsen, 1998a): Cut-and-paste

If $\qquad\qquad IV = C_{i-1}$

then $\qquad D_K(C_i, ..., C_j) = P_i, ..., P_j.$

This property allows one to truncate or extract any portion of the ciphertext blocks (Bellovin, 1996). Mao and Boyd (1995) also describe how an attacker could cut part of a message and splice it to another message and hence obtain a plaintext block, X, in between the splice, or allow him/her to falsely trick others into believing that a fake X is a valid plaintext block.

The CBC mode also leaks information due to what we call the **collision property**:

Property 3 (CBC) (Knudsen, 2000): Collision

If $\qquad\qquad C_i \quad = \quad C_j$

then $\qquad E_K(P_i \oplus C_{i-1}) \quad = \quad E_K(P_j \oplus C_{j-1})$

$$P_i \oplus C_{i-1} \quad = \quad P_j \oplus C_{j-1}$$

$$P_i \oplus P_j \quad = \quad C_{i-1} \oplus C_{j-1}$$

This property means that when an attacker obtains $2^{n/2}$ ciphertext blocks, he/she expects to see a match between two blocks, C_i and C_j, which immediately allows him to know the XOR of the two corresponding plaintext blocks, $P_i \oplus P_j$. Ferguson and Schneier (2003) also report of a similar property, which we term as the **non-collision property**, as follows:

Property 4 (CBC) (Ferguson & Schneier, 2003): Non-collision

If $\qquad\qquad C_i \quad\neq\quad C_j$

then $\quad E_K(P_i \oplus C_{i-1}) \quad\neq\quad E_K(P_j \oplus C_{j-1})$

$\qquad\qquad P_i \oplus C_{i-1} \quad\neq\quad P_j \oplus C_{j-1}$

$\qquad\qquad P_i \oplus P_j \quad\neq\quad C_{i-1} \oplus C_{j-1}$

Therefore, unequal ciphertext blocks imply that $P_i \oplus P_j \neq C_{i-1} \oplus C_{j-1}$, and since ciphertext blocks are known, this leads to an inequality formula $P_i \oplus P_j \neq c$ (c = constant) between the plaintext blocks.

CFB Mode

The CFB mode is less popular compared to the CBC mode, but also attracts wide attention due to its use by PGP-like software (Garfinkel, 1995; Zimmerman, 1995) and standards (Callas, Donnerhacke, Finney, & Thayer, 1998), which is a widely used even by cryptographers to secure their e-mails. Recently, it was demonstrated in Jallad, Katz, and Schneier (2002) and Katz and Schneier (2000) how a cut-and-splice attack also works on the CFB mode. This shows that the CFB similarly exhibits the cut-and-paste property:

We also note that the CFB mode exhibits collision and non-collision properties similar to the CBC mode:

Property 5 (CFB) [New]: Collision

If $\qquad\qquad C_i \quad=\quad C_j$ and $C_{i-1} = C_{j-1}$

then $\quad P_i \oplus E_K(C_{i-1}) \quad=\quad P_j \oplus E_K(C_{j-1})$

$\qquad\qquad P_i \quad=\quad P_j$

Property 6 (CFB) [New]: Non-collision

If $\qquad\qquad C_i \quad=\quad C_j$ and $C_{i-1} \neq C_{j-1}$

then $\quad P_i \oplus E_K(C_{i-1}) \quad=\quad P_j \oplus E_K(C_{j-1})$

$\qquad\qquad P_i \quad\neq\quad P_j$

These properties also leak information about the plaintext. The attacker simply needs to check any pairs of two consecutive ciphertext blocks, (C_{i-1}, C_i) and (C_{j-1}, C_j), in order to know if the corresponding plaintext blocks, P_i and P_j, are equal or nonequal.

The fact that the CFB mode is a stream cipher causes it to suffer from what we call the **complementation property**, as reported in Schneier (2000), where the complementation of any bit in a ciphertext block causes a complementation in the corresponding bit of the plaintext block. In particular, let $C_i[j]$ be the jth bit of ciphertext block, C_i. Then, the complementation property is summarized as follows:

Property 7 (CFB) (Schneier, 2000): Complementation

If	$C_i[j]$	$=$	$!C_i[j]$
then	$P_i[j]$	$=$	$!P_i[j]$.

This makes the CFB mode vulnerable to a **message modification attack** (Schneier, 2000) where an attacker could complement bits of the plaintext at will by simply complementing the corresponding ciphertext bits. This might have serious consequences. For example, in a money-transfer protocol, complementing the most significant bit (MSB) of the amount transferred causes a drastic change.

OFB Mode

Since the OFB is also a stream cipher, it equally exhibits the complementation property, and hence succumbs to message modification attacks.

In addition, the feedback component of the OFB mode is independent of the plaintext and ciphertext blocks. This independence causes a severe problem if the same IV is used for the encryption of different plaintext messages, and hence leaks information about the plaintexts.

Property 8 (OFB) (Ferguson & Schneier, 2003): IV-Collision

If	IV	$=$	IV'
then	X_i	$=$	X'_i
	$E_K(X_i)$	$=$	$E_K(X'_i)$

Therefore	$C_i \oplus C_i'$	$=$	$P_i \oplus E_K(X_i) \oplus P_i' \oplus E_K(X'_i)$
		$=$	$P_i \oplus P_i'$

CTR Mode

Since the CTR mode is a variant of the OFB mode, it also exhibits the complementation property of the OFB mode. This also means that in this context, the CTR mode is less secure than the CBC mode, contrary to the claims made in MacGrew (2002) and Bellare et al. (1997). Also, Ferguson and Schneier (2000) report a similar non-collision property of the CTR mode. This is based on the observation that all key blocks, K_i, are distinct since they are encryptions of distinct counters, CTR_i.

Property 9 (CTR) (Ferguson & Schneier, 2003): Non-collision

Since	CTR_i	$\neq$	CTR_j	for $i \neq j$
then	K_i	$=$	$E_K(CTR_i)$	$\neq E_K(CTR_j) = K_j$
or	$K_i \oplus K_j$	$\neq$	0	
Therefore	$C_i \oplus C_j$	$=$	$P_i \oplus K_i \oplus P_j \oplus K_j$	
		$=$	$(P_i \oplus P_j) \oplus (K_i \oplus K_j)$	
		$\neq$	$P_i \oplus P_j$	

Exploiting Modes of Operation to Attack Public-Key Protocols

In this section, we will demonstrate how to exploit properties of the modes of operation to attack public-key security protocols. Since security protocols are mainly used for insecure communication channels, it is common to assume that the intruder, *I,* can intercept any messages in the computer network, and introduce new messages into it.

Preliminaries

The protocols we will discuss use either *secret key cryptography* (Pfleeger, 1997; Schneier, 2000; Stallings, 2002; Stinson, 2002) or *public key cryptography* (Diffie & Hellman, 1976; Rivest, Shamir, & Adleman, 1978; Schneier, 2000) or both. In the former, two agents, *A* and *B,* share one common key, K_{ab}, that is used for encrypting messages between them. In the latter, each agent, *A,* possesses a public key, K_A, that is easily obtainable from a key server, *S. A* also possesses a private key, K_A^{-1}, that is the inverse of K_A and is kept secret. We denote $\{m\}_k$ to mean the message, *m,* encrypted with the key, *k.* Any agent can encrypt a message for *A* using *A*'s public key, K_A, but only *A* can decrypt this message with its private key, K_A^{-1}. This ensures confidentiality and secrecy. *A* can sign a message by encrypting it with its private key, K_A^{-1}, so that any other agent can decrypt this with *A*'s public key, K_A, to verify the identity of *A* and that the message really originated from *A*. This provides authentication.

Nonces are also used in some of the protocols described later. These are random numbers generated for use in only a single run of the protocol; hence it is expected that every protocol run would have a different nonce generated. We denote N_A and N_B to mean nonces generated by *A* and *B* respectively.

Block ciphers are commonly regarded as symmetric-key ciphers, and hence block cipher modes of operation are often associated with symmetric-key ciphers. However, we note that public-key ciphers can also encrypt in blocks and hence can also be considered as block ciphers. Therefore, modes of operation equally apply to public-key block ciphers. There is no mention of this in cryptographic literature, except for a brief mention in Menezes, Oorschot, and Vanston (1997) against using the stream cipher modes, namely

CFB and OFB, with public-key ciphers. This is because these stream cipher modes use the encryption function, E_K, for mode encryption and decryption. So if E_K is a public-key cipher, then since the encryption key, K, is public, anyone could compute E_K and perform mode decryption. Thus, stream cipher modes are unable to provide confidentiality.

Our purpose in this section is to stress that though all the other nonstream cipher modes provide confidentiality when the underlying block cipher is a public-key cipher, one should still avoid using public-key ciphers to encrypt messages whose lengths are larger than the block size because since public keys are known, then anyone can perform public-key encryptions to generate public-key encrypted blocks! This means that whereas using symmetric-key ciphers in ECB, CBC, or CFB modes allows for cut-and-paste attacks, using public-key ciphers in any mode allows for **generate-and-paste attacks**! In terms of the integrity of encrypted blocks, public-key ciphers in any mode are worse than symmetric-key ciphers used in ECB mode!

In general, public-key ciphers are never used as block ciphers (i.e., to encrypt multiple blocks), mainly because they are slower than their secret-key cipher counterparts. What we show in this section is that public-key ciphers should never be used as block ciphers, not just because of efficiency reasons, but because they would not provide any security when used in such modes.

The Needham-Schroeder Public-Key Authentication Protocol

We prove our arguments with a concrete example of an attack on the popular Needham-Schroeder public-key authentication protocol (Needham & Schroeder, 1978), upon which Kerberos' design (MIT, 2005) was based. Kerberos is used in many commercial security systems. This protocol consists of the communication of seven messages, as follows:

1. $A \rightarrow S$ A, B

2. $S \rightarrow A$ $\{K_B, B\}_{K_S^{-1}}$

3. $A \rightarrow B$ $\{N_A, A\}_{K_B}$

4. $B \rightarrow S$ B, A

5. $S \rightarrow B$ $\{K_A, A\}_{K_S^{-1}}$

6. $B \rightarrow A$ $\{N_A, N_B\}_{K_A}$

7. $A \rightarrow B$ $\{N_B\}_{K_B}$

A is the initiator, wishing to establish a session with responder, B, with the help of the trusted key server, S. In 1, A sends a message to S, containing its own identity and B's identity. This will inform S that A wishes to establish a session with B. S replies with message 2, which contains the public key, K_B of B, as well as B's identity, both signed (encrypted) with S's private key, K_S^{-1}. A generates a nonce, N_A, and sends it along with its identity to B (message 3), encrypted with B's public key. B, upon receiving this message, decrypts it to obtain N_A and A's identity. It then sends message 4 to S to request for A's public key. S returns a signed message, 5, containing A's public key as well as A's identity. B generates a nonce, N_B, and uses A's public key, K_A, to encrypt N_A and N_B, and sends them as message 6 to A. When A receives this and decrypts it to obtain N_A and N_B, it is assured that it is really talking to B since only B would be able to know what N_A is by decrypting message 3. A then encrypts N_B with B's public key and sends it as message 7 to B. B decrypts this and obtains N_B, assured that it is talking to A since only A would have been able to decrypt message 6 to obtain N_B.

Lowe (1995, 1996) noted that the Needham-Schroeder protocol is in fact an interleaving of two logically disjoint protocols: messages 1, 2, 4, and 5 are for obtaining public keys, while messages 3, 6, and 7 are for authentication between A and B. Therefore, we will adopt the convention used by Lowe (1995) that each agent initially has each other's public key, and hence concentrate our attention to only the following messages:

3. $A \rightarrow B$ $\{N_A, A\}_{K_B}$

6. $B \rightarrow A$ $\{N_A, N_B\}_{K_A}$

7. $A \rightarrow B$ $\{N_B\}_{K_B}$

Lowe (1995) presented an attack on the Needham-Schroeder protocol that exploited the nonexplicitness of its message 6, and as a countermeasure, proposed to a modified variant (Lowe, 1995) as follows:

3. $A \rightarrow B$ $\{N_A, A\}_{K_B}$

6. $B \rightarrow A$ $\{B, N_A, N_B\}_{K_A}$

7. $A \rightarrow B$ $\{N_B\}_{K_B}$

Note that only message 6 is modified by inserting the responder's identity, B.

We will also consider in this description another variant, proposed in (Mohammed, Ramli, & Daud, 2001) for wireless networks, that is based on Lowe (1995), and hence has identical messages 3, 6, and 7, differing only in the messages 1, 2, 4, and 5 used for obtaining public keys.

Our attacks on the modified Needham Schroeder public-key authentication applies to all modes of operation used, but we will limit our discussion to only the ECB and CBC modes since the other stream cipher modes, namely CFB, OFB, and CTR should not be used with public-key ciphers even for providing confidentiality (Menezes et al., 1997).

An attack in ECB mode. We first consider the protocol used in ECB mode. Our attack exploits the case where each element of a message is of a fixed size, b, equal to the block size of the public-key or secret-key block cipher used. We use I_A to represent the intruder I impersonating A. Our attack involves two simultaneous runs of the protocol, denoted by a and b respectively. We also denote, for instance, message 2 of run b by $b.2$.

Our attack on the both variants of the modified Needham-Schroeder protocol (Lowe, 1995; Mohammed et al., 2001) is as follows:

$a.3.$	$A \rightarrow I$	$\{N_A, A\}_{K_I}$
$b.3.$	$I_A \rightarrow B$	$\{N_A, A\}_{K_B}$
$b.6.$	$B \rightarrow I_A$	$\{B, N_A, N_B\}_{K_A}$
$a.6.$	$I \rightarrow A$	$\{I, N_A, N_B\}_{K_A}$
$a.7.$	$A \rightarrow I$	$\{N_B\}_{K_I}$
$b.7.$	$I_A \rightarrow B$	$\{N_B\}_{K_B}$

This attack is based on Lowe's attack (Lowe, 1995) on the original Needham-Schroeder protocol. It was claimed that due to the insertion of the responder's identity, B, into message 6, such an attack would be impeded. However, considering our current scenario, each unique plaintext block will be encrypted into just one unique ciphertext block.

The first two steps proceed as according to Lowe (1995). A initiates a session with I by sending the message $a.3$. I immediately decrypts this message, uses the decrypted components to impersonate A, and sends this to B as message 3 of an apparently new protocol run, b. B replies with message $b.6$ to A, but this is intercepted by I. Unlike the attack in Lowe (1995), I would not be able to replay this as message $a.6$ to A as A would notice that the responder's identity is B and not I. I would also not be able to decrypt the message and get hold of N_B because it has been encrypted for A's eyes only. However, we notice that essentially all I has to do is to replace the encrypted block of B in message $b.6$ with an encrypted block of its own identity, I. I could easily do this by encrypting

Figure 2. Message {B, N_A, N_B} encrypted in CBC mode

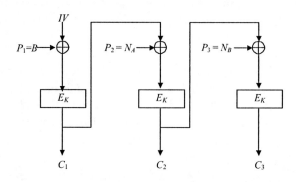

its identity, I, under A's public key, K_A, and then inserting that in place of the encrypted block of B. This forms the message $a.6$ that I can send to A. When A receives this, it would notice nothing amiss since due to the replacement, the responder's identity would show I. A replies to I with the message $a.7$ containing the encrypted N_B that I can decrypt and use to form message $b.7$ to be sent to B. Both protocol runs are now completed, and B is led to believe that A has successfully established a session with it, while A thinks it has successfully established a session with I, and does not even know of B's existence.

An attack in CBC mode. Next, we consider the case where the CBC mode is used, which is highly recommended not only for symmetric-key but also for public-key block ciphers (Menezes et al., 1997). There are three instances, depending on whether we wish to replace a block at the beginning, middle, or end of the encrypted message stream.

FIRST BLOCK. In this case, our attack works as in ECB mode. The first three steps are identical and hence after step 3, I obtains the message $b.6$, which contains the message $\{B, N_A, N_B\}$ encrypted in CBC mode. We can also view this as a stream of three ciphertext blocks, C_1, C_2, and C_3:

$$\{B, N_A, N_B\}_{K_A} = C_1, C_2, C_3$$

Again, as in the case of the ECB, I does not know the private key of A, and so is unable to decrypt it to obtain the value of N_B, or modify the encrypted B to I without affecting the ciphertext blocks, C_1 and C_2. However, by cleverly replacing the original IV with one of his choice, he can replace the identity of B in message $b.6$ with his own identity, I. For this, we analyse how $\{B, N_A, N_B\}$ is encrypted in CBC mode, as shown in Figure 2.

Since:

$$\begin{aligned} C_1 &= E_K(IV \oplus P_1) \\ \text{Then} \qquad P_1 &= IV \oplus E_K^{-1}(C_1) \quad = \quad B. \end{aligned}$$

In order to cause $P_1' = I$ instead of B, the intruder, I chooses a new $IV' = I \oplus B \oplus IV$. He then sends the message $a.6 = C_1, C_2, C_3$ to A, along with IV'. A, upon decryption, obtains the identity of the sender as:

$$\begin{aligned} P_1' &= IV' \oplus E_K^{-1}(C_1) \\ &= I \oplus B \oplus IV \oplus E_K^{-1}(C_1) \\ &= I \oplus B \oplus B \\ &= I \end{aligned}$$

and also the other plaintexts as:

$$P_2 \quad = \quad C_1 \oplus E_K^{-1}(C_2) \quad = \quad N_A$$
$$P_3 \quad = \quad C_2 \oplus E_K^{-1}(C_3) \quad = \quad N_B$$

Therefore, message $a.6$ appears to A as:

$a.6.$ $\qquad\qquad I \to A \qquad\qquad \{I, N_A, N_B\}_{K_A}$

The rest of the steps proceed as in our attack on ECB, and both protocol runs are now completed, with B thinking that A has just established a session with it, while A thinks it has established a session with I.

MIDDLE BLOCK. Replacing a middle block is harder, though still possible with more restrictions. I is able to still modify such a middle block, but is unable to choose what value it is modified to.

Again for illustration, we consider a variant of the Needham-Schroeder protocol, where the identity of the sender is inserted in the middle of message 6, of the form:

$$\{N_A, B, N_B\}_{K_A} = C_1, C_2, C_3.$$

Applying our attack to this variant also requires replacing the encrypted B block with an encryption of I. Denote the original plaintext message as:

$$M_1 \quad = \quad N_A, B, N_B$$
$$L_1 \quad = \quad C_1, C_2, C_3.$$

I then replaces the first ciphertext block, C_1 with $C_1' = E_K(IV' \oplus N_A)$ and sends:

$$L_2 \quad = \quad C_1', C_2, C_3$$

as well as a $IV' \neq IV$ to A as message 6. Upon decryption by A, the message:

$$M_2 \quad = \quad N_A, X, N_B$$

is obtained, and hence A is baffled as to why the authentication has failed even though everything appears normal. This is a nontrivial denial of service (DoS) attack in that both parties are unable to figure out why authentication keeps failing, and hence cannot detect that a DOS attack has been mounted.

LAST BLOCK. We have just demonstrated how to replace the first or middle block of a public-key CBC-encrypted message by tweaking the IV. To replace the last block of a public-key CBC-encrypted message is even easier by applying a cut-and-splice attack (Mao & Boyd, 1995).

As an illustration, consider a slightly modified variant of the Needham-Schroeder protocol, where message 6 is of the form:

$$\{N_A, N_B, B\}_{K_A} = C_1, C_2, C_3.$$

Note here that the identity of the sender, B, is put last instead of in front. To apply our attack on this protocol involves replacing the encrypted B block with the encrypted I block. Denote the original plaintext and the corresponding ciphertext messages respectively as:

$$
\begin{aligned}
M_1 &= N_A, N_B, B \\
L_1 &= C_1, C_2, C_3.
\end{aligned}
$$

Now I simply replaces the last ciphertext block, C_3 with $C_3' = E_K(I \oplus C_2)$ and sends:

$$L_2 = C_1, C_2, C_3'$$

to A as message 6. Upon decryption by A, the following message, M_2 is obtained:

$$M_2 = N_A, N_B, I$$

SUMMARY. Therefore, the CBC mode is insecure when used with public-key encryption and for most cases in the absence of IV integrity protection.

Exploiting Single-Block Encryptions

We will show in this section that the encryption of single blocks is insecure if the integrity of the block is not protected. In fact, when we think of it carefully, the encryption of a single block does not depend on previous blocks because no previous blocks exist! Therefore, in essence, the encryption of any single block is typically done in ECB mode. This observation therefore reduces the security of single-block encryptions to the security of the ECB mode!

Single-Block Encryptions Enable Known- or Chosen-IV Attacks

The ECB mode is commonly considered to be weak by the cryptographic community for the encryption of multiple-block messages. However, we note that the ECB mode is still one of the NIST's recently recommended block cipher modes of operation (NIST, 2001). There is only a brief mention of ECB's distinct-block property (NIST, 2001):

In the ECB mode, under a given key, any given plaintext block always gets encrypted to the same ciphertext block. If this property is undesirable in a particular application, the ECB mode should not be used.

without any remark on the insecurity of the ECB against block replay attacks.

It is recommended that the ECB mode only be used for the encryption of single-block messages, for example *IV*s, personal identification numbers (PINs), and challenge-response nonces (Anderson, 2001; Stallings, 2002), and that in such cases it would be appropriate and secure.

We argue here that even for encrypting single-block messages, the ECB by itself is not secure since the distinct-block property equally applies. Hence, though *IV*s are encrypted in ECB, an attacker could simply replace the encrypted ciphertext block with the encryption of an *IV* of his choice, either a known *IV* from a previous protocol session, or a chosen *IV* value obtained from a chosen-plaintext query of an encryption oracle. This allows for known-*IV* or chosen-*IV* attacks (Wagner, 1998) on the protocols for which the *IV* is being used. Therefore, though one generally considers chosen-*IV* attacks to be strong and restricted attack models, a block replay attack on the encrypted *IV* block makes such known- and chosen-*IV* attacks practical. Similarly, one could replace encrypted PIN blocks with the encryptions of known or chosen PIN values.

Abusing the IV in CTR and OFB Modes of Operation

Except for the ECB, all other standard modes use the *IV*. Though attacks on modes of operation that exploit the *IV* have been previously reported (Wagner, 1998), and similar attacks on protocols were reported in Bellovin (1996), the issue of protecting the integrity of the *IV* is still an open question (Anderson, 2001; Ferguson & Schneier, 2003; Knudsen, 2000; Schneier, 2000; Stallings, 2002) except for the case of CBC where it is mentioned in Bellovin (1996) and Menezes et al. (1997) that the integrity of the *IV* must be protected since single bit changes in the *IV* cause corresponding bit changes in the first plaintext block. But, Schneier (2000) mentions that the *IV* need not be secret and can be transmitted in the clear.

Nevertheless, we have argued in the previous section, that the integrity of the *IV* must be protected to guard against known- and chosen-*IV* attacks, because the fact that *IV*s are encrypted in ECB mode allows for block replays that make such attacks practical. In this section, we further strengthen our case by presenting a chosen-*IV* slide attack on the CTR and OFB modes.

Figure 3. Sliding the CTR mode

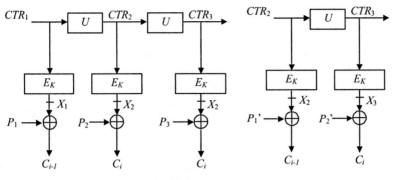

    (a) Original Encryption Sequence   (b) Slid Encryption Sequence

Chosen-IV slide attack on CTR and OFB modes. We first demonstrate a slide attack (Biryukov & Wagner, 1990) on the CTR mode. Consider the original encryption sequence as shown in Figure 3(a), with the initial counter value, $IV = CTR_I$ as usual, and whose ciphertext blocks are $C_1, C_2, ...$ An intruder, I impersonates A and mounts a chosen-IV attack and sends $IV' = CTR_2$ instead of the original IV, as well as the ciphertext blocks, $C_1, C_2, ...$ to B. We note that this has the effect that the keystream generated by B is round block out of phase with the original encryption sequence, and hence the encryption sequence at B's side is as shown in Figure 3(b).

B, upon decrypting the ciphertext blocks, obtains the plaintext blocks, $P_1', P_2', ...$, which are gibberish, since the keystream and ciphertext streams are not aligned. B replies to I with the puzzled question "What is this?", and quoting the $P_1', P_2', ...$ Since:

$$P_{i-1}' \quad = \quad C_{i-1} \oplus X_i$$
$$P_i \quad = \quad C_i \oplus X_i$$

So

$$X_i \quad = \quad C_{i-1} \oplus P_{i-1}' = C_i \oplus P_i$$

Therefore, I can calculate P_i as

$$P_i \quad = \quad C_{i-1} \oplus C_i \oplus P_{i-1}'.$$

Note that by choosing $IV' = E_K(X_0) = X_1$ in the OFB mode, a similar chosen-IV slide attack can be mounted.

Conclusion

We have presented a thorough treatment of the properties of the standard modes of operation. Our intention is that with such a list for reference by protocol implementers, this would prevent protocol attacks that exploit the inherent properties of the mode of operation used. We have shown why standard modes of operations should not be used in public-key protocols, and for most cases where the integrity of the IV is not protected, equally applies to the widely used CBC mode. We have also reduced the security of single-block encryptions to the security of the ECB mode, and shown that in the absence of IV integrity protection, one could exploit the ECB's distinct-block property to attack IVs, and hence enable known- or chosen-IV attacks. As a further proof of this, we presented chosen-IV slide attacks on the CTR and OFB modes of operation. We remark that such attacks are applicable to all other stream cipher modes that do not protect the integrity of the IV. A basic (but often left out) solution to counter the attacks discussed in this chapter is to ensure integrity protection when these modes are used. The current and future trends in proposed modes of operation are tending towards using such modes combined with authentication (integrity protection) (NIST, 2005). Of course, even having said that, one should not conclude that integrity protection guarantees no attacks can be mounted, because the interaction between these confidentiality modes and integrity protection can be quite subtle sometimes, as demonstrated in Mister and Zuccherato (2005).

References

Anderson, R. J. (2001). *Security engineering: A guide to building dependable distributed systems*. John Wiley & Sons.

Bellare, M., Desai, A., Jokipii, E., & Rogaway, P. (1997). A concrete security treatment of symmetric encryption: Analysis of the DES modes of operation. In *Proceedings of the 38th Symposium on Foundations of Computer Science, IEEE* (pp. 394-405).

Bellovin, S. M. (1996). Problem areas for the IP security protocols. In *Proceedings of the 6th USENIX Security Symposium* (pp. 1-16).

Bellovin, S. M., & Blaze, M. (2001). *Cryptographic modes of operation for the Internet*. Presented at the 2nd NIST Workshop on Modes of Operation.

Biham, E. (1994). *On modes of operation* (LNCS 809, pp. 116-120). Springer.

Biham, E. (1994a). *Cryptanalysis of multiple modes of operation* (LNCS 914, 278-292). Springer.

Biham, E. (1996). *Cryptanalysis of triple-modes of operation* (Technion Tech. Rep. No. CS885).

Biham, E. (1998). Cryptanalysis of multiple modes of operation. *Journal of Cryptology 11*(1), 45-58.

Biham, E. (1999). Cryptanalysis of triple-modes of operation. *Journal of Cryptology 12*(3), 161-184.

Biham, E., & Knudsen, L. R. (1998). *Cryptanalysis of the ANSI X9.52 CBCM mode* (LNCS 1403, pp. 100-111). Springer.

Biham, E., & Knudsen, L. R. (1998a). Cryptanalysis of the ANSI X9.52 CBCM mode. *Journal of Cryptology 15*(3), 100-111.

Biryukov, A., & Wagner, D. (1990). *Slide attacks* (LNCS 1636, 245-259). Springer.

Boyd, C. (1997). *Extensional goals for authentication protocols.* Presented at the DIMACS Workshop on Cryptographic Protocol Design and Verification.

Boyd, C., & Mathuria, A. (1997). *Key establishment protocols for secure mobile communications: A selective survey* (LNCS 1438, 344-355). Springer.

Boyd, C., & Park, D. G. (1998). Public key protocols for wireless communications. In *Proceedings of ICISC '98* (pp. 47-57). Korea Institute of Information Security and Cryptology (KIISC).

Callas, J., Donnerhacke, L., Finney, M., & Thayer, R. (1998). *OpenPGP message format* (RFC 2440).

Coppersmith, D., Johnson, D. B., & Matyas S. M. (1996). A proposed mode for triple-DES encryption. *IBM Journal of Research and Development, 40*(2), 253-262.

Diffie, W., & Hellman, M. (1976). New directions in cryptography. *IEEE Transactions on Information Theory, 22*, 644-654.

Ferguson, N., & Schneier, B. (2003). *Practical cryptography.* John Wiley & Sons.

Garfinkel, S. (1995). *PGP: Pretty good privacy.* O'Reilly & Associates.

Handschuh, H., & Preneel, B. (1999). *On the security of double and 2-key triple modes of operation* (LNCS 1636, pp. 215-230). Springer.

Jallad, K., Katz, J., & Schneier, B. (2002). Implementation of chosen-ciphertext attacks against PGP and GnuPGP. In *Proceedings of the Information Security Conference* (LNCS 2433, pp. 90-101). Springer.

Katz, J., & Schneier, B. (2000). A *chosen ciphertext attack against several e-mail encryption protocols.* Paper presented at the 9th USENIX Security Symposium.

Knudsen, L. R. (2000). *Block chaining modes of operation.* Paper presented at the 1st NIST Workshop on Modes of Operation.

Lipmaa, H., Rogaway, P., & Wagner, D. (2000). *CTR- Mode encryption.* Paper presented at the 1st NIST Workshop on Modes of Operation.

Lowe, G. (1995). An attack on the Needham-Schroeder public-key protocol. *Information Processing Letters, 56*, 131-133.

Lowe, G. (1996). *Breaking and fixing the Needham-Schroeder public-key protocol using FDR* (LNCS 1055, pp. 147-166). Springer.

Mao, W., & Boyd, C. (1993). Towards formal analysis of security protocols. In *Proceedings of IEEE Computer Security Foundations Workshop VI, IEEE Press* (LNCS 765, pp. 147-158). Springer.

Mao, W., & Boyd, C. (1994). On a limitation of BAN Logic. In *Proceedings of the Advances in Cryptology — Eurocrypt 93* (LNCS, pp. 240-247). Springer.

Mao, W., & Boyd, C. (1994a). Development of authentication protocols: Some misconceptions and a new approach. In *Proceedings of IEEE Computer Security Foundations Workshop VII*. IEEE Press.

Mao, W., & Boyd, C. (1995). On the use of encryption in cryptographic protocols. In *Proceedings of 4th IMA Conference on Cryptography and Coding* (pp. 251-262).

Mao, W., & Boyd, C. (1995a). Methodical use of cryptographic transformations in authentication protocols. *IEE Proceedings: Computers and Digital Techniques, 142*(4), 272-278.

McGrew, D. A. (2002). *Counter mode security: Analysis and recommendations.* Paper presented at the 55th IETF Conference.

Menezes, A. J., van Oorschot, P. C., & Vanston, S. A. (1997). *Handbook of applied cryptography.* CRC Press.

Mister, S., & Zuccherato, R. (2005). An attack on CFB mode encryption as used by OpenPGP. In *Proceedings of the Selected Areas in Cryptography '05* (LNCS 3897, pp. 82-94). Springer.

MIT. (2005). *Kerberos: The network authentication protocol.* Retrieved from http://web.mit.edu/kerberos/www/

Mohammed, L. A., Ramli, A. R., & Daud, M. B. (2001). How to authenticate users in wireless networks. In *Proceedings of the MMU Symposium on Information and Communication Technology (M²USIC)* (pp. 1.5(1)-1.5(4)).

Needham, R. M., & Schroeder, M. D. (1978). Using encryption for authentication of large networks and computers. *Communications of the ACM, 21*(12), 993-999.

NIST. (2001). Recommendation for block cipher modes of operation — methods and techniques. *NIST Special Publication*, SP 800-38A.

NIST. (2005). *CSRC — modes of operation.* Retrieved from http://csrc.nist.gov/CryptoToolkit/modes/

Park, D. G., Boyd, C., & Dawson, E. (2000). *Classification of authentication protocols: A practical approach* (LNCS 1975, pp. 194-208). Springer.

Pfleeger, C. P. (1997). *Security in computing.* Prentice Hall.

Rivest, R. L., Shamir, A., & Adleman, L. (1978). A method for obtaining digital signatures and public-key cryptosystems. *Communications of the ACM. 21*(2), 120-126.

Schneier, B. (2000). *Applied cryptography* (2nd ed.). John Wiley & Sons.

Stallings, W. (2002). *Cryptography and network security* (3rd ed.). Prentice Hall.

Stinson, D. (2002). *Cryptography: Theory and practice* (2nd ed.). CRC Press.

Wagner, D. (1998). *Cryptanalysis of some recently-proposed multiple modes of operation* (LNCS 1372, pp. 254-269). Springer.

Zimmerman, P. (1995). *The official PGP user's guide.* MIT Press.

Endnotes

[1]   Readers interested in the security of the modes of operation regardless of their use in protocols are referred to (Bellare, Desai, Jokipii, & Rogaway, 1997; Biham, 1994, 1994a, 1996, 1998, 1999; Biham & Knudsen, 1998, 1998a; Coppersmith, Johnson, & Matyas, 1996; Handschuh & Preneel, 1999; Schneier, 2000; Stallings, 2002).

[2]   This is sometimes also known as the cut-and-paste or cut-and-splice attack (Anderson, 2001).

Appendix

Attacking Authentication and Key-Exchange Protocols In ECB Mode

Though a block replay attack has been demonstrated in Pfleeger (1997) on money transfer protocols, we further argue that such attacks are equally applicable to authentication and key-exchange protocols. As a concrete example, we show in this Appendix how to exploit the distinct-block property of the ECB to attack the ide-mouthed-frog protocol, which provides both authentication and key exchange. We hope that this completes the evidence that the ECB allows an attacker to totally devastate security protocols and hence, should not be considered at all in protocol implementations.

The wide-mouthed-frog protocol is

1.　　$A \rightarrow S$　　　　　　$A, \{T_a, B, K_{ab}\}_{K_{as}}$

2.　　$S \rightarrow B$　　　　　　$\{T_s, A, K_{ab}\}_{K_{bs}}$

A block replay attack is described as

$a.1.$　$A \rightarrow S$　　　　　　$A, \{T_a, B, K_{ab}\}_{K_{as}}$

$a.2.$　$S \rightarrow B$　　　　　　$\{T_s, A, K_{ab}\}_{K_{bs}}$

$a'.1.$　$A \rightarrow I_S$　　　　　$A, \{T'_a, B, K'_{ab}\}_{K_{as}}$

$a''.1.$　$I_A \rightarrow S$　　　　$A, \{T'_a, B, K_{ab}\}_{K_{as}}$

$a'.2.$　$S \rightarrow B$　　　　　$\{T'_s, A, K_{ab}\}_{K_{bs}}$

Here, a denotes a protocol run of a previously established session, with the shared key, K_{ab} successfully established between A and B. a' denotes the next time A wishes to establish a session with B. However, this time round, the first message $a'.1$ is intercepted by I, who immediately replaces the encrypted block of K_{ab}' with the encrypted block of the previous session key, K_{ab}. I can do this because it can easily capture the encrypted blocks of previous protocol runs, and needs to just replace the blocks without knowing what their decrypted contents are. *I* then relays the modified message as message *a*".1 to *S*, who then sends the message *a*'.2 to *B*, and so completes the protocol run. However, *B* thinks that the session key is K_{ab} while *A* thinks it is K_{ab}'. This shows a failure of authentication and key establishment. Further, if *I* has knowledge of the previous session key, K_{ab}, then it can impersonate *A* and read all messages from *B*, send fake messages to *B*, without the knowledge of *A*.

Chapter XV

Generic Algorithm for Preparing Unbreakable Cipher:
A Short Study

R. A. Balachandar, Anna University, India

M. Balakumar, Anna University, India

S. Anil Kumar, Anna University, India

Abstract

This chapter addresses the need of cryptographic algorithm to prepare unbreakable cipher. Though the performance of symmetric key algorithms is far better than asymmetric key algorithms, it still suffers with key distribution problems. It is highly evident that there is always a demand for an algorithm to transfer the secret key in a secure manner between the participants. This chapter argues that by providing the randomness to the secret key, it would be increasingly difficult to hack the secret key. This chapter proposes an algorithm effectively utilizes the random nature of stock prices in conjunction with plain text to generate random cipher. This algorithm can be used to exchange the secret key in a secure manner between the participants.

Introduction

The goal of the chapter is to assure a secure communication between the sender and the receiver. Nowadays, most of the transactions are held across the Internet, so providing security to such transactions is extremely important. Network security is the capability to send a message electronically from the client to the server in a secure manner, so that only the intended receiver receives the secret message. Even though many protocols were developed to ensure a secure communication between the participants, they all have their own pitfalls. All these protocols effectively utilize the various existing cryptographic algorithms. With this chapter, we are providing a new cryptographic algorithm that can be used to develop a secure protocol. This chapter also addresses the problem of providing randomness to the cipher text. Cipher text generated by the symmetric key cryptosystem is unique with the secret key and can be decrypted once the secret key is hacked by the intruder. If the secret key were changing randomly with some factors, then it would be extremely difficult to hack.

This chapter utilizes the stock prices of a stock exchange to provide randomness to the cipher. The stock price does not follow any pattern and is generated by forces driving the overall market place, various sectors (aerospace, retail, etc.) and the individual stock prices. Here, we proposed a detailed procedure to prepare random key by fusing the secret key with current stock price. With this random key, it is possible to obtain a random cipher that is highly unbreakable. This procedure can be used to exchange the secret key in a secure manner between the participants. The procedure discussed here utilizes the random stock prices in conjunction with the plain text to generate random cipher. The next section provides a brief description on the objectives of cryptography.

Objectives of Cryptography

Cryptography is the study of mathematical techniques related to the aspects of information security such as confidentiality, data integrity, authentication, and nonrepudiation (Schneier, 1996). Any secure system requires fulfilling all the four aspects.

Cryptographic algorithms are used to transform plaintext or a secret message into encrypted data in which the secret message is hidden (Stallings, 2000). The act of hiding the information is called encryption. The process of transforming the encrypted data back to the plaintext is known as decryption.

Cryptographic algorithms can be classified into two types:

1. symmetric key cryptosystem and
2. asymmetric key cryptosystem

In **symmetric key cryptosystem,** one key is used for both encryption and decryption. To maintain security of the information, the key needs to be kept secret from any other entities. Second sets of algorithms are **asymmetric algorithm**, also known as public key algorithm. In this approach, one key is kept private and the other is made public. The public key can be freely distributed since the private key cannot be easily derived directly from the corresponding public key. Data encrypted using the public key can only be decrypted using the private key. The performance of asymmetric cryptography algorithms is typically not as good as a symmetric key cryptosystem as it is computationally intensive (Schneier, 1996) and therefore not usually used for data encryption. Also, the symmetric cryptosystem has its own limitations, and is discussed in the next section.

Issues and Concerns over Cryptographic Algorithms

Since same key is used for both encryption and decryption in symmetric cryptosystem, the main security importance is to get that secret key from the sender in secure fashion. Figure 1 describes symmetric key cryptosystem. Here, the secret key encrypts the message and then transports it over the network, where the secret key again is used to obtain the original message. In a private key system, the integrity of the key is extremely important and hence, key distribution becomes a major problem in this type of cryptographic algorithm. To overcome this difficulty, public key algorithms are used in conjunction with symmetric cryptosystems to take advantage of both. In this case, the message is encrypted using symmetric algorithm, and the secret key is encrypted with public key of the receiver and sent to him. This eliminates key distribution problems, but it suffers with man-in-the-middle attack, which is a computer security breach in which a malicious user intercepts, and possibly alters, data traveling along the network. Again, this can also be eliminated with the help of certification authority. But all these methodologies have already been proved to be costlier and involve a lot of overhead.

Alternatively, we can avoid the usage of asymmetric key algorithms by periodically replacing the secret key used in symmetric algorithm. The concept called "perfect forward secrecy," where keys are refreshed on a very frequent basis, helps to limit the damage, as they provide only a very small window of opportunity for attacks. Moreover,

Figure 1. Symmetric key cryptosystem

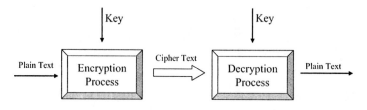

symmetric algorithms are generally faster than asymmetric as they can use smaller key sizes and generate the same security as larger key sizes in public key encryption algorithm.

If the sender uses the same key for encryption of secret message more than once, then symmetric cipher becomes a lot easier to break by **sustained data analysis attack** (Stallings, 2000) that tries all possible keys until the message can be decoded. Generating completely random, different session keys turns out to be very difficult. This difficulty can be overcome with the help of random number generators.

Stock Prices as Random Numbers

Randomness and random numbers have traditionally been used for a variety of purposes; for example, games such as dice games. With the advent of computers, people recognized the need for a means of introducing randomness into a computer program especially for the key generation in cryptographic techniques and for some classes of scientific experiments. For scientific experiments, it is convenient that a series of random numbers can be replayed for use in several experiments. However, for cryptographic use, it is important that the numbers used to generate keys are not just seemingly random, but they must be truly unpredictable also. However, the sources of random numbers exhibit limited utility in network security applications and hence there are problems both with the randomness and the precision of such numbers (Bright & Enison, 1979), to say nothing of the clumsy requirement of attaching one of these devices to every system in an Internet work (Stallings, 2000). Another alternative is to dip into a collection of good quality random numbers that have been published (Rand Corporation, 1955; Tippett, 1927). However, these collections provide a limited source of numbers compared to the potential requirements of a sizable network security application (Stallings, 2000).

Hence, cryptographic applications typically make use of algorithmic techniques for random number generation, and they chose to introduce randomness into computers in the form of pseudorandom number generators. As the name suggests, pseudorandom numbers are not truly random. Rather, they are computed from a mathematical formula, or simply taken from a precalculated list. A lot of research has gone into pseudorandom number theory and modern algorithms for generating them are so good that the numbers look exactly like they were really random. Pseudorandom numbers have the characteristic that they are predictable (Rand Corporation, 1955), meaning they can be predicted if you know where in the sequence the first number is taken from. This is extremely undesirable in the case of cryptographic techniques. So to overcome this issue we can use the stock prices of a stock market as an alternative.

The primary reason behind this is because the stock prices exhibit the property of unpredictability (Crypton, 2004). The stock prices have no pattern. Every day in the stock market, it never changes with any constant factor. No single stock price is dependant on any other. In a rising market, some stock prices fall, and in a falling market some rise (Crypton, 2004). Each and every stock price is independent, so stock prices are really random. This technique to prepare unbreakable cipher, utilizes the random property of stock prices to provide randomness to the cipher generated by symmetric cryptosystem. The same protocol can also be used for key exchange between the participants, thereby overcoming the key distribution problem of symmetric cryptosystem. With this random property of stock prices, the technique discussed here can avoid brute-force attack and the sustained data analysis attacks.

Preparing Unbreakable Cipher

The technique requires the stock prices to be used in conjunction with the key word to generate a cipher that would be highly random in nature (Crypton, 2004). The solution is straightforward. Each stock price can be considered a keying number for each letter of plain text.

The steps to be followed for preparing the cipher are as follows:

Write the plain text message in groups of five or more. Below the text, write the number that represents its position in the alphabet, 1 for "A," 2 for "B," and so on through 26 for "Z." Below these numbers put a stock price for each letter. Add the numbers and generate the cryptogram based upon a random key.

The problem is how to choose the prices in a manner that only the recipient of the coded message can able to determine the original message and nobody else. The method will, admittedly, create a list of apparent random numbers, but in actual use should have all the strength of true randomness.

For each message, the sender could select a word of eight or more from a book known both to the sender and the receiver of the message. The letters of the word then determine which stock price to use to provide a random number. A word like "ELIMINATE" would guide selection of numbers starting with the price of the first stock beginning under "E," and so on. A selected stock price should be marked in the newspaper to prevent it from being used again. If the letter "E" comes again, then select the second stock beginning under "E," and so on. Finally, both the sender and the recipient must agree upon using the stock prices from the same newspaper for the same day.

Sample Preparation of Secure Cipher

The stock prices were taken from the **August 27, 2004** edition of *The New Indian Express* using the rounded rupee price. Here, closing stock prices of Group B companies are considered. The protocol assumes that both the sender and receiver have agreed upon the common key word **ELIMINATE**. The plaint text considered is "haihellohowareu."

Keyword	E	L	I	M	I	N	A	T	E	E	L	I	M
Plaintext	h	a	i	h	e	l	l	o	h	o	w	r	u

The plain text numbers (PT numbers) are listed for every letter of the plain text based on their respective **alphabetical positions**.

PT Numbers	8	1	9	8	5	11	11	14	8	14	22	17	20

The stock prices listed are based on the stock prices of the companies whose names are starting with the respective letters of the key word. (Ex 2 for E, 25 for I and so on).

Stock Prices	2	2	25	15	6	8	8	3	19	55	18	5	2

The stock prices and PT numbers are added as shown.

AddedNumbers	10	3	34	23	11	19	19	17	27	69	40	22	22

Then the added numbers are subjected to modulo 26 operation.

Modulo 26	10	3	8	23	11	19	19	17	1	17	14	22	22

The resultant numbers are formatted to arrive at the cipher text. Since the resultant cipher is the function of stock prices and the keyword, it exhibits the property of randomness. If the same protocol is used to encrypt the secret key, then it would be extremely random. The message encrypted with that random key, it is possible to obtain a random cipher that is highly unbreakable. The steps involved in preparing the cipher have been given as a flowchart in Figure 2.

Figure 2. Flowchart for preparing cipher

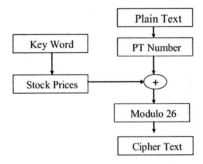

Cipher Text	j	c	h	w	k	s	s	q	a	q	n	v	v

In the receiver side, the decryption is performed. The selected stock prices would be subtracted from the encrypted numbers, and then modulo 26 operation is performed on them .If the resultant values are less than zero, then they are added with 26 to produce the numbers for the letters in the message.

Cipher Text	10	3	8	23	11	19	19	17	1	17	14	22	22
Stock Prices	2	2	25	15	6	8	8	3	19	55	18	5	2
Subtract	8	1	-17	8	5	11	11	14	-18	-38	-4	17	20
Modulo 26	8	1	-17	8	5	11	11	14	-18	-12	-4	17	20
If < 0 then Add to 26	8	1	9	8	5	11	11	14	8	14	22	17	20
Plain Text	h	a	i	h	e	l	l	o	h	o	w	r	u

The steps involved in obtaining the plain text from the cipher have been given as flowchart in the Figure 3.

Figure 3. Flowchart for obtaining plaintext from the cipher

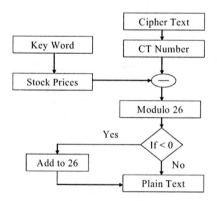

Advantages

The main drawback of the symmetric key cryptosystem is the distribution of the key between the participants (Diffie & Hellman, 1997). If the participants were in remote geographical locations, then it would be difficult to exchange the keys, as the communication channel is always prone to attack. Hence, asymmetric algorithms are widely used for exchanging the keys. The secret key is encrypted by receiver's public key, and at the receiver end it is decrypted with the intended receiver's private key. Even though this system solves the key exchange problem, it is computationally slow. Moreover, it suffers man-in-the middle attack.

Attempts were made to make the secret key change randomly, but once again generating a random number using computer system was proven to be insecure. The protocol proposed here exploits stock prices in conjunction with a key word to generate a secure cipher. As the stock prices do not follow any pattern, it is extremely random. The cipher resultant with this protocol is also random, and hence is highly unbreakable. As the procedure discussed here is used only for encryption of short messages, exchange of secret key between the sender and receiver can be done more effectively.

Conclusion

This chapter attempts to generate a secure cipher that would be highly unbreakable. The exploitation of stock prices to prepare such a cipher is highlighted here. Even though it is time consuming as it is done manually, it can be effectively simulated using some sophisticated software. By agreeing upon a common keyword, this technique will be useful for secret key management and thereby effectively eliminates the key distribution problem of symmetric key cryptosystem. It can be used in conjunction with the symmetric key cryptosystem to overcome man-in-the-middle attack encountered in conventional encryption system.

References

Bright, H., & Enison, R. (1979). Quasirandom number sequences from long-period TLP generator with remarks on application to cryptography. *ACM Computing Surveys, 11*(4), 54-67.

Crypton. (2004). An unbreakable cipher, the cryptogram. *Journal of the American Cryptogram Association*, 7.

Diffie, W., & Hellman, M. E. (1997). Exhaustive cryptanalysis of the NBS data encryption standard. *IEEE Computer, 10*, 74-84.

Rand Corporation. (1955). *A million random digits* (pp. 45-75). New York: The Free Press. Retrieved from http://www.rand.org/publications/classics/randomdigits

Schneier, B. (1996). *Applied cryptography: Protocols, algorithms and source code in C* (2nd ed., pp. 21-75). John Wiley & Sons.

Stallings, W. (2000). *Cryptography and network security: Principles and practice* (pp. 201-340). Pearson Education.

Tippett, L. H. C. (1927). Random sampling numbers. *Tracts for Computers*, (15), 35-43.

Chapter XVI

A Robust Watermarking Scheme Using Codes Based on the Redundant Residue Number System

Vik Tor Goh, Multimedia University, Malaysia

Mohammad Umar Siddiqi, International Islamic University Malaysia, Malaysia

Abstract

In this chapter, a watermarking scheme that utilizes error correction codes for added robustness is proposed. A literature survey covering various aspects of the watermarking scheme, such as the arithmetic redundant residue number system, and concepts related to digital watermarking is given. The requirements of a robust watermarking scheme are also described. In addition, descriptions and experimental results of the proposed watermarking scheme are provided to demonstrate the functionality of the scheme. The authors hope that with the completion of this chapter, the reader will have a better understanding of ideas related to digital watermarking as well as the arithmetic redundant number system.

Introduction

Companies and people alike have benefited greatly from the usage of computers in their work and daily lives. Gone are the days when interested parties would have to scour libraries and archives for references to information that they require. Today, all of these and more are accessible with the click of a mouse. The Internet has proven itself to be a limitless source of information, ranging from texts, images, sounds, and videos. Everyone can now obtain the resources that they need and use it at their pleasure, at almost no cost. Everyone is an expert, sometimes to the chagrin of real experts of the subject matter.

However, as an unforeseen consequence of this, people are ignorant to copyright issues often associated with materials obtained via the Internet. Often times, people choose to continue their activities with full knowledge that copyright laws are being violated by their actions. Solving this ever-growing problem requires a multi-prong approach ranging from passing new regulatory laws, enforcing fines on copyright violators and developing technologies that can be used in managing digital media.

One of the more promising technologies that can be used to curtail the illegal use of copyrighted materials is digital watermarking. An exciting and fast-growing field in digital watermarking focuses on the challenges involved in securing digital images. In general, a watermarking scheme attempts to hide a mark within an image that can be used for a variety of purposes such as copyright protection (Barni, Bartolini, Cappellini, & Piva, 1997; Craver, Memon, Yeo, & Yeung, 1998), fingerprinting for traitor tracking (Boneh & Shaw, 1998), copy protection and image authentication (Celik, Sharma, Saber, & Tekalp, 2002; Kundur & Hatzinakos, 1999).

Definitions and Histories

Arithmetic Redundant Residue Codes

The Chinese remainder theorem (CRT) owes its namesake to a Chinese mathematician by the name of Sun Zi, who has been credited for its initial conceptualization. The theorem first appeared in the book called *Sun Zi Suanjing* or simply Sun's Arithmetical Manual (Ding, Pei, & Salomaa, 1996, p. 2). The CRT has its many uses ranging from fields such as cryptography, computing, and coding theory.

In the field of cryptography, Shamir (1979), and later improved by Asmuth and Bloom (1983), proposed a scheme of distributing a common secret among a group of participants. Each participant has only a partial piece of the secret that cannot be used to derive the whole secret. According to Stinson (1995, p. 326), some subset of participants must cooperate to reconstitute the secret. On the other hand, for the field of computing, Asmuth and Blakley (1982) suggested a technique where a large computer file is split into several parts and stored in a few computers. The loss of a fixed number of parts not amounting to a critical level will not cause any problems in recovering the whole file. The idea was to increase the availability of the file should one or more computers fail.

In spite of that, the area of particular interest is coding theory, or more specifically, fault tolerant coding. Error correction codes based on the CRT are attractive because of its ability to perform carry-free arithmetic and lack of ordered significance among the residue digits (Miller & Rutter, 2002; Yang & Hanzo, 2001). Furthermore, according to Yang and Hanzo, both these properties suggest that these codes are highly suitable for self-checking, error detection and correction in digital processors as well as parallel processing machines.

An arithmetic residue code describes methods of representing an integer as a set of its remainders. When implemented with sufficient redundancies, the result is an arithmetic redundant residue code that can easily detect and correct errors (Krishna, Lin, & Sun, 1992). The redundant residue code uses CRT as a mean of reconstructing the integer from a set of its remainders.

Significant work concerning redundant residue codes has been carried out by numerous parties, starting with Barsi and Maestrini (1973) and Mandelbaum (1972). They introduced the initial concepts related to this error-correction technique, such as the terms *legitimate range* and *illegitimate range,* for consistency checking. In Krishna et al. (1992), a discussion of a single residue error correction algorithm is given. Besides that, Goldreich, Ron, and Sudan (2000) as well as Sun and Krishna (1992) addressed the problem of double and multiple residue error correction, respectively.

There are generally two different strategies employed to correct errors in a redundant residue code. The first method calculates the syndromes of received residues and then compares them with a set of predetermined observations. From there, conclusions are drawn and the appropriate integer recovery algorithm is carried out. This is akin to algorithms by Krishna et al. (1992) and Sun and Krishna (1992). Alternatively, the erroneous integer is recovered from the received residues and the error value is estimated using continued fractions or integer programming. The corrected integer is thus recovered by subtracting the error value from the erroneous integer. Goldreich et al. (2000) and Mandelbaum (1976) suggested schemes based on this method.

As effective as these algorithms are, they sometimes become complicated, especially when used to correct multiple errors. The error correction scheme by Sun and Krishna (1992) requires a large set of observations just to correct double errors. Likewise, integer optimization algorithms are harder to implement and when badly coded, the error correction process becomes unnecessarily time consuming. As such, an algorithm that does not rely heavily on both these correction strategies is preferable.

Digital Watermarking for Images

The precursors to digital watermarks are paper watermarks that originally appeared when the handmade paper industry started about 700 years ago in Italy. According to Kutter and Hartung (2000, p. 98), this was done to identify the producer of the paper as well as to serve as an indication of paper format, quality, and strength. These early watermarks were also used for dating and authenticating paper. It would seem that the functions of today's modern digital watermarks do not differ much from its predecessors. Some of the earliest publications in this growing field of research are by Tanaka, Nakamura, and Matsui (1990) and Caronni (1995).

The basic components of a generic digital watermarking scheme in subsequent publications consist primarily of a watermark embedding block and its counterpart, a watermark extraction block. These blocks take in several different inputs to produce their corresponding outputs. Figure 1 shows the components involved in a generic watermark-embedding scheme. In such an embedding scheme, the watermark itself can take on any form such as text, number, or an image. Besides that, if a key is used, unauthorized manipulation or removal of watermarks can be prevented.

On the other hand, a generic watermark extraction scheme is shown in Figure 2, where the inputs to such a scheme are the potentially tampered image, key, and original data. The original data refers to the inputs that are used in the embedding process such as the watermark or copyrighted image. In addition, the output of the watermark extraction process can either be the recovered watermark or a confidence measure that indicates whether the image is watermarked or otherwise. The usage of optional parameters such as keys and original data depends on the design requirements of the watermarking scheme.

Digital watermarking schemes can generally be divided into one of two types, depending on the visibility of the watermarks. *Visible watermarks* are usually patterns or logos that are visibly placed over the copyrighted material. Visible watermarks are similar to the watermarks often found on currencies. This type of watermark is usually used to label digital images found in online image databases. Although the subtlety of these watermarks makes them perfect for image previewing applications, they are sufficiently annoying to copyright violators who do not wish to give due credit or compensation to the copyright owner. Conversely, *invisible watermarks* do the exact opposite, which is to stay hidden from view. The existence of such watermarks can only be verified with the appropriate watermark extraction algorithm (Holliman & Memon, 2000). The focus for the remainder of this chapter is on invisible watermarks.

Invisible watermarking schemes can be further categorized as *robust* or *fragile* watermarks. As its name implies, robust watermarking schemes are designed to withstand a variety of image manipulation techniques. Among them are image rotation, scaling, addition of noise, and lossy compression. Cox, Kilian, Leighton, and Shamoon (1997), Podilchuk and Zeng (1998) as well as Ó Ruanaidh and Pun (1997) are among those who

Figure 1. Generic watermark embedding scheme

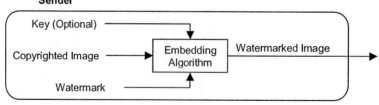

Figure 2. Generic watermark extraction scheme

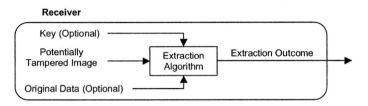

have proposed robust watermarking schemes. On the other hand, fragile watermarks are designed to be sensitive to image alterations and are used to ascertain the integrity of a given image. Fragile watermarks have been proposed by Celik, et al. (2002), as well as Yeung and Mintzer (1997).

Another characteristic that has to be taken into consideration before designing a watermarking scheme is whether any of the original data, such as those in Figure 2, are needed for the watermark extraction process. Watermarking schemes that do not require any of the original data are called *oblivious* watermarking schemes. Since they do not require additional data for the extraction process, oblivious watermarking schemes use less bandwidth (Holliman & Memon, 2000). Moreover, having either the original image or watermark at the decoder may not be convenient or even practical for some applications. Eggers, Su, and Girod (2000) as well as Liu, Gao, Cui, and Song (2002) have worked with this form of watermarking scheme. In contrast, *nonoblivious* watermarking schemes require the original data to recover the watermark. Although these schemes use more bandwidth and may be slightly more inconvenient, they are usually more robust against tampering. The highly robust watermarking scheme by Cox et al. (1997) is an example of a nonoblivious scheme.

One of the main challenges in designing an effective watermarking scheme is to inconspicuously embed the watermark in the image. With the variety of literature in digital watermarking, the comprehensive list of techniques can be overwhelming. Fortunately, all the proposed embedding techniques can actually be categorized based on their choice of workspace. Watermark embedding can be carried out either in the spatial domain or transform domains such as discrete Fourier transform (DFT), discrete cosine transform (DCT), wavelet transform, or Fourier-Mellin transform. Each of these workspaces has their own advantages and is usually more resistant to certain types of attacks as opposed to others. For example, watermarks embedded in the DCT domain can be optimised to resist JPEG compression attacks (Dugelay & Roche, 2000, p. 126). Barni, Bartolini, and Piva (2002) as well as Zhao and Koch (1995) have proposed watermarking schemes based on the DCT domain, while Bender, Gruhl, and Morimoto (1996) produced the "patchwork" algorithm that is used in the spatial domain.

Requirements of an Effective Digital Watermarking Scheme

For the purpose of copyright protection, a robust watermarking scheme is highly preferable. This is to thwart intentional or unintentional attacks on the watermarked image. In order to be effective, the watermarking scheme must fulfill a few basic but important properties. Firstly, the watermark should be *imperceptible* or rather; its presence should not interfere or degrade the protected image. On top of making the presence of the watermark known, artefacts introduced by the watermark reduce the commercial value of the image.

Secondly, the watermark embedding process should guarantee the *robustness* of the watermark against any form of attack, may it be malicious or otherwise. The list of some image modification techniques includes but is not limited to (Cox et al., 1997; Kutter & Petitcolas, 1999):

- *Signal enhancements* such as sharpening, contrast adjustment, and blurring.

- *Noise* such as additive Gaussian noise and multiplicative speckle noise.

- *Digital-to-analog* and *analog-to-digital* conversion.

- *Geometric distortions* such as rotation, translation, and scaling.

- *Collusion attacks* where combining multiple copies of the same watermarked images will destroy the watermark entirely.

- *Lossy compression* such as JPEG compression.

Up to this day, there has not been a single watermarking scheme that can resist all possible attacks. This remains to be the ultimate challenge and motivation for continued research in the field. Despite that, an effective watermarking scheme should strive to make the watermark robust enough such that even if the watermark can be removed entirely, the image would be too severely degraded and hence rendered unusable.

Lastly, results of the watermark extraction process have to be *unambiguous*. Watermarks that are recovered from a potentially tampered image should be able to verify the identity of the owner or confirm whether the image is copyrighted or not with a certain level of confidence. This property of an effective watermarking scheme is very important should it be made admissible in the court of law.

One of the strategies that can be used to make the watermark perceptually invisible is to employ a watermarking algorithm based on the human visual system (HVS). Although Delaigle, De Vleeschouwer, and Macq (1998), Kutter and Winkler (2002), as well as Podilchuk and Zeng (1998) proposed different embedding schemes, all their techniques utilize a perceptual mask based on the HVS that defines areas within an image that can be perturbed without noticeable effects.

Figure 3. Parallelism between communication system and digital watermarking

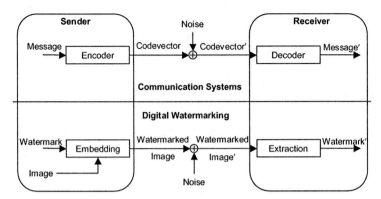

To ensure the robustness of a watermarking scheme, the watermark is usually distributed throughout the entire image. By doing so, a fair amount of redundancy is added, making sure that the watermark can still be recovered from a small sample of the image. Another way of implementing this is by formatting the watermark bits with error correction codes before the embedding process. This approach is only natural when the watermarking problem is compared to the transmission of a signal over a noisy channel, as shown in Figure 3 (Dugelay & Roche, 2000, p. 136). In this comparison, the image is considered to be the channel and the watermark as the information signal while image manipulation techniques are similar to noise. The choice of error correction codes is arbitrary but is usually chosen such that it suits the algorithm in which it is used. Baudry, Delaigle, Sankur, Macq, and Maître (2001), Loo and Kingsbury (2003) and Solanki, Jacobsen, Madhow, Manjunath, and Chandrasekaran (2004) use codes such as Bose-Chaudhuri-Hocquenghen (BCH), Reed-Solomon (RS), and turbo codes in their algorithms.

Robust Digital Watermarking Scheme

Arithmetic Redundant Residue Code

The multiple error-correction algorithm that is used in the robust digital watermarking scheme is based on the arithmetic redundant residue code. Although a thorough explanation of the algorithm is not presented here, some background and terminologies are given such that the final theorem can be understood. For further details, the paper by Goh, Tinauli, and Siddiqi (2004) can be referred to.

To begin, a set of n pairwise relatively prime positive integers $m_1, m_2, \ldots, m_i, m_{i+1}, \ldots, m_n$ called moduli is selected. Note that the term *moduli* is the plural of *modulus*. The moduli

m_i are chosen such that, the greatest common divisor, $\gcd(m_i, m_j) = 1$ for each pair of i and j with $i \neq j$ and $m_1 < m_2 < \ldots < m_i < m_{i+1} < \ldots < m_n$. From this set of n moduli, the first k moduli form a set of nonredundant moduli while the last $r = n - k$ moduli form a set of redundant moduli (Krishna et al., 1992). These sets of moduli are used to define the following:

$$M_K = \prod_{i=1}^{k} m_i \tag{1}$$

$$M = \prod_{i=1}^{n} m_i = M_K \cdot M_R \tag{2}$$

for $i = 1, 2, \ldots, k, k+1, \ldots, n$. It can be seen that M_K is the smallest product of k different m_i's. As with other error correction codes, the redundant components are used for error detection and correction. Without loss of generality, an integer X in the range of $[0, M)$ where M is as defined in (2), can be uniquely represented by a residue vector $x = \{x_1, x_2, \ldots, x_n\}$ using

$$X \equiv x_i (\text{mod } m_i) \tag{3}$$

for $i = 1, 2, \ldots, k, k+1, \ldots, n$. With (3), each of the residues x_i corresponds to X modulo m_i such that $0 \leq x_i < m_i$. However, for error correction to work, X has to be selected from the range of $[0, M_K)$ instead, where M_K is from (1). In doing so, the residue vector x can be divided into two parts, namely the first k residues called information residues and the remaining r residues called redundant residues (Krishna et al., 1992).

Without loss of generality again, when a residue vector x is given, the corresponding integer X can be uniquely determined by simultaneously solving all n linear congruences in equation (3). The problem of simultaneously solving a set of linear congruences is simplified by using the CRT, as shown in equation (4).

$$X = \sum_{i=1}^{n} x_i M_i a_i \text{ mod } M \tag{4}$$

where

$$M_i = \frac{M}{m_i} \text{ and } a_i = M_i^{-1} \text{ mod } m_i$$

for $i = 1, 2, ..., n$. The integers a_i are also known as the multiplicative inverses of $M_i \bmod m_i$. If X is selected from the range of $[0, M_K)$, any k residues out of the total n residues from the residue vector x, where $n > k$ should be sufficient in recovering the original integer X.

Now, according to Krishna et al. (1992), when the integer X is chosen from the range of $[0, M_K)$, the resulting redundant residue code can be considered linear. Furthermore, a code Ω based on a redundant residue number system has the minimum nonzero Hamming weight $wt_{min} \geq r + 1$ and minimum distance $d_{min} \geq r + 1$ (Ding et al., 1996, p. 148). Such Hamming weight and distance mean that the redundant residue code can correct up to t errors where:

$$t \leq \left\lfloor \frac{d_{min} - 1}{2} \right\rfloor$$

$\lfloor * \rfloor$ is the largest integer less than or equal to $*$. Codes with $d_{min} = r + 1$ are called maximum distance separable (MDS), and are attractive because they are optimal whereby they can correct the maximum amount of errors t, with the least number of redundancies. Since the code Ω is an MDS code, the maximum correctable errors are:

$$t \leq \left\lfloor \frac{r}{2} \right\rfloor \tag{5}$$

For the multiple error correction scheme, first consider a redundant residue code with a set of moduli m_i. An integer X is selected from the range $[0, M_K)$ and the residue vector is $x = \{x_1, x_2, ..., x_n\}$. From here onwards, let the range $[0, M_K)$ be termed as the legitimate range while its counterpart, the range $[M_K, M)$, be termed as the illegitimate range. Suppose that t errors have been introduced into the vector x when it passes through a potentially noisy system. The resulting vector is y, that is:

$$y = x + e$$
$$\{y_1, ..., y_n\} = \{x_1, ..., x_n\} + \{e_{u_1}, ..., 0, e_{u_2}, ..., e_{u_t}\}$$

where $0 \leq e_{u_j} < m_{u_j}$ for $1 \leq j \leq t$. The error values are $e_{u_1}, e_{u_2}, ..., e_{u_j}, e_{u_{j+1}}, ... e_{u_t}$ and the subscripts $u_1, u_2, ..., u_j, u_{j+1}, ..., u_t$ are the positions of errors within y. Upon receiving the vector y, error detection is first performed by determining whether y is a valid vector. This can be accomplished by computing the corresponding integer Y using a formula based on equation (4), which is:

$$Y = \sum_{i=1}^{n} y_i M_i a_i \bmod M \tag{6}$$

for $i = 1, 2, ..., n$. If the recovered Y is within the legitimate range, then y is a valid vector and no further steps need to be carried out. On the other hand, if Y is in the illegitimate range, it can then be concluded that y has errors in its residues. The multiple error correction scheme can be summed up in the following theorem.

Theorem 1. For a redundant residue number system code having the proper amount of redundancies r, such that no more $t \geq [r/2]$ errors have occurred in a received vector y, the original integer X can be found by performing the following operation:

$$X = Y \bmod Z_c \tag{7}$$

where $Z_c = M \Big/ \prod_{\alpha = u_1}^{u_t} m_\alpha$ and $u_1, u_2, ..., u_j, u_{j+1}, ..., u_t$ are the positions of the errors within y. The subscript c the index of one combination out of the $p = {}^nC_t$ possible combinations of u_j.

Since there is no way of determining a priori the positions of the errors, all possible combinations have to be taken into account when Z_c is computed. As such, equation (7) will have to be iterated at least p times to correct the errors. To demonstrate the multiple error-correcting capability of the algorithm, the following example is shown.

Table 1. Results of multiple error correction algorithm with p = 15 iterations

c	Y	Error Positions		Z_c	$X = Y \bmod Z_c$
		u_1	u_2		
1	25121455	1	2	215441	130299
2	25121455	1	3	164749	79607
3	25121455	1	4	147407	62265
4	25121455	1	5	121771	36629
5	25121455	1	6	96577	11435
6	25121455	2	3	139403	28915
7	25121455	2	4	124729	50926
8	25121455	2	5	103037	83464
9	25121455	2	6	81719	33722
10	25121455	3	4	95381	36252
11	25121455	3	5	78793	65281
12	25121455	3	6	62491	73
13	25121455	4	5	70499	23811
14	25121455	4	6	55913	16518
15	25121455	5	6	46189	40828

Consider a $(n=6, k=2)$ code using m_i of $\{11, 13, 17, 19, 23, 29\}$. From equation (5), this code can correct up to $t=2$ errors. The legitimate range is $[0, 143]$ while the illegitimate range is $[143, 30808063]$. Let $X=73$ and the equivalent residue vector is $x=\{7, 8, 5, 16, 4, 15\}$. Assume that two errors $(t=2)$ have propagated into the x during transmission at positions $u_1=3$ and $u_2=6$. Therefore, let the received vector be $y=\{7, 8, 11, 16, 4, 2\}$. From y, the computed integer Y using equation (6) is:

$$Y = \sum_{i=1}^{6} y_i M_i a_i \bmod M$$
$$= 25121455$$

The corresponding values of M_i and the multiplicative inverse a_i are shown:

$$M_i = \{2800733, 2369851, 1812239, 1621477, 1339481, 1062347\}$$
$$a_i = \{1, 9, 7, 9, 10, 26\}$$

Since the calculated value of Y is within the illegitimate range, it can be concluded that there are errors. Hence, the algorithm continues by performing equation (7) iteratively. All combinations of Z_c are calculated and the results are shown in Table 1.

The only valid result from Table 1 that is within the legitimate range of $[0, 143]$ is $X=73$. With this result, the position of the errors are determined to be $u_1=3$ and $u_2=6$. The algorithm has correctly determined the original integer.

Watermark Embedding Framework

Let C be a grayscale image of size $P_1 \times P_2$ that is to be watermarked. In addition, also let W be a watermark sequence of length N that is to be embedded into C. The grayscale image is represented by:

$$C = \{c(x, y) \mid x = 1, 2, ..., P_1, \quad y = 1, 2, ..., P_2\} \text{ and } c(x, y) \in \{0, 1, ..., 255\}$$

where $c(x, y)$ is the intensity of the pixel at the spatial coordinates of x and y. Figure 4 shows how the spatial coordinates are identified for a given image. The watermark sequence is a unique binary sequence and is given as:

$$W = \{w_h \mid h = 1, 2, ..., N\} \text{ and } w_h \in \{0, 1\}$$

Figure 4. Common axis convention used for digital image representation (Gonzalez & Woods, 1993, p. 6)

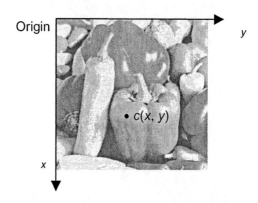

Figure 5. Different levels of partitioning in an image

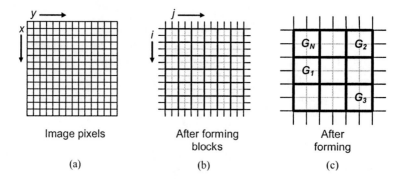

This means that the watermark sequence W is a binary bit sequence representing an ID or simply a visually meaningful image such as a logo that uniquely identifies the copyright owner.

In a blockwise watermarking scheme, the image is first divided into smaller nonoverlapping blocks of size $O_1 \times O_2$ as shown in Figure 5(b). Let these blocks be denoted as $b(i,j)$ where i and j are the spatial coordinates but in reference to the blocks instead. It can be seen that $0 \leq i < P_1/O_1$ and $0 \leq j < P_2/O_2$.

An image is essentially a collection of pixels, each having its own intensity level. These pixels are clustered together in a fixed manner, relative to each other, to form a bigger picture. Conversely, isolated pixels convey less visual information. Therefore, a visually rich image has pixels that are highly dependent on neighboring pixels in conveying its visual content. These pixels are correlated in a certain manner that cannot be varied much without degrading the visual quality to an unacceptable manner. It is this very property that is used as a means to embed the watermark.

Figure 6. Diagram showing various possibilities of how adjacent blocks can be grouped for comparison: (a) left-and-right; (b) top-and-bottom; and (c) rectangle

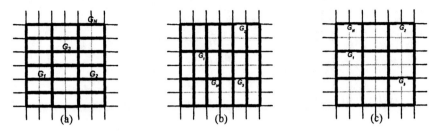

Now, instead of measuring the correlation of one pixel to another, the correlation of a group of pixels to another group is measured. Each group of pixels is represented by its mean intensity. This is because minor modifications to the image, such as addition of random noise, will not cause significant change to the mean intensity of pixels. If more modification is carried out, it can be assumed that the adjacent group of pixels will also be affected in roughly the same manner. As a result, the overall relationship between the groups is maintained or changes are kept to a minimal level.

Let the group of pixels be the $O_1 \times O_2$ block partitioned earlier. The mean value of each block $b(i,j)$ is denoted as $\mu_{b(i,j)}$. It can be calculated by using the following:

$$\mu_{b(i,j)} = \frac{\sum\limits_{(x,y)\in b(i,j)} c(x,y)}{O_1 \times O_2}$$

where x and y are the spatial coordinates of pixels that constitute the block $b(i,j)$. Besides that, the correlation between the blocks can be calculated using any function that provides information on how they are related to each other. In this watermarking scheme, the function used to calculate the correlation of these blocks is the *standard deviation*.

In order to obtain the correlation, blocks adjacent to each other are used. All the $O_1 \times O_2$ blocks are then grouped together as in Figure 5(c). The groups can actually be of any shapes and sizes, with some examples shown in Figure 6. Regardless of how these blocks are grouped together, it should be noted that one group of q blocks will be used to embed a single watermark bit. Therefore, N groups are pseudorandomly selected from different parts of the image using the embedding key ψ. This ensures that the watermark is dispersed throughout the image, reducing the visual distortion caused by the watermarking scheme. Let the set of pseudorandomly selected groups be $\Gamma = \{\Gamma_1, \Gamma_2, ..., \Gamma_h, \Gamma_{h+1}, ..., \Gamma_N\}$. This can be seen in Figure 6.

If nonadjacent blocks are grouped together, the correlation between these blocks is harder to maintain. This is due to the fact that varying levels of modification can be applied to different parts of the image without actually degrading the visual quality.

Figure 7. A segmented axis used in the watermark embedding process

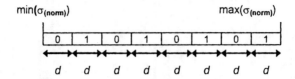

Unfortunately, this changes the way the nonadjacent blocks relate to each other during the extraction process. On the other hand, modifications are usually quite uniform within an area, allowing for a more accurate recovery of the watermark.

The block partition size O_1 and O_2 as well as the number of contiguous blocks q in a set must be carefully selected such that:

$$N \le \frac{1}{\alpha q}\left(\frac{P_1}{O_1} \cdot \frac{P_2}{O_2}\right) \tag{8}$$

where $a \ge 1$. This ensures that sufficient space is available within the image to hold the watermark. The parameter a is used to make certain that not all the pixels of the image are changed to embed the watermark. By doing so, the chances of watermark removal are reduced and distortions are also minimized.

The standard deviation of the mean intensities in a group Γ_h is defined as σ_h and calculated using:

$$\sigma_h = \left\{\frac{1}{q}\sum_{b(i,j)\in G_h}\left[A_h - \mu_{b(i,j)}\right]^2\right\}^{\frac{1}{2}} \tag{9}$$

where

$$A_h = \frac{1}{q}\sum_{b(i,j)\in G_h}\mu_{b(i,j)}$$

Next, let the set $\sigma = \{\sigma_1, \sigma_2, ..., \sigma_h, \sigma_{h+1}, ..., \sigma_N\}$ and the normalized version be $\sigma_{(norm)} = \{\sigma_{1(norm)}, \sigma_{2(norm)}, ..., \sigma_{h(norm)}, \sigma_{h+1(norm)}, ..., \sigma_{N(norm)}\}$ where the mean has been set to zero and variance to one. The standard deviation σ_h for $h = 1, 2, ..., N$ needs to be changed to embed the watermark bits. To determine the amount of change, the axis in Figure 7 is used.

$\max(\sigma_{(norm)})$

The axis is spanned by the minimum and maximum values of $\sigma_{(norm)}$. It is also segmented into ε disjoint cells of equal sizes with each interval having the width of

$$d = \frac{\max\left(\sigma_{(norm)}\right) - \min\left(\sigma_{(norm)}\right)}{\varepsilon}$$

An alternating sequence of zeros and ones representing the binary digits are then assigned to each of the cells. The kth watermark bit is embedded by adding a small deviation $\Delta s_{k(norm)}$ to $\sigma_{k(norm)}$ (Wong, Au, & Yeung, 2003). If $\sigma_{k(norm)}$ falls within the cell that has a binary digit that matches the kth watermark bit, only a small deviation that moves $\sigma_{k(norm)}$ to the centre of the cell is needed. On the other hand, if the cell's watermark bit does not match the kth watermark bit, a deviation of $\Delta \sigma_{k(norm)}$ is needed to move $\sigma_{k(norm)}$ to the centre of the nearest cell that does.

Moving $\sigma_{k(norm)}$ to the centre of a cell ensures that maximum watermark robustness is achieved. This is because the distance to the next cell in either direction is furthest at the centre. It will take a distortion of $d/2$ to toggle the watermark bit, resulting in an error while extracting the watermark (Wong et al., 2003). As such, a larger value of d is preferable in order to maintain the robustness of the watermark. Unfortunately, a large d may lead to visible artefacts.

Once the deviation $\Delta \sigma_h$ for $h = 1, 2, ..., N$ has been determined, the old standard deviation σ_h has to be changed to s^*_h. Observe from (9) that s_h is dependent on $\mu_{b(i,j)}$. Therefore, to obtain σ^*_h, the mean values $\mu_{b(i,j)}$ for $b(i,j) \in G_h$ will have to be changed accordingly. Let $\Delta \mu_{b(i,j)}$ be the value that needs to be added to $\mu_{b(i,j)}$, giving the new mean of $\mu^*_{b(i,j)}$. Mathematically:

$$\mu^*_{b(i,j)} = \mu_{b(i,j)} + \Delta \mu_{b(i,j)} \tag{10}$$

for $b(i,j) \in G_h$ and $h = 1, 2, ..., N$. With $\mu^*_{b(i,j)}$, the relation between $\Delta \sigma_h$ and σ_h is given as:

$$\left(\sigma^*_h\right)^2 = \sigma_h^2 + \Delta \sigma_h \tag{11}$$

The last term is:

$$\Delta \sigma_h = \frac{1}{q} \sum_{b(i,j) \in G_h} \left[2\left(A_h - \mu_{b(i,j)}\right)\left(\delta - \Delta \mu_{b(i,j)}\right) + \left(\delta - \Delta \mu_{b(i,j)}\right)^2 \right] \tag{12}$$

where the average value of $\Delta\mu_{b(i,j)}$ for $b(i,j) \in G_h$ is:

$$\delta = \frac{1}{q} \sum_{b(i,j)\in G_h} \Delta\mu_{b(i,j)} \qquad (13)$$

With equation (13), the parameter $\Delta\mu_{b(i,j)}$ for $b(i,j) \in G_h$ needs to be varied to obtain the closest estimation of the desired deviation $\Delta\sigma_h$. The range of values for $\Delta\mu_{b(i,j)}$ without causing the new mean intensity to have invalid grayscale levels is:

$$\left(0 - \mu_{b(i,j)}\right) \le \Delta\mu_{b(i,j)} \le \left(255 - \mu_{b(i,j)}\right)$$

Although extreme values of $\Delta\mu_{b(i,j)}$ can be used to obtain a better estimation of the desired deviation $\Delta\sigma_h$, visual distortions become visible. As such, $\Delta\mu_{b(i,j)}$ is limited to the range $[-t, t]$. t is usually a single digit integer.

To find the most suitable values of values $\Delta\mu_{b(i,j)}$ for $b(i,j) \in G_h$, all possible combinations of $\Delta\mu_{b(i,j)}$ are tested. Each different set of combinations having q values is tested by substituting it into equation (12). The estimated results are then compared with the desired deviation $\Delta\sigma_{b(i,j)}$ and the combination that produces the smallest error is used.

After determining the best combination of $\Delta\mu_{b(i,j)}$, the mean intensities of each block in the group Γ_h for $h = 1, 2, ..., N$ will have to be changed accordingly. The simplest way of accomplishing this is by uniformly adding the amount $\Delta\mu_{b(i,j)}$ to the intensity of every pixel in the *block b(i, j)* $\in G_h$. This is given as:

$$c^*(x,y) = c(x,y) + \Delta\mu_{b(i,j)} \qquad (14)$$

where $c^*(x, y)$ is the watermarked pixel for $(x, y) \in b(i, j)$. The result of the embedding process is the watermarked image C^*.

Watermark Extraction Framework

Since the integrity of the watermarked image C^* cannot be determined prior to extracting the watermark, let it be C'. The potentially tampered version of the watermarked image is represented by:

$$C' = \left\{c'(x,y) \mid 0 \le x < P_1, 0 \le y < P_2\right\} \text{ and } c'(x,y) \in \{0, 1, ..., 255\}$$

The copyright information, however, can still be recovered from C' with the key ψ. To extract the watermark, the same processes as the embedding algorithm are carried out. Firstly, the image C' is partitioned into smaller nonoverlapping $O_1 \times O_2$ blocks. The blocks are then clustered into nonoverlapping groups. Next, with the key ψ, the groups with the embedded watermark bits are selected to form the set $\Gamma = \{\Gamma_1, \Gamma_2, ..., \Gamma_h, \Gamma_{h+1}, ..., \Gamma_N\}$. The entire process can be seen from Figure 5.

Continuing with the extraction algorithm, the set of standard deviation $\sigma = \{\sigma_1, \sigma_2, ..., \sigma_h, \sigma_{h+1}, ..., \sigma_N\}$ and the normalized version $\sigma_{(norm)}$ are obtained. An axis similar to that in Figure 7 is generated and used to recover the watermark bits. Watermark extraction is performed by reversing the rules used to embed watermark bits. If $\sigma_{h(norm)}$ falls into a cell, the bit representing that cell is the hth watermark bit. The same process is repeated until all watermark bits w_h, are extracted for $h = 1, 2, ..., N$. With the watermark bits w'_h, the recovered watermark sequence is W'.

Watermark Embedding with Error Correction Codes

In order to increase the robustness of the watermark by utilizing error correction codes, the watermark will have to be properly formatted first. Since an error correction scheme based on the Chinese remainder theorem (CRT) is used mainly for integers, the watermark will have to be a sequence of integers instead. This sequence can either be a series of integers or a grayscale logo. In any case, let the watermark be:

$$L = \{L_v \mid v = 1, 2, ..., F\} \text{ and } L_v \in \{0, M_K - 1\}$$

The copyrighted image of size $P_1 \times P_2$ is called C and is represented by:

$$C = \{c(x, y) \mid x = 1, 2, ..., P_1, \quad y = 1, 2, ..., P_2\} \text{ and}$$

Figure 8. Block diagrams describing the modified watermark embedding process

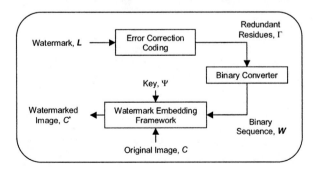

Additionally, a set of n moduli $m_1, \ldots, m_k, m_{k+1} \ldots, m_n$ is chosen such that $\gcd(m_i, m_j) = 1$ for each pair of i and j with $i \neq j$ and $m_1 < m_2 < \ldots < m_k < m_{k+1} < \ldots < m_n$. The *legitimate range* is therefore $[0, M_K)$ where M_K is as defined from equation (1). The key ψ is also chosen to prevent unauthorized removal of the watermark. Note that the key and the moduli are needed at the receiver to extract the watermark. Error correction capability is implemented by formatting the watermark such that it carries redundant information. Each integer of the watermark L is made redundant using equation (15).

$$L_v \equiv l_{v_i} \pmod{m_i}$$
(15)

Therefore, a single integer, L_v is represented by its residue vector. The resultant residue vectors are then concatenated together to form a set of redundant residues given as:

$$\begin{aligned} \Gamma &= \{l_1, l_2, \ldots, l_F\} \\ &= \{l_{v_i} \mid v = 1, 2, \ldots, F, \quad i = 1, 2, \ldots, n\} \end{aligned}$$

The set of redundant residues Γ consists of $F \cdot n$ integers. Besides that, each of residues in Γ is within the range of $0 \leq l_{v_i} < m_n$ where m_n is the largest modulus.

The set of redundant residues Γ consists of integers. These integers are changed into a binary bitstream so that it can be embedded into an image using the watermark embedding framework presented earlier. This is accomplished by using a fixed length binary representation of the integer where each integer is represented by s bits. The binary sequence is therefore given as:

$$W' = \{w'_h \mid h = 1, 2, \ldots, N\} \text{ and } w'_h \in \{0, 1\}$$

Figure 9. Block diagrams of the watermark extraction algorithm. Error correction is included to increase the robustness of the watermark.

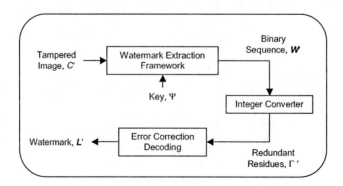

Table 2. Examples of watermarks **L**, *and their corresponding residues* **G** *when the moduli is {11, 13, 17, 19}*

No.	L	Γ
1	{62, 48, 44, 52, 56, 84}	{7, 10, 11, 5, 4, 9, 14, 10, 0, 5, 10, 6, 8, 0, 1, 14, 1, 4, 5, 18, 7, 6, 16, 8}
2	{84, 17, 5, 65, 124, 133}	{7, 6, 16, 8, 6, 4, 0, 17, 5, 5, 5, 5, 10, 0, 14, 8, 3, 7, 5, 10, 1, 3, 14, 0}
3	{133, 37, 22, 124, 34, 92}	{1, 3, 14, 0, 4, 11, 3, 18, 0, 9, 5, 3, 3, 7, 5, 10, 1, 8, 0, 15, 4, 1, 7, 16}

Figure 10. Watermarked images: (a) "Lena" with PSNR = 43.85 dB and; (b) "Baboon" with PSNR = 43.07 dB

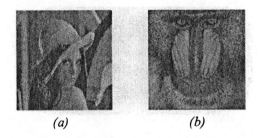

(a)   *(b)*

where

$$N = s \times F \times n \tag{16}$$

By substituting equation (16) into equation (8), the following is obtained:

$$N \leq \frac{1}{\alpha \, q}\left(\frac{P_1}{O_1} \cdot \frac{P_2}{O_2}\right)$$

$$F \leq \frac{1}{\alpha \, q}\left(\frac{P_1}{O_1} \cdot \frac{P_2}{O_2}\right)\frac{1}{s \, n} \tag{17}$$

where $a \geq 1$. The size of the watermark **L** has been carefully chosen such that equation (17) remains true.

Once the watermark has been properly formatted, it can then be embedded into the image C, using the algorithm and techniques described earlier. The entire watermark embedding process is summed up in Figure 8.

Watermark Extraction with Error Correction Codes

If the watermarked version of the copyrighted image is C', let the potentially tampered version be C'. The watermark extraction process begins by recovering all N embedded bits using the techniques described ealier. These bits are represented as:

$$W' = \left\{ w'_h \mid h = 1, 2, ..., N \right\} \text{ and } w'_h \in \{0, 1\}$$

The binary sequence is then converted back into a sequence of integers. The sequence of integers is given as:

$$\Gamma' = \left\{ l_{v_i} \mid v = 1, 2, ..., F, \quad i = 1, 2, ..., n \right\}$$

If some of the recovered bits differ from the original, changing them back into integers will yield erroneous results. As such, error correction is performed by using the decoding algorithm explained earlier. Note that the decoding algorithm will terminate if there are more than t errors. However, for this watermarking scheme, a less accurate solution is preferable instead of terminating the decoding algorithm prematurely. Therefore, to prevent premature termination, a flip of a fair coin is used to choose the solution when there is more than one possible solution that falls within the legitimate range.

After decoding, all watermark integers L_v for $v = 1, 2, ..., F$ are recovered and joined together to form the watermark L. The watermark extraction process is summarized in Figure 9.

Experimental Results and Discussions

To test the robustness of the watermarking scheme, the watermarked images are tested against several common image manipulation techniques. These images have the dimensions of 256×256 pixels and each pixel can have any one of the 256 distinct gray levels. For these tests, the watermarking scheme was set up such that it could correct up to $t = 1$ error. Therefore, according to equation (5), r has to be at least two to correct a single error. Any combination of n and k giving $r = 2$, should suffice, but the most optimal setting that allows an integer to be represented with the least number of residues is $n = 4$ and $k = 2$.

For a ($n = 4$, $k = 2$) code, the moduli that was selected to be used for all the robustness tests were $m_1 = 11$, $m_2 = 13$, $m_3 = 17$ and $m_4 = 19$. With these moduli, the integer sequence that uniquely identifies the copyright owner can only have values from the legitimate range of [0, 143]. Besides that, all the residues representing the integers in the set Γ will be in the range of [0, 19]. As such, the minimum number of bits needed to represent the residues in Γ is $s = 5$.

Using the optimal setting for the watermark embedding algorithm, the parameters are set as $O_1 = 8$, $O_2 = 8$, $t = 3$, $a = 2$, and $\varepsilon = 25$. In addition, $q = 4$ blocks are grouped together as a *rectangle*. According to equation (17), the only value of F that satisfies the inequality is $F = 6$. Hence, six integers from the legitimate range of [0, 143] are selected to be the watermark L. Table 2 shows some examples of watermarks and their corresponding residue vector.

Figure 10 shows both the watermarked version of "Lena" and "Baboon." Once again, visual inspection of the images will not reveal any obvious degradation as a result of embedding the watermarks. The high PSNR values also confirm this observation.

One of the easiest image manipulation techniques that can be applied to any copyrighted image is JPEG compression. The advantage of JPEG compression is that while the overall size of the image file is reduced, the image integrity is still maintained at an acceptable level. Unfortunately, JPEG compression sometimes destroys embedded watermarks. Most image editing software use the default value of 75 for the quality factor (QF) setting. Therefore, well-designed watermarking schemes should, at the least, be able to recover watermarks from JPEG compressed images with QF = 75. Some examples of JPEG compressed images can be seen in Figure 11.

The graph shown in Figure 12 shows the robustness of the watermark when the image is JPEG compressed with different QF. It can be seen that the proposed scheme clearly achieves the minimum requirement of QF = 75. Note that 10 trials with different keys ψ and watermark L are performed for each manipulation technique to obtain the average symbol error rate. It can be seen that the symbol error rate suddenly increases, such as the one experienced by "Boy" when QF = 50. This can be attributed to the fact that for some key ψ, the pseudorandomly selected groups of blocks Γ_h where $h = 1, 2, ..., N$ are not suitable for watermark embedding.

The addition of noise also disrupts the watermark extraction process. An attack of this sort can be tested on the watermarked images by using an additive zero-mean Gaussian noise. The variance of the zero-mean Gaussian noise is adjusted such that various PSNR levels can be attained in the noisy images. Some examples of images with additive Gaussian noise can be seen from Figure 13.

The result of the test is shown in Figure 14. It can be seen that while the watermarking scheme performs well for some images, the otherwise is also true for others. All the images used in the test have roughly the same visual characteristics such as equal amount of textured and homogenous regions. As such, it would seem that the inability of the algorithm to accurately recover the watermark is not due to the visual properties of the images but rather a poor choice of watermark embedding location.

Figure 11. JPEG compressed images of: (a) "Lena" with QF = 30 and PSNR = 31.24 dB as well as; (b) "Baboon" with QF = 30 and PSNR = 24.76 dB

(a)   *(b)*

Figure 12. Results of test for a sample of six images under JPEG compression attack

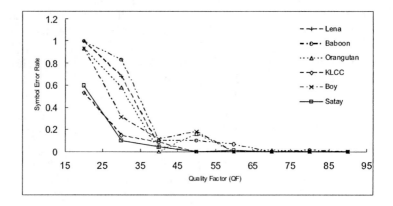

Besides that, images are often subjected to resizing operations. Resizing an image usually results in an image that is either larger or smaller than the original. For the watermark extraction algorithm to work, a resized image needs to be resized back to the original dimensions. Therefore, all resized images are changed back to the dimensions of 256 × 256 pixels before watermark extraction. Images that have been reduced in size usually lose more information compared to those that have been enlarged. This can be clearly seen from Figure 15, where one has been reduced in size while the other has been enlarged.

Figure 16 shows the effects of varying the scaling factor from 0.5 to 5. The watermark extraction algorithm generally produces better results when images are enlarged as opposed to images that have been reduced in size.

Figure 13. Images with additive zero-mean Gaussian noise where: (a) "Lena" with PSNR = 30 dB and; (b) "Baboon" with PSNR = 30 dB

(a)   *(b)*

Figure 14. Results of test for a sample of six images with additive zero-mean Gaussian noise

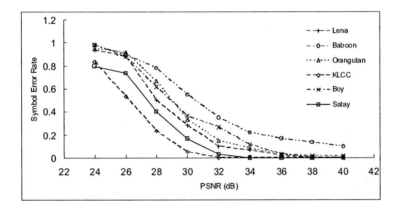

Blurring an image by means of an average filter will usually cause a loss in high-frequency details such as edges in the image. It is often used as a technique to remove noise from a corrupted image. However, when used on a watermarked image, this technique can almost remove the entire watermark, especially with filter sizes of five and above. Some samples of blurred images are shown in Figure 17 while the symbol error rate graph is in Figure 18.

Performance Evaluation of Watermarking Scheme

To evaluate the performance or effectiveness of this watermarking scheme, an empirical comparison between the proposed algorithm with other similar algorithms is carried out.

Figure 15. "Lena" images that have been rescaled back to the dimensions of 256 ' 256 pixels where: (a) the scaling factor was originally 0.3 with PSNR = 24.01 dB and; (b) the scaling factor was originally 3 with PSNR = 30.97 dB

(a)   *(b)*

Figure 16. Results of test for a sample of six images under resizing attack

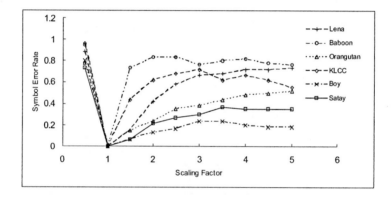

To maintain consistency, a grayscale image of "Lena" with the dimensions of 512×512 pixels is also used for this evaluation.

The scheme is set up such that it can correct a single error, that is $t = 1$. For this, a ($n = 4$, $k = 2$) code with the moduli $m_1 = 11$, $m_2 = 13$, $m_3 = 17$, $m_4 = 19$ is used. The other parameters of the watermarking scheme are similar to those in Section 0, that is $O_1 = 8$, $O_2 = 8$, $t = 3$, $q = 4$, $a = 2$, $\varepsilon = 25$ and $s = 5$. Now, according to equation (17), the most suitable watermark length for L is $F = 24$. Therefore, the total length of the redundant residue Γ is $F \times n = 96$. The next step in the watermarking process, as in Figure 8, is to change the integers in Γ to binary digits. The binary sequence W is then embedded into the image and the quality of the watermarked image can be seen from Figure 19(b).

To carry out the comparisons, a few assumptions have to be made. Firstly, the parameters used to tune each watermarking scheme are assumed to be optimum and produce the best

Figure 17. "Baboon" images that have been blurred with a lowpass filter of: (a) size 3 and PSNR = 22.46 dB while; (b) the filter size is 5 and PSNR = 20.83 dB

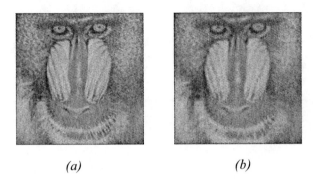

(a)   *(b)*

Figure 18. Results of test for a sample of six images under blurring attack

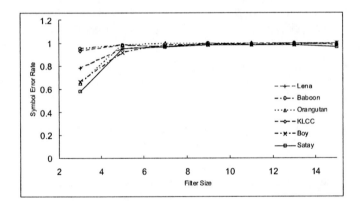

results for their respective algorithm. Therefore, the results of the comparison are treated as is; disregarding the tuning parameters that may actually have influenced the performance the respective schemes. In addition, if the watermarked image used in some schemes is not that of "Lena," the results by these schemes are still assumed to be valid for comparison.

The first test used to evaluate the performance of the proposed watermarking scheme is the JPEG compression test. As it can be seen from Figure 20, the watermark is recovered for QF ≥ 30, using the proposed scheme. The slight difference in results when Figure 20 is compared to Figure 12 can be explained by the fact that only a single trial is used to obtain these readings, as opposed to 10 trials used in the earlier tests.

Works by Zhu, Clarke, and Ferreira (2004), Yang and Chen (2004) as well as Kang, Huang, Shi, and Zhu (2004) use various types of error correction codes to increase the robustness of their watermarking scheme. The choice of codes used in each scheme is a result of

Figure 19. (a) Original image of "Lena"; and (b) watermarked version of "Lena" with PSNR = 43.7 dB

(a)   *(b)*

different design parameters. Briefly, Zhu et al. (2004) use Reed-Solomon (RS) codes while both Kang et al. (2004) as well as Yang and Chen (2004) use turbo codes. The chart in Table 3 lists down the performance of these schemes under different QF settings in a simulated JPEG compression attack. The values presented by Zhu et al. are obtained using another image instead of "Lena."

The values in Table 3 are plotted against the QF settings and shown in Figure 21. As the plot indicates, the performance of the proposed scheme does not fair too badly against the others. As with the other techniques, the proposed scheme can recover watermarks from the "Lena" image that have been JPEG compressed with QF setting of 30 and above. However, there is a significant drop in the recovery rate when the image is compressed with a QF of 20. The other techniques do not have this limitation.

Another image manipulation technique often used as a measure of a scheme's effectiveness is the addition of noise. An additive zero-mean Gaussian noise is used to degrade the quality of the "Lena" image, and results for various noise levels can be seen in Figure 22. All the watermark integers can be correctly recovered for noise levels of 32 dB and above using the proposed scheme.

The comparison between the proposed scheme and the scheme by Yang and Chen (2004) is shown in Table 4 and Figure 23, respectively. The noise level at which both schemes can recover all watermark information differs only by about 2 dB. Despite that, the symbol error rate for the proposed scheme increases more steadily than the scheme by Yang and Chen for equivalent noise levels below 30 dB.

The averaging tests that have been carried out thus far are products of codes being run within MATLAB. It is interesting to note that the averaging filter in MATLAB introduces a dark border around the image. The border can be seen in Figure 24(a). Now, if an image editing software such as Paint Shop Pro (PSP) is used to carry out the averaging, the border is nonexistent. This is evident in Figure 24(b). The presence of the dark border affects the quality of the recovered watermark. The performance of the watermarking scheme against averaging filters of varying sizes is shown in Figure 25. The two plots are results of implementing the averaging filter in MATLAB and PSP.

Figure 20. Results of test when watermarked "Lena" is under JPEG compression attack

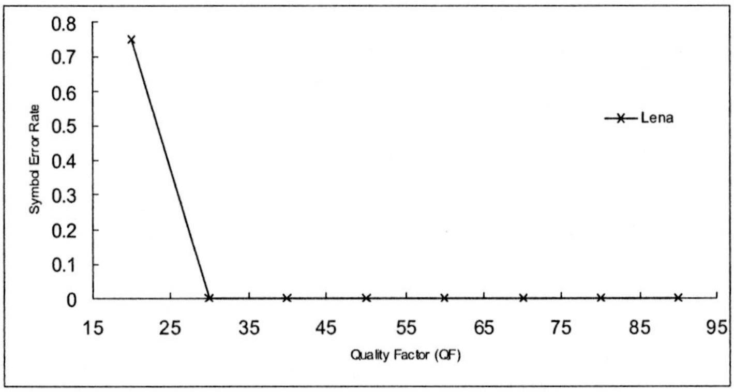

Table 3. Symbol error rate for four different watermarking schemes under JPEG compression attack

QF	Proposed Scheme	Zhu et al. (2004)	Yang & Chen (2004)	Kang et al. (2004)
20	0.75	0	0.25	0
30	0	0	0.15	0
40	0	0	0.02	0
50	0	0	0	0
60	0	0	0	0
70	0	0	0	0
80	0	0	0	0
90	0	0	0	0

The difference between a MATLAB-averaged image and a PSP-averaged image is quite significant, especially for a filter of size 3×3. Unfortunately, a perfect watermark is still not recoverable for the "Lena" image, regardless of the software that is used to carry out the smoothing operation. The proposed scheme is compared to works carried out by Fu, Shen, and Lu (2004). Their watermarking scheme uses the Bose-Chaudhuri-Hocquenghen (BCH) coding technique to embed the watermarks. Table 5 shows the comparison between the schemes.

Recovering the watermark from a PSP-averaged image is comparable to the scheme due to Fu et al.

Finally, the quality of images watermarked using these various schemes is compared. The PSNR value for Yang and Chen (2004) is not available and the bar chart in Figure 26 reflects this.

Figure 21. Recovery rate of four different watermarking schemes under JPEG compression attack

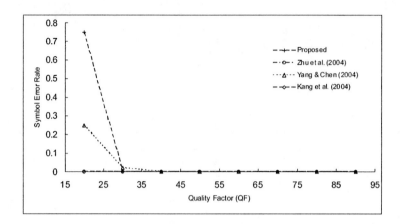

Figure 22. Results of test when watermarked "Lena" is under additive zero-mean Gaussian noise attack

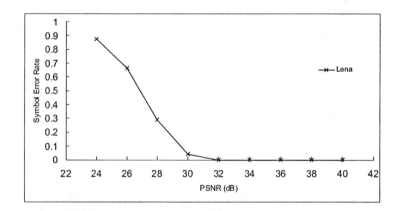

Among all the techniques, the proposed scheme produces the best output. Despite that, the other schemes also hold up quite well in this comparison, with the exception of Zhu et al. (2004). It should be kept in mind, however, the unreliability of PSNR values as an indicator of image degradation levels.

Overall, the comparisons seem to indicate that the proposed watermarking scheme is robust against a fixed set of image tampering techniques. It should be remembered that various other parameters are not taken into account in these comparisons and as such, the results may not reflect the actual effectiveness of the various schemes.

Table 4. Symbol error rate for two different watermarking schemes under Gaussian noise attack

PSNR (dB)	Proposed Scheme	Yang & Chen (2004)
24	0.88	0.26
26	0.67	0.20
28	0.29	0.08
30	0.04	0
32	0	0
34	0	0
36	0	0
38	0	0
40	0	0

Figure 23. Recovery rate of two different watermarking schemes under Gaussian noise attack

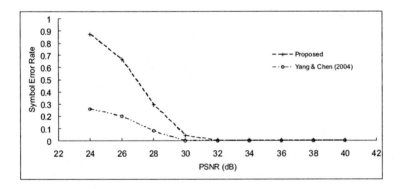

Figure 24. The presence of a thin dark border on the top and right of the image can be seen in (a), where averaging filter is implemented in MATLAB, while (b) has no border when the averaging filter is applied using Paint Shop Pro.

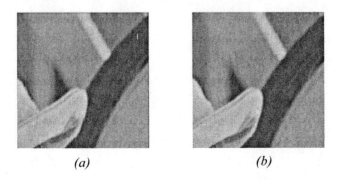

(a)   *(b)*

*Figure 25. Results of test with watermarked "Lena" when averaging filter is applied
to image. Two implementations of the averaging filter are tested.*

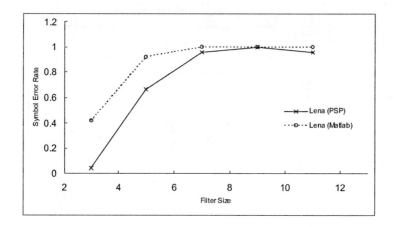

*Table 5. Symbol error rate for two different watermarking schemes under image
smoothing attack*

Filter Size	Proposed Scheme		Fu et al. (2004)
	with Matlab	With PSP	
3×3	0.467	0.042	0.010

Figure 26. The quality of watermarked images for four different watermarking schemes

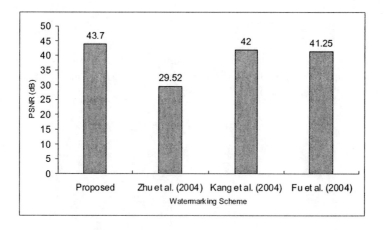

Conclusion and Recommendations

The need to protect the rights of copyright owners in today's day and age has become even more urgent with prevalence of computers and the Internet. Copyrighted materials such as music, videos, and digital images are being used indiscriminately without compensating the owners. A possible solution in tackling this problem is with the development of better rights management tools such as digital watermarking.

This chapter is the culmination of work and research carried out to make digital watermarking for grayscale images a viable copyright protection mechanism. The requirements of an effective watermarking scheme have been described in detail. To reiterate, an effective oblivious invisible watermarking scheme should be able to make the watermark unobtrusive and robust against tampering.

As a strategy to achieve these requirements, the proposed watermarking scheme uses error correction coding. The novel error correction scheme is based on the Chinese remainder theorem (CRT), often times referred to as the redundant residue number system. The advantage of using this error correction scheme is its ability to correct the maximum number of errors with the least number of redundancies. Besides that, the algorithm responsible for correcting errors is simple to implement and does not require any complicated optimization techniques.

Another approach in satisfying the requirements of an effective watermarking scheme is to develop a watermark embedding and extraction framework that can also be used together with error correction codes. The proposed framework is an oblivious invisible watermarking scheme that is applied blockwise. The scheme essentially measures how each block of pixels relates to other blocks around it and alters that relationship such that a single watermark bit can be embedded. Some parameters in the scheme are fixed and cannot be changed without changing the program itself. As a result, the watermarking scheme cannot change these parameters to exploit image characteristics that may actually allow more change without degrading the final watermarked version. Future implementation of this watermarking scheme may use a perceptual mask based on the human visual system (HVS) to determine the bound instead (Delaigle et al., 1998; Pérez-Gonzáles & Hernández, 1999).

Both the proposed error correction code and the watermarking framework are combined together to form a robust watermarking scheme. Since the error correction codes deal mainly with integers, the watermark is made up of a sequence of integers that uniquely identifies the copyright owner. An error-coded version of the watermark is then changed into binary digits and embedded into the image using the watermarking framework.

While the watermarking framework attempts to recover embedded bits as accurately as possible, errors that cannot be avoided are kept to a minimum with the error correction codes. The error tolerance of this watermarking scheme is not as high as other watermarking schemes that utilize error correction codes. This could be explained by the fact that other schemes implement bit-level error correction codes while this scheme uses integer level error correction codes. A possible solution would be to develop a technique that actually embeds integers instead of bits into the image. Alternatively, the error correction scheme could be modified to work for binary data.

The results of the comparison are also used as indicators to gauge the performance of the proposed watermarking scheme relative to others. The proposed scheme holds up quite well when compared to the other schemes. However, it could be further improved by making it more tolerant against misalignment or jitter attacks. The presence of a thin dark border is sufficient in significantly reducing the recovery rate.

Overall, both the error correction scheme and watermarking scheme with error correction capabilities have been shown to work well. Examples and experimental results have been presented to support the schemes. Although the watermarking scheme does not hold up as well as the schemes that are used for comparisons, it does demonstrate the feasibility of using the relationship between blocks of pixel to embed the watermark. A future revision of the scheme could perhaps use another measure of relationship instead of *standard deviation*. This may allow for more watermark data to be embedded.

With the completion of this chapter, it can be seen that the development of a watermarking scheme that can withstand all forms of image tampering is quite demanding. Realization of such a scheme from both the information theoretic and algorithmic aspect still remains to be a challenge among the digital watermarking research community. Hopefully, this challenge will continue to spur more examination into this interesting field of research.

References

Asmuth, C. A., & Blakley, G. R. (1982). Pooling, splitting and reconstituting information to overcome total failure of some channels of communication. *Proceedings of the 1982 Symposium on Security and Privacy,* New York (pp. 156-169).

Asmuth, C., & Bloom, J. (1983). A modular approach to key safeguarding. *IEEE Transactions on Information Theory, 29*(2), 208-210.

Barni, M., Bartolini, F., Cappellini, V., & Piva, A. (1997). Robust watermarking of still images for copyright protection. *Proceedings of the 13th International Conference on Digital Signal Processing, Santorini* (pp. 499-502).

Barni, M., Bartolini, F., & Piva, A. (2002). Multichannel watermarking of color images. *IEEE Transactions Circuits and Systems for Video Technology, 12*(3), 142-156.

Barsi, F., & Maestrini, P. (1973). Error correcting properties of redundant residue number systems. *IEEE Transactions on Computers, 22*(3), 307-315.

Baudry, S., Delaigle, J. F., Sankur, B., Macq, B., & Maître, H. (2001). Analyses of error correction strategies for typical communication channels in watermarking. *Signal Processing, 81*(6), 1239-1250.

Bender, W., Gruhl, D., Morimoto, N., & Lu, A. (1996). Techniques for data hiding. *IBM Systems Journal, 35*(3-4), 313-336.

Boneh, D., & Shaw, J. (1998). Collusion-secure fingerprinting for digital data. *IEEE Transactions on Information Theory, 44*(5), 1897-1905.

Caronni, G. (1995). Assuring ownership rights for digital images. *Proceedings of Reliable IT Systems VIS '95, Germany* (pp. 251-263).

Celik, M. U., Sharma, G., Saber, E., & Tekalp, A. M. (2002). Hierarchical watermarking for secure image authentication with localization. *IEEE Transactions on Image Processing, 11*(6), 585-595.

Cox, I. J., Kilian, J., Leighton, F. T., & Shamoon, T. (1997). Secure spread spectrum watermarking for multimedia. *IEEE Transactions on Image Processing, 6*(12), 1673-1687.

Craver, S., Memon, N., Yeo, B. L., & Yeung, M. M. (1998). Resolving rightful ownerships with invisible watermarking techniques: limitations, attacks, and implications. *IEEE Journal on Selected Areas in Communications, 16*(4), 573-586.

Delaigle, J. F., De Vleeschouwer, C., & Macq, B. (1998). Watermarking algorithm based on a human visual model. *Signal Processing, 66*(3), 319-335.

Ding, C., Pei, D., & Salomaa, A. (1996). *Chinese remainder theorem: Applications in computing, coding, cryptography.* Singapore: World Scientific Publishing.

Dugelay, J. L., & Roche, S. (2000). A survey of current watermarking techniques. In S. Katzenbesser & F. A. P. Petitcolas (Eds.), *Information hiding: Techniques for steganography and digital watermarking* (pp. 121-148). Boston: Artech House.

Eggers, J. J., Su, J. K., & Girod, B. (2000). A blind watermarking scheme based on structured codebooks. *Proceedings of IEE Seminar on Secure Images and Image Authentication, London,* 4/1-4/6.

Fu, Y., Shen, R., & Lu, H. (2004). Optimal watermark detection based on support vector machines. *Springer-Verlag Lecture Notes in Computer Science, 3173,* 552-557.

Goh, V. T., Tinauli, M., & Siddiqi, M. U. (2004). A novel error correction scheme based on the Chinese Remainder Theorem. *Proceedings of the 9th International Conference on Communication Systems (ICCS 2004),* Singapore (pp. 461-465).

Goldreich, O., Ron, D., & Sudan, M. (2000). Chinese remaindering with errors. *IEEE Transactions on Information Theory, 46*(4), 1330-1338.

Gonzalez, R. C., & Woods, R. E. (1993). *Digital image processing.* Upper Saddle River, NJ: Addison-Wesley.

Holliman, M., & Memon, N. (2000). Counterfeiting attacks on oblivious block-wise independent invisible watermarking schemes. *IEEE Transactions on Image Processing, 9*(3), 432-441.

Kang, X., Huang, J., Shi, Y. Q., & Zhu, J. (2004). Robust watermarking with adaptive receiving. *Lecture Notes in Computer Science, 2939,* 396-407.

Krishna, H., Lin, K. Y., & Sun, J. D. (1992). A coding theory approach to error control in redundant residue number systems — Part I: Theory and single error correction. *IEEE Transaction on Circuit and Systems, 39*(1), 8-17.

Kundur, D., & Hatzinakos, D. (1999). Digital watermarking for telltale tamper proofing and authentication. *Proceedings of the IEEE, 87*(7), 1167-1180.

Kutter, M., & Hartung, F. (2000). Introduction to watermarking techniques. In S. Katzenbesser & F. A. P. Petitcolas (Eds.), *Information hiding: Techniques for steganography and digital watermarking* (pp. 97-120). Boston: Artech House.

Kutter, M., & Petitcolas, F. (1999). A fair benchmark for image watermarking systems. *Proceedings of SPIE, Security and Watermarking of Multimedia Contents, 3657*, 223-226.

Kutter, M., & Winkler, S. (2002). A vision-based masking model for spread-spectrum image watermarking. *IEEE Transactions on Image Processing, 11*(1), 16-25.

Liu, Y., Gao, W., Cui, M., & Song, Y. (2002). General blind watermark schemes. *Proceedings of Second International Conference on Web Delivering of Music (WEDELMUSIC '02),* Darmstadt (pp. 143-149).

Loo, P., & Kingsbury, N. (2003). Watermark detection based on the properties of error control codes. *IEEE Proceedings: Vision, Image and Signal Processing, 150*(2), 115-121.

Mandelbaum, D. M. (1972). Error correction in residue arithmetic. *IEEE Transaction on Computers, 21*(6), 538-545.

Mandelbaum, D. M. (1976). On a class of arithmetic codes and a decoding algorithm. *IEEE Transaction on Information Theory, 22*(1), 85-88.

Miller, D. F., & Rutter, E. A. (2002). Error control in residue number systems. *Applicable Algebra in Engineering, Communication and Computing, 13*(4), 301-312.

Ó Ruanaidh, J. J. K, & Pun, T. (1997). Rotation, scale and translation invariant digital image watermarking. *Proceedings of IEEE International Conference on Image Processing (ICIP 97),* Santa Barbara (pp. 536-539).

Pérez-Gonzáles, F., & Hernández, J. (1999). A tutorial on digital watermarking. *Proceedings of the 33rd Annual International Carnahan Conference on Security Technology,* Madrid (pp. 286-292).

Podilchuk, C. I., & Zeng, W. (1998). Image-adaptive watermarking using visual models. *IEEE Journal on Selected Areas in Communications, 16*(4), 525-539.

Shamir, A. (1979). How to share a secret. *Communications of the ACM, 22*(11), 612-613.

Solanki, K., Jacobsen, N., Madhow, U., Manjunath, B. S., & Chandrasekaran, S. (2004). Robust image-adaptive data hiding using erasure and error correction. *IEEE Transactions on Image Processing, 13*(12), 1627-1639.

Stinson, D. R. (1995). *Cryptography: Theory and practice.* Boca Raton, FL: CRC Press.

Sun, J. D., & Krishna, H. (1992). A coding theory approach to error control in redundant residue number systems— Part II: Multiple error detection and correction. *IEEE Transaction on Circuit and Systems, 39*(1), 18-34.

Tanaka, K., Nakamura, Y., & Matsui, K. (1990). Embedding secret information into a dithered multilevel image. *Proceedings of the 1990 IEEE Military Communications Conference (MILCOM '90),* Monterey (pp. 216-220).

Wong, P. H. W., Au, O. C., & Yeung, Y. M. (2003). A novel blind multiple watermarking technique for images. *IEEE Transactions on Circuits and Systems for Video Technology, 8*(13), 813-829.

Yang, L. L., & Hanzo, L. (2001). Redundant residue number system based error correction codes. *Proceedings of the 54th Vehicular Technology Conference (VTC 2001),* Atlantic City (pp. 1472-1476).

Yang, Q., & Chen, K. (2004). Digital image authentication based on turbo codes. *Lecture Notes in Computer Science, 3311*, 276-285.

Yeung, M. M., & Mintzer, F. (1997). An invisible watermarking technique for image verification. *Proceedings of IEEE International Conference on Image Processing (ICIP 97),* Santa Barbara (pp. 680-683).

Zhao, J., & Koch, E. (1995). Embedding robust labels into images for copyright protection. *Proceedings of the International Congress on Intellectual Property Rights for Specialized Information, Knowledge and New Technologies,* Vienna (pp. 242-251).

Zhu, H., Clarke, W. A., & Ferreira, H. C. (2004). Watermarking for JPEG image using error correction coding. *Proceedings of the 7th Conference in Africa (AFRICON 2004),* Botswana (pp. 191-196).

Chapter XVII

A Framework for Electronic Bill Presentment and Off-Line Message Viewing

Ezmir Mohd Razali, Multimedia University, Malaysia

Ismail Ahmad, Multimedia University, Malaysia

G. S. V. Radha Krishna Rao, Multimedia University, Malaysia

Kenneth Foo Chuan Khit, NetInfinium Sdn. Bhd., Malaysia

Abstract

A security framework for secure message delivery and off-line message viewing of electronic bills is presented. This framework is implementable toward smart applications such as electronic bill presentment and payment systems.

Introduction

The Internet has revolutionised the biller-consumer interaction through the use of electronic billing systems that facilitate online payments. Traditionally, the system required presentation of bills through paper statements for products/services provided and settlement of bills through cheques sent through snail mail. This process obviously is quite time consuming. The electronic bill ensures prompt delivery of the billing statements with online guidance and instructions for payments via e-mail/interactive Web sites, cuts down on bill delivery costs, ensures prompt payment processing, and hence seems to be better favoured as compared against the traditional paper-dependent manual system. Despite the obvious benefits, it has been found that a majority of consumers are apprehensive about using these electronic systems. Security and privacy issues surrounding the transfer of financial information are cited as one of their primary concern. They fear that the confidentiality and integrity of data transferred can be compromised when transacted electronically.

This chapter argues that electronic bill presentment is still viable, and security concerns can be eliminated by adopting the security framework for secure massage delivery and online message viewing. This effort will help increase the trust over electronic commerce and specifically to electronic billing systems. The ERI framework has been named as such based on the first letters of the author's names.

Motivation and Background

The growth of various Internet-based communication technologies has not managed to stall the popularity of electronic mail or e-mail. Since the 1970s, e-mail has remained the communication tool of choice for many professions all over the world (Berghel, 1997; Oppliger, 2004). One technical advantage of e-mail over alternative means of communication is the speed that e-mail can be transmitted notwithstanding geographical distances. Another obvious advantage of e-mail is that it does not require scheduled endpoint connectivity. As such, both senders and receivers are able to interact with their messages in an autonomous fashion. Another important characteristic is that e-mail is both paperless and archivable (Berghel, 1997; Oppliger, 2004).

These important characteristics have attributed to e-mail being investigated as a medium for transmitting bill statements, invoices, and other confidential information (Carenini, Ng, Zhou, & Zwart, 2005).

The term "secure messaging" refers to the ability to provide data confidentiality, data integrity, data origin authentication, and nonrepudiation of origin services for e-mail (Oppliger, 2004). Despite the positive attributes that e-mail offers, security of e-mail is still a primary concern, especially with respect to using e-mail as a medium to deliver confidential information. E-mail messages are generally not protected as they move across the Internet. It would be possible for e-mail messages to be misdelivered, intercepted, or even read by unauthorized persons. Additionally, e-mail contents can be covertly changed without the knowledge of the original sender. It can be lamented that ordinary Internet e-mail simply lacks the capability to assure integrity, privacy, and authenticity. This sentiment is echoed in Simson et al. (Simson, Margrave, Schiller, Nordlander, & Miller, 2005).

Fortunately, we have seen numerous efforts to make secure Internet e-mail possible. These include the initiatives by the Internet Activities Board's privacy task force, which started work in the 1980s to develop standards designed to provide end-to-end encryption for e-mail, which later became known as privacy enhanced mail (PEM). Following that, the development of secure multipurpose Internet mail extensions (S/MIME) was introduced. Although S/MIME is supported in many e-mail clients today, its presence in Web-based mail systems is yet to be felt (Simson et al., 2005). Another initiative to carry out rudimentary message signing, sealing, and key management, known as PGP, was introduced in 1991. As explained at length in Simson et al. (2005), the major differences between the efforts were the systems' paradigm to certification. PEM specified a centralized public key infrastructure (PKI) with a single root, whereas PGP supports independently certified keys belonging to other users as well as trust certification statements made by other users. PGP now interoperates with popular e-mail systems such as Microsoft Outlook and Eudora.

However, the widespread availability of software that implements cryptographically secured e-mail did not result in the increased usage of secure e-mail. In a secure messaging user survey conducted by Simson et al. (2005), a majority of the respondents felt that receipts from online merchants should be digitally signed, and those arriving from banks and credit card companies should be digitally signed and sealed. This is a clear desire for the need of mail security. Interestingly, the survey also found out that the majority of the respondents were not aware of the cryptographic capabilities of the software they were using. In terms of usability, a large number of the respondents felt that they did not use cryptography either because they did not know how or they did not care or felt that it is a waste of time. The authors came to a conclusion that as a result of the survey, they recommended that online merchants and other corporations send digitally signed e-mail using certificates issued by well known certificate authorities (CA) wherever possible. Given this background, one could argue that secure messaging is a solved problem. Unfortunately, this is not yet the case; there are still several missing pieces. Certified mail schemes based on trusted systems look fine in theory, but their usefulness and security are often overestimated (Oppliger, 2004).

The growth in popularity for using e-mail has made many organizations think of innovative ways of employing e-mail in conducting their daily business. According to Philip Ginzboorg (2000) it is envisaged that the change in technology will influence the way delivery and payment arrangement of services are carried out. It was also highlighted in Ginzboorg (2000) that most of the payments made by residential users over the Internet are made through credit card companies. The most common way to facilitate this is when the buyer's Web browser and the seller's Web server establish an encrypted communication link over which the buyer sends his or her credit card number. This is achieved by the browser and the server using the (secure socket layer) SSL protocol. The SSL protocol, introduced by Netscape in 1994, is a general purpose protocol that provides privacy of communication. Further to this, in 1996 credit card companies specified a suite of protocols called secure electronic transaction (SET) for performing network payments. It was further forecasted in Ginzboorg (2000) that charging and billing by a third party will become a commonality in time to come. Third-party billing is to the advantage of both buyers and sellers. To a buyer, the advantage is that the billing service provider combines services of several sellers into one subscription, with all charges presented in a single bill. To a seller, it is easier to enter the market if the jobs of managing subscriptions, monitoring the service usage, and collecting the money from the buyers can be outsourced.

There is business opportunity in providing charging and billing as a service for companies that sell information.

Given the popularity of e-mail as well as the growing trend towards electronic charging and billing over the Internet, we envisaged that e-mail and electronic billing will soon converge. In our opinion, bill presentment and payment over e-mail will be something as common as doing credit card transactions over the Internet. The technical problem of overcoming the issues of privacy, confidentiality, and authenticity of the information transmitted via e-mail remains a major stumbling block to a widespread adoption of bill presentment and payment via e-mail.

In the next section, we propose a framework called the ERI framework for secure message delivery and off-line viewing that could be used to provide a secure means of delivering messages such as bills statements, invoices, and other confidential information via e-mail, overcoming the security issues that plagued the use of e-mail. These messages are received via ordinary e-mail clients. Once downloaded on the recipients' computer, the message would remain secure and could only be accessed by the authorized recipient. The contents of a protected e-mail remain protected via an encryption scheme that we will discuss in greater details in subsequent sections. This assures that wherever the e-mail travels, online or off-line, the contents remain protected. If the person to whom the e-mail was forwarded does not have access privileges by the author of the e-mail, then he will not be able to view the e-mail.

The accompaniment of a specialized attachment reader for the e-mail will allow the e-mail to be read off-line after the e-mail has been downloaded to the receiver's computer. This attachment reader, equipped with personalized access privileges and decryption mechanism, needs to be downloaded once only into the users' computer as a plug-in to provide a seamless method of accessing the contents of the e-mail. The users will be completely oblivious of the mechanism that is used by the reader when viewing the protected e-mail.

ERI Framework Overview

Our proposed secure message delivery over online SMTP medium and off-line message-viewing framework is known as ERI framework (Figure 1). At the sender side, the message must be encrypted to ensure confidentiality, and it is further enhanced by introducing OTP as a means to prevent replay attacks. The sender also must sign and hash the message to authenticate and preserve the integrity of the message. A checksum is used to verify the integrity of the viewer application, which is uniquely owned by the intended recipient.

The strength of this framework lies in the security features implementation in viewer application Detailed architecture model of viewer application is shown in Figure 2, and details of every component are given in Table 1.

Figure 1. ERI framework for secure message delivery over online SMTP medium and off-line message viewing

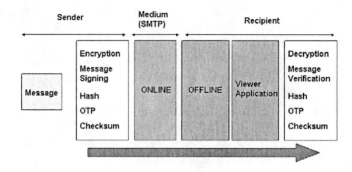

Figure 2. Viewer application architecture model

User Interface	
Login Manager	
Encryption/Decryption Engine	
Hash Engine	Public Key Storage
Application Manager	User Profile Manager
OTP Manager	

OTP: User 1, User 2, User 3

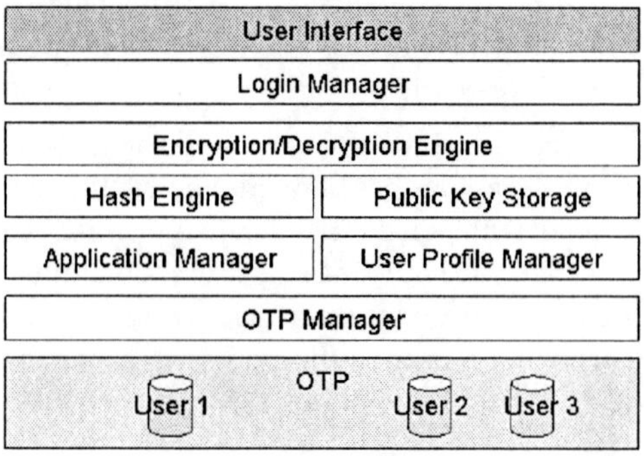

Table 1. Description of viewer application architecture model components

User Interface	Contains GUI for user to interact with the application
Log-in Manager	Check number of log in attempts and log user activities.
Encryption/ Decryption Engine	Perform encryption and decryption based on user password, server's public key, and OTP
Hash Engine	Perform hashing and dehashing to ensure message integrity
Public Key Storage	Store server's public key
User Profile Manager	Maintain user ID, message ID, and OTP DB for every user
Application Manager	Manage viewer application ID and checksum calculation. Perform application integrity check every time application runs
OTP Manager	Perform lookup and verifying user access to OTP DB.
OTP	Store OTP DB for each user

Figure 3. Overview of ERI framework implementation

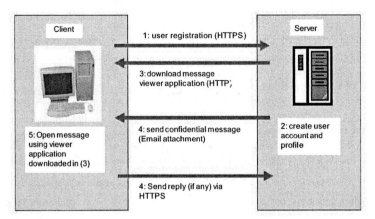

ERI Framework Implementation

To implement ERI framework, a user (recipient) has to register to the server (sender) via secure hypertext transmission protocol, HTTPS. Upon completion, server will register the user's profile in the database and send the viewer application for user to download. Before the server can send the confidential information to the user as an e-mail attachment, the message is formatted in such a way that it can only be opened using the viewer application downloaded by the user previously. Once e-mail is delivered, user can download the attachment and view the content using a special viewer application.

User Registration

A user launches a browser and accesses the server's address or uniform resource locator (URL) and fills in the registration form via HTTPS. A user is required to fill in these two important parameters: (1) password and (2) set of personal information. The user is recommended to select a well-defined password as described in URL-1. The personal information is used for password recovery.

User Profile Account and Viewer Application Generation

Upon completion of user registration, the server generates the following items associated with user's profile: (1) password-based symmetric key, k_1 (2) user ID and (3) user's one-time password (OTP) database (DB). The first and third items are stored in the server database with user ID as its primary key. The key (k_1) is generated from user's password during registration (from previous section), and it will be used to encrypt and decrypt the attachment that is going to be sent to the user. An OTP database is a set of unique passwords to be used only once during the encryption and decryption (symmetric) process. Once any particular password has been used in OTP DB, it will not be selected again. Items (1) to (3) are unique to one particular user, and different sets will be generated for each different user.

After the user profile items have been generated, the server then generates unique parameters for viewer application: (1) viewer application ID, and (2) viewer application checksum (ck_1). Application ID is used to uniquely identify each viewer application and to keep track of all viewer applications installed by the user (user is allowed to install multiple viewer applications in multiple computers). The application is now ready for user to download via HTTPS.

Viewer Application Download and Installation

The server will not send the viewer application straight away for the user to download. Instead, an installer manager program will be downloaded first to check the presence of previously installed viewer application in the user's PC. This is to prevent multiple viewer application installations when the same PC is shared by many users. If the installer manager program verifies that no viewer application has been previously installed, the server will resume the viewer application full download and installation process.

Once downloading has finished, the following items are generated and installed in user's PC: (1) server public key, k_{2PUB} (2) OTP DB. The value of this OTP DB matches exactly

Figure 4. Relationship ID between ERI framework components in user's PC (Recipient)

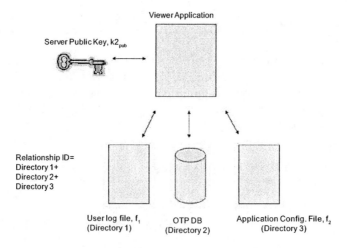

with OTP DB generated in section 2.2, (3) user log profile, f_1. To track user activities with viewer application (i.e., number of attempts keying the wrong password for decryption process) and (4) application configuration file, f_2. It contains several configuration parameters of viewer application (i.e., number of allowable decryption attempts by the user).

Unique relation ID is created between items (2) to (4), as shown in Figure 4. They are put across different directories to provide application integrity protection. Only when all the components are present in the correct directory can the viewer application be launched.

In case the viewer application has already been installed by another user, full installation will not proceed. In this case, only OTP DB and userID will be installed for the new user. A special flag will be set to indicate that the viewer application would need to send the applicationID to the server for this user. The installer manager program can detect the previously installed viewer application in the local PC by checking the presence of server public key k_{2PUB}.

Message Encryption and Delivery

When the server has a confidential message that needs to be sent to the user, the message must first be hashed using MD5 algorithm. Message ID is also generated to uniquely represent the message. Three levels of encryption are performed by the server:

Encryption Level 1

The server will look up the OTP DB corresponding to the respective user ID and generate a random number for OTP index. The OTP index will be used to retrieve a specific OTP. That OTP is used to encrypt the message, message ID, message hash value, user's viewer application ID, and checksum using symmetric algorithm (i.e., Blowfish or AES).

Figure 5. Encryption structure of the message

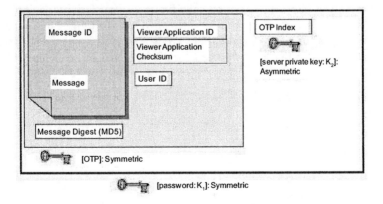

An application ID and checksum are used to make sure that only the viewer application belonging to that particular user can open up the message. A user with multiple viewer applications will have a multiple set of viewer application IDs and checksums sent together. This is to ensure that the user is capable of opening the attachment using all computers that have been installed with viewer applications.

Encryption Level 2

The OTP index generated in level-1 encryption is encrypted under the server private key (K_{2PRIV}) by using asymmetric algorithm (i.e., RSA). The item can be decrypted by the user's viewer application by using server public key (K_{2PUB}) described in the previous section.

Encryption Level 3

Results from encryption Level 1 and Level 2 are encrypted under user's password k_1 (from the "User Profile Account" section). The encrypted message is sent to the user as an e-mail attachment only after this is done. The whole process is illustrated in Figure 5.

Message Decryption and Viewing

A user opens his e-mail message and downloads the attachment. When the user clicks the attachment to open it, viewer application is launched and relationship ID (between OTP DB, f_1 and f_2) is calculated and compared with the relationship ID calculated earlier in previous section. If everything is in place, the viewer application will perform decryption Level 1.

Decryption Level 1

The user will be asked for a password to decrypt the message. User is only allowed to try up to a maximum number of attempts specified in f_2. User activities will be logged in f_1 to make sure that the user will not be allowed to run the application again after exceeding a specific number of attempts. Once a correct password is entered, the viewer application will convert the password to a symmetric key and use it to decrypt the outer envelop of the message.

Figure 6. User registration and viewer application download algorithm

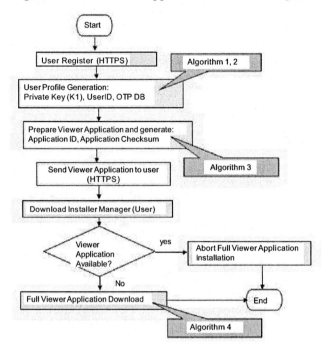

Decryption Level 2

Once the outermost envelop is successfully decrypted, the viewer application will retrieve the server public key (K_{2PUB}) from the local keystore. K_{2PUB} is used to decrypt the next envelope, which contains OTP index. With the OTP index, the viewer application will look up the corresponding OTP in the user's OTP DB.

Decryption Level 3

The selected OTP is used to decrypt the next envelope, containing the message digest, viewer application ID, and its checksum. Next, viewer application performs a message digest verification to ensure message integrity. Then, application must perform its own integrity check by calculating its checksum against the one sent by the server. The value must be equal to pass the verification process

ERI Framework Model Algorithms

User Registration and Viewer Application Download (Server and Client)

Algorithm 1: Generate user's private key, K_1

Input:	User password of at least 7 characters
Output:	Password-based symmetric key (blowfish) stored in the server's database
Method:	1. Request user to enter password (6 characters long at least) 2. Hash password entered using hashing algorithm (MD5) 3. Use the hash password as a key specification 4. Generate blowfish symmetric key using the given key specification in (3) 5. The generated is stored under User ID primary key in the database

Algorithm 2: Generate OTP DB

Input:	Information unique to user (i.e. name, identity card number, user id, address)
Output:	Randomly and uniquely generated password list for the user
Method:	1. Get user's unique information (name, identity card number, user id, address) 2. Hash user's unique information from step 1 using hashing algorithm (MD5) and store the first password in a text file 3. Randomly increment value of user's hashed password from step 2 and store the second password in a same text file 4. Repeat step 3 until sufficient amount of password is achieved (i.e. say to 100 password list) 5. The OTP DB is named according to User ID and stored in a directory specified in a server 6. Alternatively, the value of the text file can be serialized and stored in a database under User ID primary key

Algorithm 3: Generate viewer application information to the user

Input:	-
Output:	Unique ID and checksum value for viewer application
Method:	1. Generate random number for application ID and store in the database under user ID 2. Serialized viewer application and perform checksum calculation 3. Store checksum value (from step 2) and store under application ID (from step 1) in the database

Algorithm 4: Viewer application installation in a client's machine

Input:	-
Output:	Viewer application, OTP DB, user log file and application configuration file, server public key
Method:	1. Install viewer application in a default installation directory (specified by user) 2. Retrieve OTP DB from the installation package and install OTP DB locally. OTP DB can be installed together in a specific directory under the installation directory 3. Create a text file for user log file. The file is unique for the user and name with UserIDlog.txt and store in a specified directory in a local hard drive 4. Create a text file for application configuration file and store in a specified directory in a local hard drive 5. Read the file location in step 2,3, and 4, and hash the value to form a file relationship ID 6. Store the relationship ID and store in user log file created in step 3. 7. Store public key in a text file in a specified directory in a local hard drive

Figure 7. Message encryption and delivery algorithm from server to client

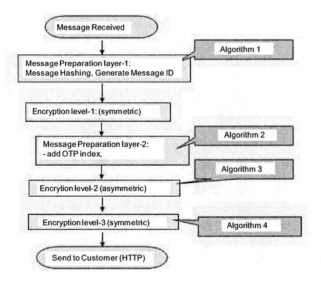

Message Encryption and Delivery (Server)

Algorithm 1: Message preparation

Input:	Message to be sent to the user
Output:	message hash value, message ID,
Method:	1. Serialize message and hash it using MD5 hashing algorithm 2. Generate a random number for Message ID

Algorithm 2: Encryption level-1 (OTP index, Symmetric)

Input:	message hash value, message ID, message, user's viewer application ID and its checksum
Output:	First envelope of encryption under OTP; OTP index
Method:	1. Generate random OTP index number (between 1 – 100) 2. Retrieve OTP from the generated OTP index of step 1 from user's OTP DB 3. Use OTP from step 2 as a key specification to generate 'session' symmetric key for encryption/decryption. 4. Encrypt all inputs using key generated in step 3

Algorithm 3: Encryption level-2 (Server private key K_{2PRIV}, asymmetric)

Input:	OTP index
Output:	OTP index encrypted under server's private key K_{2PRIV}
Method:	1. Get OTP index generated previously 2. Retrieve server private key K_{2PRIV} from database 3. Encrypt OTP index from step 1 using server private key K_{2PRIV} from step 2 using RSA encryption algorithm

Algorithm 4: Encryption level-3 (User password K_1, symmetric)

Input:	Output from algorithm 2 and 3
Output:	Third level encryption using K_1
Method:	1. Retrieve password-based symmetric key generated in algorithm 1 of section 3.1 from the database 2. Encrypt output of algorithm 2 and 3 using password-based symmetric key from step 1 as key by using Blowfish symmetric encryption

Figure 8. Attachment download and message viewing algorithm at client's machine

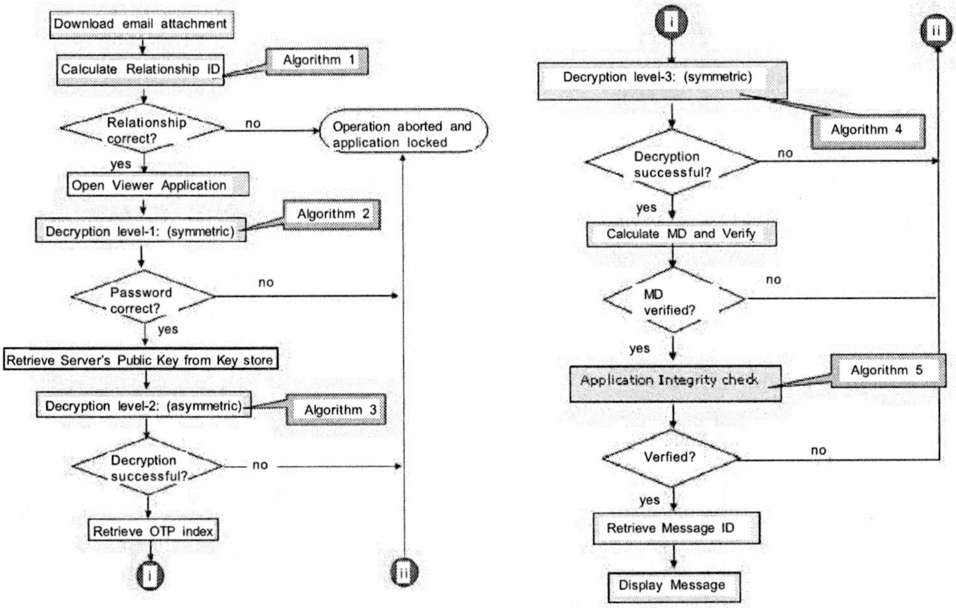

Attachment Download and Message Viewing (User's Machine)

Algorithm 1: Viewer application integrity check

Input:	-
Output:	Relationship ID
Method:	1. Locate user's OTP DB, user's log file and application configuration file 2. Calculate run-time relationship ID and compare with the previous calculated value stored in application configuration file 3. Proceed if relationship is correct

Algorithm 2: Decryption level-1 (Password based decryption k_1, symmetric)

Input:	User's Password
Output:	Encrypted OTP index, Encrypted message
Method:	1. Ask user to enter password to decrypt the first layer envelope 2. Record number of login attempts. If more wrong attempts have been made than the pre-determined value (stored in application configuration file), user status will be mark as 'block access' in user's log file. User will be block from using the viewer application in the future. To unblock it, the user has to contact the server admin, and have to re-download the viewer application again. If the password was correctly entered, the process continues. 3. Hash the password with MD5 hashing algorithm 4. Use user's password from step 1 as a key specification to generate symmetric key for decryption 5. Decrypt the first layer envelope

Algorithm 3: Decryption level-2 (Server's public key k_{2PUB}, asymmetric)

Input:	Server's Public Key, Encrypted OTP index
Output:	OTP index
Method:	1. Retrieve server's public key 2. Decrypt OTP index envelope 3. Retrieve OTP index

Algorithm 4: Decryption level-3 (OTP, symmetric)

Input:	OTP index (from algorithm 3), Encrypted message (from algorithm 2)
Output:	Message data, message hash code, Viewer application ID and checksum
Method:	1. Get OTP index from the output of algorithm 3 2. Use OTP index from step 1 to retrieve corresponding OTP for decryption in OTP DB stored in client's machine 3. Get the selected OTP from step 2 and decrypt third layer envelope

Algorithm 5: Bill and application integrity check

Input:	Message data, message hash code, Viewer application ID and checksum
Output:	-
Method:	1. Serialized the decrypted message and hash using the same algorithm as in algorithm 1 of section 3.2 2. Compare run-time hash value calculated by client side from step 1 3. …with original value sent by the server (algorithm 1 of section 3.2). If value is similar, the process continues. Otherwise, the process aborted 4. Serialized viewer application and calculate the checksum by using same algorithm as in algorithm 1 of section 3.1 5. Compare run-time value in step 3 with the original value sent by the server (algorithm 1 of section 3.1). If value is similar, the process continues. Otherwise, the process aborted

ERI Framework Sample Application

Initial program startup for server to generate a private and public key (Figure 9).

User's Registration

User enters the password during registration process. The password will used as a key to perform encryption and decryption of the message. Once registered, OTP and user ID for the user are generated (Figure 10).

Figure 9. Generate server public and private key pair (RSA 1024bit). Server public and private keys are stored in the database.

Viewer Application Download

Next, client will download the user application and following files are generated and stored in a specified directory in a client's machine (Figure 11):

- *userId*.db   : user's profile

- *userId*.db.otp   : user's OTP list

- *userId*.pwdCheck   : application configuration file

- server.pub.asc   : server's public key

Figure 10. Generate OTP. Shown here using 10 set of passwords. User Id, OTP list and hashed password are stored in the database.

Figure 11. Viewer application download emulation

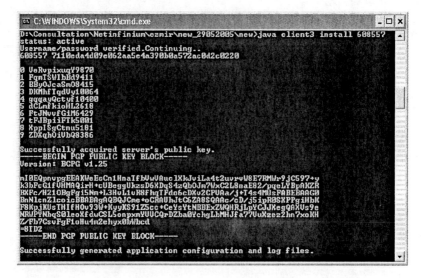

Figure 12. Running the application

Figure 13. Original message to encrypt

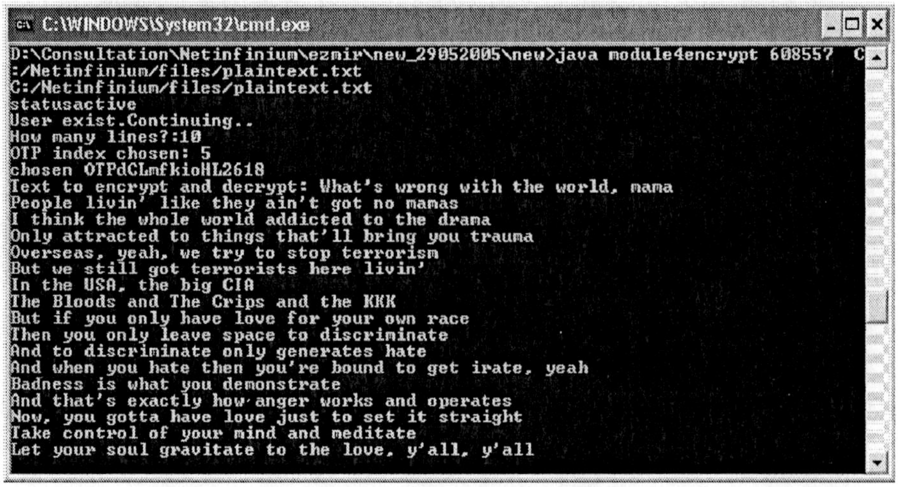

Running Viewer Application

When viewer application is running, it will first check for the presence of log file and application configuration file (Figure 12).

Encryption by the Server

See Figure 13 through Figure 16.

Decryption by User Using Viewer Application

See Figure 17 through Figure 19.

Figure 14. 1ˢᵗ Encryption: Using OTP-based Blowfish of plaintext above (ciphertext 1)

Figure 15. 2ⁿᵈ Encryption: Encrypt OTP index using server's private key (ciphertext 2)

Figure 16. Combine ciphertext 1 and 2, encrypt both of them using hashed user's password. Table userId *was added to the database to store the resulting ciphertext.*

Figure 17. User enters the password to decrypt the encrypted message received from the server

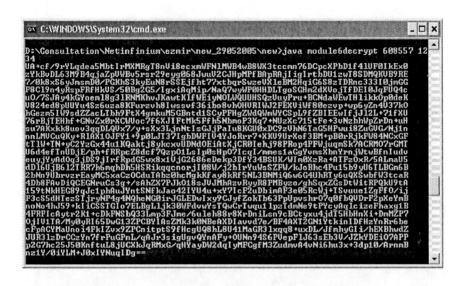

Figure 18. 1ˢᵗ level decryption: Extract ciphertext 1 and ciphertext 2

Figure 19. Decrypt OTP index using server's public key and decrypt the encrypted bill using the selected OTP

Conclusion

We proposed a framework that could be used to provide a secure means of delivering messages and other confidential information via e-mail, overcoming the security issues that plagued the use of e-mails. These messages are received via ordinary e-mail clients. Once downloaded on the recipients' computer would remain secure and could only be accessed by the authorized recipient. The contents of a protected e-mail remain protected via an encryption scheme. This assures that wherever the e-mail travels, online or off-line, the contents remain protected. If the person to whom the e-mail was forwarded does not have access privileges by the author of the e-mail, then he will not be able to view the e-mail. The accompaniment of a specialized attachment reader for the e-mail will allow the e-mail to be read off-line after the e-mail has been downloaded to the receiver's computer. This attachment reader, equipped with personalized access privileges and decryption mechanism, needs to be downloaded once only into the users' computer, which acts as a plug-in to provide a seamless method of accessing the contents of the e-mail. The users will be completely oblivious of the mechanisms that are used by the reader when viewing the protected e-mail.

Acknowledgments

This research work is a collaborative effort between Multimedia University, Malaysia and NetInfinium Sdn. Bhd. Malaysia. The authors are grateful to NetInfinium Sdn. Bhd. towards allowing this work to be published. Appreciation is due to Mr. Lee See Sheong of NetInfinium Sdn. Bhd. for useful discussions.

References

Berghel, H. (1997). E-mail: The good, the bad and the ugly. *Communications of the ACM, 40*(4), 11-15.

Carenini, G., Ng, R., Zhou, X., & Zwart, E. (2005). Discovery and regeneration of hidden e-mails. In *Proceedings of the 2005 ACM symposium on Applied computing*, Santa Fe, New Mexico (pp 503-510).

Garfinkel, S. L., Margrave, D., Schiller, J. I., Nordlander, E., & Miller, R. C. (2005). E-mail and security: How to make secure e-mails easier to read. In *Proceedings of the SIGCHI Conference on Human Factors in Computing Systems*, Portland, Oregon (pp. 701-710).

Ginzboorg, P. (2000). Seven comments on charging and billing. *Communications of the ACM, 43*(11), 89-92.

Oppliger, R. (2004). Certified mail: The next challenge for secure messaging. *Communications of the ACM, 47*(8), 75-79.

Secure Computing.com. Retrieved from http://www.securecomputing.com/gateway/one_time_password.cfm

Propagation and Delegation of Rights in Access Controls and Risk Assessment Techniques

Saravanan Muthaiyah, George Mason University, USA
and Multimedia University, Malaysia

Abstract

Access control methods have been improvised over time, but one area that remains quite grey is the concept of assessing risk levels before any type of access rights are granted. This is relatively a new paradigm in the research of semantic Web security, and new methodologies for this effort are being studied. In this chapter, we will see how qualitative risk assessment (Nissanke & Khayat, 2004) and quantitative risk assessment are carried out. The purpose is to have different methods of assessment for better grant of access control rights and permissions. New examples based on the model described (Nissanke & Khayat, 2004) are used to illustrate the concept. A new quantities technique is also added to complement the qualitative techniques.

Introduction

This chapter introduces the concept of access control and its objectives in fulfilling security requirements for the computing world. The main arrears in access control, namely **DAC, MAC,** and **RBAC,** will be covered, thus giving enough background knowledge to the reader on existing policies and framework. Hence, the reader will be able to comprehend the concept of task delegation with regard to access control policies and how delegated tasks or roles can affect existing risk levels in an organization. **Measuring risk** has a two fold benefit: one is that it enables security officials to be prepared with more accurate security measures with higher granularity, and secondly, this will certainly be useful for security plans for mitigating potential risks.

However, measuring risk is easier said than done. Being subjective in its nature, we are unable to say which technique is the best. In finance-related research, models have been introduced, such as VAR (value at risk), to accurately measure risk based on volatility of share prices in the market. There is a gap of knowledge in computer science in this area and as such, this chapter introduces two novel ways of measuring risk. The assumption is that we take the real world approach in understanding risk or, in other words, there are risks that we can measure and there are risks that cannot be measured. For the former, a two-dimension approach will be used, which will be referred to as **quantitative approach (QTA)**, and for the latter, risk graphs coupled with task delegation (role assignment) framework will be used, which will be referred to as **qualitative approach (QLA)**.

Background

What is Access Control?

Security policies or technologies devised to prevent unauthorized usage or access can be regarded as access control. Access controls can be physical, technical, or administrative, and can be categorized as preventive or detective. Access control is a preventive control that attempts to avoid unwanted events from taking place whereas detective controls attempt to find out about events after they have taken place. Audit trails, intrusion detection methods, and checksums are examples of detective control techniques.

Access Control Objectives?

Nowadays, databases contain extensive information that is sensitive and proven to be highly valuable. If the data is accessed by unauthorized users, it can be detrimental to the organization that is the gatekeeper of that data. Organizations today are faced with challenges such as maintaining privacy and guaranteeing trust to its patrons. Technologies today make it easier to share information between databases, and the ability to properly protect it becomes more and more challenging. The macroobjective of access control is to determine the confidentiality, integrity, and availability of data.

How Access Control Fulfills: Privacy, Authentication, and Integrity

Hackers and masqueraders seem to be the culprits who take advantage of the vulnerability of systems. They are a threat to the confidentiality, privacy, and integrity of data items. Trojan horses are also becoming increasingly popular. They can be programmed to copy confidential files to unprotected areas of the system. This happens unknowingly when legitimate users who have authorized access to certain files try to execute them. The Trojan horse becomes a resident on the system of the legitimate user when executed, and will copy confidential files to unprotected areas regularly.

Privacy and Confidentiality

The Bell-Lapadula model has been used for enforcing confidentiality, and it defines relationships that exist between objects (i.e., files and records) and subjects (i.e., persons and devices). Here the described relationship is the assigned access level or privilege and the level of sensitivity of objects. It can also be referred to as security clearance of the subject and security classification of the object.

Access such as read, write, or read and write are common types of subjects' access on objects. **Bell-LaPadula** also enforces the lattice principle, which states that subjects are allowed write access to objects if its level is the same or higher than the object. Read access to objects is given if object is at the same or lower level. Read/write access is for objects that are at the same level as the subject. This can prevent writing higher-classified data into a lower-classified file or disclosing higher-classified data to lower-classified individuals.

Authentication

Authentication is indeed a very tedious process and possibly the most difficult part of the access control administration. Using personal identity or physical attributes of individuals (i.e., biometric identification) has been a good way. Access control for authentication in a heterogeneous environment can be difficult as we have to be sure that people are whom they claim to be. The implementation of **Kerberos** in distributed network environments has id necessary, but the cost and performance indicators have to be looked into.

Integrity

Access control is a mechanism that provides integrity to systems. Integrity is to take precaution and to protect data from intentional or unintentional accidental changes. The security program should ensure that data is maintained in the state that users expect it to be. No user should be able to modify data in such a way that it could corrupt existing records and render the organizational data unreliable. In the military, navigational data, weapons, and data on logistics (i.e., fuel, food, and supplies) are crucial data and if tampered with, could result in a disaster. Commercial systems also require high-level integrity for accounting data, production, and inventory and payroll. Three basic principles to establish integrity controls are giving access on a need-to-know basis, separation of duties, and rotation of duties. Once again the Bell-Lapadula model is useful here.

Types of Access Control: DAC, MAC, and RBAC

There have been several types of access control concepts. Discretionary access controls (DAC) is one that does allow access rights of a user to be propagated from one user to another or from one subject to another. Access rights that a subject has will be sufficient to allow access of an object. However, DAC has some weaknesses, such as information from one object can be read by a subject and can then be written to another object by that subject if access is unrestricted. Suppose this does not happen because we trust our users, but it will still be possible for Trojan horses.

Mandatory access controls (MAC), on the other hand, do restrict the access of subjects to objects using security labels. The label-based policy is used to assign security levels to data, security clearance to users and, in a database, users who have clearance only can access the data. Role-based access control (RBAC), uses roles of users to give access rights. This is how it is done in the real world, especially in a distributed system.

This model has been developed to support a number of tasks including single sign-on (SSO). Here a user's responsibilities are more important rather than who the user is. In DAC, an individual's user ownership of data is more important and so it is not a good fit. MAC, which uses security labels, also requires users have security clearance and objects to have security classifications. Therefore, a new access control model was needed, and RBAC provided that need.

Propagation of Rights in Access Control

Assignment of rights and access based on roles of users has been a major contribution of RBAC. A user's rights can be propagated from one user to another user in DAC, but it is indeed critical to grant rights to a user based on level of risks. The risk level is related to the role that has been assigned to the user by virtue of the task that has to be carried out. The user should be able to perform all the assigned tasks within his domain and with this he gains all rights to whatever the domain permits. The assumption here is that a set of fixed permissions are assigned to each of these roles. Even if the role changes dynamically, it would mean that anytime a task could be delegated by one user to another, permissions should also change. For example, in a bank, the branch manager (B) can assign a task to his manager (M). When this happens, the manager (M) would have inherited some of the roles of his superior (B). RBAC does not take this into consideration and so this will complement all other studies on permission role assignment should in order for better security models. This introduces application of domain-oriented data modeling, task policy, and task delegation.

Risk Assessment: A Real-World Approach

Risk is potential harm that can affect us in an adverse way. There are many definitions for risk, but there have been only a few methods to actually measure risk. Risk in business transactions such as impersonation, collateral access to business systems, and misuse of personal data is popular on the Web. Risk can be divided into two main types, which are systematic and unsystematic risk. Systematic risk cannot be quantified but unsystematic risk can be measured.

With adopting the risk-ordering relation, we can categorize the risk into various risk bands (RB) so that it becomes easier for us to see relative levels of risk. With this we can propagate tasks after weighing them on the risk scale. If a user is given rights to carry out certain tasks and if the task is propagated, the scale would indicate the relative level of risk and, based on that, access can be allowed. Since risk is difficult to be quantified and the concept of risk is as problematic as defining it, we are using a scale method to overcome this problem (Williams, Walker, & Dorofee, 1997).

QLA (Qualitative Approach: Risks cannot be Measured)

Statecharts have been widely used for modeling reactive systems and is an extension of finite-state machines with enhanced capabilities such as hierarchical decomposition of system's states, explicit representation of concurrency and broadcast communication. Statecharts is a kind of directed graph, with nodes denoting states and arrows denoting labeled transitions (Harel, 1987). A formal method used to show various risk levels, referred to as risk band (RB), is called a risk graph.

This method was introduced (Nissanke & Khayat, 2004) to scale risk. In our example (Figure 2b), there are six risk bands. RB 6 is the lowest level of risk and RB 1 is the highest level of risk.

Any task that falls under RB 1 would have a higher level of risk compared to the task that falls under RB 6. When a task is delegated, it can be placed in any one of these risk bands. Also, the risk graph clearly shows the concept of relative risk. This means that RB 1 has a relatively higher risk compared to RB 6. Comparable and noncomparable risks are also shown in the risk graph. Task 1 (T1) and Task 3 (T3) are comparable risk and because of this, they share the same risk band, which is RB 6. Noncomparable risks, for example, are T2 and T8.

The following diagram shows a risk graph with multiple roles in a banking environment. Role functions in this case would be teller (T), manager (M), and branch manager (B). Each of these roles has its own role that can be delegated. When the manager's task is performed by his superior, who is the branch manager, the risk band in our example, RB = 2, shows the same level of risk between them, although the branch manager has higher level of authority. This is because by default, it is the job of the manager to assist loan decisions and not the function of the branch manager. On the other hand, if the teller assists loan decisions, the risk band for the teller will fall under RB = 4.

When tasks are actually propagated, their movements should be recorded on a scale, as the one described, for systematic risks where we cannot quantitatively measure the risk. As a result, we can only compare the relative levels of risk as whether they are higher or lower. Then the tasks that are placed on the risk scale should be used for granting rights to provide access. If a user is given rights to carry out certain tasks and if the task was propagated, the scale would indicate if the new level of risk for that task, and based on those new rights, can be allowed.

QTA (Quantitative Approach: Risks can be Measured)

In this approach, we can estimate the risk using a two-dimensional model. In reality, there can be multiple factors that affect risk levels; however, in the next example, only two

Figure 1. Risk ordering relation and risk graph (Nissanke & Khayat, 2004)

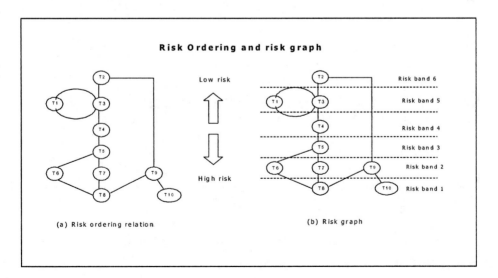

Figure 2. Risk graph of the permissions in the banking environment

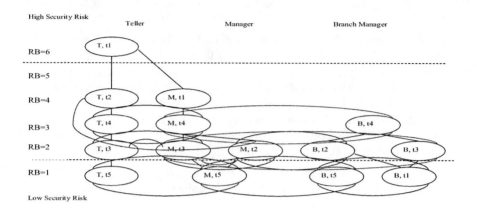

Table 1. Tasks of business side defined in a banking environment

Task Name	Representation	Brief Description	Authorized Roles
t1	(decide, loan)	Make Loan Decisions	Branch Manager (B)
t2	(asst, loan)	Assist Loan Decisions	Manager (M)
t3	(pre, cust)	Prepare Loan Application	Teller (T)
t4	(vault, cust)	Vault Transaction for Customer	Teller (T)
t5	(trans, cust)	Teller Transaction for Customer	Teller (T)

factors will be discussed, that is, risk levels (RB) and transaction value ($). So, the function for risk curve is as follows: Risk curve $= f\{$transaction value ($), risk levels (RB)$\}$.

The three points in the graph, which are E1, E2, and E3, are equilibrium points for risk levels and transaction values. Such values can also be obtained by calculating the gradient of the slope for the risk curve. Table 1 shows some elasticity levels and access level security for these values, and Table 2 shows how the gradient values can be calculated.

Here the risk band can be developed from an index based on consumer perception of risk based on trust factors and nontrust factors as shown in the following table.

Figure 3. Risk curve with three equilibrium points

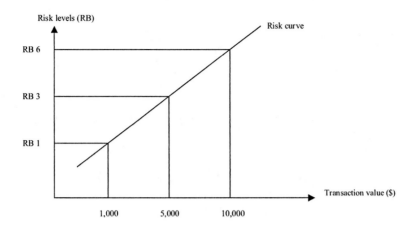

Table 2. Elasticity values and access level security granted

Equilibrium values	Elasticity levels	Access level security
E = 0	Perfectly inelastic	Very low
E = 1	uniform	Equal
E > 1	Elastic	Higher
E < 1	Inelastic	Lower
E = infinite	Perfectly elastic	Very high

Table 3. Elasticity values and for movement on the risk curve

Movement in RB	Changes in risk level and evaluating equilibrium values
RB1 to RB3	Change in transaction value ($) Change in risk level = 5000-1000 / 1000 3-1 / 1 = 2
RB3 to RB6	Change in transaction value ($) Change in risk level = 10000-5000 / 5000 6-3 / 3 = 1

Table 4. Source: Craig Van Slyke and France Belanger. E-Business Technologies, *Supporting the Net-Enhanced Organization, 2003.*

Perceptions other than trust	Perceptions based on trust
Relative advantage	Predictability
Complexity	Reliability
Compatibility	Technical competence
Result demonstrability	**Fiduciary responsibility**
Visibility	
Trialability	

Conclusion

E-commerce has accelerated enormously through the advancement of network computing and the evolution of the Internet. The advent of payment systems and virtual marketplace has increased B2C participation worldwide and thus risk assessment for unregulated environments, such as pervasive computing, mobile computing, and Web services, is becoming increasingly important. A formal technique or method-of-risk assessment is, therefore, important so that access rights can be granted without any ambiguities or inconsistencies. The use of risk assessment techniques becomes important, and new concepts such as risk graphs, risk relations, and risk bands are useful in that way. Both quantitative and qualitative techniques that have been discussed provide a formal methodology for addressing risk issues for e-commerce in general and Web services in particular.

References

Barka, E., & Sandhu, R. (2000, December). Framework for role-based delegation models. In *Proceedings of the 16ᵗʰ IEEE Annual Computer Security Applications Conference* (pp. 168-175), New Orleans, LA.

Lawton, G. (2002). Invasive software: Who's inside your computer? *IEEE Computer Magazine, 35*(7), 15-18.

Harel, D. (1987), Statecharts: A visual formalism for complex systems. *Science of Computer Programming, 8*(3), 231-274.

Holdrege & Srisresh (2001). Protocol complications with the IP network address translator. In *RFC 3027* (pp. 1-20).

Huston, G. (2003). Measuring IP network performance. *The Internet Protocol Quarterly Journal*, 6(1), 2-19.

Khayat, E., & Nissanke (2003). Risk-based security analysis of permissions in RBAC. In *Proceedings of the 2ⁿᵈ International Workshop on Security in Information Systems, WOSIS 2004,* Porto, Portugal (pp. 342-350) April, 2004.

Sandhu, R., Ferraiolo, D., & Kuhn, R. (2000, July). The NIST model for tole-based access control: Towards a unified standard. In *Proceedings of 5ᵗʰ ACM Workshop on Role-Based Access Control*, Berlin, Germany (pp. 47-64).

Stallings, W. (2003). The session initiation protocol. *The Internet Protocol Quarterly Journal*, 6(1), 20-40.

Van Slyke, C., & Belanger, F. (2003). *E-business technologies, supporting the net-enhanced organization.*

Williams, R. C., Walker, J. A., & Dorofee, A. J. (1997). Putting risk management into practice. *IEEE Software*, May/June, 75-82.

Chapter XIX

IPSec Overhead in Dual Stack IPv4/IPv6 Transition Mechanisms:
An Analytical Study

M. Mujinga, University of Fort Hare, South Africa

Hippolyte Muyingi, University of Fort Hare, South Africa

Alfredo Terzoli, Rhodes University, South Africa

G. S. V. Radha Krishna Rao, University of Fort Hare, South Africa

Abstract

Internet protocol version 6 (IPv6) is the next generation Internet protocol proposed by the Internet Engineering Task Force (IETF) to supplant the current Internet protocol version 4 (IPv4). Lack of security below the application layer in IPv4 is one of the reasons why there is a need for a new IP. IPv6 has built-in support for the Internet protocol security protocol (IPSec). This chapter reports work done to evaluate implications of compulsory use of IPSec on dual stack IPv4/IPv6 environment.

Introduction and Background

The Internet protocol (IP) is the protocol that operates at the backbone of the Internet, and networking in general. The initial IP was first published in 1981, in RFC 791 [DARPA IP Spec., 1981] and is now generally known as IPv4. Internet protocol version 6 (IPv6) is the next generation Internet protocol proposed by the IETF in RFC 2460 (Deering & Hinden., 1998; Doraswamy & Harkins, 1999), published in 1998 to supplant IPv4. IP security (IPSec) is provided by a set of protocols, the main protocols being authentication header (AH) and encapsulating security payload (ESP) protocols (Kent & Atkinson, 1998). IPSec operates at the network layer in a way that is completely transparent to the applications, and much more powerful, because the applications do not need to have any knowledge of IPSec to be able to use it (Farrel, 2004). In IPv4, IPSec headers are inserted after the IPv4 header and before the next-layer protocol header. While with IPv6, this is applied in the form of additional extension headers (Loshin, 2003). This obviously increases the overhead of an IP datagram, and since this protocol is mandatory on IPv6, this overhead becomes increasingly significant.

There was some research done on the performance implications of IPSec deployment. In Ronan et al. (2004), the authors evaluated the performance overheads under a range of different bandwidth and different processors, on throughput and processor; single and dual, when communicating over a secured VPN on IPv4 infrastructure, using Linux 2.6.1 kernel. The findings showed that the overhead differs from one processor type to the other, and this was consistent when dual processors were used of the same type. The other work (Ariga et al., 2000) evaluated the performance of data transmissions with IPv4 and IPv6 networks. The results showed that IPSec obviously degrades the network performance in terms of throughput and end-to-end delay for the large data transmission and for the actual application. The authors concentrated on digital video (DV) transmission as the application. Their results showed that, for large data transmissions, when authentication and encryption are applied, the throughput degrades to 1/9 compared with the throughput without authentication or encryption.

Dual stack translation mechanism (DSTM) was our primary method in the IPv6 experiments; 6to4 in particular. 6to4 is a tunneling addressing mechanism that enables communication between two IPv6 computers that live in an IPv4 environment (Carpenter & Moore, 2001). In this paper, we will investigate the cost in terms of performance when transmitting traffic on computer networks, with IPSec enabled on IPv4 and IPv6. Our research focuses on Windows IPv6 and IPSec implementations, and evaluates a variety of IP traffic over HTTP, FTP, TFTP, and ICMP protocols. We evaluated the additional frame overhead induced by IPSec on both IPv4 and IPv6 on these protocols, noting also its impact on average round-trip times. This is achieved by comparing traffic with IPSec on and IPSec off. The research we are conducting will give an insight into the quantitative expense, which the mandatory use of IPSec will bring into our networks, and we will give a model of how and when to use it on your network. Knowing when and how to deploy IPSec efficiently will help to save two of our most valued resources in the Internet community: the scarce and expensive bandwidth and computer processing power.

Table 1. List of experimental equipment

Hardware	Software
Domain Controller Server	Windows Server 2003 SP1
File Server	Windows XP Professional SP2
Web Server	Finisar Surveyor 5.5
2 Client computers	
10/100 Fast Ethernet Switch	

Experimental Details

Our network consists of five computers, of which three are servers running Windows 2003 Server SP1 and two clients running Windows XP Professional SP 2. All nodes have Microsoft TCP/IP version 6 protocol stack enabled. We configured IPSec on the domain controller. We are using a third-party protocol analyzer for packet capturing and analysis.

All the computers used have the following system properties:

- CPU: 2.8 GHz

- RAM: 1.1 GB

- HD Size: 112 GB

Our experimental test bed consists of equipment with the specifications, as available in Table 1.

There were a number of tests that were carried out, and there are two main sections of tests, that is, those conducted to determine the traffic overhead and those conducted to determine the delay using the round-trip times and download times in the case of HTTP and FTP.

Frame Overhead

Frame overhead are bits that are added at regular intervals to a digital signal at the sending end or intermediary gateways of a digital link. We determined the frame overhead induced by applying different IPSec protocols and algorithms in our first set of experiments.

Round-Trip Time

Round-trip time (RTT) is a measure of the time it takes for a packet to travel from a computer, across a network to another computer, and back. RTT is computed by the sending side recording the clock when it transmits a packet, and then recording the clock again when an acknowledgment or a reply arrives. By subtracting the two values, we obtain a single estimate of the round-trip time. A collection of these values for a period of time gives the average RTT.

Download Time

The download time is the time it takes to download a file or a Web page from the remote server or computer to the local computer. We calculated this by subtracting the time the first frame of the downloaded file is received from the time the last frame is received.

Applications/Protocols Tested

ICMP

Internet control message protocol (ICMP) is a required protocol tightly integrated with IP. ICMP uses IP as if ICMP were a higher-level protocol, that is, ICMP messages are encapsulated in IP datagrams. ICMP is also not dependent on either TCP or UDP. Ping is an application that tests host responses over a network connection. Ping uses the network layer to send packets to a remote address. If there are network connectivity problems or the host has problems, the ping will fail, indicating that a problem exists. Additional tests may be needed at that point to determine the cause of the problem.

HTTP

The hypertext transfer protocol (HTTP) is an application-level protocol for distributed, collaborative, hypermedia information systems used to transfer data across the Internet. HTTP has been in use by the World Wide Web global information initiative since 1990. The current version of HTTP is HTTP/1.1. We used HTTP to test how IPSec performs on TCP.

FTP

File transfer protocol (FTP) is a procedure used to upload and download files to and from your FTP server. FTP is a special way to login to another Internet site for the purposes of retrieving and/or sending files, and is the best way of sending files from one computer to another over the Internet using TCP.

TFTP

Trivial file transfer protocol (TFTP) is a simple UDP-based protocol used for transferring files between computers. TFTP is used where user authentication and the need to view directories on remote computers are not required. Its two major uses are to bootstrap diskless machines that are being installed over the network, and to install images that reside in firmware. This type of communication also needs to be protected to improve network security.

Frame Structure

IPv4

The minimum size of an IPv4 Ethernet frame is 64 bytes, which includes the minimum frame payload of 46 bytes plus the Ethernet header of 18 bytes, including 4 bytes for cyclical redundancy check (CRC). The maximum frame size for IPv4 Ethernet is 1518 bytes, given by an Ethernet maximum transmission unity (MTU) of 1,500 bytes plus the Ethernet header.

IPv6

An IPv4 Ethernet frame using 6to4 has a minimum size of 86 bytes, comprised of 68 bytes of frame payload plus 18 bytes of Ethernet header, including 4 bytes of CRC. There are fundamental differences on how IPSec affects IPv4 and IPv6. The default MTU size for IPv6 packets on an Ethernet is 1280 octets.

IPSec transform sets

An IPSec transform specifies a single IPSec security protocol (either AH or ESP) with its corresponding security algorithms and mode. Since our tests are based on a single network, that is, point–to–point communication within a site, we chose to use the transport mode for the tests. Therefore, all IPSec transform sets are based on transport mode IPSec that protects the IP payload only with the IP header visible. A transform set is a combination of individual IPSec transforms designed to enact a specific security policy for protecting a particular traffic flow. Table 2 shows the available IPSec transform sets in Windows Server 2003. Windows IPSec implementation provides two integrity algorithms: SHA1 and MD5, and two encryption algorithms: 3DES and DES. Hence, all our IPSec transform sets are based on these four algorithms and in transport mode.

Table 2. IPSec transform sets in Windows Server 2003

Transform Set	AH algorithm	ESP Algorithm
AH Only		
1	AH-MD5	None
2	AH-SHA1	None
ESP Only		
3	None	ESP-SHA1
4	None	ESP-MD5
5	None	ESP-SHA1-3DES
6	None	ESP-MD5-3DES
7	None	ESP-SHA1-DES
8	None	ESP-MD5-DES
AH and ESP Encryption		
9	AH-MD5	ESP-DES
10	AH-MD5	ESP-DES
11	AH-SHA1	ESP-DES
12	AH-SHA1	ESP-DES
AH and ESP Integrity		
13	AH-MD5	ESP-SHA1
14	AH-MD5	ESP-MD5
15	AH-SHA1	ESP-SHA1
16	AH-SHA1	ESP-MD5
BOTH		
17	AH-MD5	ESP-SHA1-3DES
18	AH-MD5	ESP-MD5-3DES
19	AH-SHA1	ESP-SHA1-3DES
20	AH-SHA1	ESP-MD5-3DES
21	AH-MD5	ESP-SHA1-DES
22	AH-MD5	ESP-MD5-DES
23	AH-SHA1	ESP-SHA1-DES
24	AH-SHA1	ESP-MD5-DES

There are 24 possible IPSec transform sets in Windows IPSec implementation, and we experimented with all of them on IPv4 and IPv6.

Test Considerations

Our tests were on both IP protocols, IPv4 and IPv6. For all tests we carried out plain benchmarking tests, that is, performance tests were performed without enabling IPSec and we used these results as a baseline for comparing with IPSec tests results as outlined in Kaeo and Van Herck (2006). IPv6 tests were carried out using 6to4 because it is applicable on the global Internet and intrasite networks, while intrasite automatic tunnel addressing protocol (ISATAP) provides IPv6 connectivity within an IPv4 intranet. However, we conducted preliminary experiments using ISATAP and realized that it has the same frame overhead impact as 6to4.

Results and Discussion

Frame Overhead Tests on ICMP

The first protocol we measured IPSec frame overhead was ICMP, using the ping application on the different sizes of packets: 1 byte, 8 bytes, 32 bytes, 128 bytes, 512 bytes, 2,048 bytes, 8,192 bytes, 32,768 bytes, and 65,500 bytes, of which 1 to 512 bytes are nonfragmented packets and the rest are fragmented. We started the ping program on one client sending to the other client, while capturing the communication using the protocol analyzer on the sending computer. This procedure was conducted with IPSec off first and then IPSec on, using different transform sets on IPv4 and IPv6.

IPSec overhead tests on IPv4

The observations we made after capturing packets of different sizes is that AH, applied on its own, adds an additional 24 bytes to each packet sent on IPv4. Even if the packet is fragmented, only 24 bytes are added on the first fragment. These 24 bytes are made of the following sections of the AH header, as captured by our protocol analyzer.

1 byte – Next header
1 byte – Payload length

Table 3. Ethernet frame protected by AH in transport mode

Ethernet header	IPv4 header	AH header	Data Variable	Ethernet Trail
14	20	24		4

Table 4. AH header format

Next header	Payload length	Reserved	SPI	Authentication data
1	1	2	4	16

2 bytes – Reserved

4 bytes – Security parameters index

16 bytes – Authentication data

Table 3 shows the structure of the frame protected by AH protocol in transport mode, the sizes are in bytes. Table 4 shows the AH header sections.

The additional bytes due to IPSec headers are the same for all packet sizes, fragmented and nonfragmented. The overhead is the same irrespective of the hash function used, that is, MD5 or SHA1. ESP-only transform sets add an overhead of 36 bytes using both properties (integrity and encryption) of ESP. This is divided into the following sections:

- Security association identifier – 4 bytes

- Sequence number – 4 bytes

- Opaque transform data – 28 bytes

The overhead for applying ESP integrity only is 28 bytes, made up of

- Security association identifier – 4 bytes

- Sequence number – 4 bytes

- Opaque transform data – 20 bytes

The overhead for using both IPSec protocols is the summation of the overhead added by each protocol. For instance, the overhead of AH and ESP fully implemented is 60 bytes

Table 5. IPSec Frame overhead bytes

Transform Set Description	Additional Bytes
AH only	24
ESP Integrity only	28
ESP Integrity and Encryption	36
AH and ESP Integrity	48
AH and ESP Encryption	52
AH and ESP	60

Figure 1. Impact of AH, ESP, and BOTH IPSec transform sets on IPv4 overhead

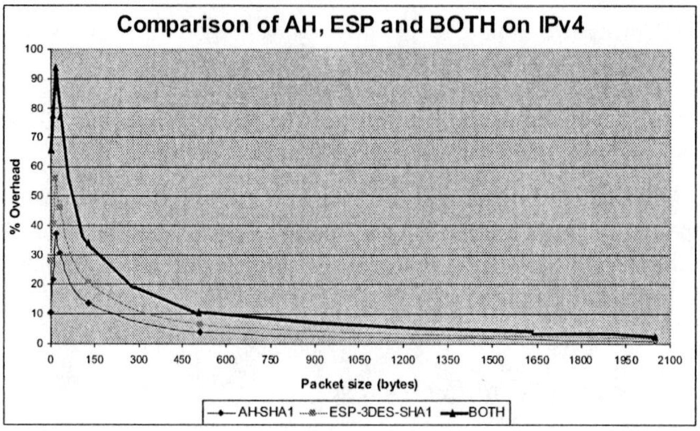

(24 AH and 36 ESP). We calculated the percentage impact of the overhead using the formula:

$$\text{Percentage overhead} = \frac{\text{IPSec Frame Size - IPSec disabled Frame Size}}{\text{IPSec disabled Frame Size}} * 100$$

The additional bytes added by IPSec headers using different IPSec transforms sets are shown in Table 5.

Figure 1 shows the impact of each of the two security protocols enabled separately and both fully implemented. It compares the percentage of the overhead discussed previously on the original packet transmitted with three different IPSec transform sets namely; AH only, ESP only, and AH and ESP both applied.

The overhead starts low on packet sizes of 1 byte, because some overhead bytes are used as padding bytes, which reduces the overall overhead of IPSec headers on the packets that need padding. All packets less than 18 bytes require padding for them to be transmitted over the network and they all have a frame size of 64 bytes. That means the percentage of IPSec overhead increases from 1 byte and reaches the maximum on 18 bytes packet. Then it starts to fall on packet sizes of more than 18 bytes. By comparison, the overhead of 18-bytes packets using the transform sets shown in Figure 1 is as follows; AH only gives 38%, ESP only gives 56%, and both protocols gives 94%. This shows that there is quite a significant increase in overhead when using ESP only compared to AH only on IPv4 on small packets.

The overhead of using both protocols on 18 bytes packets is 94%, which is the aggregate of AH and ESP overheads. The overhead falls sharply as packet size increases to the level of about 0.04% for packets of 65,000 bytes, because IPv4 IPSec headers are applied on the first fragment only. Hence, the additional overhead bytes are constant and they are spread over an increasing common denominator, that is, the cumulative size of all fragments. This trend applies to all three IPSec transform sets.

Understandably, AH only has a lower overhead as compared to ESP only, which in turn has a lower overhead compared to both protocols applied. Applying ESP only instead of AH only increases the overhead by 7.64% on average across all the packet sizes we experimented with. Using both protocols instead of ESP only increases the overhead by 15.67% on average, and using both protocols instead of AH only increases the overhead by 23.31%.

The use of ESP protocol only in an IPSec transform gives two options of IPSec transform sets, namely; ESP with integrity only, and a complete ESP that has both integrity and encryption. Figure 2 shows the impact of these ESP transform sets.

ESP integrity using either MD5 or SHA1 algorithms results in the same overhead impact. The same applies for a complete ESP implementation that has integrity and encryption: irrespective of the algorithms used, the overhead is the same on ICMP packets. ESP integrity only overhead is relatively lower than that of ESP with integrity and encryption. Applying ESP integrity and encryption increases the overhead by almost 12% compared to ESP integrity only on smallest packet size that does not need padding, 18 bytes. On average the overhead increases by 5% from packet sizes of 1 byte to 65,500 bytes.

For all different IPSec transform sets on IPv4, the impact of the overhead relatively is the same on very large packets, for example, in our experiments, the impact of the overhead is almost constant at 0.04% across all different transform sets with packet size of 65,500 bytes.

Figure 2. Impact of ESP transform sets on IPv4 overhead

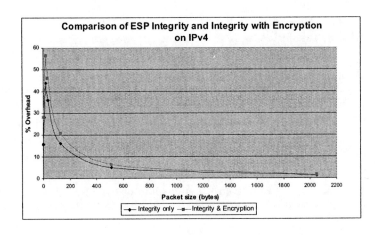

Figure 3. Impact of AH, ESP, and BOTH IPSec transform sets on IPv6 overhead

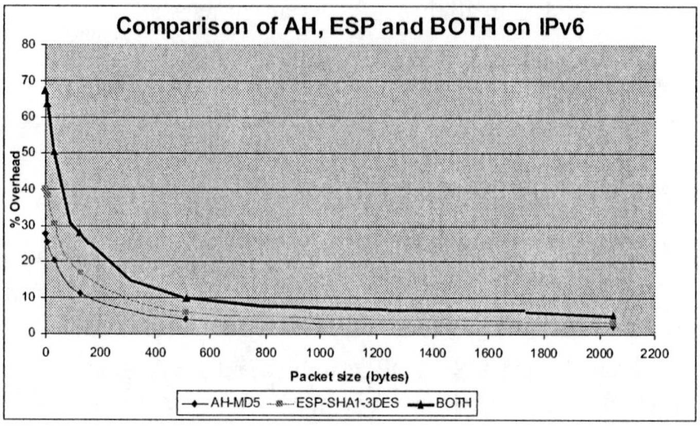

IPSec Overhead on IPv6

IPSec overhead on IPv6 adds the same number of bytes (for IPSec headers) as IPv4 on all IPSec transform sets. Figure 3 shows the percentage impact of overhead on ICMP packets of different sizes. As was the case on IPv4, AH only has a lower overhead as compared to ESP only, which in turn has a lower overhead compared to both protocols applied. Unlike IPv4, there is no increase in the overhead on very small packets, because no padding bits are necessary when using IPv6. Since the minimum frame payload of IPv6 Ethernet exceeds the IPv4 Ethernet minimum payload. The impact of the overhead is higher from the first packet size of 1 byte, and it gradually decreases as the packet size increases. The first significant difference of how IPSec affects IPv6 as compared to that on IPv4 is that IPSec headers are applied on all fragments, while on IPv4 they were applied on the first fragment only. This makes the overhead have a more significant impact on IPv6. Secondly, unlike the constant overhead percentage on packets of 65,500 bytes on IPv4 using different transform sets, IPv6 has a constant different value for each security policy from 32,768 bytes and larger.

On fragmented packets the IPSec protocol headers are applied on every fragment on IPv6 protocol; hence, the percentage overhead does not decrease sharply as it does on IPv4. Consequently, the overhead on large packets on IPv6 is higher than that on IPv4. Applying ESP only instead of AH only increases the overhead by 5.77% on average across all the packet sizes, while using both protocols instead of ESP only increases the overhead by 11.82% on average, and using both protocols instead of AH only increases the overhead by 17.59%.

Figure 4 shows the impact of two ESP only implementations of IPSec: ESP with integrity only and ESP with both integrity and encryption. Significant difference in the two settings can be noticed on the last point, which is relatively higher than the difference in IPv4 protocol in Figure 2 due to the previously mentioned fact of IPSec headers applied on every fragment in IPv6.

We also compared how the IPSec overhead impacts on IPv4 and IPv6, using the default three transform sets: AH only, ESP only, and both protocols. Figure 5 illustrates this comparison.

Figure 4. Impact of ESP transform sets on IPv6 overhead

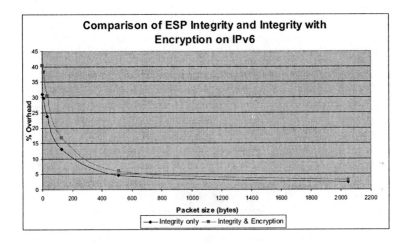

Figure 5. Comparison of IPSec transform sets on IPv4 and IPv6 overhead

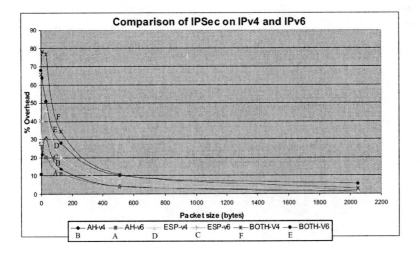

Comparison of IPSec overhead impact on IPv4 and IPv6 gave the trend shown in Figure 5. The overhead has a higher impact on IPv4 as compared to IPv6 for smaller packets that are not fragmented. Comparing IPv4 and IPv6 average values shows that general IPSec have a higher overhead on IPv4 than IPv6. This can be attributed to the fact that IPSec headers' sizes are the same on both IP protocols, while there is a huge difference in the frame sizes of these IP protocols. IPv6 fragmented packets have a higher overhead as compared to IPv4, because in IPv4 the IPSec header is applied on the first fragment only, while in IPv6 it is applied on each fragment.

We noticed that the maximum frame size of 1,518 bytes is never exceeded in IPv4 even after turning IPSec on. The additional overhead of using IPSec headers will occupy part of the payload data; hence, reducing the payload of each fragment on fragmented IPv4 packets. This differs from how fragmented packets are handled in IPv6. In IPv6 the same payload data size is maintained and the additional bytes added by IPSec headers increase the frame size directly.

IPSec headers sizes are constant for both IPv4 and IPv6, but the way these headers are applied is different. Therefore, their effects are also different on both protocols. For instance, on IPv4 the overhead is applied on the first fragment only where a packet needs fragmentation. This obviously means the burden of the overhead is higher on IPv6 than it is on IPv4. On both IP protocols, there is no difference in the frame size when using either SHA1 or MD5 for data integrity and DES or 3DES for data confidentiality.

Round-Trip Time Tests on ICMP

From the RTT values recorded when testing IPSec overhead, we also computed the average RTT for each IPSec transform set. Figure 6 shows the average RTT of ICMP messages on IPv4; the comparison includes the RTT of packets with IPSec disabled.

Figure 6. Impact of IPSec on ICMP Average RTT on IPv4

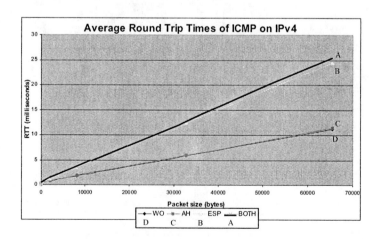

Firstly, for all transform sets the RTT increases as packet sizes increases. This is because a larger packet obviously needs more time to reach its destination across the network and come back to the source. The graph shows that there is an insignificant difference between the RTT of transmissions with IPSec disabled and IPSec with AH only.

There is also an insignificant difference between the RTT of IPSec with ESP only and IPSec with both headers implemented, especially on smaller packets, but the difference becomes slightly significant on very large packets. The huge difference between these two sets of transform sets: AH only and without IPSec compared to ESP and both headers applied, suggests that a longer processing time is required when an encryption algorithm is used in an IPSec transform.

The average RTTs for IPv6 shows a different picture from those of IPv4, as shown in Figure 7. There is a gradual increase in RTT from transmission without IPSec to AH only, ESP only, and finally both headers applied. The trend portrayed in IPv4 of a huge difference between transform sets with an encryption algorithm and those without an encryption algorithm does not apply in IPv6. This is because IPSec has ESP with null encryption in IPv6 while IPv4 ESP has functional encryption. Even though this is a case of ESP only, both IPSec protocols have a longer RTT as compared to AH only and disabled IPSec transmissions.

Frame Overhead Tests on HTTP

We conducted frame overhead tests of IPSec on HTTP using different Web page sizes that contain only text on IPv4 protocol. The Web page sizes we considered are 1 KB, 5 KB, 20 KB, 60 KB, and 100KB. This experiment was conducted by capturing the HTTP requests on the client machine that was requesting Web pages from the Web server. The first fragment has the HTTP header of 228 bytes in a typical Ethernet frame of 1,518 bytes,

Figure 7. Impact of IPSec on ICMP average RTT on IPv6

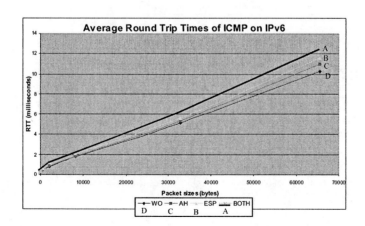

Figure 8. Impact of AH, ESP and BOTH transform sets on HTTP overhead

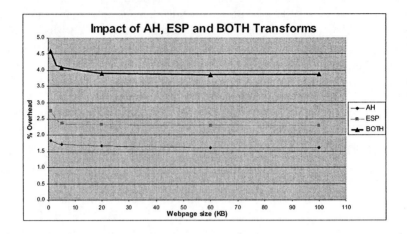

Figure 9. Impact of ESP transform sets on HTTP overhead

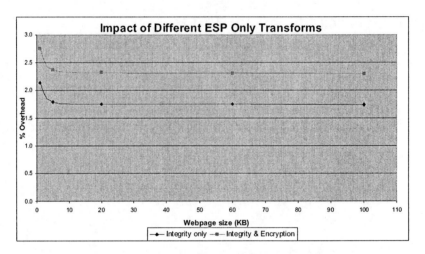

with 1,232 bytes of payload data. The HTTP header is on the first fragment only, and for the other fragments the HTTP header size is added to the payload. AH only adds an overhead of 24 bytes, ESP only adds 36 bytes, and with both protocols applied, the overhead is cumulative as was the case in ICMP. The first comparison shows the percentage overhead of the three main security policies: AH only, ESP only, and both applied, in Figure 8. The graph shows the impact of IPSec using the following transforms: AH with MD5 or SHA1, followed by ESP with both integrity and encryption, and lastly both protocols applied. The overhead of AH is lower than that of ESP and both protocols

Figure 10. Impact of IPSec transform sets using on HTTP overhead

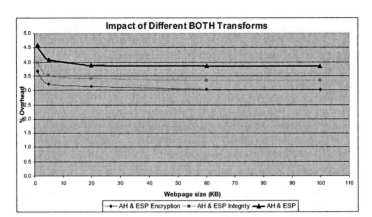

Figure 11. Impact of different IPSec protocols on HTTP download times

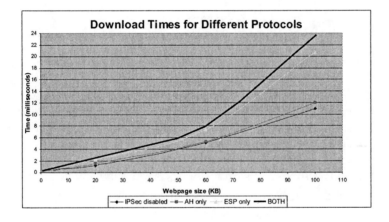

because AH uses only one cryptographic algorithm to provide its security services while ESP uses two: one for integrity and the other for encryption.

The overhead is also higher on smaller Web pages as compared to larger pages. For AH, the overhead starts higher for a Web page of 1 KB and slightly drops for 5 KB Web pages, but for ESP and both it drops sharply because they add a larger overhead than AH. On the same note, ESP's overhead is lower than that of both protocols applied together.

On an average the overhead increases by almost 1 percentage point when using ESP instead of AH, and it further increases on an average by at least 1.5 percentage points.

The overhead increases by a margin of 2.5 percentage points when both protocols are used instead of AH only. This is quite a significant impact and should be taken into account in deploying IPSec. The overhead starts higher on smaller packets but it drops as packet size increases and becomes almost constant. This is because IPSec protects every fragment on fragmented packets; therefore, the same overhead is spread evenly on all the fragments, and on nonfragmented packets the impact is relatively higher. Comparing the two ESP-only transform-sets implementations of IPSec gives the picture in Figure 9.

Figure 9 shows that there is quite a huge difference in the IPSec overhead when using the two ESP-only transform sets on HTTP. ESP with integrity and encryption induce an additional 0.6 percentage point on average on the overhead as compared to ESP with integrity only.

Figure 10 compares the impact of IPSec transform sets in the category of a full implementation of both protocols. There are three different implementations, namely AH and ESP encryption, AH and ESP integrity, and AH and ESP integrity and encryption. The graph shows that there is no huge differences in the overhead when these transform sets are applied separately. The overall overhead increases by almost 1 percentage point from the least expensive transform set to the most expensive set.

Download Time Tests on HTTP

We compared the time it takes to download Web pages of different sizes, first with IPSec disabled then with different IPSec transform sets. The Web page sizes we used are as follows: 1 KB, 5 KB, 20 KB, 60 KB, and 100 KB. This test was conducted by requesting these Web pages from the Web server and capturing the packets between the server and the requesting client. The protocol analyzer was running on the client. We took the time the first frame is received and the time the last frame is received, and the difference between the two was recorded as the download time. Even though the times were not uniform, the trend for different IPSec transform sets was relatively clear.

There was a slight difference between the download times of AH only transform sets using MD5 and SHA1. The average download time of all the Web page files tested shows that SHA1 has more average download time than MD5 by 1 second. Figure 11 shows the download times for different IPSec transform sets with different protocols. AH only transform uses SHA1 algorithm, ESP only transform uses 3DES and SHA1, and both protocols transform uses MD5 for AH and 3DES and SHA1 for ESP. These transform sets are compared against the download times of Web pages with IPSec disabled.

There is a small difference in the download times between the times without IPSec and IPSec using AH only transform set. There is a difference of 1.2 milliseconds in the average download times of the two sets. On the other hand, there is also a small difference between ESP only and both protocols transform sets' download times. For all transform sets, the download times increase gradually from Web page size of 1 KB to 60 KB, but beyond this size the download times increase sharply. According to Sullivan (2005), the average size of the Web pages on the Internet is 60 KB. Figure 11 confirms the argument that as the more Web page sizes exceed 60 KB, the longer they take to download from the server;

Figure 12. Impact of ESP on HTTP download times

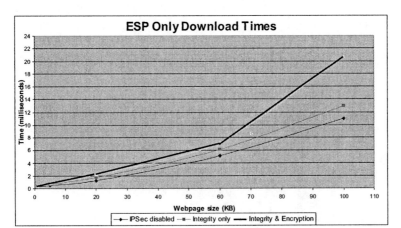

Figure 13. Impact of IPSec on HTTP download times using both protocols

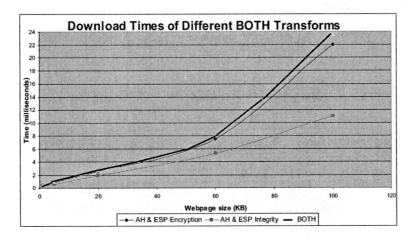

hence, performance is compromised. Therefore, in the case where IPSec is enabled using ESP only or both IPSec protocols, the cost in terms of performance is very significant for pages above 60 KB. The other reason why the download time increases sharply might be the use of an encryption algorithm, because in the sets without encryption the times do not increase that much.

Figure 12 shows the download times obtained when using the IPSec transform sets available when using ESP only. ESP integrity only transform was using MD5 algorithm, which has a slightly lower average download time than SHA1. The download times of ESP

Figure 14. Comparison of different IPSec protocols on FTP overhead

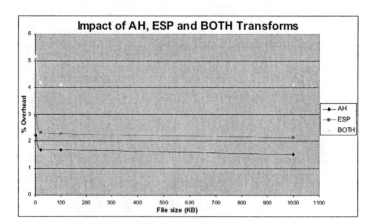

integrity only are higher than those of AH only using the same algorithm, if we compare ESP integrity only in Figure 12 and AH only in Figure 11.

Figure 13 compares the download times of different IPSec transform sets of both protocols applied. The download times without IPSec encryption are significantly lower compared to encryption turned on, as can be seen in the graph. This is because encryption generally requires more processing time on the encrypting system, in our case on the Web server. This delays the transmission of a Web page request to the requesting client. There is a slight increase in download time from ESP encryption applied and both IPSec protocols fully implemented.

Frame overhead tests on FTP

Our tests included frame overhead tests of IPSec on FTP using different clear text file sizes. FTP tests were conducted using IPv4 protocol since there is no support for FTP on Windows IPv6 protocol. We considered the following sizes: 1 KB, 20 KB, 100 KB, 1 MB, 5 MB, and 10 MB, but in this section we will show sizes up to and including 1 MB only because the trend beyond 1 MB is constant. This experiment was conducted by capturing the FTP file requests on the client machine that was requesting files from the file server using a Web browser. The FTP packet fragment of 1,518 bytes consists of 1,460 bytes of data, and the rest are headers.

First we compared the impact of AH only, ESP only, and both protocol transforms on FTP, this shown in Figure 14. AH only adds an overhead of 24 bytes, ESP only adds 36 bytes, and with both protocols applied, the overhead is also cumulative as was the case in ICMP and HTTP. The transforms used in Figure 14 use the following algorithms: AH with MD5 or SHA1, ESP with both integrity and encryption, and lastly both protocols applied. For all transforms the overhead drops sharply from the file size of 1 KB to 20 KB because the

Figure 15. Impact of ESP transform sets on FTP overhead

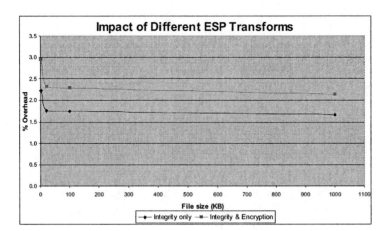

Figure 16. Impact of IPSec using both protocols on FTP overhead

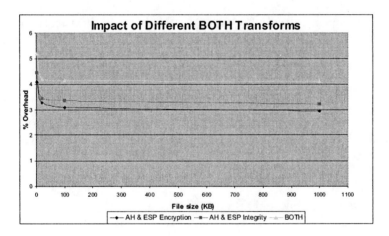

frame size of a 1 KB FTP file (1,370 bytes, of IPSec both protocols transform set) is far lower than the fragment size (1,514 bytes); hence, the percentage of 24 bytes is higher on 1 KB compared to 20 KB fragments. This trend applies to all the three transform sets on the graph. On average AH only adds an overhead of almost 2%, ESP only adds an overhead of almost 2.5% and both protocols adds an average overhead of 4.5%, that is, the cumulative overhead of AH and ESP.

The overhead of fragmented packets is almost constant as file sizes increase because the IPSec headers are applied on every transmitted fragment. AH overhead is lower than that of ESP and both protocols, as was the case on HTTP, because AH uses only one cryptographic algorithm to provide its security services while ESP uses two: one for integrity and the other for encryption.

When comparing the overhead of using different ESP transform sets of integrity only and integrity with encryption, we get the trend shown in Figure 15. On average, ESP integrity only adds an overhead of almost 2% on FTP, and ESP with both integrity and encryption adds an overhead of about 2.5%. The same trend shown in Figure 14 of the overhead remaining almost constant on fragmented packets applies also on ESP-only transform sets shown in Figure 15.

Figure 16 compares the overhead added by using different IPSec transform sets that utilize both IPSec protocols. It shows a significant increase in overhead when both IPSec protocols are fully implemented as compared to both protocols with partial ESP implementation.

The overhead increases by almost 1 percentage point. We noticed that there is a very small difference in download times when using DES for encryption and 3DES in ESP protocol, but this difference is really insignificant.

Download Times Tests on FTP

FTP download time tests were more uniform with a more clearly visible trend than that of HTTP tests. We used the following file sizes for this test: 1 KB, 20 KB, 100 KB, 5 MB, and 10 MB. We recorded the time it took to download all the frames of a particular download, that is, for the first frame and the last frame, and computed the difference, which we recorded as the download time. First we compared the times of IPSec disabled and IPSec using different protocols, as shown in Figure 17.

Figure 17 shows that there is the smallest of differences in download times between IPSec AH only and IPSec disabled. There is a difference of 4 milliseconds in the average values of these two sets, which is very insignificant. The other two transforms, ESP only and

Figure 17. Impact of IPSec on FTP download times

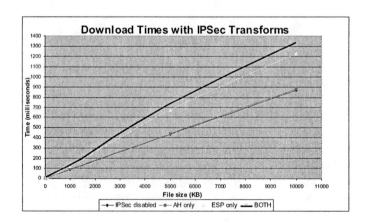

Figure 18. Impact of ESP transform sets on FTP download times

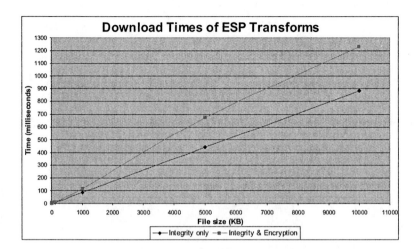

both protocols, do have a small difference in their download times, but it is more significant than the first two sets. Unlike the trend in HTTP download times, FTP times increase gradually as the packet size increases. But still, there is significant differences between IPSec transform sets with ESP encryption and those without ESP encryption, confirming that ESP encryption needs more processing on the processing node.

Figure 18 compares the download times of FTP using ESP only transform sets. In ESP integrity only, we used SHA1 algorithms, and full ESP uses SHA1 and 3DES. On average there is a difference of 100 milliseconds between ESP with integrity only and ESP with both integrity and encryption; this is a very significant performance cost consideration when deploying IPSec.

When comparing download times that use a full implementation of IPSec with different set algorithms, we get the trend shown in Figure 19. The algorithms used in these transform sets are AH uses SHA1 through out, ESP encryption uses 3DES, and integrity uses MD5. The transform set without encryption also has a lower download time compared to those with ESP encryption, and download times increase as file sizes increase.

Frame Overhead Tests On TFTP

We also tested the IPSec frame overhead impact on TFTP using different clear text file sizes using IPv4. We considered the following sizes: 4 bytes, 14 bytes, 200 bytes, 1 KB, 20 KB, 100 KB, 1 MB, and 10 MB, but in the graphs we will show sizes up to and including 1 KB only because the trend beyond 1 KB is exactly the same as that of 1 KB. This

Figure 19. Impact of IPSec using both protocols on FTP download times

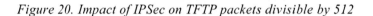

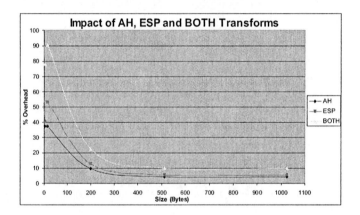

Figure 20. Impact of IPSec on TFTP packets divisible by 512

experiment was conducted by capturing the TFTP file requests from a third-party TFTP server. The data packet consists of a TFTP header with 2 bytes for opcode and 2 bytes for the block number including the transport and network headers.

Figure 20 shows the impact of IPSec on TFTP using the transform sets of AH only, ESP only, and both protocols, using packet sizes divisible by 512. IPSec headers added on TFTP traffic are of the same size as those added on FTP. For the packet sizes we tested, we chose 4 bytes, which is small enough to require padding, 14 bytes is the size that does not need padding, at which the overhead is at its maximum. Theoretically, the overhead starts low on packet sizes of 1 byte, in our case 4 bytes, because some overhead bytes are used as padding bytes, which reduces the overall overhead of IPSec headers on the packets that need padding. All packets less than 14 bytes require padding for them to

Figure 21. Impact of IPSec on TFTP packets not divisible by 512

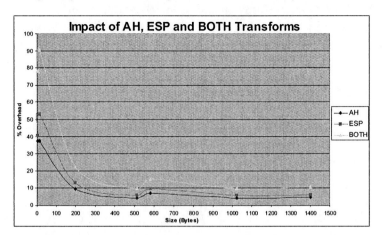

be transmitted over the network, and they all have a frame size of 64 bytes. That means the percentage of IPSec overhead increases from 4 bytes and reaches the maximum on a 14 bytes packet. Then it starts to fall on packet sizes of more than 14 bytes. As long as the packet size is increasing in blocks of 512 bytes, the overhead becomes constant on all packets between 512 bytes and 32 MB.

This trend does not apply on packet sizes that are not divisible by 512, as the overhead will be higher if a packet is fragmented due to the overhead in the last fragment, which is not proportional; hence, the trend changes to that shown in Figure 21. This means that the overhead is higher the lower the last fragment is to 512 bytes; otherwise, if divisible by 512 the overhead is at its lowest. And on the same note, the overhead is also the fewer the number of blocks or fragments.

Figure 21 shows the comparison of the trend for IPSec overhead for packets divisible and not divisible by 512 bytes. We used the following sizes: 4 bytes, 14 bytes, 200 bytes, 512 bytes, 580 bytes, 1024 bytes, and 1400 bytes.

Conclusion

Our experiments showed that the impact of IPSec overhead on all protocols we tested is higher for smaller packets as compared to larger packets for both IPv4 and IPv6, except in cases where the packet is small enough for padding bits in IPv4. This is because part of IPSec overhead is used to replace the padding bits that were otherwise needed in the absence of IPSec. We also noticed that the use of both IPSec protocols increases the overhead cumulatively as the overhead of each protocol.

The tests also showed that irrespective of the integrity algorithm used in both AH and ESP protocols, between SHA1 and MD5, the IPSec header size does not change for all

IPSec transform sets tested. Hence, the percentage overhead for both algorithms is the same. But they affect the round-trip time and download time differently. The use of SHA1 increases the round-trip time and download time because SHA1 is more secure than MD5.

The use of 3DES or DES algorithms for encryption in ESP protocol does apply the same overhead on both IPv4 and IPv6. But they differ on the round-trip time and download time in that 3DES increases the above two metrics because it is more secure than DES; hence, they are implemented differently.

References

Ariga, S., Nagahashi, K., Minami, M., Esaki, H., & Murai, J. (2000, July 18-21). Performance evaluation of data transmission using IPSec over IPv6 networks. In *INET 2000 Proceedings — The Internet Global Summit: Global Distributed Intelligence for Everyone, the 10th Annual Internet Society Conference*, Pacifico Yokohama Conference Center, Yokohama, Japan.

Carpenter, B., & Moore, K. (2001). *Connection of IPv6 domains via IPv4 Clouds*. RFC 3056, February.

DARPA. (1981). *Internet protocol specification*. RFC 791, September.

Deering, S., & Hinden, R. (1998). *Internet protocol, version 6 specification*. RFC 2460, December.

Doraswamy, N., & Harkins, D. (1999). IPSec: *The new security standard for the Internet, intranets, and virtual private networks*. Englewood, NJ: Prentice Hall PTR.

Farrel, A. (2004). *The Internet and its protocols: A comparative approach*. Amsterdam: Morgan Kaufmann.

Kaeo, M., & Van Herck, T. (2006). *Methodology for benchmarking IPSec devices*. Internet-Draft (draft-ietf-bmwg-ipsec-meth-00), November 2005, Expires: May 5.

Kent, S., & Atkinson, R. (1998). *IP authentication header*. RFC 2402, November.

Kent, S., & Atkinson, R. (1998). *IP encapsulating security payload*. RFC 2406, November.

Kent, S., & Atkinson, R. (1998). *Security architecture for the Internet protocol*. RFC 2401, November.

Loshin, P. (2003). *IPv6: Theory, protocol, and practice* (2nd ed.). Amsterdam: Morgan Kaufmann.

Ronan, J., et al. (2004, March). *Performance implications of IPSec deployment*. Telecommunications Software & Systems Group (TSSG), Waterford Institute of Technology, Ireland.

Sullivan, T. (2005). Retrieved November 2005, from http://www.pantos.org/atw/35654.html

Chapter XX

An Approach for Intentional Modeling of Web Services Security Risk Assessment

Subhas C. Misra, Carleton University, Canada

Vinod Kumar, Carleton University, Canada

Uma Kumar, Carleton University, Canada

Abstract

In this chapter, we provide a conceptual modeling approach for Web services security risk assessment that is based on the identification and analysis of stakeholder intentions. There are no similar approaches for modeling Web services security risk assessment in the existing pieces of literature. The approach is, thus, novel in this domain. The approach is helpful for performing means-end analysis, thereby, uncovering the structural origin of security risks in WS, and how the root-causes of such risks can be controlled from the early stages of the projects. The approach addresses "why" the process is the way it is by exploring the strategic dependencies between the actors of a security system, and analyzing the motivations, intents, and rationales behind the different entities and activities in constituting the system.

Introduction

The area of *Web services* (WS) has currently emerged as an approach for integrating Web-based applications. To facilitate this, several standards have been proposed, for example, simple object access protocol (SOAP) for data transfer, Web service definition language (WSDL) for providing a description of different available services, and extensible markup language (XML) for tagging data in such a way that users can create their customized applications. In the WS world, information can be transmitted between two service end points using SOAP messages. Security in WS has, therefore, gained importance, as the WS-based systems are susceptible to attacks by malicious users. For example, malicious users have the potential to intrude into the integrity and confidentiality of messages transmitted using SOAP. Several mechanisms are commonly available to address these security issues. An example is the use of secure socket layer (SSL), and transport layer security (TLS) to provide authentication, integrity, and confidentiality of information. Transport layer security can be provided using IPSec. Several pieces of literature are available in the area of architecting secured WS-based systems. A recent example is the work done by Gutierreze et al. (Gutierrez, Fernandez-Medina, & Piattini, 2005), who proposed an architecture-based process for the development of WS security. This process helps in identifying, defining, and analyzing the security requirements of a WS-based system using an architecture approach. Recently, different researchers have explored model-based assessment of security risk. (Alghathbar, Wijesekera, & Farkas, 2005; Dimitrakos, Ritchie, Raptis, & Stolen, 2002; Fernandez, Sorgente, & Larrondo-Petrie, 2005; Lodderstedt, Bastin, & Doser, 2002; Lund, Hogganvik, Seehusen, & Stolen, 2003; Swiderski & Snyder, 2004; Villarroel, Fernandez, Trujillo, & Piattini, 2005).

Fletcher et. al. (1995), Labuschangne (1999), and Martel (2002) have advocated that the field of security risk analysis has evolved through three generations. The *first generation* of risk analysis techniques date back to those associated with the advent of centralized mainframes. A brief overview of them can be had from Martel's thesis (Martel, 2002), and Labuschagne's paper (Labuschagne, 1999). Most of these approaches are checklist based, ad hoc, and assume that the risk scenarios are static and they do not change. There are different commercial tools available that support these ad hoc approaches (e.g., @RISK, and RiskPAC (Labuschagne, 1999)).

The *second generation* of risk analysis tools and techniques emerged with the growth of LANs, and distributed computing. COBRA Risk Consultant (COBRA, 2005) and Tivoli Secure Way Risk Manager (TSRM) (Tivoli, 2005) are two examples. While the former supports ISO 17799 compliant risk analysis, the later supports enterprise-wide risk management, whereby organizations are able to correlate security information from different sources in an enterprise. The second generation of the risk analysis techniques and tools are concerned more with the combined effects of threats rather than individual elements of threat. These techniques and tools attempt to view security from a holistic viewpoint of equipment, software, and data.

The *third generation* is what we have currently. Today security is no longer limited to local area networks, and individual standalone networks and data. Current security needs are cross-organizational because of interorganizational communication via the Internet, and extranets for organization-to-organization communication. Today data of one enterprise is transmitted over several third-party networks. Additionally, there are new types of attacks that emerge everyday. Martel (2002) provides an approach for risk analysis of current day security issues. She proposed a model wherein a global risk value is dynamically determined for a specific asset/exposure pair with the changes in the environment. Discussions of other such third-generation risk analysis approaches can be found in Swiderski and Snyder (2004) Dimitrakos et al. (2002), Lund et al. (2003), Lodderstedt et al. (2002), Fernandez et al. (2005), Villarroel et al. (2005), and Alghathbar et al. (2005). They are not individually elaborated over here, but most of them work based on dataflow diagramming and UML profiling approaches. These approaches help to address "what" the requirements are, and not "why" those requirements are needed. A critical comparative analysis has been done by rigorous review of the different existing pieces of literature, the summary of which is listed in Table 1.

In this chapter, we present a new approach for modeling information systems security risk assessment. The approach is based on the analysis of the strategic dependencies between the actors of a system. The purpose of this chapter is to introduce an approach that can help in modeling issues while performing WS security risk assessment. In this chapter, we have outlined the approach, and illustrated it with an example. We have not considered all possible aspects of WS security in this chapter. Therefore, we encourage further evaluation of the approach for modeling different scenarios possible in WS security.

Table 1. Comparative analysis of the traditional security modeling approaches (in general) and the stated approach (Misra, Kumar, & Kumar, 2005a)

	Traditional modeling approaches	**Proposed approach**
1.	Model late phase security requirements.	Models early phase security requirements.
2.	Indicates: "what" steps a process consists of and "how" those steps to be done.	Indicates: "why" the process is the way it is.
3.	Do not capture the motivations, intents and rationales behind the activities.	Captures the motivations, intents, and rationales behind the activities.
4.	Do not capture the intentional structure of a process and the organization that embeds it.	Captures the intentional structure of a process and he organization that embeds it.
5.	Process performers are concerned with models that describe "hows". Process managers are concerned with models that indicate "whats."	Process engineers are concerned with models that describe "whys" as they are concerned with modifying the processes.
6.	Model functional security requirements.	Models nonfunctional security requirements.
7.	They cannot reason about the opportunities and vulnerabilities of the system under consideration.	It helps to incorporate the issues of trust, vulnerability, change, and risk explicitly in the process of systems analysis and design.

Background

Several risk assessment methodologies tailored towards specific domains are available in the existing pieces of literature (Aagedal, Braber, Dimitrakos, Gran, Raptis, & Stolen, 2002). For instance, SEISMED is a methodology that provides a set of guidelines on IT security risk analysis for health care IT personnel, and ODESSA is a methodology that provides health care data security. There are several other risk assessment methodologies in the domain of health care that are used for specific purposes, viz., ISHTAR, RAMME, CPRI, and TRA (Aagedal et al., 2002). Several attempts have been made for over a decade to make the existing schemes align into one framework that is acceptable to all for testing IT security functionality. The Common Criteria (CC) project successfully aligns the criteria followed by Europe, Canada, and America (Common Criteria Organization, 2002). Gradually, it is replacing all regional and national criteria with a common set followed worldwide and accepted by the International Standard Organization (ISO). However, CC does not provide any specific methodology for risk analysis. On the other hand, a new project, CORAS, run during 2001-2003, provides a concrete methodology focusing on the IT security risk assessment process (Aagedal et al., 2002).

Other methodologies (projects) in related areas include surety analysis (SA), control objectives for information and related technology (COBIT), and CCTA risk analysis and management methodology (CRAMM). SA provides a methodology based on the creation of an explicit model that includes various aspects of the behavior of a system (Sandia National Laboratories, 2002). RSDS is a tool-supported methodology that has been applied in the analysis of various reactive systems in the domain of chemical process control and automated manufacturing (Reactive System Design Support, 2002). COBIT project addresses the good management practices for security and control in IT for worldwide endorsement by various organizations (Control Objectives for Information and Related Technology, 2002). CRAMM is a risk analysis methodology that was developed with an aim of providing a structured approach to manage computer security for all systems (Barber & Davey, 1992).

We now present the three projects, and their related works on security, that had a major influence on our modeling approach.

CORAS

The most influential of the projects for our work is the CORAS methodology (Vraalsen Braber, Hogganvik, Lund, & Stolen, 2004), which bases itself on the following risk-management methodologies: hazard and operability (HazOp), fault tree analysis (FTA), failure mode and effect criticality analysis (FMECA), Markov analysis, and CRAMM. These methodologies are, to a great extent, complementary to one another. As we adopt ideas of CORAS in our approach, we, in turn, partially adopt the ideas of these methodologies. CORAS project introduced a unified modeling language (UML) Version 2.0 profile for security risk assessment. The profile includes a metamodel that describes different security risk components (e.g., assets, and vulnerabilities), and relations between them. Also, the profile includes mapping of the components to UML modeling elements. To perform a high-quality risk assessment, one should clearly understand the organization of the system being assessed. Description of the target system should be done in the first stage of the risk management process. As CORAS uses UML to model security-related elements in order to achieve uniformity, CORAS suggests using UML to describe other aspects of the system. However, according to CORAS project, security-related elements should be depicted in separate diagrams that do not include other structural elements of the target system.

SecureUML

SecureUML is a modeling language based on UML. It helps in the model-driven development of secure systems. The approach bases on role-based access control. This approach helps to improve the productivity while developing secure distributed systems. SecureUML can integrate the specification of access control into application models (Lodderstedt et al., 2002).

Tropos

Tropos is an agent-oriented software engineering methodology that is capable of modeling both the organizational aspects of a system, and the late and early phase requirements of the system itself. It has been shown by Mouratidis et al. (Mouratidis, Giorgini, Manson, & Philip, 2002), and Mouratidis et al. (Mouratidis, Giorgini, & Manson, 2003) how the extensions of Tropos methodology can be used to accommodate different security concerns of the system under development in the requirements analysis phase.

Intentional Modeling

Issues of Traditional Conceptual Modeling Techniques

As stated earlier, most of the recent initiatives conducted in the area of model-based security risk are based on dataflow diagramming, and UML profiling. We now briefly review some of those pieces of work, some of which were already mentioned in the earlier sections, while providing an overview of work done in the area of security.

Swiderski, and Snyder (2004) describe how dataflow-diagramming techniques can be used for threat modeling. Dimitrakos et al. (2002) proposed a model-based security risk analysis technique that uses UML for modeling security risk. Lund et al. (2003) proposed a UML profile for use in security assessment. Lodderstedt et al. (2002) proposed SecureUML, a UML-based modeling language for use in the area of security modeling.

Similar other recent works in the uses of UML on the area of security modeling have been proposed by Fernandez et al. (2005), Villarroel et al. (2005), and Alghathbar et al. (2005). However, each of these conventional works has the following *issues*:

- Traditional conceptual security modeling techniques help to model the late phase requirements. However, they do not model early phase requirements.

- Such techniques indicate "what" steps a security process consists of, and "how" those steps are to be done. They do not indicate "why" a security process is the way it is.

- The traditional techniques do not capture the motivations, intents, and rationales behind the security activities.

- Those techniques do not capture the intentional structure of a security process, and the organization that embeds it.

- The traditional modeling techniques model functional requirements of a security process. They do not model nonfunctional requirements.

- The traditional modeling techniques cannot reason about the opportunities and vulnerabilities. They do not help to incorporate the issues of trust, vulnerability, change, and risk explicitly in the process of security systems analysis and design.

To address these issues, we proposed an agent-oriented security risk modeling approach (Misra, Kumar, & Kumar, 2005b). Our approach helps to explore the strategic dependencies between the actors of a security system being modeled. This helps to uncover the structural origin of security issues in a system. This approach extends the concept of i* (Chung, Nixon, Yu, & Mylopoulos, 2000; Donzelli & Bresciani, 2003; Gans, Jarke, Kethers, Lakemeyer, Ellrich, Funken, & Meister, 2001; Misra et al., 2005a; Misra et al., 2005b; Misra, Kumar & Kumar, 2005c; Misra, Kumar & Kumar, 2005d; Misra, Kumar & Kumar, 2005e; Misra, Kumar & Kumar, 2005f; Yu & Mylopoulos, 1994; Yu, 1999) for use in the domain of security modeling. In particular, our approach helps for security risk identification and analysis. This approach is further described.

The stated approach is demonstrated with the help of a *case study* as described next. The case study is hypothetical, and is amalgamated modification of the examples used in Giorgini et al. (Giorgini, Massacci, & Mylopoulos, 2003), and Yu and Liu (2000).

Case Study

The last few years have seen an upsurge in electronic commerce and electronic banking. Most of the major vendors supporting electronic payments are concerned about offering their customers an assurance of security of their personal sensitive information entered online. Let us consider a simple example of one such company, X, and see how it secures its online business of selling product Y.

Customers of company X are offered the ability to buy their products online using a smart card. Customers have the option of either walking to one of the satellite counters of the company, giving their card to the merchant, who can then use the cards to process the payment, or the customers can themselves enter or swipe the card using an input device (e.g., a card reader). To prevent the card information from being eavesdropped, the sensitive information is encrypted using the SSL protocol. However, such an encryption mechanism does not necessarily protect the customer-sensitive information to be stolen manually by the merchants. On the other hand, it might so happen that the information supplied by the customer is fraudulent.

Company X issues a smart card, uniquely to each of its customers, that they can either use at the card reader in a suitable terminal, or that they can use to enter their information manually. The cards issued to the customers are manufactured by a third-party vendor of company X. Similarly, the hardware and software supporting the entire system are built by another third-party vendor. The sensitive data is owned by a separate division of company X.

Although there are different scenarios that can be generated from this case study, in the interest of brevity, we will show only a few of them to illustrate our approach. Similarly, as will be seen next, there are many scenarios that are uncovered through the modeling exercise, but are not explicitly stated in the case study statement. Such instances resonate the usefulness of such a modeling exercise.

Recommendation: The Intentional Modeling Approach

The concepts associated with modeling actor dependencies have their roots in requirements engineering (RE). RE methodologies can be used to model organizational goals, processes, relationships, and actors. In order to perform very good quality risk assessment, one is required to understand the organization clearly.

In this section, we discuss the actor dependency concept using i* (see, for example, Chung et al., 2000; Donzelli & Bresciani, 2003; Gans et al., 2001; Misra et al., 2005a; Misra et al., 2005b; Misra et al., 2005c; Misra et al., 2005d; Misra et al., 2005e; Misra et al., 2005f; Sutcliffe & Minocha, 1999; and Yu, 1999, to learn more about this area of research and its applicability to various domains). Although i* is a "brain-child" of software RE research, it can be used as a powerful tool to model organizational tasks, processes, actors, and goals. The framework allows requirements engineers to model, in detail, current processes, and to modify them in order to optimize, improve, and increase enterprise productivity. All these benefits could be obtained quite early, even when the project is yet to start. i* explores "why" processes are performed in the existing way. Moreover, it is much easier to obtain real and understandable requirements using i* modeling. Expected behavior of the software, and its rationale, could also be modeled using i*. Furthermore, i* does not take directly into account precision, completeness, and consistency as UML does. In contrast, i* principally takes into account the actors' interests, goals, rationale, tasks, and concerns.

In this work, we have used i* to model both requirements and risk management elements that help managers to identify, monitor, analyze, and control risks, all from the point of view of project goals. i* provides a qualitative analysis of project viability under several scenarios. In our context, this analysis will allow for verifying that all required actions to control risks have been taken into account (i.e., if project goals can be satisfied in all the studied scenarios). For any project, requirements can be modeled as goals and softgoals to be reached during project development.

In order to model and solve this problem, two actor-dependency diagrams are used: the strategic dependency model (SD), and the strategic rationale model (SR). In the interest of brevity, only brief introductions of SD and SR are provided.

SD diagrams are used to model dependencies between actors, while SR diagrams are used to model, internally, why each actor has those dependencies. In other words, SD describes dependencies at a higher level of abstraction than SR, since SR shows an internal description of an actor, and supports those dependencies.

All dependencies comprise of a "depender," a "dependee," and a "dependum." "Depender" depends on a "dependee" to get "dependum." The most important elements in SD diagrams are

- **Goal dependency:** It is used to model when one actor depends on another to make a tangible condition come true. Dependee has freedom to choose how to achieve this goal.

- **Task dependency:** It is used to model when one actor depends on another to perform an activity. In this case, there is an implicit (usually not shown) depender's goal, which explains why this task must be performed.

- **Resource dependency:** It is used to model when one actor depends on another for the availability of an entity. Depender assumes that obtaining this resource will be straightforward.

Figure 1. SD diagram for a Web services-based card payment System

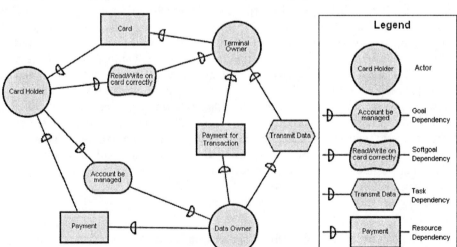

Figure 2. Example of different types of actors

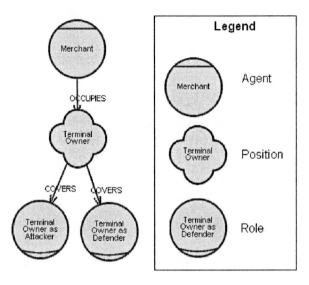

*   **Softgoal dependency:** It is used to model when one actor depends on another to realize a fuzzy condition. In this case, *fuzzy* means there is no clear criteria for such a condition to be true. In this case, dependee collaborates, but depender will decide how to achieve the softgoal.

Figure 1 is an example of an SD model. It represents the dependencies between actors of a smart card payment system supporting Web services. Goal dependency "Account be Managed" indicates that Cardholder needs his account to be managed, and it is up to Data Owner how to manage the account. Data Owner, from the other side, expects payment from the Card Holder that is represented by resource dependency "Payment" between the two actors. Dependency "Read/Write on Card Correctly" is a softgoal dependency, as it is hard to determine what "correctly" means. Task dependency "Transmit Data" indicates data owner needs terminal owner to transmit data; terminal owner does not have freedom for completing the task.

Actors can be modeled as a generalized relationship among agents, position and role (Dubois, Yu, & Petit, 1998). In general, agents represent physical manifestation of actors. Agents occupy a *position* in SD diagrams. In fact, a *position* is a generalization of an agent. Furthermore, positioned agents can have or cover several roles. Figure 2 shows an example of different types of actors.

SR diagrams focus inside actors. In fact, SR diagrams show both external and internal information. External information is modeled using the same elements of SD diagrams (e.g., goals, softgoals, resources, and tasks). Internal information is represented basi-

Figure 3. SR diagram for a Web services-based card payment system

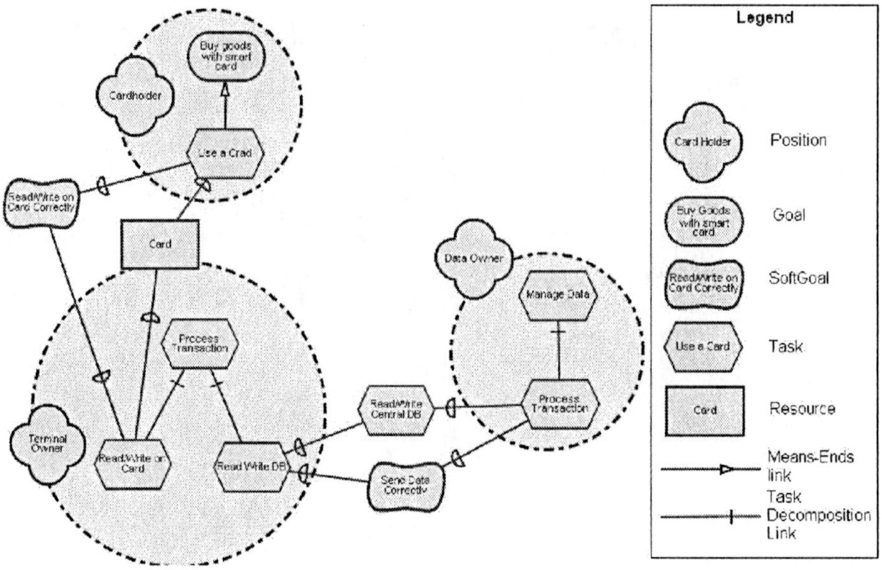

cally using the same elements but arranged hierarchically in either a *means-end* or a *task-decomposition* relationship.

Internal elements of SR respond to external dependency relationships among actors. In general, external goals, tasks, softgoals, and resources are attached to internal tasks. Internal tasks might be decomposed into subtasks, subgoals, and subsoftgoals (task-decomposition relationships). Moreover, internal goals might depend on other subtasks (means-end relationships). Finally, internal softgoals might obtain either negative or positive contribution from tasks and other subsoftgoals.

Figure 3 illustrates the SR diagram for various actors of our Web services-based card payment system case. Card holder has an internal goal, "Buy goods with a smart card." S/he uses a card to do this. So s/he has internal task "Use a Card." The goal "Buy goods with a smart card" and the task "Use a card" are linked with means-ends link. Terminal owner has a major task, "Process transaction." The task is divided into two separate subtasks: "Read/write on card" and "Read write DB," related with the task "Process

Figure 4. Representation of task elements corresponding to the exploitation vulnerabilities in the Web services-based card payment system

Figure 5. Representation of attacks that make the dependency totally unviable in our Web services-based card payment system example. The link is labeled as a break *link.*

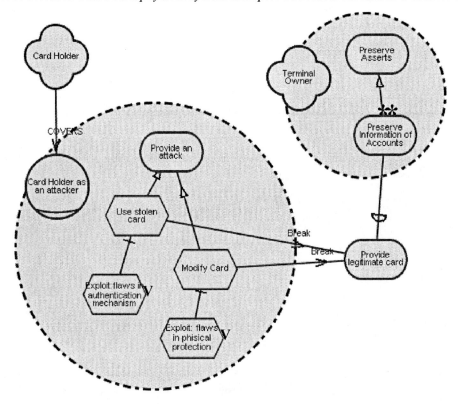

Figure 6. Depiction of risk values

transaction" by task decomposition links. "Read/write on card" is associated with the card holder. The external softgoal, "Read/write on card correctly," depends on this task. The external task, "Read\write central DB," as well is softgoal "Send data correctly" is dependency going from data owner to terminal owner. However, a more detailed view presents us that both "Read/write central DB" and "Send data correctly" depend on the internal task of terminal owner "Read write on DB." The dependencies between internal and external elements of SR Diagram allow performing more detailed modeling.

In any security risk management process, there are two main tasks: (a) the identification of the security risks and vulnerabilities, and their analysis, and (b) their evaluation to

Figure 7. Depiction of treatment *measures in an SR diagram in our Web services-based card payment system example.*

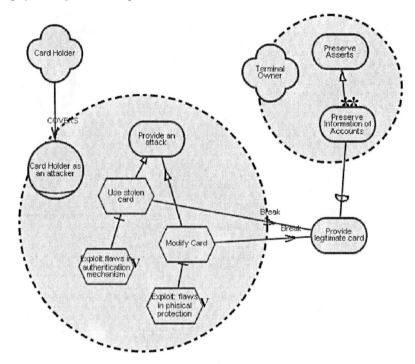

identify their potential for damage. We now show how we can address these two concerns in our approach.

To conduct an attack, an attacker must exploit vulnerabilities. Thus, exploitations of vulnerabilities are subtasks of the task associated with the attack, and they are linked with task decomposition links. We note task elements corresponding to the exploitation of vulnerabilities by letter "V" on the right of the element, as shown in Figure 4.

If one actor depends on another actor who is an attacker, the attacker may provide a number of attacks to make the dependency not viable. Making a dependency not viable is depicted by a contribution link connecting to the dependum. The links originate from the tasks associated with the attacks. For attacks that make dependency totally unviable, the link is labeled as a *break* link. This can be seen in the example in Figure 5.

The next important step in any risk management process is to determine the values of risks. In our approach, we have seen that a risk is associated with an attack. To estimate a risk value, we need to estimate possible frequency of the attack associated with the risk. Then we need to take into consideration values of all the assets that can be affected by the attack.

If we use discrete risk values, we can represent risk values by the exclamation mark ("!") at the top of a task element associated with an attack. For example, three exclamation marks depict that risk value is high, whereas one exclamation mark depicts that the risk value is low. Figure 6 shows an example of how risk value is depicted.

If continuous risk values are used, the values can be depicted as numbers on the top of the corresponding task element.

If we want to assign value to an asset or a security feature, we assign a value to the corresponding goal or softgoal. We represent values on the top of i* goal and softgoal elements. If we use discreet values, we represent values as star marks ("*"). We draw more for assets and security features having larger value. If we use continuous value, we represent them as numbers.

To protect their assets, in other words, to reduce security risks, actors may want to provide countermeasures against possible attacks. An actor who provides defensive measures plays a role "Actor as a defender." The countermeasures are represented as internal tasks of defending actors. The aim of treatment measure is to fix some vulnerability, and thus to reduce the impact or the frequency of the attack. To show that a treatment measure is aimed at fixing vulnerability, we draw a negative contribution link connecting the task representing the treatment measure with the task representing exploitation of the vulnerability. Figure 7 illustrates how treatment measures are depicted in SR diagram.

Conclusion and Future Trends

We have described an approach that can be used for reasoning opportunities, vulnerabilities, threats, and risks that are associated with WS-based security systems.

There have been several initiatives undertaken to model security risks from different perspectives. So far, most of the pieces of literature describe different strategies for modeling as per the security requirements of a system under development. The development of a system from the perspective of the intentions of the actors of the system, and how they interact between each other, is interesting and necessary for a comprehensive management of security risks of a system. The actor dependency-based approach that we have illustrated in this chapter is helpful to address this need. However, this approach is developed considering the general security risks of a system. We believe that this approach can, as well, be used for modeling all aspects of security risk issues that might occur. However, it is necessary to consider specific cases of WS security, and analyze how well the presented approach in this chapter can help in addressing the modeling of those cases. Addressing all possible security issues is complex. Different issues need to be considered from different perspectives. Therefore, we believe that the aspect of intentional modeling of WS security has the potential for its growth as an independent field. We also believe that intensive work in this area has the strong potential to lead to the development of a new modeling language for use in the area of WS security.

Acknowledgments

The authors thank the anonymous referees for their valuable comments, which helped to strengthen the quality of this chapter. The authors also thank the referees and the audience of the 3rd International Workshop on Security in Information Systems (WOSIS 2005), Miami, Florida, for their valuable feedback and comments, where some portions of the work presented in this chapter appeared in the workshop proceedings. This chapter was written from the inspiration obtained by the authors while presenting their preliminary work in WOSIS 2005.

References

Aagedal, J. O., Braber, F. D., Dimitrakos, T., Gran, B. A., Raptis, D., & Stolen, K., (2002, September 17-20). Model-based risk assessment to improve enterprise security. In *Proceedings of the Fifth International Enterprise Distributed Object Computing Conference (EDOC 2002),* Lausanne, Switzerland.

Alghathbar, K., Wijesekera, D., & Farkas, C. (2005). Return on security investment (ROSI): A practical quantitative model. In *Proceedings of International Workshop on Security in Information Systems,* Miami, FL, USA (pp. 239-252).

Barber, B., & Davey, J. (1992). The use of the CCTA risk analysis and management methodology (CRAMM) in health information systems. In *Medinfo 92,* Amsterdam, North Holland (pp. 1589-1593).

Chung, L., Nixon, B. A., Yu, E., & Mylopoulos, J. (2000). *Non-functional requirements in software engineering.* Kluwer Academic Publishers, USA. ISBN 0792386663.

COBRA. (2005). *COBRA risk consultant.* Retrieved August 21, 2006, from http://www.riskworld.net/

Common Criteria Organization. (2002). *Common criteria for information technology security evaluation.* Retrieved August 21, 2006, from http://www.commoncriteria.org

Control Objectives for Information and Related Technology. (2002). *COBIT.* Retrieved from http://www.isaca.org/ct-denld.htm

Dimitrakos, T., Ritchie, B., Raptis, D., & Stolen, K. (2002). Model-based security risk analysis for Web applications: The CORAS approach. In *Proceedings of Euroweb 2002,* Oxford, U.K.

Donzelli, P., & Bresciani, P. (2003). An agent-based requirements engineering framework for complex socio-technical systems. In *Proceedings of SELMAS 2003,* Portland, OR, USA.

Dubois, E., Yu, E.,0 & Petit, M. (1998). From early to late formal requirements: A process control case study. In *Proc. 9th International Workshop on Software Specification and Design,* Ise-Shima, Japan (pp. 34-42).

Fernandez, E. B., Sorgente, T., & Larrondo-Petrie, M. M. (2005). A UML-based methodology for secure systems: The design stage. In *Proceedings of International Workshop on Security in Information Systems*, Miami, FL (pp. 207-216).

Fletcher, S., Jansen, R., Lim, J., Halbgenacher, R., Murphy, M., & Flyss, G. (1995). Software system risk assessment and assurance. In *Proceedings of the New Security Paradigms Workshop*, San Diego, CA.

Gans, G., Jarke, M., Kethers, S., Lakemeyer, G., Ellrich, L., Funken, C., & Meister, M. (2001). Requirements modeling for organization networks: A (dis)trust-based approach. In *Proceedings of the 5th IEEE International Symposium on Requirements Engineering*, Toronto, Canada.

Giorgini, P., Massacci, F., & Mylopoulos, J. (2003). *Requirement engineering meets security: A case study on modelling secure electronic transactions by VISA and Mastercard* (Technical Report DIT-03-027). Informatica e Telecomunicazioni, University of Trento, Italy.

Gutierrez, C., Fernandez-Medina, E., & Piattini, M. (2005). Towards a process for Web services security. In *Proceedings of the 3rd International Workshop on Security in Information Systems* (WOSIS 2005), Miami, FL (pp. 298-308).

Labuschagne, L. (1999). *Risk analysis generations — The evolution of risk analysis*. Retrieved January 29, 2002, from http://csweb.rau.ac.za/deth/research/article_page.htm

Lodderstedt, T., Bastin, D., & Doser, J. (2002). SecureUML: A UML-based modeling language for model-driven security. In *Proceedings of the 5th International Conference on Unified Modeling Language,* Dresden, Germany.

Lund, M. S., Barber, F. D., Stolen K., & Vraalsen, F. (2004). *A UML profile for the identification and analysis of security risks during structured brainstorming* (Report # STF40 A03067). SINTEF, Norway.

Lund, M. S., Hogganvik, I., Seehusen, F., & Stolen, K. (2003). *UML profile for security assessment* (Report # STF40 A03066). SINTEF Telecom and Informatics, Norway.

Martel, S. (2002). A New Model for Computer Network Security Risk Analysis. MA.Sc. thesis. Carleton University, Canada.

Misra, S. C., Kumar, V., & Kumar, U. (2005a). How can i* complement UML for modeling organizations? In *Proceedings of the 18th IEEE Canadian Conference on Electrical and Computer Engineering* (CCECE 2005), Saskatoon, Saskatchewan, Canada (pp. 2319-2321).

Misra, S. C., Kumar, V., & Kumar, U. (2005b, May 24-25). An approach for modeling information systems security risk assessment. In *Proceedings of the 3rd International Workshop on Security in Information Systems* (WOSIS 2005), Miami, FL , USA (pp. 253-262).

Misra, S.C., Kumar, V., & Kumar, U. (2005c, May 25-28). A strategic modeling technique for change management in organizations undergoing BPR. In *Proceedings of the 7th International Conference on Enterprise Information Systems (ICEIS 2005)* (Vol. 3, pp. 447-450). Miami, FL.

Misra, S. C., Kumar, V., & Kumar, U. (2005d, May 25-28). Modeling strategic actor relationships to support risk analysis and control in software projects. In *Proceedings of the 7th International Conference on Enterprise Information Systems (ICEIS 2005*, Miami, FL (Vol. 3, pp. 288-293).

Misra, S. C., Kumar, V., & Kumar, U. (2005e, May 1-4). Goal-oriented or scenario-based requirements engineering (RE) technique: What should a practitioner select? In *Proceedings of the 18th IEEE Canadian Conference on Electrical and Computer Engineering (CCECE 2005),* Saskatoon, Saskatchewan, Canada (pp. 2314-2318).

Misra, S. C., Kumar, V., & Kumar, U. (2005f, April 20-22). Strategic modeling of risk management in industries undergoing BPR. In *Proceedings of the 8th International Conference on Business Information Systems (BIS 2005)*, Poznan, Poland (pp. 85-103).

Mouratidis, H., Giorgini, P., Manson, G., & Philip, I. (2002). A natural extension of tropos methodology for modelling security. In *Proceedings of the Agent Oriented Methodologies Workshop (OOPSLA 2002)*, Seattle, WA.

Mouratidis, H., Giorgini, P., & Manson, G. (2003). An ontology for modelling security: The tropos approach. *Lecture Notes in Computer Science, 2773*, 1387-1394. USA: Springer-Verlag.

Sandia National Laboratories. (2002). *Surety analysis*. Retrieved from http://www.sandia.gov

Schechter, S. E. (2004). *Computer security and risk: A quantitative approach*. PhD thesis, Computer Science, Harvard University.

Standards Australia. (1999). *AS/NZS 4360: Risk management*. Standards Australia. Standard. AS/NZS 4360.

Sutcliffe, A. G., & Minocha, S. (1999). Linking business modeling to socio-technical system design. In *Proceedings of CaiSE '99* (pp. 73-87). Heidelberg, Germany.

Swiderski, F., & Snyder, W. (2004). *Threat modeling*. USA: Microsoft Press.

Tivoli. (2005). *Tivoli secure way risk manager*. Retrieved March 14, 2003, from http://www-306.ibm.com/software/tivoli/products/security-compliance-mgr/

Villarroel, R., Fernandez, E., Trujillo, J., & Piattini, M. (2005). Towards a UML 2.0/OCL extension for designing secure data warehouses. In *Proceedings of International Workshop on Security in Information Systems*, Miami, FL, USA (pp. 217-228).

Vraalsen, F., Braber, F. D., Hogganvik, I., Lund, S., & Stolen, K. (2004). *The CORAS tool-supported methodology* (SINTEF Report. Report # STF90A04015). SINTEF ICT, Norway.

Yu, E. (1999). Strategic modeling for enterprise integration. In *Proceedings of the 16th World Congress of International Federation of Automatic Control,* Beijing, China (pp. 127-132). Pergamon, Elsevier Sciences.

Yu, E., & Liu, L. (2000). Modelling trust in the i* strategic actors framework. In *Proceedings of the 3rd International Workshop on Deception, Fraud, and Trust in Agent Societies*, Barcelona, Catalonia, Spain.

Yu, E. S. K., & Mylopoulos, J. (1994, May 16-21). Understanding "why" in software process modeling, analysis, and design. In *Proceedings of the 16th International Conference in Software Engineering*, Sorrento, Italy (pp. 548-565).

About the Authors

G. Radhamani received her PhD from Multimedia University, Malaysia and MSc, MPhil (computer science) degrees from PSG College of Technology, India. She was working with Dr. G. R.Damodaran College of Science, India, and is currently in the Faculty of Information Technology, Multimedia University, Cyberjaya, Malaysia. She has published several papers in international journals and conferences. She is a senior member of IEEE and CSI. Her research interests are XML databases, computer security, and mobile computing.

G. S. V. Radha Krishna Rao, is currently associated with the Faculty of Information Technology, Multimedia University, Malaysia. He obtained his master's degree and PhD from Andhra University, India. He worked in various capacities in the IT industry, such as systems analyst, programmer analyst, and senior software engineer, and is a current postdoctoral research fellow at Telkom Center of Excellence in Developmental e-Commerce at the University of Fort Hare, South Africa. His research interests include information security, rural telecommunications, microwaves, WiMax, network processors, hyperthreading technology, databases, and operating systems. He has authored and edited his books, and published/presented research papers in international journals/conferences. He is a senior member of IEEE and a member of ACM.

* * *

Ismail Ahmad, an alum of Queensland University of Technology, Australia, is currently associated with the Faculty of Information Technology at Multimedia University, Malaysia. Currently pursuing his PhD in the security field, Ahmad has 11 years of experience in the IT field. His research interests include distributed file systems, database systems, and computer security, and Ahmad has published/presented widely in national/international journal/conferences.

S. Anil Kumar is doing his bachelor's degree in IT at the Sri Krishna College of Information Technology, Coimbatore, Tamilnadu, India. The author shows his maximum interests in network security and Web services. Anilkumar has published several papers in national level seminars in network security and he is holding an excellent academic record in his career. He is keen to pursue higher studies and doctorate from reputed universities.

R. Anitha is working as an assistant professor in the Department of Mathematics & Computer Applications, PSG College of Technology, Coimbatore, India. She graduated in mathematics from Holy Cross College, Madurai Kamarajar University. She pursued her master's degree from the same university and earned her MPhil degree from Sree Avinashilingam Home Science College, Coimbatore. She was awarded a doctorate degree from Bharathiar University, Coimbatore. She has been guiding candidates for the PhD programme since 1999. Her areas of interest include queueing theory, graph theory, cryptography, advanced data structures and algorithm, and design and analysis of algorithms. She has 18 years of teaching experience.

Maryam Arvandi's first BSc in midwifery was from University of Tehran, Iran in 1992. After 7 years of exciting work, she felt a need for a new challenge in a field that showed a great potential for the future's high-tech world. To follow her interest, she received her second BSc (Hons.) in computer science and MASc in electrical and computer engineering from Ryerson University, Toronto, Canada (2003 and 2005, respectively). Her main interest in data security has led her to work under the supervision of Professor Alireza Sadeghian, specifically in "Analysis of Neural Network Based Ciphers."

Win Aye received a BCTech (Bachelor of Computer Technology) and an MCTech (Master of Computer Technology) from the University of Computer Studies, Yangon (UCSY, Myanmar) in 1995 and 1999, respectively. She is currently working toward a PhD at the Center of Excellence Laboratory in the Faculty of Information Technology at Multimedia University, Malaysia. She has been in the teaching profession at UCSY since 1995. Currently, she is a lecturer in the Department of Hardware Technology at UCSY. Her research interests include control engineering, multicast transmission, multicast security, and network security.

R. A. Balachandar pursued his bachelor's degree in electrical and electronics engineering in 2001 and a master's degree in computer science and engineering in 2003. Balachandar has teaching experience for two years and currently, he is working as a senior research fellow at Madras Institute of Technology, Anna University, Chennai, Tamil Nadu in the field of Grid computing sponsored by the Centre for Development of Advanced Computing (CDAC), India. His areas of interest are Grid computing, Semantic

Web services, and network security. Balachandar has published a paper in the National Conference at Allahabad in the field of network security. He is very keen to discuss the latest trends in semantic Grid computing and to analyze the scope of integrating security components with grid infrastructures.

M. Balakumar is studying his bachelor's degree in IT at Sri Krishna College of Information Technology, Coimbatore, Tamilnadu, India. His areas of interest are cryptography and networking. The author has published several papers in national level seminars in the field of security. Because of his attitude and research interests, Balakumar has also received an offer of employment with IBS Software Services Private Ltd., Trivandrum. In addition to that, he is consistently maintaining his academic excellence throughout his career.

Chua Fang Fang received a Bachelor of Information Technology (Hons.) majoring in software engineering from Multimedia University, Malaysia (2003). She then received her Master of Information Technology from the University of Melbourne, Australia (2004). After graduation, she joined Multimedia University as a lecturer and is currently pursuing her PhD. Her research interests include intelligent agents, information systems, knowledge management, e-learning, and AI in education.

Vik Tor Goh received a BEng (Hons.) in electronics engineering from Multimedia University, Malaysia (2002). After graduation, he joined Multimedia University as a teaching assistant and is currently pursuing a MEngSc. He has been a certified information systems security professional (CISSP) since September 2005. His research interests include digital watermarking, steganography, cryptography, and error control coding.

Bok-Min Goi received a BEng in electrical engineering from the University of Malaya (UM) and an MEngSc degree from Multimedia University (MMU), Malaysia (1998 and 2002, respectively). Since 2002, he has been working as a lecturer in the Faculty of Engineering, MMU. Currently, he is the chairman of MMU's Centre for Cryptography and Information Security (CCIS). His current research interests include cryptology, hash function, authentication and key exchange protocols, and embedded systems design.

Biju Issac is a lecturer in the School of IT and Multimedia in Swinburne University of Technology (Sarawak Campus), Malaysia. He is also the head of the Network Security Research group in the iSECURES Research Lab at Swinburne University Sarawak. His research interests are in wireless and network security, wireless mobility, and IPv6 networks. He is an electronics and communication engineer with a master's degree in computer applications. Currently, he is doing a part-time PhD in networking and mobile communications in UNIMAS, Malaysia. He has published papers in IEEE and IEE Conferences and has in-depth teaching experience.

S. S. Jamuar received his BSc engineering degree in electronics and communication from Bihar Institute of Technology, Sindri (1967), and MTech and PhD Degrees in electrical engineering from Indian Institute of Technology, Kanpur, India (1970 and 1977, respectively). He worked as a research assistant, senior research fellow, and senior research assistant from 1969 to 1975 at IIT Kanpur. During 1975-76, he was with Hindustan Aeronautics Ltd., Lucknow. Subsequently, he joined the Lasers and Spectroscopy Group in the Physics Department at IIT Kanpur, where he was involved in the design of various types of laser systems. He joined as lecturer in the Electrical Engineering Department at Indian Institute of Technology Delhi in 1977, where he became assistant professor in 1980. He was a professor in the Department of Electrical Engineering at IIT Delhi from 1991 to 2003. He was attached to Bath College of Further Education, Bath (UK), Aalborg University, Aalborg (Denmark) during 1987 and 2000. He was a consultant to UNESCO during 1996 in Lagos State University, Lagos (Nigeria). He was with University Putra Malaysia during 1996-97 in the Faculty of Engineering. Presently, he is a professor in the Electrical and Electronic Engineering Department in the Faculty of Engineering, University Putra Malaysia since 2001. He has been teaching and conducting research in the areas of electronic circuit design, instrumentation, and communication systems. He has more than 40 papers in international journals and has attended several international conferences and presented papers. He recently received a Taiwan patent on "A Simulation Circuit Layout Design for Low Voltage, Low Power and High Performance Type II Current Conveyor." He is recipient of Meghnad Saha Memorial Award 1976 from IETE, Distinguished Alumni Award from BIT Sindri in 1999, and Best Paper Award in the *IETE journal of Education 2004* from IETE. He is senior member of IEEE and fellow of Institution of Electronics and Telecommunications Engineering (India). He is on the editorial board of *Wireless Personnel Communication Journal*. He is presently the chapter chair for IEEE CASS Chapter in Malaysia.

F. Mary Magdalene Jane received her MCA from Gobi Arts College, Gobi, India and an MPhil from Manonmaniam Sundaranar University, Tirunelveli, India. She is a lecturer in computer science with PSGR Krishnammal College for Women, Coimbatore, India. Her research interests focus on mobile computing and security in computing. She is a member of the Computer Society of India.

Kenneth Foo Chuan Khit is in charge of setting the vision and timeframe for product rollouts. A former application engineer, Khit has had extensive experience in software development and applications. He is now based at the Cyberjaya Division, Malaysia, where he heads the research and development arm of NetInfinium.

Uma Kumar, MSc, MS, PhD, is a full professor of management science and technology management and director of the Research Centre for Technology Management at Carleton University, Canada. She has been the director of graduate programs of the Eric Sprott School of Business, Carleton University. Dr. Kumar's research is in the area of management of technology including forecasting and monitoring technology, efficiency in new product development through e-commerce, quality in R&D, managing R&D internationally, R&D and innovation policy, performance metrics in e-commerce, and

ERP adoption and implementation. Dr. Kumar has published over 90 articles in journals and refereed proceedings. Her eight papers have won best paper awards at prestigious conferences. She has won Carleton's prestigious Research Achievement Award, and twice has won the Scholarly Achievement Award. Dr. Kumar is the recipient of a number of research grants from reputed research funding agencies.

Vinod Kumar received his graduate education from the University of California, Berkeley, and the University of Manitoba. He has been the director of the Sprott School of Business–Carleton University for 10 years, and is currently the head of the Manufacturing Systems Centre, an organized research unit at Carleton University, Canada. He is a professor of technology and operations management. Before joining academia in the early eighties, Dr. Kumar worked for manufacturing industries for over 15 years in India, the U.S., and Canada in various line and staff management positions. He is a member of a number of professional organizations. Dr. Kumar's research is in enterprise system adoption and implementation, e-commerce technology strategy, supply chain management, improving performance of production and operation systems, manufacturing flexibility, technology transfer, quality in R&D, and innovation management in defence and high tech sector. Dr. Kumar has published over 120 articles in refereed journals and proceedings. He has won several Best Paper Awards in prestigious conferences. Dr. Kumar has also obtained the Scholarly Achievement Award of Carleton University for the academic years 1985-86 and 1987-88, and Research Achievement Award for the year 1993 and 2001. He is on the editorial board of two international journals. In addition, Dr. Kumar has also served for several years on the Board of Governors and the Senate for Carleton University and on the Board of the Ontario Network of e-Commerce.

Rosalind Deena Kumari graduated with a BEng in electronics & communication eng. from Gulbarga University, Karnataka, India (1991), and completed a Master in Information Technology (MIT) from University of Malaya, Malaysia (2002). She has been a lecturer for the past 11 years, and is currently a lecturer at the faculty of IT in Multimedia University, Malaysia. Her areas of interest are network security, DIDS, Congestion control, and ad hoc networks.

Subhas C. Misra held several positions in several organizations including senior project advisor in Super Net Solutions, Scarborough, Ontario, Canada, software developer in Nortel Networks, Ottawa, Canada, and assistant executive engineer in the Indian Telephone Industries, Mankapur, India. He has several years of experience working on R&D projects in software engineering, project management, quality engineering, risk management, and project management. He has published several technical papers in different international journals, and is a regular speaker in reputed conferences. He has also offered several tutorials in the allied areas. Subhas received several prestigious academic awards that include Best Paper Award for one of his published papers. He received his MTech in computer science and data processing from the Indian Institute of Technology (IIT), Kharagpur, India, and MS in computer science from the University of New Brunswick, Fredericton, Canada. He is also completing his PhD in IT management from the Eric Sprott School of Business, Carleton University, Canada.

Sudip Misra is a postdoctoral researcher at Cornell University, Ithaca, NY, USA. Prior to this, he received his doctoral, master's, and bachelor's degrees from Carleton University, University of New Brunswick (Fredericton, Canada), and Indian Institute of Technology (Kharagpur, India), respectively. He has several years of experience working in academia, government, and the private sectors. Misra has worked in R&D projects in project management, architecture, software design, and product engineering roles at Nortel Networks, Canada, Atreus Systems Corporation, Canada, and the Government of Ontario, Canada. His current research interests include algorithm design and experimentation for high-performance and high-speed Telecommunication Networks.

Lawan A. Mohammed is a lecturer in the School of IT and Multimedia in Swinburne University of Technology (Sarawak Campus), Malaysia. He is also the head of Smartcard Research group in the iSECURES Research Lab at Swinburne University Sarawak. His main research focuses on the design of authentication protocols for secure e-commerce, wireless and mobile networks, cryptography, and smart card. After finishing his master's degrees in computer science and operations research, he received his PhD in computer and communication systems engineering from University Putra Malaysia (UPM) in 2004. He has published papers in IEEE and IEE Conferences and is an experienced researcher.

M. Mujinga is from Zimbabwe and is currently a master's student associated with Telkom Center of Excellence at Computer Science Department of University of Fort Hare, South Africa.

Saravanan Muthaiyah is currently a senior lecturer at Multimedia University, Cyberjaya, Malaysia. He had formerly worked for IBM World Trade Corporation and University Malaya before joining MMU. He is a Fulbright Scholar and has authored a book in Information Systems that was published by Prentice Hall in 2004. He is sound in finance, accounting, and information technology.

Hippolyte Muyingi earned his electrical engineering doctorate from Vrije Universiteit Brussels (VUB), Belgium in 1988. For the past 5 years, since his arrival at the University of Fort Hare in South Africa, he has been progressively involved at the leadership level in setting up a Postgraduate Programme in the Computer Science Department through the Telkom Centre of Excellence programme. Around 10 postgraduate students are completing the program every year. A research culture is growing. Five MSc graduates completed in December 2005. As a UN specialist between 1998-2001, his 3-year experience with the United Nations Development Programme (UNDP) in Rwanda has been a rich source of knowledge and ideas in trying to uplift the quality of life for disadvantaged communities in developing countries. Based on that, Professor Muyingi came up with a research niche area that is "developmental e-commerce/communication for rural communities" in the SA Eastern Cape province and in Africa at large. The problem to be addressed is "How ICT can become a medium for income generation for rural users rather than a source of expenditure they cannot afford." This challenge is the basic idea behind the "2nd generation of Telecentre." A very poor and remote community region on the

Eastern coast has been selected as a target to implement and investigate ways to bridge the digital divide for disadvantaged people in the two-economy system of South Africa. Starting his professional career as a Lecturer in 1979, Professor Muyingi published extensively and regularly. He is involved in several R&D as well as professional body activities.

Kamesh Namuduri received his BE in electronics and communication engineering from Osmania University, India (1984), MTech in computer science from University of Hyderabad (1986), and a PhD in computer science and engineering from the University of South Florida (1992). He has worked with C-DoT, a telecommunication firm in India from 1984 to 1986. Currently, he is with the Electrical and Computer Engineering Department at Wichita State University, USA, as an assistant professor. His areas of research interest include information security, image/video processing and communications, and ad hoc sensor networks. He is a senior member of IEEE.

Richard S. Norville studied at Wichita State University under Dr. Namuduri. There he received a Master of Science in electrical and computer engineering in May 2005, a Bachelor of Science in Mathematics in May 2005, and a Bachelor of Science in computer science in Dec 2003. He is currently employed at Lockheed Martin Corporation, Integrated Systems & Solutions Department, as a software engineer. His interests include network and computer security.

Ravi Pendse is an associate vice president for academic affairs and research, Wichita State Cisco fellow, and director of the Advanced Networking Research Center at Wichita State University, USA. He has received a BS in electronics and communication engineering from Osmania University, India (1982), an MS in electrical engineering from Wichita State University (1985), and a PhD in electrical engineering from Wichita State University (1994). He is a senior member of IEEE. His research interests include ad hoc networks, voice over IP, and aviation security.

Raphael C.-W. Phan is director of the information security research (iSECURES) at the laboratory at Swinburne University of Technology (Sarawak Campus), Malaysia. Phan researches on cryptology, security protocols, smartcard security, and digital watermarking. He has published in refereed journals by IEE, IEEE, and Elsevier, and internationally refereed cryptology conferences published by Springer, Germany. He is general chair of Mycrypt '05 and Asiacrypt '07, program chair of International Workshop on Information Security & Hiding (ISH '05), and technical program committee member of Mycrypt '05, International Conference on Information Security & Cryptology (ICISC '05) and International Conference on Applied Cryptography & Network Security (ACNS '06).

Ezmir Mohd Razali is currently associated with Multimedia University, Malaysia. An alumni of Multimedia University, Razali is also pursuing his PhD at Multimedia University. His research includes network protocol design, Web services, mobile technology Java, and .NET. He is published in international/national conferences/journals.

Alireza Sadeghian received a BASc (Hons.) in electrical engineering from Tehran Polytechnic University, and MAc and PhD degrees in electrical and computer engineering from the University of Toronto, Canada. Since 1999, he has been on the staff of the Department of Computer Science, Ryerson University, Canada, where he holds the position of associate professor. He is the author of more than 20 technical papers in the areas of information security, cryptography, computational intelligence, knowledge-based expert systems, and nonlinear modeling.

Robin Salim holds a degree in the IT field from Multimedia University, Malaysia. Currently, he is doing research in Network Intrusion Detection System on Intel-based Network Processing Unit funded under Intel, USA research grant. At the same time, he is also a postgraduate student in Multimedia University, working in the field of network security specializing in network intrusion detection.

E. S. Samundeeswari received her MCA degree from PSG College of Technology, Coimbatore, India, and the MPhil degree from the Bharathiar University, Coimbatore, India. She is currently doing research in process management. She is a lecturer (Selection Grade) in computer science, Vellalar College for Women, Erode, India. Her current research interests are concurrent engineering, process model, and workflow. She is a member of ISTE, New Delhi, India.

R. S. Sankarasubramanian is working as a lecturer in the Department of Mathematics & Computer Applications, PSG College of Technology, Coimbatore, India. He obtained his graduation in special mathematics from The American College, Madurai, and pursued his master's degree in applied mathematics from Thiagarajar College of Engineering, Madurai. He has 7 years of teaching experience. His areas of interest include applied mathematics, cryptography, computer graphics, and security in computing.

Amitabh Saxena is a PhD student at La Trobe University, Australia. His research interests are electronic payment systems, group oriented cryptography, network security, number theory and complexity theory. His thesis is in the area of secure and trustworthy group communication.

Mohammad Umar Siddiqi received BSc Eng and MSc Eng degrees from Aligarh Muslim University (AMU Aligarh) in 1966 and 1971 respectively, and a PhD from the Indian Institute of Technology Kanpur (IIT Kanpur) in 1976, all in electrical engineering. He has been in the teaching profession throughout, first at AMU Aligarh, then at IIT Kanpur. In 1998, he joined Multimedia University, Malaysia. Currently, he is a professor in the Faculty of Engineering at International Islamic University, Malaysia. He has published more than 90 papers in international journals and conferences. His research interests are in error control coding and cryptography.

Ben Soh is a professor working at La Trobe University, Australia. His research interests are dependable e-commerce systems, network and Web security, intrusion detection systems, and next generation Internet. As a principal investigator, La Trobe's Dr. Ben Soh leads a team that recently won an ARC Linkage Grant to develop a new transport layer protocol to provide secure broadband Internet connection via satellite to rural regions.

Alfredo Terzoli obtained a laurea cum laude in physics from the University of Pavia, Italy. At the time, the laurea was the highest academic qualification in Italy. With his industry/academic background, he is currently project director of the Telkom Centre of Excellence in Distributed Multimedia at Rhodes University and research coordinator of the Telkom Centre of Excellence in Developmental e-commerce at the University of Fort Hare.

Dennis M. L. Wong received his BEng (Hons.) in electronics engineering and communications in 1997 from The University of Liverpool, UK. He furthered his research in the area of signal processing and communications, and was awarded his PhD in July 2004 from the same institution. Currently, he is an engineering lecturer at the School of Engineering, Swinburne University of Technology (Sarawak Campus), Malaysia. His main research expertise is pattern classification problems in signal processing and telecommunications. Currently, he is also working on security and privacy issues related to radio frequency identification and digital watermarking schemes.

Isaac Woungang received an MASc and a PhD, all in applied mathematics, from the Université du Sud, Toulon-Var, France (1990 and 1994, respectively). In 1999, he received an MASc from INRS-Materials and Telecommunications, University of Quebec, Canada. From 1999 to 2002, he worked as a software engineer at Nortel. Since 2002, he has been with Ryerson University, Canada, where he is now an assistant professor of computer science. In 2004, he co-founded DABNEL (Distributed Applications and Broadband Networks Laboratory) R&D group. His research interests are telecommunications network design, network security, and error-correcting codes.

Shuwei Wu received his Bachelor's in Computer Science from Zongfhan University, China, in 1992. In 2003, he received his master's degree in electrical engineering from Ryerson University, Toronto, Canada, with majors in AI, cryptography and network security. Since 2004, he has been with the Ministry of Community and Services, Toronto, Canada, where he is now a programmer analyst.

Wei-Chuen Yau is a lecturer in the Faculty of Engineering at Multimedia University, Malaysia. He received his BS and MS degrees in electrical engineering from National Cheng Kung University, Tainan, Taiwan (1999 and 2001, respectively). He is currently pursuing his PhD study in IT at Multimedia University. His research interests include network security, cryptography, and intrusion detection.

Chan Gaik Yee is currently a lecturer in Multimedia University, Malaysia. She joins the Faculty of Information Technology, MMU, purely with the aim of contributing her knowledge and expertise towards academic research and development. After graduating with a Master of Science, majoring in MIS, from the Texas Tech University, USA (1992), she worked in the information technology industry for more than 10 years in Malaysia. Throughout her working life in the industry, she gained the practical industry skill sets and experiences from playing the role as college lecturer, system analyst, project leader/manager, senior system consultant, and assistant vice president. She has lead in the analysis, designing, development, and implementation of systems such as change management system, hospital support services system, Web-based customer support system, and multimedia-based e-learning system.

Index

Symbols

3F rule 2
802.1x 7

A

access control 82, 328, 329
access control methods 328
access control objectives 329
accountable-subgroup multisignatures
   (ASM) 220
active responses 135
ad hoc 3
advanced encryption standard 3
agent 112
agent technologies 112
aggregate signature 219
Aircrack 7
Airsnort 16
anomaly based intrusion 210
anomaly detection 134
anomaly detection model 232
applications 57
architectures 95
ARP 5

ARP poisoning 25
association 4
authentication 2, 32, 86, 143, 263
authentication protocol 142, 240
authentication techniques 32
authentication times 142
authenticator 11
authorization 88
availability 131

B

backward chaining 227
basic service set 3
beacon 4
BI environment 204
bilinear pairings 222
biometric 29
bit flipping 26
block cipher 240
brute-force attack 266
business 94
business intelligence (BI) 204
business intelligence security 204

C

Cain and Abel 25
CCMP 1, 8
central analysis server (CAS) 233
chain signatures 218
"chained signatures" 218
cipher block chaining (CBC) 239
cipher modes 239
CISCO 5
code on demand 75
communication 94
communication architectures 98
completeness 146
Computational Diffie-Hellman problem
   (CDHP) 219
conceptual modeling 363
conceptual modeling approach 363
confidentiality 131, 263
cooperative agent network 233
countermeasures 165
cracking 2
cryptography 33, 97
cryptosystems 186

D

DAC 329
data encryption 32
data integrity 208
database 60
denial of service 136
DHCP 2
digital signatures 184
direct sequence spread spectrum 3
distributed DoS 22
distributed intrusion detection systems
   231
DoS attacks 17
download time 341
DriftNet 18
Dual Stack IPv4/IPv6 338
dual stack translation mechanism (DSTM)
   339

E

e-business 165
e-business systems 165
e-commerce 94
e-mail protocols 184
EAP 2
EAPOL 12
eavesdropping 5
electronic article surveillance (EAS) 60
electronic bill presentment 306
electronic billing systems 306
electronic bills 306
electronic codebook (ECB) mode 239
elliptic curve digital signature algorithm
   184
elliptic curve digital signature algorithm
   (ECDSA) 184
encryption 2, 32, 97
ERI framework 309
Ethereal 18
EtherPEG 18
exploiting 239
extended service set 3

F

false negative 136
false positive 136
filtering 2
flooding 2
forensic 137
forward chaining 227
forward secrecy 65
forwarding 2
frame overhead 340
FreeRADIUS 14
frequency hopping spread spectrum 3
FTP 339

G

generic algorithm 262
GPS 17
graph isomorphism (GI) 144

H

hacker 7
hash-lock 65
heterogeneous e-business systems 165
honey pots 28
host-based 132
HTTP 339

I

ICMP 339
identity based chained signatures 229
IEEE 802.11 2
IEEE802.11 wireless LAN 1
illegitimate range 273
imperceptible 276
independent basic service set 3
information 94
infrastructure mode 3
initialisation vector (IV) 239
initialization vector 6
integrity 115, 131, 263
integrity check sum value 6
intentional modeling 363
Internet authentication server 14
Internet Engineering Task Force (IETF) 338
intruder 263
intrusion detection (ID) 129, 204, 210, 231
intrusion detection system 129
intrusion prevention (IP) techniques 204
intrusion prevention system 130
IPSec 25
IPSec Overhead 338
IPv4 339
IPv6 339

K

k-element aggregate extraction problem
   (k-EAEP) 219
key generation 93
key management cryptographic algorithms
93

L

LEAP 12
legitimate range 273

liability 218
Link Ferret software 16
Linux 14

M

MAC 329
Mac Makeup 23
MAC spoofing 23
malicious 115
man-in-the middle attack 269
MapToGroup mapping 224
Michael 8
misuse detection model 232
misused detection scheme 134
MITM 24
mobile agent systems 112
mobile agent technology 112
mobile agents 75
mobile code 75
mobile code technology 75
mobility 2
mode of operation 244
MS-CHAPv2 12
multicast communication 93

N

NAT 2
NetBIOS 26
NetStumbler 17
network interface card 6
network-based 132
network-based intrusion detection 133
neural network-based cipher 32
neural networks 32
node authentication 142
NP-complete 145

O

oblivious watermarking 275
off-line message viewing 306
orthogonal frequency division
   multiplexing 3

P

packet analyzers 18
Packetyzer 18
pairing-based cryptography 222
passive responses 135
PEAP 12
ping flood attack 22
privacy 57
protocol version 6 (IPv6) 338
protocols 143
prover 150
pseudocode 142
public key 104

Q

qualitative approach (QLA) 329
quantitative approach (QTA) 329

R

radio frequency 2
radio frequency identification 57
radio frequency identification (RFID)
    systems 57
RADIUS server 1, 2
RBAC 329
RC4 5
reader 60
redundant residue codes 273
redundant residue number System 271
remote evaluation 75
repudiation 263
RFID 58
RFID systems 57
risk assessment 363
risk assessment techniques 328
robust watermarking scheme 271
rogue access points 21
round-trip time (RTT) 340

S

safeguard 57
scalability 137
scanning 4
secret key 262, 263

secure message delivery 306
secure messaging 307
secure multicast communication
    protocols 93
secure trust transfer 218
security 1, 32, 57, 75, 94, 363
security attacks 2
security framework 306
security issues 75
security protocols 239
security risk assessment 363
security safeguards 2
security threats 112
service set identifier 4
session hijacking 24
signature based intrusion 210
signature-based intrusion detection
    system 139
simple object access protocol (SOAP) 165
smart tags 61
Smurf attack 22
soundness 146
stream ciphers 7
subtle interactions 239
supplicant 11
sustained data analysis attacks 266
symmetric cipher 32

T

TCP SYN flooding 22
technologies 94
temporal key integrity protocol 3
TFTP 339
TKIP 1
transition mechanisms 338
transponder 60
transport layer security 12
Tripwire 137
trust 218
trust transfer 218
trusted third party (TTP) 185

U

UDDI 171
UDP 11
unbreakable cipher 262

universal description, discovery, and
integration 165

V

verifiable encryption 184
verifiable encryption of elliptic curve
    digital signatures 184
verifiably encrypted signatures (VES) 219
verifier 150
virtual private network 11
vulnerabilities 2

W

war driving 2
watermarking scheme 271
Web services 165, 363
Web services architecture 166
Web services description language
    (WSDL) 165
Web services security 165
Web services security risk 363
Web services security risk assessment 363
WEP 2
WEP encryption options 1
Windows 13
wireless 32
wireless bridge 2
wireless LAN setup 1
wireless router 2
wireless station 2
wireless Web security 32
wireless Web services environments 32
WLAN 2
WPA 11

X

XML 167

Z

zero knowledge 146
zero-day attack 140
zero-knowledge proof (ZKP) 142

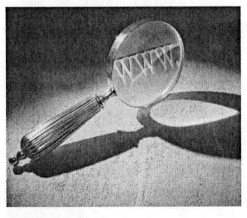